Windows Server 2012 R2: Essentials & Configuration

Pocket Consultant

William R. Stanek
Author and Series Editor

PUBLISHED BY
Microsoft Press
A Division of Microsoft Corporation
One Microsoft Way
Redmond, Washington 98052-6399

Library of Congress Control Number: 2013955479
ISBN: 978-0-7356-8257-3

Printed and bound in the United States of America.

First Printing

Microsoft Press books are available through booksellers and distributors world-wide. If you need support related to this book, email Microsoft Press Book Support at mspinput@microsoft.com. Please tell us what you think of this book at http://www.microsoft.com/learning/booksurvey.

Microsoft and the trademarks listed at http://www.microsoft.com/en-us/legal/intellectualproperty/trademarks/en-us.aspx are trademarks of the Microsoft group of companies. All other marks are property of their respective owners.

The example companies, organizations, products, domain names, email addresses, logos, people, places, and events depicted herein are fictitious. No association with any real company, organization, product, domain name, email address, logo, person, place, or event is intended or should be inferred.

Acquisitions Editor: Anne Hamilton
Developmental Editor: Karen Szall
Project Editor: Rosemary Caperton
Editorial Production: Online Training Solutions, Inc. (OTSI)
Technical Reviewer: Bob Hogan; Technical Review services provided by Content Master, a member of CM Group, Ltd.
Copyeditor: Victoria Thulman (OTSI)
Indexer: Krista Wall (OTSI)
Cover: Best & Company Design

Contents

What do you think of this book? We want to hear from you!

Microsoft is interested in hearing your feedback so we can continually improve our
books and learning resources for you. To participate in a brief online survey, please visit:

microsoft.com/learning/booksurvey

What do you think of this book? We want to hear from you!

Microsoft is interested in hearing your feedback so we can continually improve our
books and learning resources for you. To participate in a brief online survey, please visit:

microsoft.com/learning/booksurvey

Acknowledgments

To my readers—thank you for being there with me through many books and many years. It has been an honor and a privilege to be your pocket consultant.

To my wife—for many years, through many books, many millions of words, and many thousands of pages she's been there, providing support and encouragement and making every place we've lived a home.

To my kids—for helping me see the world in new ways, for having exceptional patience and boundless love, and for making every day an adventure.

To Anne, Karen, Martin, Lucinda, Juliana, and many others who've helped out in ways both large and small.

Special thanks to my son Will for not only installing and managing my extensive dev lab for all my books since *Windows 8 Pocket Consultant* but also for performing check reads of all those books.

—William R. Stanek

Introduction

Welcome to *Windows Server 2012 R2 Pocket Consultant: Essentials & Configuration*. Over the years, I've written about many different server technologies and products, but the one product I like writing about the most is Windows Server. Anyone transitioning to Windows Server 2012 R2 from Windows Server 2012 might be surprised at just how much has been updated, because changes both subtle and substantial have been made throughout the operating system. For anyone transitioning to Windows Server 2012 R2 from Windows Server 2008 R2 or an earlier release of Windows Server, I'll let you know right up front that I believe Windows Server 2012 and Windows Server 2012 R2 are the most significant updates to Windows Server since the introduction of Windows 2000 Server.

The good news is Windows Server 2012 R2 builds off the same code base as Windows 8.1. This means that you can apply much of what you know about Windows 8.1 to Windows Server 2012 R2, including how Windows works with touchscreen devices. Although you might not install Windows Server 2012 R2 on touchscreen computers, you can manage Windows Server 2012 R2 from your touchscreen computers. If you do end up managing it this way, understanding the touchscreen options and the revised interface options will be crucial to your success. For this reason, I discuss both the touchscreen options and the traditional mouse and keyboard techniques throughout this book.

When you are working with touchscreen computers, you can manipulate on-screen elements in ways that weren't possible previously. You can enter text by using the on-screen keyboard and also in the following ways:

- **Tap** Tap an item by touching it with your finger. A tap or double-tap of elements on the screen generally is the equivalent of a mouse click or double-click.

- **Press and hold** Press your finger down and leave it there for a few seconds. Pressing and holding elements on the screen generally is the equivalent of a right-click.

- **Swipe to select** Slide an item a short distance in the opposite direction compared to how the page scrolls. This selects the items and also might bring up related commands. If pressing and holding doesn't display commands and options for an item, try using swipe to select instead.

- **Swipe from edge (slide in from edge)** Starting from the edge of the screen, swipe or slide in. Sliding in from the right edge displays the charms. Sliding in from the left edge shows open apps and allows you to easily switch between them. Sliding in from the top or bottom edge shows commands for the active element.

- **Pinch** Touch an item by using two or more fingers, and then move the fingers toward each other. Pinching zooms out.

- **Stretch** Touch an item by using two or more fingers, and then move the fingers away from each other. Stretching zooms in.

Because I've written many top-selling Windows Server books, I was able to bring a unique perspective to this book—the kind of perspective you gain only after working with technologies for many years. As you've probably noticed, a great deal of information about Windows Server 2012 R2 is available on the web and in other printed books. You can find tutorials, reference sites, discussion groups, and more to make using Windows Server 2012 R2 easier. However, the advantage of reading this book is that much of the information you need to learn about Windows Server 2012 R2 is organized in one place and presented in a straightforward and orderly fashion. This book has everything you need to customize Windows Server 2012 R2 installations, master Windows Server 2012 R2 configurations, and maintain Windows Server 2012 R2 servers.

In this book, I teach you how features work, why they work the way they do, and how to customize them to meet your needs. I also offer specific examples of how certain features can meet your needs, and how you can use other features to troubleshoot and resolve issues you might have. In addition, this book provides tips, best practices, and examples of how to optimize Windows Server 2012 R2. This book won't just teach you how to configure Windows Server 2012 R2, it will teach you how to squeeze every last bit of power out of it and make the most from the features and options it includes.

Unlike many other books about administering Windows Server 2012 R2, this book doesn't focus on a specific user level. This isn't a lightweight beginner book. Regardless of whether you are a beginning administrator or a seasoned professional, many of the concepts in this book will be valuable to you, and you can apply them to your Windows Server 2012 R2 installations.

Who is this book for?

Windows Server 2012 R2 Pocket Consultant: Essentials & Configuration covers all editions of Windows Server 2012 R2. The book is designed for the following readers:

- Current Windows system administrators
- Accomplished users who have some administrator responsibilities
- Administrators upgrading to Windows Server 2012 R2 from previous versions
- Administrators transferring from other platforms

To pack in as much information as possible, I had to assume that you have basic networking skills and a basic understanding of Windows Server. With this in mind, I don't devote entire chapters to explaining Windows Server architecture, Windows Server startup and shutdown, or why you want to use Windows Server. I do, however, cover configuration, remote management, directory services, security, and much more.

I also assume that you are fairly familiar with Windows commands and procedures and the Windows user interface. If you need help learning Windows basics, you should read other resources (many of which are available from Microsoft Press).

How this book is organized

Rome wasn't built in a day, and this book wasn't intended to be read in a day, in a week, or even in a month. Ideally, you'll read this book at your own pace, a little each day as you work your way through all the features Windows Server 2012 R2 has to offer. This book is organized into 10 chapters. The chapters are arranged in a logical order, taking you from planning and deployment tasks to configuration and maintenance tasks.

Ease of reference is an essential part of this hands-on guide. This book has an expanded table of contents and an extensive index for finding answers to problems quickly. Many other quick-reference features have also been added to the book, including quick step-by-step procedures, lists, tables with fast facts, and extensive cross references.

As with all *Pocket Consultants*, *Windows Server 2012 R2 Pocket Consultant: Essentials & Configuration* is designed to be a concise and easy-to-use resource for managing Windows servers. This is the readable resource guide that you'll want on your desktop at all times. The book covers everything you need to perform the essential administrative tasks for Windows servers. Because the focus is on giving you maximum value in a pocket-size guide, you don't have to wade through hundreds of pages of extraneous information to find what you're looking for. Instead, you'll find exactly what you need to get the job done, and you'll find it quickly.

In short, the book is designed to be the one resource you turn to whenever you have questions regarding Windows Server administration. To this end, the book zeroes in on daily administration procedures, frequently performed tasks, documented examples, and options that are representative though not necessarily inclusive. One of my goals is to keep the content so concise that the book remains compact and easy to navigate while at the same time ensuring that it is packed with as much information as possible.

Conventions used in this book

I've used a variety of elements to help keep the text clear and easy to follow. You'll find code listings in monospace type. When I tell you to actually enter a command or text, the command or text appear in **bold** type. When I introduce and define a new term in a paragraph of text, I put it in *italics*.

NOTE Group Policy now includes both policies and preferences. Under the Computer Configuration and User Configuration nodes, you find two nodes: Policies and Preferences. Settings for general policies are listed under the Policies node. Settings for general preferences are listed under the Preferences node. When referencing settings under the Policies node, I sometimes use shortcut references, such as User Configuration \Administrative Templates\Windows Components, or specify that the policies are found in the Administrative Templates for User Configuration under Windows Components. Both references tell you that the policy setting being discussed is under User Configuration rather than Computer Configuration and can be found under Administrative Templates\Windows Components.

Other conventions include the following:

- **Best Practices**   To examine the best technique to use when working with advanced configuration and maintenance concepts
- **Caution**   To warn you about potential problems you should look out for
- **Important**   To highlight important concepts and issues
- **More Info**   To provide more information on a subject
- **Note**   To provide additional details on a particular point that needs emphasis
- **Real World**   To provide real-world advice when discussing advanced topics
- **Security Alert**   To point out important security issues
- **Tip**   To offer helpful hints or additional information

I truly hope you find that *Windows Server 2012 R2 Pocket Consultant: Essentials & Configuration* provides everything you need to perform the essential administrative tasks on Windows servers as quickly and efficiently as possible. You are welcome to send your thoughts to me at *williamstanek@aol.com.* Follow me on Twitter at WilliamStanek and on Facebook at *www.facebook.com/William.Stanek.Author.*

Other resources

No single magic bullet for learning everything you'll ever need to know about Windows Server 2012 R2 exists. Even though some books are offered as all-in-one guides, there's simply no way one book can do it all. With this in mind, I hope you use this book as it is intended to be used—as a concise and easy-to-use resource. It covers everything you need to perform core administration tasks for Windows servers, but it is by no means exhaustive.

Your current knowledge will largely determine your success with this or any other Windows resource or book. As you encounter new topics, take the time to practice what you've learned and read about. Seek out further information as necessary to get the practical hands-on know-how and knowledge you need.

I recommend that you regularly visit the Microsoft website for Windows Server (*microsoft.com/windowsserver/*) and *support.microsoft.com* to stay current with the latest changes. To help you get the most out of this book, you can visit my corresponding website at *williamstanek.com/windows.* This site contains information about Windows Server 2012 R2 and updates to the book.

Errata and book support

We've made every effort to ensure the accuracy of this book and its companion content. Any errors that have been reported since this book was published are listed at:

http://aka.ms/wsR2pc_EC/errata

If you find an error that is not already listed, you can report it to us through the same page.

If you need additional support, email Microsoft Press Book Support at:

mspinput@microsoft.com

Please note that product support for Microsoft software is not offered through the addresses above.

We want to hear from you

At Microsoft Press, your satisfaction is our top priority, and your feedback our most valuable asset. Please tell us what you think of this book at:

http://aka.ms/tellpress

The survey is short, and we read every one of your comments and ideas. Thanks in advance for your input!

Stay in touch

Let's keep the conversation going! We're on Twitter: *http://twitter.com/MicrosoftPress*.

CHAPTER 1

Windows Server 2012 R2 administration

Windows Server 2012 R2 is a powerful, versatile, full-featured server operating system that builds on the enhancements that Microsoft provided in Windows Server 2012. Windows Server 2012 R2 and Windows 8.1 share a number of common features because they were part of a single development project. These features share a common code base and extend across many areas of the operating systems, including management, security, networking, and storage. Because of this, you can apply much of what you know about Windows 8.1 to Windows Server 2012 R2.

This chapter covers getting started with Windows Server 2012 R2 and explores the extent to which the architectural changes affect how you work with and manage Windows Server 2012 R2. Throughout this chapter and the other chapters of this book, you'll also find discussions of the many security features and enhancements. These discussions explore all aspects of computer security, including physical security, information security, and network security. Although this book focuses on Windows Server 2012 R2 administration, the tips and techniques it presents can help anyone who supports, develops for, or works with the Windows Server 2012 R2 operating system.

Windows Server 2012 R2 and Windows 8.1

Before you deploy Windows Server 2012 R2, you should carefully plan the server architecture. As part of your implementation planning, you need to look closely at the software configuration that will be used and modify the hardware configuration on a per-server basis to meet related requirements. For additional flexibility in server deployments, you can deploy servers by using one of three installation types:

- **Server With A GUI installation**   An installation option that provides full functionality—also referred to as a *full-server installation*. You can configure a server to have any allowed combination of roles, role services, and features, and a full user interface is provided for managing the server. This installation option provides the most dynamic solution and is recommended for deployments of Windows Server 2012 R2 in which the server role might change over time.

- **Server Core installation**   A minimal installation option that provides a fixed subset of roles but does not include the Server Graphical Shell, Microsoft Management Console, or Desktop Experience. You can configure a Server Core installation with a limited set of roles. A limited user interface is provided for managing the server, and most management is done locally at a command prompt or remotely by using management tools. This installation option is ideally suited to situations in which you want to dedicate servers to a specific server role or combination of roles. Because additional functionality is not installed, the overhead caused by other services is reduced, providing more resources for the dedicated role or roles. Generally, the limited interface also is inherently more secure than other installation types.

- **Server With Minimal Interface installation**   An intermediate installation option where you perform a full-server installation and then remove the Server Graphical Shell. This leaves a minimal user interface, Microsoft Management Console, Server Manager, and a subset of Control Panel for local management. This installation option is ideally suited to situations in which you want to carefully control the tasks that can be performed on a server and the roles and features installed, but you still want the convenience of the graphical interface.

You choose the installation type during installation of the operating system. In a significant change from earlier releases of Windows Server, you can change the installation type after you've installed a server. A key difference between the installation types relates to the presence of the graphical management tools and the graphical shell. A Server Core installation has neither, a full-server installation has both, and a minimal-interface installation has only the graphical management tools.

> **MORE INFO**   Several server features and roles require the graphical shell. They include Fax Server, Remote Desktop Session Host, Windows Deployment Services, and the Internet Printing user interface. Additionally, in Event Viewer, the Details view requires the graphical shell, as does the graphical interface for Windows Firewall.

Like Windows 8.1, Windows Server 2012 R2 has the following features:

- **Modularization for language independence and disk imaging for hardware independence**   Each component of the operating system is designed as an independent module you can easily add or remove. This functionality provides the basis for the configuration architecture in Windows Server 2012 R2. Microsoft distributes Windows Server 2012 R2 on media with Windows Imaging (WIM) format disk images that use compression and single-instance storage to dramatically reduce the size of image files.

- **Preinstallation and preboot environments**   The Windows Preinstallation Environment (Windows PE) replaces MS-DOS as the preinstallation environment and provides a bootable startup environment for installation, deployment, recovery, and troubleshooting. The Windows Preboot Environment provides a startup environment with a boot manager that lets you choose which boot application to run to load the operating system. On systems with multiple operating systems, you access pre–Windows 7 operating systems in the boot environment by using the legacy operating system entry.

- **User account controls and elevation of privileges**   User Account Control (UAC) enhances computer security by ensuring true separation of standard user and administrator user accounts. Through UAC, all applications are run by using either standard user or administrator user privileges, and a security prompt is displayed by default whenever you run an application that requires administrator privileges. The way the security prompt works depends on Group Policy settings. Additionally, if you log on by using the built-in Administrator account, typically elevation prompts are not provided.

In Windows 8.1 and Windows Server 2012 R2, features with common code bases have identical management interfaces. In fact, just about every Control Panel utility that is available in Windows Server 2012 R2 is identical to or nearly identical to its Windows 8.1 counterpart. Of course, exceptions exist in some cases for standard default settings. Because Windows Server 2012 R2 does not use performance ratings, Windows servers do not have Windows Experience Index scores. Because Windows Server 2012 R2 does not use Sleep or related states, Windows servers do not have sleep, hibernate, or resume functionality. Because you typically do not want to use extended power management options on Windows servers, Windows Server 2012 R2 has a limited set of power options.

Windows Server 2012 R2 does not include the Windows Aero enhancements, Windows Sidebar, or other user-interface enhancements, because Windows Server 2012 R2 is designed to provide optimal performance for server-related tasks and is not designed for extensive personalization of the desktop appearance. That said, when you are working with a full-server installation, you can add the Desktop Experience feature and then enable some Windows 8.1 features on your server.

The Desktop Experience provides Windows desktop functionality on the server. Windows features added include Windows Media Player, desktop themes, Video for Windows (AVI support), Windows Defender, Disk Cleanup, Sync Center, Sound Recorder, Character Map, and Snipping Tool. Although these features allow a server to be used like a desktop computer, they can reduce the server's overall performance.

NOTE Windows Defender for Windows Server 2012 R2 has been upgraded to a more fully featured program. Windows Defender now protects against viruses, spyware, rootkits, and other types of malware. Rootkit detection helps to safeguard computers from malware that inserts itself into non-Microsoft drivers. If Windows Defender detects that a non-Microsoft driver has been infected, it prevents the driver from starting. Microsoft drivers are protected at startup as part of other security features. Note also that Windows Defender is available on Server Core installations, though without the user interface. If you add Windows Defender as an option on a Server Core installation, the program is enabled by default.

Because the common features of Windows 8.1 and Windows Server 2012 R2 have so many similarities, I will not cover changes in the interface from previous operating system releases, discuss how UAC works, and so on. You can find extensive coverage of these features in *Windows 8.1 Pocket Consultant: Essentials & Configuration* (Microsoft Press, 2013), which I encourage you to use in conjunction with this book. In addition to its coverage of broad administration tasks, *Windows 8.1 Pocket Consultant: Essentials & Configuration* examines how to customize the operating system and Windows environment, configure hardware devices, manage user access and global settings, troubleshoot system problems, and much more. This book, alternatively, focuses on directory services administration, user administration, and server management.

Getting to know Windows Server 2012 R2

The Windows Server 2012 R2 operating system includes several different editions. All Windows Server 2012 R2 editions support multiple processor cores. It is important to point out that although an edition might support only one discrete-socketed processor (also referred to as a *physical processor*), that one processor could have eight processor cores (also referred to as *logical processors*).

Introducing Windows Server 2012 R2

Windows Server 2012 R2 is a 64-bit–only operating system. In this book, I refer to 64-bit systems designed for the x64 architecture as *64-bit* systems. Because the various server editions support the same core features and administration tools, you can use the techniques discussed in this book regardless of which Windows Server 2012 R2 edition you're using.

When you install a Windows Server 2012 R2 system, you configure the system according to its role on the network, as the following guidelines describe:

- Servers are generally assigned to be part of a workgroup or a domain.
- *Workgroups* are loose associations of computers in which each individual computer is managed separately.

- *Domains* are collections of computers you can manage collectively by means of *domain controllers*, which are Windows Server 2012 R2 systems that manage access to the network, to the directory database, and to shared resources.

NOTE In this book, *Windows Server 2012 R2* and *Windows Server 2012 R2 family* refer to all editions of Windows Server 2012 R2. The various server editions support the same core features and administration tools.

Windows 8.1 and Windows Server 2012 R2 also support a workplace configuration. A *workplace* is a loose association of computers that grants access to certain internal network resources and business apps. Workplaces have specific benefits:

- If users have Windows 8.1 devices from which they want to access corporate resources, those devices can use a workplace configuration to remotely connect to a computer at work. Users can then change their network passwords and connect to internal websites. Users also can use workplaces as an alternative way to access Outlook Web Access (OWA). Here, users connect to the workplace and then access OWA by using the internal URL (rather than an external URL).
- If administrators have Windows 8.1 devices from which they want to access corporate resources, those devices can use a workplace configuration to remotely connect to servers and perform assigned tasks by using administration links.

You implement workplaces by installing the Windows Server Essentials Experience role on servers running Windows Server 2012 R2. Because the Windows Server Essentials Experience role is designed to be used in single-domain deployments of Active Directory Domain Services (AD DS), you should not deploy this role in AD DS implementations with multiple domains.

Windows 8.1 and Windows Server 2012 R2 also support Work Folders, a similar but distinctly different feature. Work Folders allow users to synchronize their corporate data to their devices and vice versa. Those devices can be joined to the corporate domain or a workplace. To deploy Work Folders, the administrator adds the File And Storage Services\File and iSCSI Services\Work Folders role service to a server and then configures Work Folders by using Server Manager. Unlike workplaces, Work Folders can be used in multidomain environments.

Working with Windows Server 2012 R2

Windows Server 2012 R2 uses a Start screen. Start is a window, not a menu. Programs can have Tiles on the Start screen. Tapping or clicking a Tile runs the program. When you press and hold or right-click on a program, an options panel usually is displayed. The charms bar is an options panel for Start, Desktop, and PC Settings. With a touch UI, you can display the charms by sliding in from the right side of the screen. With a mouse and keyboard, you can display the charms by pointing to the hidden button in the upper-right or lower-right corner of the Start, Desktop, or PC Settings screen; or by pressing Windows key+C.

Tap or click the Search charm to display the Search panel. Any text entered while on the Start screen is entered into the Search box in the Search panel. The search box can be focused on Everywhere, Settings, or Files. When focused on Everywhere, you can use Search to quickly find installed programs, settings, and files. When focused on Settings, you can use Search to quickly find settings and options in Control Panel. When focused on Files, you can use Search to quickly find files.

One way to quickly open a program is by typing the file name of the program, and then pressing Enter. This shortcut works as long as the Everywhere search box is in focus (which it typically is by default). In an Everywhere search, any matches for programs are listed first, followed by any matches for settings and finally, any matches for files.

Pressing the Windows key toggles between the Start screen and the desktop (or, if you are working with PC Settings, between Start and PC Settings). On Start, there's a Desktop Tile that you can tap or click to display the desktop. You also can display the desktop by pressing Windows key+D or, to peek at the desktop, press and hold Windows key+Comma. From Start, you access Control Panel by tapping or clicking the Control Panel Tile. From either Start or the desktop, you can display Control Panel by pressing Windows key+I and then clicking the Control Panel option. Additionally, because File Explorer is pinned to the desktop taskbar by default, you typically can access Control Panel on the desktop by following these steps:

1. Open File Explorer by tapping or clicking the taskbar icon.
2. Tap or click the leftmost arrow button in the address list.
3. Tap or click Control Panel.

Start and Desktop have a convenient menu that you can display by right-clicking the lower-left corner of the Start screen or the desktop. Alternatively, you can press Windows key+X. Options on the menu include Computer Management, Device Manager, Event Viewer, System, Task Manager, Windows Command Prompt, and Command Prompt (Admin). On the Start screen, the button in the lower-left corner shows a Windows icon, and tapping or clicking the thumbnail opens the desktop. On the desktop, tapping or clicking this button opens Start. Right-clicking the button is what displays the shortcut menu.

REAL WORLD By default with Windows Server 2012 R2, the command prompt and the administrator command prompt are options on the shortcut menu that is displayed when you right-click in the lower-left corner or press Windows key+X. The alternative is for the Windows PowerShell command prompt and the administrator Windows PowerShell command prompt to be displayed on this menu. To configure which options are available, on the desktop, press and hold or right-click the taskbar, and then click Properties. In the Taskbar And Navigation Properties dialog box, on the Navigation tab, select or clear the Replace Command Prompt With Windows PowerShell... check box as appropriate.

Shut Down and Restart are options of Power settings now. This means to shut down or restart a server, you follow these steps:

1. Display Start options by sliding in from the right side of the screen or moving the mouse pointer to the lower-right or upper-right corner of the screen.
2. Tap or click Settings, and then tap or click Power.
3. Tap or click Shut Down or Restart as appropriate.

Alternatively, if configured as a power option, you can press the server's physical power button to initiate an orderly shutdown by logging off and then shutting down. If you are using a desktop-class system and the computer has a sleep button, the sleep button is disabled by default, as are closing the lid options for portable computers. Additionally, servers are configured to turn off the display after 10 minutes of inactivity.

Windows 8.1 and Windows Server 2012 R2 support the Advanced Configuration and Power Interface (ACPI) 5.0 specification. Windows uses ACPI to control system and device power state transitions, putting devices in and out of full-power (working), low-power, and off states to reduce power consumption.

The power settings for a computer come from the active power plan. You can access power plans in Control Panel by tapping or clicking System And Security and then tapping or clicking Power Options. Windows Server 2012 R2 includes the Power Configuration (Powercfg.exe) utility for managing power options from the command prompt. At a command prompt, you can view the configured power plans by entering **powercfg /l**. The active power plan is marked with an asterisk.

The default, active power plan in Windows Server 2012 R2 is called *Balanced*. The Balanced plan is configured to do the following:

- Never turn off hard disks (as opposed to turning off hard disks after a specified amount of idle time).
- Disable timed events to wake the computer (as opposed to enabling wake on timed events).
- Enable USB selective suspend (as opposed to disabling selective suspend).
- Use moderate power savings for idle PCI Express links (as opposed to maximum power savings being on or off).
- Use active system cooling by increasing the fan speed before slowing processors (as opposed to using passive system cooling to slow the processors before increasing fan speed).
- Use minimum processor and maximum processor states if supported (as opposed to using a fixed state).

NOTE Power consumption is an important issue, especially as organizations try to become more earth friendly. Saving power also can save your organization money and, in some cases, allow you to install more servers in your data centers. If you install Windows Server 2012 R2 on a laptop—for testing or for your personal computer, for example—your power settings will be slightly different, and you'll also have settings for when the laptop is running on battery.

Power management options

When working with power management, important characteristics to focus on include the following:

- Cooling modes
- Device states
- Processor states

ACPI defines active and passive cooling modes. These cooling modes are inversely related to each other:

- *Passive cooling* reduces system performance but is quieter because there's less fan noise. With passive cooling, Windows lessens power consumption to reduce the operating temperature of the computer but at the cost of system performance. Here, Windows reduces the processor speed in an attempt to cool the computer before increasing fan speed, which would increase power consumption.

- *Active cooling* allows maximum system performance. With active cooling, Windows increases power consumption to reduce the temperature of the machine. Here, Windows increases fan speed to cool the computer before attempting to reduce processor speed.

Power policy includes an upper and lower limit for the processor state, referred to as the *maximum processor state* and the *minimum processor state*, respectively. These states are implemented by making use of a feature of Advanced Configuration and Power Interface (ACPI) 3.0 and later versions called *processor throttling*, and they determine the range of currently available processor performance states that Windows can use. By setting the maximum and minimum values, you define the bounds for the allowed performance states, or you can use the same value for each to force the system to remain in a specific performance state. Windows reduces power consumption by throttling the processor speed. For example, if the upper bound is 100 percent and the lower bound is 5 percent, Windows can throttle the processor within this range as workloads permit to reduce power consumption. In a computer with a 3-gigahertz (GHz) processor, Windows would adjust the operating frequency of the processor between .15 GHz and 3.0 GHz.

Processor throttling and related performance states were introduced with Windows XP and are not new, but these early implementations were designed for computers with discrete-socketed processors and not for computers with processor cores. As a result, they are not effective in reducing the power consumption of computers with logical processors. Windows 7 and later releases of Windows reduce power consumption in computers with multicore processors by taking advantage of a feature of ACPI 4.0 called *logical processor idling* and by updating processor throttling features to work with processor cores.

Logical processor idling is designed to ensure that Windows uses the fewest number of processor cores for a given workload. Windows accomplishes this by consolidating workloads onto the fewest cores possible and suspending inactive processor cores. As additional processing power is required, Windows activates inactive processor cores. This idling functionality works in conjunction with management of process performance states at the core level.

ACPI defines processor performance states, referred to as *p-states*, and processor idle sleep states, referred to as *c-states*. Processor performance states include P0 (the processor/core uses its maximum performance capability and can consume maximum power), P1 (the processor/core is limited below its maximum and consumes less than maximum power), and P*n* (where state *n* is a maximum number that is processor-dependent, and the processor/core is at its minimal level and consumes minimal power while remaining in an active state).

Processor idle sleep states include C0 (the processor/core can execute instructions), C1 (the processor/core has the lowest latency and is in a nonexecuting power state), C2 (the processor/core has longer latency to improve power savings over the C1 state), and C3 (the processor/core has the longest latency to improve power savings over the C1 and C2 states).

> **MORE INFO**   ACPI 4.0 was finalized in June 2009, and ACPI 5.0 was finalized in December 2011. Computers manufactured prior to this time will likely not have firmware that is fully compliant, and you will probably need to update the firmware when a compatible revision becomes available. In some cases, and especially with older hardware, you might not be able to update a computer's firmware to make it fully compliant with ACPI 4.0 or ACPI 5.0. For example, if you are configuring the power options and you don't have minimum and maximum processor state options, the computer's firmware isn't fully compatible with ACPI 3.0 and likely will not fully support ACPI 4.0 or ACPI 5.0 either. Still, you should check the hardware manufacturer's website for firmware updates.

Windows switches processors/cores between any p-state and from the C1 state to the C0 state nearly instantaneously (fractions of milliseconds) and tends not to use the deep sleep states, so you don't need to worry about performance impact to throttle or wake up processors/cores. The processors/cores are available when they are needed. That said, the easiest way to limit processor power management is to modify the active power plan and set the minimum and maximum processor states to 100 percent.

Logical processor idling is used to reduce power consumption by removing a logical processor from the operating system's list of nonprocessor-affinitized work. However, because processor-affinitized work reduces the effectiveness of this feature, you'll want to plan carefully prior to configuring processing affinity settings for applications. Windows System Resource Manager allows you to manage processor resources through percent processor usage targets and processor affinity rules. Both techniques reduce the effectiveness of logical processor idling.

Windows saves power by putting processor cores in and out of appropriate p-states and c-states. On a computer with four logical processors, Windows might use p-states 0 through 5, where P0 allows 100 percent usage, P1 allows 90 percent usage, P2 allows 80 percent usage, P3 allows 70 percent usage, P4 allows 60 percent usage, and P5 allows 50 percent usage. When the computer is active, logical processor 0 would likely be active with a p-state of 0 through 5, and the other processors would likely be at an appropriate p-state or in a sleep state. Figure 1-1 shows an example. Here, logical processor 1 is running at 90 percent, logical processor 2 is running at 80 percent, logical processor 3 is running at 50 percent, and logical processor 4 is in the sleep state.

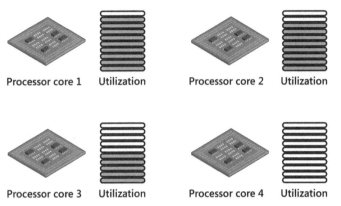

Processor core 1   Utilization   Processor core 2   Utilization

Processor core 3   Utilization   Processor core 4   Utilization

FIGURE 1-1 Processor cores working at different p-states have different usage patterns.

REAL WORLD ACPI 4.0 and ACPI 5.0 define four global power states. In G0, the working state in which software runs, power consumption is at its highest and latency is at its lowest. In G1, the sleeping state, in which software doesn't run, latency varies with sleep state and power consumption is less than the G0 state. In G2 (also referred to as S5 sleep state), the soft off state where the operating system doesn't run, latency is long and power consumption is very near zero. In G3, the mechanical off state, where the operating system doesn't run, latency is long, and power consumption is zero. There's also a special global state, known as S4 nonvolatile sleep, in which the operating system writes all system context to a file on nonvolatile storage media, allowing system context to be saved and restored.

Within the global sleeping state, G1, are sleep-state variations. S1 is a sleeping state where all system context is maintained. S2 is a sleeping state similar to S1 except that the CPU and system-cache contexts are lost and control starts from a reset. S3 is a sleeping state where all CPU, cache, and chip-set context are lost and hardware maintains memory context and restores some CPU and L2 cache configuration context. S4 is a sleeping state in which it is assumed that the hardware has powered off all devices to reduce power usage to a minimum and only the platform context is maintained. S5 is a sleeping state in which it is assumed that the hardware is in a soft off state, where no context is maintained and a complete boot is required when the system wakes.

Devices also have power states. D0, the fully on state, consumes the highest level of power. D1 and D2 are intermediate states that many devices do not use. D3hot is a power-saving state, where the device is software enumerable and can optionally preserve device context. D3 is the off state, where the device context is lost and the operating system must reinitialize the device to turn it back on.

Networking tools and protocols

Windows Server 2012 R2 has a suite of networking tools that includes Network Explorer, Network And Sharing Center, and Network Diagnostics. Figure 1-2 shows Network And Sharing Center.

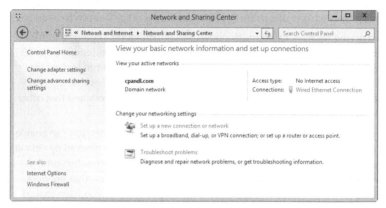

FIGURE 1-2 Network And Sharing Center provides quick access to sharing, discovery, and networking options.

Understanding networking options

The sharing and discovery configuration in Network And Sharing Center controls basic network settings. When network discovery settings are turned on and a server is connected to a network, the server can see other network computers and devices and is visible on the network. When sharing settings are turned on or off, the various sharing options are allowed or restricted.

In Windows 8.1 and Windows Server 2012 R2, networks are identified as one of the following network types:

- **Domain** A network in which computers are connected to the corporate domain to which they are joined

- **Work** A private network in which computers are configured as members of a workgroup and are not connected directly to the public Internet

- **Workplace** A private network in which computers are configured as members of a workplace to which devices can connect over the public Internet (Windows 8.1 only)

- **Home** A private network in which computers are configured as members of a homegroup and are not connected directly to the public Internet

- **Public** A public network in which computers are connected to a network in a public place, such as a coffee shop or an airport, rather than an internal network

These network types are organized into three categories: private, domain, and public. Each network category has an associated network profile. Because a computer saves sharing and firewall settings separately for each network category, you can use different block and allow settings for each network category. When you connect to a network, a dialog box is displayed in which you can specify the network category. If you select Private, and the computer determines that it is connected to the corporate domain to which it is joined, the network category is set as Domain Network.

Based on the network category, Windows Server configures settings that turn discovery on or off. The On (enabled) state means that the computer can discover other computers and devices on the network and that other computers on the network can discover the computer. The Off (disabled) state means that the computer cannot discover other computers and devices on the network and that other computers on the network cannot discover the computer.

Using Advanced Sharing Settings in Network And Sharing Center, you can enable discovery and file sharing. However, discovery and file sharing are blocked by default on a public network, which enhances security by preventing computers on the public network from discovering other computers and devices on that network. When discovery and file sharing are disabled, files and printers you have shared from a computer cannot be accessed from the network. Additionally, some programs might not be able to access the network.

Working with networking protocols

To allow a server to access a network, you must install TCP/IP networking and a network adapter. Windows Server uses TCP/IP as the default wide area network (WAN) protocol. Normally, networking is installed during installation of the operating system. You can also install TCP/IP networking through local area connection properties.

The TCP and IP protocols make it possible for computers to communicate across various networks and the Internet by using network adapters. Windows 7 and later releases of Windows have a dual IP-layer architecture in which both Internet Protocol version 4 (IPv4) and Internet Protocol version 6 (IPv6) are implemented and share common transport and network layers. IPv4 has 32-bit addresses and is the primary version of IP used on most networks, including the Internet. IPv6, alternatively, has 128-bit addresses and is the next-generation version of IP.

NOTE DirectAccess clients send only IPv6 traffic across the DirectAccess connection to the DirectAccess server. Thanks to the NAT64/DNS64 support, DirectAccess clients can initiate communications with IPv4-only hosts on the corporate intranet. NAT64/DNS64 work together to translate incoming connection traffic from an IPv6 node to IPv4 traffic. The NAT64 translates the incoming IPv6 traffic to IPv4 traffic and performs the reverse translation for response traffic. The DNS64 resolves the name of an IPv4-only host to a translated IPv6 address.

REAL WORLD The TCP Chimney Offload enables the networking subsystem to offload the processing of a TCP/IP connection from the computer's processors to its network adapter as long as the network adapter supports TCP/IP offload processing. Both TCP/IPv4 connections and TCP/IPv6 connections can be offloaded. For Windows 7 and later releases of Windows, TCP connections are offloaded by default on 10 gigabits per second (Gbps) network adapters, but they are not offloaded by default on 1-Gbps network adapters. To offload TCP connections on a 1-Gbps or 10-Gbps network adapter, you must enable TCP offloading by entering the following command at an elevated, administrator command prompt: **netsh int tcp set global chimney=enabled**. You can check the status of TCP offloading by entering **netsh int tcp show global**. Although TCP offloading works with Windows Firewall, TCP offloading won't be used with IPsec, Windows virtualization (Hyper-V), network load balancing, or the Network Address Translation (NAT) service. To determine whether TCP offloading is working, enter **netstat-t** and check the offload state. The offload state is listed as *offloaded* or *inhost*.

Windows also uses receive-side scaling and network direct memory access (NetDMA). You can enable or disable receive-side scaling by entering **netsh int tcp set global rss=enabled** or **netsh int tcp set global rss=disabled**, respectively. To check the status of receive-side scaling, enter **netsh int tcp show global**. You can enable or disable NetDMA by setting a DWord value under the EnableTCPA registry entry to **1** or **0**, respectively. This registry entry is found under HKEY_LOCAL_MACHINE\SYSTEM \CurrentControlSet\Services\Tcpip\Parameters.

IPv4's 32-bit addresses are commonly expressed as four separate decimal values, such as 127.0.0.1 or 192.168.10.52. The four decimal values are referred to as *octets* because each represents 8 bits of the 32-bit number. With standard unicast IPv4 addresses, a variable part of the IP address represents the network ID, and a variable part of the IP address represents the host ID. A host's IPv4 address and its media access control (MAC) address used by the host's network adapter have no correlation.

IPv6's 128-bit addresses are divided into eight 16-bit blocks delimited by colons. Each 16-bit block is expressed in hexadecimal form, such as FEC0:0:0:02BC:FF:BECB:FE4 F:961D. With standard unicast IPv6 addresses, the first 64 bits represent the network ID, and the last 64 bits represent the network interface. Because many IPv6 address blocks are set to 0, a contiguous set of 0 blocks can be expressed as "::", a notation referred to as *double-colon notation*. Using double-colon notation, the two 0 blocks in the previous address can be compressed as FEC0::02BC:FF:BECB:FE4F:961D. Three or more 0 blocks would be compressed in the same way. For example, FFE8:0:0:0:0:0:0:1 becomes FFE8::1.

When networking hardware is detected during installation of the operating system, both IPv4 and IPv6 are enabled by default; you don't need to install a separate component to enable support for IPv6. The modified IP architecture in Windows 7 and later releases of Windows is referred to as the *Next Generation TCP/IP stack*, and it includes many enhancements that improve the way IPv4 and IPv6 are used.

For Windows 8.1 and Windows Server 2012 R2, Group Policy Preferences have been updated to support IPv6 addresses for TCP/I Printers and VPN connections. Item-level Targeting options also allow you to configure IPv6 address ranges.

For traffic routing between virtual and physical networks, Windows Server 2012 R2 includes Windows Server Gateway, which is integrated with Hyper-V Network Virtualization. You can use Windows Server Gateway to route network traffic regardless of where resources are located, allowing you to support integration of public and private cloud services with your internal networks in addition to multitenant implementations with Network Address Translation (NAT) and virtual private network (VPN) connections.

Domain controllers, member servers, and domain services

When you install Windows Server 2012 R2 on a new system, you can configure the server to be a member server, a domain controller, or a stand-alone server. The differences between these types of servers are extremely important. Member servers are part of a domain but don't store directory information. Domain controllers are distinguished from member servers because they store directory information and provide authentication and directory services for the domain. Stand-alone servers aren't part of a domain. Because stand-alone servers have their own user databases, they authenticate logon requests independently.

Working with Active Directory

Windows Server 2012 R2 supports a multimaster replication model. In this model, any domain controller can process directory changes and then replicate those changes to other domain controllers automatically. Windows Server distributes an entire directory of information, called a *data store*. Inside the data store are sets of objects representing user, group, and computer accounts in addition to shared resources such as servers, files, and printers.

Domains that use Active Directory are referred to as *Active Directory domains*. Although Active Directory domains can function with only one domain controller, you can and should configure multiple domain controllers in the domain. This way, if one domain controller fails, you can rely on the other domain controllers to handle authentication and other critical tasks.

Microsoft changed Active Directory in several fundamental ways for the original release of Windows Server 2008. As a result, Microsoft realigned the directory functionality and created a family of related services, including the following:

- **Active Directory Certificate Services (AD CS)** AD CS provides functions necessary for issuing and revoking digital certificates for users, client computers, and servers. AD CS uses certificate authorities (CAs), which are responsible for confirming the identity of users and computers and then issuing certificates to confirm these identities. Domains have enterprise root CAs, which are the certificate servers at the root of certificate hierarchies for domains and the most trusted certificate servers in the enterprise, and subordinate CAs, which are members of a particular enterprise certificate hierarchy. Workgroups have stand-alone root CAs, which are the certificate servers at the root of nonenterprise certificate hierarchies, and stand-alone subordinate CAs, which are members of a particular nonenterprise certificate hierarchy.

■ **Active Directory Domain Services (AD DS)**   AD DS provides the essential directory services necessary for establishing a domain, including the data store that stores information about objects on the network and makes that information available to users. AD DS uses domain controllers to manage access to network resources. After users authenticate themselves by logging on to a domain, their stored credentials can be used to access resources on the network. Because AD DS is the heart of Active Directory and is required for directory-enabled applications and technologies, I typically refer to it simply as *Active Directory* rather than Active Directory Domain Services or AD DS.

■ **Active Directory Federation Services (AD FS)**   AD FS complements the authentication and access-management features of AD DS by extending them to the World Wide Web. AD FS uses web agents to provide users with access to internally hosted web applications and proxies to manage client access. After AD FS is configured, users can use their digital identities to authenticate themselves over the web and access internally hosted web applications with a web browser such as Internet Explorer.

■ **Active Directory Lightweight Directory Services (AD LDS)**   AD LDS provides a data store for directory-enabled applications that do not require AD DS and do not need to be deployed on domain controllers. AD LDS does not run as an operating system service and can be used in both domain and workgroup environments. Each application that runs on a server can have its own data store implemented through AD LDS.

■ **Active Directory Rights Management Services (AD RMS)**   AD RMS provides a layer of protection for an organization's information that can extend beyond the enterprise, allowing email messages, documents, intranet webpages, and more to be protected from unauthorized access. AD RMS uses a certificate service to issue rights account certificates that identify trusted users, groups, and services; a licensing service that provides authorized users, groups, and services with access to protected information; and a logging service to monitor and maintain the rights management service. After trust is established, users with a rights account certificate can assign rights to information. These rights control which users can access the information and what they can do with it. Users with rights account certificates can also access protected content to which they've been granted access. Encryption ensures that access to protected information is controlled both inside and outside the enterprise.

Microsoft introduced additional changes in Windows Server 2012 R2. These changes include a new domain functional level, called *Windows Server 2012 R2 domain functional level*, and a new forest functional level, called *Windows Server 2012 R2 forest functional level*. The many other changes are discussed in Chapter 7, "Using Active Directory."

Using read-only domain controllers

Windows Server 2008 and later releases support read-only domain controllers (RODCs) and restartable AD DS. An RODC is an additional domain controller that hosts a read-only replica of a domain's Active Directory data store. RODCs are ideally suited to the needs of branch offices, where a domain controller's physical security cannot be guaranteed. Except for passwords, RODCs store the same objects and attributes as writable domain controllers. These objects and attributes are replicated to RODCs through unidirectional replication from a writable domain controller that acts as a replication partner.

Because RODCs by default do not store passwords or credentials other than for their own computer account and the Kerberos Target (Krbtgt) account, RODCs pull user and computer credentials from a writable domain controller that is running Windows Server 2008 or later. If allowed by a password replication policy that is enforced on the writable domain controller, an RODC retrieves and then caches credentials as necessary until the credentials change. Because only a subset of credentials is stored on an RODC, this limits the number of credentials that can possibly be compromised.

IMPORTANT Any domain user can be delegated as a local administrator of an RODC without granting any other rights in the domain. An RODC can act in the role of a global catalog but cannot act in the role of an operations master. Although RODCs can pull information from domain controllers running Windows Server 2003, RODCs can pull updates of the domain partition only from a writable domain controller running Windows Server 2008 or later in the same domain.

Using restartable Active Directory Domain Services

Restartable AD DS is a feature that allows an administrator to start and stop AD DS. In the Services console, the Active Directory Domain Services service is available on domain controllers, allowing you to easily stop and restart AD DS in the same way as for any other service that is running locally on the server. While AD DS is stopped, you can perform maintenance tasks that would otherwise require restarting the server, such as performing offline defragmentation of the Active Directory database, applying updates to the operating system, or initiating an authoritative restore. While AD DS is stopped on a server, other domain controllers can handle authentication and logon tasks. Cached credentials, smart cards, and biometric logon methods continue to be supported. If no other domain controller is available and none of these logon methods applies, you can still log on to the server by using the Directory Services Restore Mode account and password.

All domain controllers running Windows Server 2008 or later support restartable AD DS—even RODCs. As an administrator, you can start or stop AD DS by using the Domain Controller entry in the Services utility. Because of restartable AD DS, domain controllers running Windows Server 2008 or later have three possible states:

- **Active Directory Started** Active Directory is started, and the domain controller has the same running state as a domain controller running Windows 2000 Server or Windows Server 2003. This allows the domain controller to provide authentication and logon services for a domain.

- **Active Directory Stopped** Active Directory is stopped, and the domain controller can no longer provide authentication and logon services for a domain. This mode shares some characteristics of both a member server and a domain controller in Directory Services Restore Mode. As with a member server, the server is joined to the domain. Users can log on interactively by using cached credentials, smart cards, and biometric logon methods. Users can also log on over the network by using another domain controller for domain logon. As with Directory Services Restore Mode, the Active Directory database (Ntds.dit) on the local domain controller is offline. This means you can perform offline AD DS operations, such as defragmentation of the database and application of security updates, without having to restart the domain controller.

- **Directory Services Restore Mode** Active Directory is in restore mode. The domain controller has the same restore state as a domain controller running Windows Server 2003. This mode allows you to perform an authoritative or nonauthoritative restore of the Active Directory database.

When working with AD DS in the Stopped state, you should keep in mind that dependent services are also stopped when you stop AD DS. This means that File Replication Service (FRS), Kerberos Key Distribution Center (KDC), and Intersite Messaging are stopped before Active Directory is stopped, and that even if they are running, these dependent services are restarted when Active Directory restarts. Further, you can restart a domain controller in Directory Services Restore Mode, but you cannot start a domain controller in the Active Directory Stopped state. To get to the Stopped state, you must first start the domain controller in the customary way and then stop AD DS.

Name-resolution services

Windows operating systems use name resolution to make it easier to communicate with other computers on a network. Name resolution associates computer names with the numerical IP addresses that are used for network communications. Thus, rather than using long strings of digits, users can access a computer on the network by using a friendly name.

Current Windows operating systems natively support three name-resolution systems:

- Domain Name System (DNS)
- Windows Internet Name Service (WINS)
- Link-Local Multicast Name Resolution (LLMNR)

The sections that follow examine these services.

Using Domain Name System

DNS is a name-resolution service that resolves computer names to IP addresses. Using DNS, the fully qualified host name computer84.cpandl.com, for example, can be resolved to an IP address, which allows it and other computers to find one another. DNS operates over the TCP/IP protocol stack and can be integrated with WINS, Dynamic Host Configuration Protocol (DHCP), and Active Directory Domain Services.

DNS organizes groups of computers into domains. These domains are organized into a hierarchical structure, which can be defined on an Internet-wide basis for public networks or on an enterprise-wide basis for private networks (also known as *intranets* and *extranets*). The various levels within the hierarchy identify individual computers, organizational domains, and top-level domains. For the fully qualified host name computer84.cpandl.com, *computer84* represents the host name for an individual computer, *cpandl* is the organizational domain, and *com* is the top-level domain.

Top-level domains are at the root of the DNS hierarchy; they are also called *root domains*. These domains are organized geographically, by organization type, and by function. Normal domains, such as cpandl.com, are also referred to as *parent domains*. They're called parent domains because they're the parents of an organizational structure. Parent domains can be divided into subdomains that can be used for groups or departments within an organization.

Subdomains are often referred to as *child domains*. For example, the fully qualified domain name (FQDN) for a computer within a human resources group could be jacob.hr.cpandl.com. Here, *jacob* is the host name, *hr* is the child domain, and *cpandl.com* is the parent domain.

Active Directory domains use DNS to implement their naming structure and hierarchy. Active Directory and DNS are tightly integrated, so much so that you should install DNS on the network before you install domain controllers that use Active Directory. During installation of the first domain controller on an Active Directory network, you're given the opportunity to install DNS automatically if a DNS server can't be found on the network. You are also able to specify whether DNS and Active Directory should be fully integrated. In most cases, you should respond affirmatively to both requests. With full integration, DNS information is stored directly in Active Directory. This allows you to take advantage of Active Directory's capabilities.

The difference between partial integration and full integration is very important:

- **Partial integration** With partial integration, the domain uses standard file storage. DNS information is stored in text-based files that end with the .dns extension, and the default location of these files is %SystemRoot%\System32 \Dns. Updates to DNS are handled through a single authoritative DNS server. This server is designated as the primary DNS server for the particular domain or an area within a domain called a *zone*. Clients that use dynamic DNS updates through DHCP must be configured to use the primary DNS server in the zone. If they aren't, their DNS information won't be updated. Likewise, dynamic updates through DHCP can't be made if the primary DNS server is offline.

- **Full integration** With full integration, the domain uses directory-integrated storage. DNS information is stored directly in Active Directory and is available through the container for the *dnsZone* object. Because the information is part of Active Directory, any domain controller can access the data, and a multimaster approach can be used for dynamic updates through DHCP. This allows any domain controller running the DNS Server service to handle dynamic updates. Furthermore, clients that use dynamic DNS updates through DHCP can use any DNS server within the zone. An added benefit of directory integration is the ability to use directory security to control access to DNS information.

REAL WORLD Windows Server 2012 R2 allows DNS clients to register both address (A) and pointer (PTR) records or only A records. A records are used for name-to-IP address lookups, also known as forward lookups; PTR records are used for IP address-to-name lookups, also known as reverse lookups. Being able to register only A records is useful when reverse lookups haven't been configured and you don't want DNS clients to repeatedly try to register PTR records.

If you look at the way DNS information is replicated throughout the network, you can see more advantages to full integration with Active Directory. With partial integration, DNS information is stored and replicated separately from Active Directory. Having two separate structures reduces the effectiveness of both DNS and Active Directory and makes administration more complex. Because DNS is less efficient than Active Directory at replicating changes, you might also increase network traffic and the amount of time it takes to replicate DNS changes throughout the network.

To enable DNS on the network, you need to configure DNS clients and servers. When you configure DNS clients, you tell the clients the IP addresses of DNS servers on the network. Using these addresses, clients can communicate with DNS servers anywhere on the network, even if the servers are on different subnets.

When the network uses DHCP, you should configure DHCP to work with DNS. To do this, you need to set the DHCP scope options 006 DNS Servers and 015 DNS Domain Name. Additionally, if computers on the network need to be accessible from other Active Directory domains, you need to create records for them in DNS.

DNS records are organized into zones; as mentioned earlier in this chapter, a zone is simply an area within a domain.

When you install the DNS Server service on an RODC, the RODC is able to pull a read-only replica of all application directory partitions that are used by DNS, including *ForestDNSZones* and *DomainDNSZones*. Clients can then query the RODC for name resolution as they would query any other DNS server. However, as with directory updates, the DNS server on an RODC does not support direct updates. This means that the RODC does not register name server (NS) resource records for any Active Directory–integrated zone that it hosts. When a client attempts to update its DNS records against an RODC, the server returns a referral to a DNS server that the client can use for the update. The DNS server on the RODC should receive the updated record from the DNS server that receives details about the update by using a special replicate-single-object request that runs as a background process.

Windows 7 and later releases add support for DNS Security Extensions (DNSSEC). The DNS client running on these operating systems can send queries that indicate support for DNSSEC, process related records, and determine whether a DNS server has validated records on its behalf. On Windows servers, this allows your DNS servers to securely sign zones and to host DNSSEC-signed zones. It also allows DNS servers to process related records and perform both validation and authentication.

Using Windows Internet Name Service

WINS is a service that resolves computer names to IP addresses. Using WINS, the computer name COMPUTER84, for example, can be resolved to an IP address that enables computers on a Microsoft network to find one another and transfer information. WINS is needed to support pre–Windows 2000 systems and earlier applications that use NetBIOS over TCP/IP, such as the .NET command-line utilities. If you don't have pre–Windows 2000 systems or applications on the network, you don't need to use WINS.

WINS works best in client/server environments in which WINS clients send single-label (host) name queries to WINS servers for name resolution and WINS servers resolve the query and respond. When all your DNS servers are running Windows Server 2008 or later, deploying a Global Names zone creates static, global records with single-label names that do not rely on WINS. This allows users to access hosts by using single-label names rather than FQDNs and removes the dependency on WINS. To transmit WINS queries and other information, computers use NetBIOS. NetBIOS provides an application programming interface (API) that allows computers on a network to communicate. NetBIOS applications rely on WINS or the local LMHOSTS file to resolve computer names to IP addresses. On pre–Windows 2000 networks, WINS is the primary name resolution service available. On Windows 2000 and later networks, DNS is the primary name resolution service and WINS has a different function. This function is to allow pre–Windows 2000 systems to browse lists of resources on the network and to allow Windows 2000 and later systems to locate NetBIOS resources.

To enable WINS name resolution on a network, you need to configure WINS clients and servers. When you configure WINS clients, you tell the clients the IP addresses for WINS servers on the network. Using the IP addresses, clients can communicate with WINS servers anywhere on the network, even if the servers are on different subnets. WINS clients can also communicate by using a broadcast method through which clients broadcast messages to other computers on the local network segment that are requesting their IP addresses. Because messages are broadcast, the WINS server isn't used. Any non-WINS clients that support this type of message broadcasting can also use this method to resolve computer names to IP addresses.

When clients communicate with WINS servers, they establish sessions that have the following three key parts:

- **Name registration** During name registration, the client gives the server its computer name and its IP address and asks to be added to the WINS database. If the specified computer name and IP address aren't already in use on the network, the WINS server accepts the request and registers the client in the WINS database.

- **Name renewal** Name registration isn't permanent. Instead, the client can use the name for a specified period known as a *lease*. The client is also given a time period within which the lease must be renewed, which is known as the *renewal interval*. The client must reregister with the WINS server during the renewal interval.

- **Name release** If the client can't renew the lease, the name registration is released, allowing another system on the network to use the computer name, IP address, or both. The names are also released when you shut down a WINS client.

After a client establishes a session with a WINS server, the client can request name-resolution services. The method used to resolve computer names to IP addresses depends on how the network is configured. The following four name-resolution methods are available:

- **B-node (broadcast)** Uses broadcast messages to resolve computer names to IP addresses. Computers that need to resolve a name broadcast a message to every host on the local network, requesting the IP address for a computer name. On a large network with hundreds or thousands of computers, these broadcast messages can use up valuable network bandwidth.

- **P-node (peer-to-peer)** Uses WINS servers to resolve computer names to IP addresses. As explained earlier, client sessions have three parts: name registration, name renewal, and name release. In this mode, when a client needs to resolve a computer name to an IP address, the client sends a query message to the server and the server responds with an answer.

- **M-node (mixed)** Combines b-node and p-node. With m-node, a WINS client first tries to use b-node for name resolution. If the attempt fails, the client then tries to use p-node. Because b-node is used first, this method has the same problems with network bandwidth usage as b-node.

- **H-node (hybrid)** Also combines b-node and p-node. With h-node, a WINS client first tries to use p-node for peer-to-peer name resolution. If the attempt fails, the client then tries to use broadcast messages with b-node. Because peer-to-peer is the primary method, h-node offers the best performance on most networks. H-node is also the default method for WINS name resolution.

If WINS servers are available on the network, Windows clients use the p-node method for name resolution. If no WINS servers are available on the network, Windows clients use the b-node method for name resolution. Windows computers can also use DNS and the local files LMHOSTS and HOSTS to resolve network names.

When you use DHCP to assign IP addresses dynamically, you should set the name resolution method for DHCP clients. To do this, you need to set DHCP scope options for the 046 WINS/NBT Node Type. The best method to use is h-node. You'll get the best performance and reduce traffic on the network.

Using Link-Local Multicast Name Resolution

LLMNR fills a need for peer-to-peer name-resolution services for devices with an IPv4 address, an IPv6 address, or both, allowing IPv4 and IPv6 devices on a single subnet without a WINS or DNS server to resolve each other's names—a service that neither WINS nor DNS can fully provide. Although WINS can provide both client/server and peer-to-peer name-resolution services for IPv4, it does not support IPv6 addresses. DNS, alternatively, supports IPv4 and IPv6 addresses, but it depends on designated servers to provide name-resolution services.

Windows 7 and later releases support LLMNR. LLMNR is designed for both IPv4 and IPv6 clients in configurations where other name-resolution systems are not available, such as the following:

- Home or small office networks
- Ad hoc networks
- Corporate networks where DNS services are not available

LLMNR is designed to complement DNS by enabling name resolution in scenarios in which conventional DNS name resolution is not possible. Although LLMNR can replace the need for WINS in cases where NetBIOS is not required, LLMNR is not a substitute for DNS because it operates only on the local subnet. Because LLMNR traffic is prevented from propagating across routers, it cannot accidentally flood the network.

As with WINS, you use LLMNR to resolve a host name, such as COMPUTER84, to an IP address. By default, LLMNR is enabled on all computers running Windows 7 and later releases, and these computers use LLMNR only when all attempts to look up a host name through DNS fail. As a result, name resolution works like the following for Windows 7 and later releases:

1. A host computer sends a query to its configured primary DNS server. If the host computer does not receive a response or receives an error, it tries each configured alternate DNS server in turn. If the host has no configured DNS servers or fails to connect to a DNS server without errors, name resolution fails over to LLMNR.

2. The host computer sends a multicast query over User Datagram Protocol (UDP) requesting the IP address for the name being looked up. This query is restricted to the local subnet (also referred to as the *local link*).

3. Each computer on the local link that supports LLMNR and is configured to respond to incoming queries receives the query and compares the name to its own host name. If the host name is not a match, the computer discards the query. If the host name is a match, the computer transmits a unicast message containing its IP address to the originating host.

You can also use LLMNR for reverse mapping. With a *reverse mapping*, a computer sends a unicast query to a specific IP address, requesting the host name of the target computer. An LLMNR-enabled computer that receives the request sends a unicast reply containing its host name to the originating host.

LLMNR-enabled computers are required to ensure that their names are unique on the local subnet. In most cases, a computer checks for uniqueness when it starts, when it resumes from a suspended state, and when you change its network interface settings. If a computer has not yet determined that its name is unique, it must indicate this condition when responding to a name query.

REAL WORLD   By default, LLMNR is automatically enabled on computers running Windows 7 and later releases. You can disable LLMNR through registry settings. To disable LLMNR for all network interfaces, create and set the following registry value to 0: HKLM/SYSTEM/CurrentControlSet/Services/Dnscache/Parameters/EnableMulticast.

To disable LLMNR for a specific network interface, create and set the following registry value to 0: HKLM/SYSTEM/CurrentControlSet/Services/Tcpip/Parameters/AdapterGUID /EnableMulticast.

Here, *AdapterGUID* is the globally unique identifier (GUID) of the network-interface adapter for which you want to disable LLMNR. You can enable LLMNR again at any time by setting these registry values to 1. You also can manage LLMNR through Group Policy.

Frequently used tools

Many utilities are available for administrating Windows Server 2012 R2 systems. The tools you use the most include the following:

- **Control Panel** A collection of tools for managing system configuration. You can organize Control Panel in different ways according to the view you're using. A *view* is simply a way of organizing and presenting options. You change the view by using the View By list. Category view is the default view, and it provides access to tools by category, tool, and key tasks. The Large Icons and Small Icons views are alternative views that list each tool separately by name.

- **Graphical administrative tools** The key tools for managing network computers and their resources. You can access these tools by selecting them individually from the Administrative Tools program group.

- **Administrative wizards** Tools designed to automate key administrative tasks. You can access many administrative wizards in Server Manager—the central administration console for Windows Server 2012 R2.

- **Command-line utilities** You can start most administrative utilities from the command prompt. In addition to these utilities, Windows Server 2012 R2 provides others that are useful for working with Windows Server 2012 R2 systems.

To learn how to use any of the .NET command-line tools, type **NET HELP** at a command prompt followed by the command name, such as **NET HELP SHARE**. Windows Server 2012 R2 then provides an overview of how the command is used.

Windows PowerShell

For additional flexibility in your command-line scripting, you might want to use Windows PowerShell. Windows PowerShell is a full-featured command shell that can use built-in commands called *cmdlets*, built-in programming features, and standard command-line utilities. A command console and a graphical environment are available.

Although the Windows PowerShell console and the graphical scripting environment are installed by default, several other Windows PowerShell features are not installed by default. They include the Windows PowerShell 2.0 engine, which is provided for backward compatibility with existing Windows PowerShell host applications, and Windows PowerShell Web Access, which lets a server act as a web gateway for managing the server remotely by using Windows PowerShell and a web client.

REAL WORLD You can install these additional Windows PowerShell features by using the Add Roles And Features Wizard. On the desktop, tap or click the Server Manager button on the taskbar. This option is included by default. In Server Manager, tap or click Manage, and then tap or click Add Roles And Features. This runs the Add Roles And Features Wizard, which you use to add these features. Note, however, that with Windows Server 2012 R2, not only can you disable a role or feature, but you also can remove the binaries needed for that role or feature. Binaries needed to install roles and features are referred to as *payloads*.

The Windows PowerShell console (Powershell.exe) is a 32-bit or 64-bit environment for working with Windows PowerShell at the command line. On 32-bit versions of Windows, you'll find the 32-bit executable in the %SystemRoot% \System32\WindowsPowerShell\v1.0 directory. On 64-bit versions of Windows, you'll find the 32-bit executable in the %SystemRoot%\SysWow64\WindowsPowerShell \v1.0 directory, and the 64-bit executable in the %SystemRoot%\System32 \WindowsPowerShell\v1.0 directory.

On the desktop, you can open the Windows PowerShell console by tapping or clicking the Windows PowerShell button on the taskbar. This option is included by default. On 64-bit systems, the 64-bit version of Windows PowerShell is started by default. If you want to use the 32-bit Windows PowerShell console on a 64-bit system, you must select the Windows PowerShell (x86) option.

You can start Windows PowerShell from a Windows command shell (Cmd.exe) by entering the following:

```
powershell
```

NOTE The directory path for Windows PowerShell should be in your command path by default. This ensures that you can start Windows PowerShell from a command prompt without first having to change to the related directory.

After starting Windows PowerShell, you can enter the name of a cmdlet at the prompt, and the cmdlet will run in much the same way as a command-line command. You can also execute cmdlets in scripts. Cmdlets are named by using verb-noun pairs. The verb tells you what the cmdlet does in general. The noun tells you what specifically the cmdlet works with. For example, the Get-Variable cmdlet gets all Windows PowerShell environment variables and returns their values, or it gets a specifically named environment variable and returns its value. The common verbs associated with cmdlets are as follows:

- **Get-** Queries a specific object or a subset of a type of object, such as a specified performance counter or all performance counters
- **Set-** Modifies specific settings of an object
- **Enable-** Enables an option or a feature
- **Disable-** Disables an option or a feature
- **New-** Creates a new instance of an item, such as a new event or service
- **Remove-** Removes an instance of an item, such as an event or event log

At the Windows PowerShell prompt, you can get a complete list of cmdlets by entering **get-help *-***. To get Help documentation on a specific cmdlet, enter **get-help** followed by the cmdlet name, such as **get-help get-variable**. Windows PowerShell V3 and later use online and updatable Help files. Because of this, you might see only basic syntax for cmdlets and functions. To get full Help details, you'll have to either use online Help or download the Help files to your computer. For online Help, add the -online option to your get-help command, as shown here:

```
get-help get-variable -online
```

Use the Update-Help cmdlet to download and install the current Help files from the Internet. Without parameters, Update-Help updates the Help files for all modules installed on the computer. However, Update-Help does the following:

- Downloads files only once a day
- Installs files only when they are newer than the ones on the computer
- Limits the total size of uncompressed Help files to 1 GB

You can override these restrictions by using the -Force parameter. You can save Help files to the local computer by using Save-Help.

All cmdlets also have configurable aliases that act as shortcuts for executing a cmdlet. To list all aliases available, enter **get-alias** at the Windows PowerShell prompt. You can create an alias that invokes any command by using the following syntax:

```
new-item -path alias:AliasName -value:FullCommandPath
```

Here *AliasName* is the name of the alias to create, and *FullCommandPath* is the full path to the command to run, such as the following:

```
new-item -path alias:sm -value:c:\windows\system32\compmgmtlauncher.exe
```

This example creates the alias *sm* for starting Server Manager. To use this alias, you simply type **sm** and then press Enter when you are working with Windows PowerShell. It's important to note that Windows PowerShell 3 and later versions automatically import required modules the first time you use a related command. With Windows PowerShell 2, you needed to explicitly import a module before you could run any of its commands.

REAL WORLD Generally speaking, anything you can enter at a command prompt also can be entered at the Windows PowerShell prompt. This is possible because Windows PowerShell looks for external commands and utilities as part of its usual processing. As long as the external command or utility is found in a directory specified by the PATH environment variable, the command or utility is run as appropriate. However, keep in mind that the Windows PowerShell execution order could affect whether a command runs as expected. For Windows PowerShell, the execution order is 1) alternate built-in or profile-defined aliases, 2) built-i Windows n or profile-defined functions, 3) cmdlets or language keywords, 4) scripts with the .ps1 extension, and 5) external commands, utilities, and files. Thus, if any element in 1 through 4 of the execution order has the same name as a command, that element will run instead of the expected command.

Windows Remote Management

The Windows PowerShell remoting features are supported by the WS-Management protocol and the Windows Remote Management (WinRM) service that implements WS-Management in Windows. Computers running Windows 8 and later, and also Windows Server 2012 or later, include WinRM 3.0 or later. If you want to manage a Windows server from a workstation, you need to be sure that WinRM 3.0 and Windows PowerShell are installed and that the server has a WinRM listener enabled.

A Microsoft Internet Information Services (IIS) extension, installable as a Windows feature called *WinRM IIS Extension*, lets a server act as a web gateway for managing the server remotely by using WinRM and a web client.

Enabling and using WinRM

You can verify the availability of WinRM 3.0 and configure Windows PowerShell for remoting by following these steps:

1. Tap or click Start, and then point to Windows PowerShell. Start Windows PowerShell as an administrator by pressing and holding or right-clicking the Windows PowerShell shortcut and then selecting Run As Administrator.

2. The WinRM service is configured for manual start by default. You must change the startup type to Automatic and start the service on each computer you want to work with. At the Windows PowerShell prompt, you can verify that the WinRM service is running by using the following command:

   ```
   get-service winrm
   ```

   As shown in the following example, the value of the *Status* property in the output should be *Running*:

   ```
   Status    Name          DisplayName
   ------    ----          -----------
   Running   WinRM         Windows Remote Management
   ```

   If the service is stopped, enter the following command to start the service, and then configure it to start automatically in the future:

   ```
   set-service -name winrm -startuptype automatic -status running
   ```

3. To configure Windows PowerShell for remoting, enter the following command:

   ```
   Enable-PSRemoting -force
   ```

   You can enable remoting only when your computer is connected to a domain or a private network. If your computer is connected to a public network, you need to disconnect from the public network and connect to a domain or private network and then repeat this step. If one or more of your computer's connections has the Public Network connection type but you are actually connected to a domain or private network, you need to change the network connection type in Network And Sharing Center and then repeat this step.

In many cases, you are able to work with remote computers in other domains. However, if the remote computer is not in a trusted domain, the remote computer might not be able to authenticate your credentials. To enable authentication, you need to add the remote computer to the list of trusted hosts for the local computer in WinRM. To do so, enter the following:

```
winrm set winrm/config/client '@{TrustedHosts="RemoteComputer"}'
```

Here *RemoteComputer* is the name of the remote computer, such as the following:

```
winrm set winrm/config/client '@{TrustedHosts="CorpServer56"}'
```

When you are working with computers in workgroups or homegroups, you must use HTTPS as the transport or add the remote machine to the TrustedHosts configuration settings. If you cannot connect to a remote host, verify that the service on the remote host is running and is accepting requests by running the following command on the remote host:

```
winrm quickconfig
```

This command analyzes and configures the WinRM service. If the WinRM service is set up correctly, you'll get output similar to the following:

```
WinRM already is set up to receive requests on this machine.
WinRM already is set up for remote management on this machine.
```

If the WinRM service is not set up correctly, you receive errors and need to respond affirmatively to several prompts that allow you to automatically configure remote management. When this process is complete, WinRM should be set up correctly.

Whenever you use Windows PowerShell remoting features, you must start Windows PowerShell as an administrator by pressing and holding or right-clicking the Windows PowerShell shortcut and then selecting Run As Administrator. When starting Windows PowerShell from another program, such as the command prompt, you must start that program as an administrator.

Configuring WinRM

When you are working with an elevated, administrator command prompt, you can use the WinRM command-line utility to view and manage the remote management configuration. Enter **winrm get winrm/config** to display detailed information about the remote management configuration.

If you examine the configuration listing, you'll notice there is a hierarchy of information. The base of this hierarchy, the Config level, is referenced with the path winrm/config. Then there are sublevels for client, service, and WinRS, referenced as winrm/config/client, winrm/config/service, and winrm/config/winrs, respectively. You can change the value of most configuration parameters by using the following command:

```
winrm set ConfigPath @{ParameterName="Value"}
```

Here *ConfigPath* is the configuration path, *ParameterName* is the name of the parameter you want to work with, and *Value* sets the value for the parameter, as shown in the following example:

```
winrm set winrm/config/winrs @{MaxShellsPerUser="10"}
```

Here, you set the *MaxShellsPerUser* parameter under winrm/config/winrs. This parameter controls the maximum number of connections to a remote computer that can be active per user. (By default, each user can have only five active connections.) Keep in mind that some parameters are read-only and cannot be set in this way.

WinRM requires at least one listener to indicate the transports and IP addresses on which management requests can be accepted. The transport must be HTTP, HTTPS, or both. With HTTP, messages can be encrypted by using NTLM or Kerberos encryption. With HTTPS, Secure Sockets Layer (SSL) is used for encryption. You can examine the configured listeners by entering **winrm enumerate winrm/config /listener**. As Listing 1-1 shows, this command displays the configuration details for configured listeners.

LISTING 1-1 Sample configuration for listeners

```
Listener
    Address = *
    Transport = HTTP
    Port = 80
    Hostname
    Enabled = true
    URLPrefix = wsman
    CertificateThumbprint
    ListeningOn = 127.0.0.1, 192.168.1.225
```

By default, your computer is probably configured to listen on any IP address. If so, no output will be displayed. To limit WinRM to specific IP addresses, the computer's local loopback address (127.0.0.1) and assigned IPv4 and IPv6 addresses can be explicitly configured for listening. You can configure a computer to listen for requests over HTTP on all configured IP addresses by entering the following:

```
winrm create winrm/config/listener?Address=*+Transport=HTTP
```

You can listen for requests over HTTPS on all IP addresses configured on the computer by entering the following:

```
winrm create winrm/config/listener?Address=*+Transport=HTTPS
```

Here, the asterisk (*) indicates all configured IP addresses. Note that the *CertificateThumbprint* property must be empty to share the SSL configuration with another service.

You can enable or disable a listener for a specific IP address by entering the following:

```
winrm set winrm/config/listener?Address=IP:192.168.1.225+Transport=HTTP @
{Enabled="true"}
```

or

```
winrm set winrm/config/listener?Address=IP:192.168.1.225+Transport=HTTP @
{Enabled="false"}
```

You can enable or disable basic authentication on the client by entering the following:

```
winrm set winrm/config/client/auth @{Basic="true"}
```

or

```
winrm set winrm/config/client/auth @{Basic="false"}
```

You can enable or disable Windows authentication using either NTLM or Kerberos (as appropriate) by entering the following:

```
winrm set winrm/config/client @{TrustedHosts="<local>"}
```

or

```
winrm set winrm/config/client @{TrustedHosts=""}
```

In addition to managing WinRM at the command line, you can manage the service by using Group Policy. As a result, Group Policy settings might override any settings you enter.

CHAPTER 2

Deploying Windows Server 2012 R2

- Server roles, role services, and features for Windows Server 2012 R2 **32**
- Full-server, minimal-interface, and Server Core installations **40**
- Installing Windows Server 2012 R2 **44**

Servers are the heart of any Windows network. One of your primary responsibilities as an administrator is to manage these resources. Windows Server 2012 R2 comes with several integrated management tools. The one you'll use for handling core system administration tasks is Server Manager. Server Manager provides setup and configuration options for the local server in addition to options for managing roles, features, and related settings on any remotely manageable server in the enterprise. Tasks you can use Server Manager to perform include the following:

- Adding servers for remote management
- Initiating remote connections to servers
- Configuring the local server
- Managing installed roles and features
- Managing volumes and shares on file servers
- Configuring Network Interface Card (NIC) Teaming
- Viewing events and alerts
- Restarting servers

Server Manager is great for general system administration, but you also need a tool that gives you granular control over system environment settings and properties. This is where the System utility comes into the picture. You can use this utility to do the following:

- Change a computer's name.
- Configure application performance, virtual memory, and registry settings.
- Manage system and user environment variables.
- Set system startup and recovery options.

Server roles, role services, and features for Windows Server 2012 R2

Windows Server 2012 R2 uses the same configuration architecture as Windows Server 2012. You prepare servers for deployment by installing and configuring the following components:

- **Server roles**   A server role is a related set of software components that allows a server to perform a specific function for users and other computers on a network. A computer can be dedicated to a single role, such as Active Directory Domain Services (AD DS), or provide multiple roles.

- **Role services**   A role service is a software component that provides the functionality for a server role. Each role can have one or more related role services. Some server roles, such as Domain Name System (DNS) and Dynamic Host Configuration Protocol (DHCP), have a single function, and installing the role installs this function. Other roles, such as Network Policy and Access Services, and Active Directory Certificate Services (AD CS), have multiple role services that you can install. With these server roles, you can choose which role services to install.

- **Features**   A feature is a software component that provides additional functionality. Features, such as BitLocker Drive Encryption and Windows Server Backup, are installed and removed separately from roles and role services. A computer can have zero or more features installed, depending on its configuration.

You configure roles, role services, and features by using Server Manager, a Microsoft Management Console (MMC). Some roles, role services, and features are dependent on other roles, role services, and features. As you install roles, role services, and features, Server Manager prompts you to install other roles, role services, or features that are required. Similarly, if you try to remove a required component of an installed role, role service, or feature, Server Manager warns that you cannot remove the component unless you also remove dependent roles, role services, or features.

Because adding or removing roles, role services, and features can change hardware requirements, you should carefully plan any configuration changes and determine how they affect a server's overall performance. Although you typically want to combine complementary roles, doing so increases the workload on the server, so you need to optimize the server hardware accordingly. Table 2-1 provides an overview of the primary roles and the related role services you can deploy on a server running Windows Server 2012 R2.

TABLE 2-1 Primary Roles and Related Role Services for Windows Server 2012 R2

ROLE	DESCRIPTION
Active Directory Certificate Services (AD CS)	Provides functions necessary for issuing and revoking digital certificates for users, client computers, and servers. Includes these role services: Certification Authority, Certification Enrollment Policy Web Service, Certification Authority Web Enrollment, Network Device Enrollment Service, and Online Responder.
Active Directory Domain Services (AD DS)	Provides functions necessary for storing information about users, groups, computers, and other objects on the network, and makes this information available to users and computers. Active Directory domain controllers give network users and computers access to permitted resources on the network.
Active Directory Federation Services (AD FS)	Complements the authentication and access management features of AD DS by extending them to the World Wide Web.
Active Directory Lightweight Directory Services (AD LDS)	Provides a data store for directory-enabled applications that do not require AD DS and do not need to be deployed on domain controllers.
Active Directory Rights Management Services (AD RMS)	Provides controlled access to protected email messages, documents, intranet pages, and other types of files. Includes these role services: Active Directory Rights Management Server and Identity Federation Support.
Application Server	Allows a server to host distributed applications built by using ASP.NET, Enterprise Services, and Microsoft .NET Framework 4.5. Includes COM+ Network Access, TCP Port Sharing, and other role services.
DHCP Server	DHCP provides centralized control over IP addressing. DHCP servers can assign dynamic IP addresses and essential TCP/IP settings to other computers on a network.
DNS Server	DNS is a name-resolution system that resolves computer names to IP addresses. DNS servers are essential for name resolution in Active Directory domains.

ROLE	DESCRIPTION
Fax Server	Provides centralized control over sending and receiving faxes in the enterprise. A fax server can act as a gateway for faxing and allows you to manage fax resources, such as jobs and reports, and fax devices on the server or on the network.
File And Storage Services	Provides essential services for managing files and storage, and the way they are made available and replicated on the network. A number of server roles require some type of file service. Includes these role services and subservices: BranchCache for Network Files, Data Deduplication, Distributed File System (DFS), DFS Namespaces, DFS Replication, File Server, File Server Resource Manager, Services for Network File System (NFS), File Server VSS Agent Service, Internet SCSI (iSCSI) Target Server, iSCSI Target Storage Provider, Server for NFS, Storage Services, and Work Folders.
Hyper-V	Provides services for creating and managing virtual machines that emulate physical computers. Virtual machines have separate operating system environments from the host server.
Network Policy and Access Services (NPAS)	Provides essential services for managing network access policies. Includes these role services: Network Policy Server (NPS), Health Registration Authority (HRA), and Host Credentials Authorization Protocol (HCAP).
Print And Document Services	Provides essential services for managing network printers, network scanners, and related drivers. Includes these role services: Print Server, Distributed Scan Server, Internet Printing, and LPD Service.
Remote Access	Provides services for managing routing and remote access to networks. Use this role if you need to configure virtual private networks (VPNs), network address translation (NAT), and other routing services. Includes these role services: DirectAccess and VPN (RAS), Routing, and Web Application Proxy.

ROLE	DESCRIPTION
Remote Desktop Services	Provides services that allow users to run Windows-based applications that are installed on a remote server. When users run an application on a terminal server, the execution and processing occur on the server, and only the data from the application is transmitted over the network. Includes Remote Desktop role services: Connection Broker, Gateway, Licensing, Session Host, Virtualization Host, and Web Access.
Volume Activation Services	Provides services for automating the management of volume license keys and volume key activation.
Web Server (IIS)	Used to host websites and web-based applications. Websites hosted on a web server can have both static content and dynamic content. You can build web applications hosted on a web server by using ASP.NET and .NET Framework 4.5. When you deploy a web server, you can manage the server configuration by using Microsoft Internet Information Services (IIS) modules and administration tools. Includes several dozen role services.
Windows Deployment Services (WDS)	Provides services for deploying Windows computers in the enterprise. Includes these role services: Deployment Server and Transport Server.
Windows Server Essentials Experience	Provides services for deploying workplaces, which are remotely accessible through a web gateway. Requires single-domain installation.
Windows Server Update Services (WSUS)	Provides services for Microsoft Update, allowing you to distribute updates from designated servers. Includes role services: WID Database, WSUS Services, and Database.

Table 2-2 provides an overview of the primary features you can deploy on a server running Windows Server 2012 R2. Unlike early releases of Windows, Windows Server 2012 R2 does not install some important server features automatically. For example, you must add Windows Server Backup to use the built-in backup and restore features of the operating system.

TABLE 2-2 Primary Features for Windows Server 2012 R2

FEATURE	DESCRIPTION
Background Intelligent Transfer Service (BITS)	Provides intelligent background transfers. When this feature is installed, the server can act as a BITS server that can receive file uploads from clients. This feature isn't necessary for downloads to clients that are using BITS. Additional subfeatures include IIS Server Extension and Compact Server.
BitLocker Drive Encryption	Provides hardware-based security to protect data through full-volume encryption that prevents disk tampering while the operating system is offline. Computers that have Trusted Platform Module (TPM) can use BitLocker Drive Encryption in Startup Key or TPM-Only mode. Both modes provide early integrity validation.
BitLocker Network Unlock	Provides support for network-based key protectors that automatically unlock BitLocker-protected operating system drives when a domain-joined computer is restarted.
BranchCache	Provides services needed for BranchCache client and server functionality. Includes HTTP protocol, Hosted Cache, and related services.
Client for NFS	Provides functionality for accessing files on UNIX-based NFS servers.
Data Center Bridging	Supports a suite of IEEE standards for enhancing LANs and enforcing bandwidth allocation.
Enhanced Storage	Provides support for Enhanced Storage Devices.
Failover Clustering	Provides clustering functionality that allows multiple servers to work together to provide high availability for services and applications. Many types of services can be clustered, including file and print services. Messaging and database servers are ideal candidates for clustering.
Group Policy Management	Installs the Group Policy Management Console (GPMC), which provides centralized administration of Group Policy.
Ink and Handwriting Services	Provides support for use of a pen or stylus and handwriting recognition.

FEATURE	DESCRIPTION
IP Address Management Server	Provides support for central management of the enterprise's IP address space and the related infrastructure servers.
Internet Printing Client	Provides functionality that allows clients to use HTTP to connect to printers on web print servers.
iSNS Server Service	Provides management and server functions for iSCSI devices, allowing the server to process registration requests, deregistration requests, and queries from iSCSI devices.
LPR Port Monitor	Installs the LPR Port Monitor, which allows printing to devices attached to UNIX-based computers.
Media Foundation	Provides essential functionality for Windows Media Foundation.
Message Queuing	Provides management and server functions for distributed message queuing. A group of related subfeatures also is available.
Multipath I/O	Provides functionality necessary for using multiple data paths to a storage device.
.NET Framework 4.5	Provides application programming interfaces (APIs) for application development. Replaces .NET 3.5 as the default framework. Only the framework and TCP Port Sharing are installed by default. Other subfeatures include: ASP.NET 4.5, HTTP Activation, Message Queuing Activation, Named Pipe Activation, and TCP Activation.
Network Load Balancing	Network Load Balancing provides failover support and load balancing for IP-based applications and services by distributing incoming application requests among a group of participating servers. Web servers are ideal candidates for load balancing.
Peer Name Resolution Protocol (PNRP)	Provides Link-Local Multicast Name Resolution (LLMNR) functionality that allows peer-to-peer, name-resolution services. When you install this feature, applications running on the server can use LLMNR to register and resolve names.
Quality Windows Audio Video Experience	A networking platform for audio/video (AV) streaming applications on IP home networks.
RAS Connection Manager Administration Kit	Provides the framework for creating profiles for connecting to remote servers and networks.

FEATURE	DESCRIPTION
Remote Assistance	Allows a remote user to connect to the server to provide or receive Remote Assistance.
Remote Differential Compression	Provides support for differential compression by determining which parts of a file have changed and replicating only the changes.
Remote Server Administration Tools (RSAT)	Installs role-management and feature-management tools that can be used for remote administration of other Windows Server systems. Options for individual tools are provided, or you can install tools by top-level category or subcategory.
Remote Procedure Call (RPC) over HTTP Proxy	Installs a proxy for relaying RPC messages from client applications to the server over HTTP. RPC over HTTP is an alternative to having clients access the server over a VPN connection.
Simple TCP/IP Services	Installs additional TCP/IP services, including Character Generator, Daytime, Discard, Echo, and Quote of the Day.
SMB 1.0/CIFS File Sharing Support	Provides support for legacy file shares and clients.
Simple Mail Transfer Protocol (SMTP) Server	SMTP is a network protocol for controlling the transfer and routing of email messages. When this feature is installed, the server can act as a basic SMTP server. For a full-featured solution, you need to install a messaging server, such as Microsoft Exchange Server.
Simple Network Management Protocol (SNMP) Services	SNMP is a protocol used to simplify management of TCP/IP networks. You can use SNMP for centralized network management if your network has SNMP-compliant devices. You can also use SNMP for network monitoring via network management software.
User Interfaces And Infrastructure	Allows you to control the user experience and infra-structure options (Graphical Management Tools And Infrastructure, Desktop Experience, or Server Graphical Shell).
Windows Biometric Framework	Provides functionality required for using fingerprint devices.

FEATURE	DESCRIPTION
Windows Internal Database	Allows the server to use relational databases with Windows roles and features that require an internal database, such as AD RMS, Universal Description, Discovery, and Integration (UDDI) Services, WSUS, Windows SharePoint Services, and Windows System Resource Manager.
Windows PowerShell	Allows you to manage the Windows PowerShell features of the server. Windows PowerShell and the Windows PowerShell Integrated Scripting Environment (ISE) are installed by default.
Windows PowerShell Web Access	Allows the server to act as a web gateway for remotely managing servers in a web browser.
Windows Process Activation Service	Provides support for distributed, web-based applications that use HTTP and non-HTTP protocols.
Windows Standards-Based Storage Management	Provides support for managing standards-based storage, and includes management interfaces and extensions for Windows Management Instrumentation (WMI) and Windows PowerShell.
Windows Server Backup	Allows you to back up and restore the operating system, system state, and any data stored on a server.
Windows TIFF IFilter	Focuses on text-based documents, which means thatsearching is more successful for documents that contain clearly identifiable text (for example, black text on a white background).
WinRM IIS Extension	Provides an IIS–based hosting model. WinRM IIS Extension can be enabled at either the website or virtual-directory level.
Windows Internet Name Service (WINS) Server	A name-resolution service that resolves computer names to IP addresses. Installing this feature allows the computer to act as a WINS server.
Wireless LAN Service	Allows the server to use wireless networking connections and profiles.
WoW64 Support	Supports WoW64, which is required on a full-server installation. Removing this feature converts a full-server installation to a Server Core installation.
XPS Viewer	A program you can use to view, search, set permissions for, and digitally sign XPS documents.

NOTE Desktop Experience is now a subfeature of the top-level feature called User Interfaces And Infrastructure. Desktop Experience provides Windows desktop functionality on the server. Windows features added include Windows Media Player, desktop themes, Video for Windows (AVI support), Disk Cleanup, Sync Center, Sound Recorder, Character Map, and Snipping Tool. Although these features allow a server to be used like a desktop computer, they can reduce the server's overall performance.

As an administrator, you might be asked to install or uninstall dynamic-link libraries (DLLs), particularly if you work with IT development teams. The utility you use to work with DLLs is Regsvr32. This utility is run at the command line. After you open a Command Prompt window, you install or register a DLL by entering **regsvr32 name.dll**, as in this example:

```
regsvr32 mylibs.dll
```

If necessary, you can uninstall or unregister a DLL by entering **regsvr32 /u name.dll**, as in this example:

```
regsvr32 /u mylibs.dll
```

Windows File Protection prevents the replacement of protected system files. You can replace only DLLs installed by the Windows Server operating system as part of a hotfix, service pack update, Windows update, or Windows upgrade. Windows File Protection is an important part of the Windows Server security architecture.

Full-server, minimal-interface, and Server Core installations

Windows Server 2012 R2 supports full-server, minimal-interface, and Server Core installations. Full-server installations, also referred to as *Server With A GUI Installations*, have the Graphical Management Tools And Infrastructure and Server Graphical Shell features (which are part of the User And Infrastructure feature) and the WoW64 Support framework installed. Minimal-interface installations, also referred to as Server With Minimal Interface Installations, are full-server installations with the Server Graphical Shell removed. Server Core installations have a limited user interface and do not include any of the User Interfaces And Infrastructure features or the WoW64 Support framework.

As discussed in "Changing the installation type" section later in this chapter, the installation type can be changed at any time. With a full-server installation, you have a complete working version of Windows Server 2012 R2 that you can deploy with any permitted combination of roles, role services, and features. With a minimal-interface installation, you also can deploy any permitted combination of roles, role services, and features. However, with a Server Core installation, you have a minimal installation of Windows Server 2012 R2 that supports a limited set of roles and role combinations. The supported roles include AD CS, AD DS, AD LDS, DHCP Server, DNS Server, File Services, Hyper-V, Media Services, Print And Document Services, Routing And Remote Access Server, Streaming Media Services, Web Server (IIS), and Windows Server Update Server. In its current implementation, a Server Core installation is not a platform for running server applications.

Although all three installation types use the same licensing rules and can be managed remotely by using any available and permitted remote-administration technique, full-server, minimal-interface, and Server Core installations are completely different when it comes to local console administration. With a full-server installation, you're provided with a user interface that includes a full desktop environment for local console management of the server. With a minimal interface, you have only Microsoft Management Consoles, Server Manager, and a subset of Control Panel available for management tasks. Missing from both a minimal-interface installation and a Server Core installation are File Explorer, the taskbar, the notification area, Internet Explorer, a built-in Help system, themes, Metro-style apps, and Windows Media Player.

Navigating Server Core

With a Server Core installation, you get a user interface that includes a limited desktop environment for local console management of the server. This minimal interface includes the following:

- Windows Logon screen for logging on and logging off
- Notepad (Notepad.exe) for editing files
- Registry Editor (Regedit.exe) for managing the registry
- Task Manager (Taskmgr.exe) for managing tasks and starting new tasks
- Command prompt (Cmd.exe) for administration using the command line
- Windows PowerShell prompt for administration using Windows PowerShell
- File Signature Verification tool (Sigverif.exe) for verifying digital signatures of system files
- System Information (Msinfo32.exe) for getting system information
- Windows Installer (Msiexec.exe) for managing Windows Installer
- Date And Time control panel (Timedate.cpl) for viewing or setting the date, time, and time zone
- Region And Language control panel (Intl.cpl) for viewing or setting regional and language options, including formats and the keyboard layout
- Server Configuration utility (Sconfig.exe), which provides a text-based menu system for managing a server's configuration

When you start a server with a Server Core installation, you can use the Windows Logon screen to log on just as you do with a full-server installation. In a domain, the standard restrictions apply for logging on to servers, and anyone with appropriate user rights and logon permissions can log on to the server. On servers that are not acting as domain controllers and for servers in workgroup environments, you can use the NET USER command to add users, and the NET LOCALGROUP command to add users to local groups for the purposes of logging on locally.

After you log on to a Server Core installation, you have a limited desktop environment with an administrator command prompt. You can use this command prompt for administration of the server. If you accidentally close the command prompt, you can open a new command prompt by following these steps:

1. Press Ctrl+Alt+Delete, and then click Task Manager.
2. In Task Manager, click More Details.
3. On the File menu, tap or click Run New Task.
4. In the Create New Task dialog box, enter **cmd** in the Open box, and then click OK.

You can use this technique to open additional Command Prompt windows, too. Although you can work with Notepad and Regedit by entering **notepad.exe** or **regedit.exe** instead of **cmd**, you can also start Notepad and Regedit directly from a command prompt by entering **notepad.exe** or **regedit.exe** as appropriate.

The Server Configuration utility (Sconfig) provides a text-based menu system that makes it easy to do the following:

- Configure domain or workgroup membership.
- Change a server's name.
- Add a local Administrator account.
- Configure remote management features.
- Configure Windows Update settings.
- Download and install Windows updates.
- Enable or disable Remote Desktop.
- Configure network settings for TCP/IP.
- Configure the date and time.
- Log off, restart, or shut down.

When you are logged on, you can display the Windows Logon screen at any time by pressing Ctrl+Alt+Delete. In a Server Core installation, the Windows Logon screen has the same options as it does in a full-server installation, allowing you to lock the computer, switch users, log off, change a password, or start Task Manager. At the command prompt, you have all the standard commands and command-line utilities available for managing the server. However, commands, utilities, and programs run only if all of their dependencies are available in the Server Core installation.

Although a Server Core installation supports a limited set of roles and role services, you can install most features. Windows Server 2012 R2 also supports the .NET Framework, Windows PowerShell, and Windows Remote Management (WinRM). This support allows you to perform local and remote administration by using Windows PowerShell. You also can use a Remote Desktop client to manage a Server Core installation remotely. Some of the common tasks you might want to perform when you are logged on locally are summarized in Table 2-3.

COMMAND	TASK
Cscript Scregedit.wsf	Configure the operating system. Use the /cli parameter to list available configuration areas.
ipconfig /all	List information about the computer's IP address configuration.
Netdom RenameComputer	Set the server's name.
Netdom Join	Join the server to a domain.
Netsh	Provide multiple contexts for managing the configuration of networking components. Enter netsh interface ipv4 to configure IPv4 settings. Enter netsh interface ipv6 to configure IPv6 settings.
Pnputil.exe	Install or update hardware device drivers.
Sc query type=driver	List installed device drivers.
Serverweroptin.exe	Configure Windows Error Reporting.
Slmgr −ato	Windows Software Licensing Management tool used to activate the operating system. Runs `Cscript slmgr.vbs −ato`
Slmgr −ipk	Install or replace the product key. Runs `Cscript slmgr.vbs −ipk`
SystemInfo	List the system configuration details.
Wecutil.exe	Create and manage subscriptions to forwarded events.
Wevtutil.exe	View and search event logs.
Winrm quickconfig	Configure the server to access requests for WS-Management from other computers. Runs `Cscript winrm.vbs quickconfig` Enter without the quickconfig parameter to see other options.
Wmic datafile where name="FullFilePath" get version	List a file's version.
Wmic nicconfig index=9 call enabledhcp	Set the computer to use dynamic IP addressing rather than static IP addressing.

COMMAND	TASK
Wmic nicconfig index=9 call enablestatic("IPAddress"), ("SubnetMask")	Set a computer's static IP address and network mask.
Wmic nicconfig index=9 call setgateways("GatewayIPAddress")	Set or change the default gateway.
Wmic product get name /value	List installed Windows Installer (MSI) applications by name.
Wmic product where name="Name" call uninstall	Uninstall an MSI application.
Wmic qfe list	List installed updates and hotfixes.
Wusa.exe PatchName.msu /quiet	Apply an update or hotfix to the operating system.

Installing Windows Server 2012 R2

You can install Windows Server 2012 R2 on new hardware or as an upgrade. When you install Windows Server 2012 R2 on a computer with an existing operating system, you can perform a clean installation or an upgrade. With a clean installation, the Windows Server 2012 R2 Setup program replaces the original operating system on the computer, and all user or application settings are lost. With an upgrade, the Setup program performs a clean installation of the operating system and then migrates user settings, documents, and applications from the earlier version of Windows.

Windows Server 2012 R2 supports only 64-bit architecture. You can install the operating system only on computers with 64-bit processors. Before you install Windows Server 2012 R2, you should be sure that your computer meets the minimum requirements of the edition you plan to use. Microsoft provides both minimum requirements and recommended requirements. If your computer doesn't meet the minimum requirements, you will not be able to install Windows Server 2012 R2. If your computer doesn't meet the recommended requirements, you will experience performance issues.

Windows Server 2012 R2 requires at least 10 gigabytes (GB) of disk space for installation of the base operating system. Microsoft recommends that a computer running Windows Server 2012 R2 have 32 GB or more of available disk space. Additional disk space is required for paging and dump files and also for the features, roles, and role services you install. For optimal performance, you should have at least 10 percent of free space on a server's disks at all times.

When you install Windows Server 2012 R2, the Setup program automatically makes recovery options available on your server as an advanced boot option. In addition to a command line for troubleshooting and options for changing the startup behavior, you can use System Image Recovery to perform a full recovery of the computer by using a system image created previously. If other troubleshooting techniques fail to restore the computer and you have a system image for recovery, you can use this feature to restore the computer from the backup image.

Performing a clean installation

Before you start an installation, you need to consider whether you want to manage the computer's drives and partitions during the setup process. If you want to use the advanced drive setup options that Setup provides for creating and formatting partitions, you need to start the computer by using the distribution media. If you don't start by using the distribution media, these options won't be available, and you'll be able to manage disk partitions at a command prompt only by using the DiskPart utility.

You can perform a clean installation of Windows Server 2012 R2 by following these steps:

1. Start the Setup program by using one of the following techniques:

   - For a new installation, turn on the computer with the Windows Server 2012 R2 distribution media in the computer's disc drive, and then press any key when prompted to start Setup from your media. If you are not prompted to boot from the disc drive, you might need to select advanced boot options and then boot from the media rather than from the hard disk, or you might need to change the computer's firmware settings to allow starting and loading the operating system from media.

   - For a clean installation over an existing installation, you can boot from the distribution media, or you can start the computer and log on by using an account with administrator privileges. When you insert the Windows Server 2012 R2 distribution media into the computer's disc drive, Setup should start automatically. If Setup doesn't start automatically, use File Explorer to access the distribution media, and then double-tap or double-click Setup.exe.

2. If you started the computer by using the distribution media, choose your language, time and currency formats, and keyboard layout when prompted. Only one keyboard layout is available during installation. If your keyboard language and the language edition of Windows Server 2012 R2 you are installing are different, you might see unexpected characters as you type. Be sure that you select the correct keyboard language to avoid this. When you are ready to continue with the installation, tap or click Next.

3. Click Install Now to start the installation. After Setup copies the temporary files to the computer, choose whether to get updates for Setup during the installation. If you started Setup after logging on to an existing installation of Windows, click either Go Online To Install Updates Now or No, Thanks.

4. With volume and enterprise licensed editions of Windows Server 2012 R2, you might not need to provide a product key during installation. With retail editions, however, you need to enter a product key when prompted. Tap or click Next to continue. The Activate Windows When I'm Online check box is selected by default to ensure that you are prompted to activate the operating system the next time you connect to the Internet.

    NOTE You must activate Windows Server 2012 R2 after installation. If you don't activate Windows Server 2012 R2 in the allotted time, you get an error stating "Your activation period has expired" or that you have a "Non-genuine version of Windows Server 2012 R2 installed." Windows Server 2012 R2 will then run with reduced functionality. You need to activate and validate Windows Server 2012 R2 as necessary to regain full functionality.

5. On the Select The Operating System You Want To Install page, options are provided for full-server and Server Core installations. Make the appropriate selection, and then tap or click Next.

6. The license terms for Windows Server 2012 R2 have changed from previous releases of Windows. After you review the license terms, tap or click I Accept The License Terms, and then tap or click Next.

7. On the Which Type Of Installation Do You Want page, choose the type of installation you want Setup to perform. Because you are performing a clean installation to replace an existing installation or configure a new computer, click Custom Install Windows Only (Advanced) as the installation type. If you started Setup from the boot prompt rather than from Windows itself, the Upgrade option is disabled. To upgrade rather than perform a clean install, you need to restart the computer and boot the currently installed operating system. After you log on, you then need to start the installation.

8. On the Where Do You Want To Install Windows page, select the disk or disk and partition on which you want to install the operating system. There are two versions of the Where Do You Want To Install Windows page, so you need to keep the following in mind:

    ■ When a computer has a single hard disk with a single partition encompassing the whole disk or a single area of unallocated space, the whole disk partition is selected by default, and you can tap or click Next to choose this as the install location and continue. With a disk that is completely unallocated, you might want to create the necessary partition before installing the operating system, as discussed in the "Creating, formatting, deleting, and extending disk partitions during installation" section later in this chapter.

    ■ When a computer has multiple disks or a single disk with multiple partitions, you need to select an existing partition to use for installing the operating system or create a partition. You can create and manage partitions, as discussed in the "Creating, formatting, deleting, and extending disk partitions during installation" section later in this chapter.

- If a disk has not been initialized for use or if the firmware of the computer does not support starting the operating system from the selected disk, you need to initialize it by creating one or more partitions on the disk. You cannot select or format a hard disk partition that uses FAT or FAT32 or has other incompatible settings. To work around this issue, you might want to convert the partition to NTFS. When working with this page, you can access a command prompt to perform any necessary preinstallation tasks. See the "Creating, formatting, deleting, and extending disk partitions during installation" section later in this chapter.

9. If the partition you select contains a previous Windows installation, Setup provides a prompt stating that existing user and application settings will be moved to a folder named Windows.old and that you must copy these settings to the new installation to use them. Tap or click OK.

10. Tap or click Next. Setup starts the installation of the operating system. During this procedure, Setup copies the full disk image of Windows Server 2012 R2 to the location you selected and then expands it. Afterward, Setup installs features based on the computer's configuration and the hardware it detects. This process requires several automatic restarts. When Setup finishes the installation, the operating system will be loaded, and you can perform initial configuration tasks such as setting the administrator password and server name.

REAL WORLD Servers running core installations of Windows Server are configured to use DHCP by default. As long as the server has a network card and a connected network cable, a Server Core installation should be able to connect to your organization's DHCP servers and obtain the correct network settings. However, many enterprise data centers do not use or provide DHCP for servers, and assign static IP addresses. You can configure the server by using Sconfig, which provides menu options for configuring domain/workgroup membership, the computer name, remote management, Windows Update, Remote Desktop, network settings, date and time, logoff, restart, and shutdown.

Alternatively, you can configure the server by using individual commands. If you want to use a static IP address, use Netsh to apply the settings you want. After networking is configured correctly, enter **Slmgr –ipk** to set the product key and **Slmgr –ato** to activate Windows. Enter **timedate.cpl** to set the server's date and time. If you want to enable remote management by using the WS-Management protocol, enter **winrm quickconfig**.

Next, you'll probably want to set the name of the computer. To view the default computer name, enter **echo %computername%**. To rename the computer, use Netdom RenameComputer with the following syntax: **netdom renamecomputer** *currentname* **/newname:***newname*, where *currentname* is the current name of the computer and *newname* is the name you want to assign. An example is **netdom renamecomputer win-k4m6bnovlhe /newname:server18**. You'll need to restart the computer, and you can do this by entering **shutdown /r**.

When the computer restarts, you can join it to a domain by using Netdom Join. For the syntax, enter **netdom join /?**.

Performing an upgrade installation

Although Windows Server 2012 R2 provides an upgrade option during installation, an upgrade isn't what you think it is. With an upgrade, Setup performs a clean installation of the operating system and then migrates user settings, documents, and applications from the earlier version of Windows.

During the migration portion of the upgrade, Setup moves folders and files from the previous installation to a folder named Windows.old. As a result, the previous installation will no longer run.

NOTE You cannot perform an upgrade installation of Windows Server 2012 R2 on a computer with a 32-bit operating system, even if the computer has 64-bit processors. You need to migrate the services being provided by the computer to other servers and then perform a clean installation. The Windows Server Migration tools might be able to help you migrate your server. These tools are available on computers running Windows Server 2012 R2.

You can perform an upgrade installation of Windows Server 2012 R2 by following these steps:

1. Start the computer, and log on by using an account with administrator privileges. When you insert the Windows Server 2012 R2 distribution media into the computer's DVD-ROM drive, Setup should start automatically. If Setup doesn't start automatically, use File Explorer to access the distribution media and then double-tap or double-click Setup.exe.

2. Because you are starting Setup from the current operating system, you are not prompted to choose your language, time and currency formats, or keyboard layout, and only the current operating system's keyboard layout is available during installation. If your keyboard language and the language of the edition of Windows Server 2012 R2 you are installing are different, unexpected characters might be displayed as you type.

3. Choose Install Now to start the installation. After Setup copies the temporary files to the computer, choose whether to get updates during the installation. Click either Go Online To Install Updates Now or No, Thanks.

4. With volume-licensed and enterprise-licensed editions of Windows Server 2012 R2, you might not need to provide a product key during installation of the operating system. With retail editions, however, you are prompted to enter a product key. Tap or click Next to continue. The Automatically Activate Windows When I'm Online check box is selected by default to ensure that you are prompted to activate the operating system the next time you connect to the Internet.

5. On the Select The Operating System You Want To Install page, options are provided for full-server and Server Core installations. Make the appropriate selection, and then tap or click Next.

6. The license terms for Windows Server 2012 R2 have changed from previous releases of Windows. After you review the license terms, tap or click I Accept The License Terms, and then tap or click Next.

7. On the Which Type Of Installation Do You Want page, you need to select the type of installation you want Setup to perform. Because you are performing a clean installation over an existing installation, select Upgrade. If you started Setup from the boot prompt rather than from Windows itself, the Upgrade option is disabled. To upgrade rather than perform a clean install, you need to restart the computer and boot the currently installed operating system. After you log on, you can start the installation.

8. Setup will then start the installation. Because you are upgrading the operating system, you do not need to choose an installation location. During this process, Setup copies the full disk image of Windows Server 2012 R2 to the system disk. Afterward, Setup installs features based on the computer's configuration and the hardware it detects. When Setup finishes the installation, the operating system will be loaded, and you can perform initial configuration tasks such as setting the administrator password and server name.

Performing additional administration tasks during installation

Sometimes you might forget to perform a preinstallation task prior to starting the installation. Rather than restarting the operating system, you can access a command prompt from Setup or use advanced drive options to perform the necessary administrative tasks.

Using the command line during installation

When you access a command prompt from Setup, you access the Windows Preinstallation Environment (Windows PE) used by Setup to install the operating system. During installation, on the Where Do You Want To Install Windows page, you can access a command prompt by pressing Shift+F10. As Table 2-4 shows, the Windows PE gives you access to many of the same command-line tools that are available in a standard installation of Windows Server 2012 R2.

TABLE 2-4 Command-Line Utilities in the Windows Preinstallation Environment

COMMAND	DESCRIPTION
ARP	Displays and modifies the IP-to-physical address translation tables used by the Address Resolution Protocol (ARP).
ASSOC	Displays and modifies file extension associations.
ATTRIB	Displays and changes file attributes.
CALL	Calls a script or script label as a procedure.
CD/CHDIR	Displays the name of or changes the current directory.
CHKDSK	Checks a disk for errors and displays a report.
CHKNTFS	Displays the status of volumes. Sets or excludes volumes from automatic system checking when the computer is started.
CHOICE	Creates a list from which users can select one of several choices in a batch script.
CLS	Clears the console window.
CMD	Starts a new instance of the Windows command shell.
COLOR	Sets the colors of the command-shell window.
CONVERT	Converts FAT volumes to NTFS.
COPY	Copies or combines files.
DATE	Displays or sets the system date.
DEL	Deletes one or more files.
DIR	Displays a list of files and subdirectories within a directory.
DISKPART	Invokes a text-mode command interpreter so that you can manage disks, partitions, and volumes by using a separate command prompt and commands that are internal to DISKPART.
DISM	Services and manages Windows images.
DOSKEY	Edits command lines, recalls Windows commands, and creates macros.
ECHO	Displays messages or turns command echoing on or off.
ENDLOCAL	Ends localization of environment changes in a batch file.
ERASE	Deletes one or more files.
EXIT	Exits the command interpreter.
EXPAND	Uncompresses files.
FIND	Searches for a text string in files.
FOR	Runs a specified command for each file in a set of files.

COMMAND	DESCRIPTION
FORMAT	Formats a floppy disk or hard drive.
FTP	Transfers files.
FTYPE	Displays or modifies file types used in file name extension associations.
GOTO	Directs the Windows command interpreter to a labeled line in a script.
HOSTNAME	Prints the computer's name.
IF	Performs conditional processing in batch programs.
IPCONFIG	Displays TCP/IP configuration.
LABEL	Creates, changes, or deletes the volume label of a disk.
MD/MKDIR	Creates a directory or subdirectory.
MORE	Displays output one screen at a time.
MOUNTVOL	Manages a volume mount point.
MOVE	Moves files from one directory to another directory on the same drive.
NBTSTAT	Displays the status of NetBIOS.
NET ACCOUNTS	Manages user account and password policies.
NET COMPUTER	Adds or removes computers from a domain.
NET CONFIG SERVER	Displays or modifies the configuration of a server service.
NET CONFIG WORKSTATION	Displays or modifies the configuration of a workstation service.
NET CONTINUE	Resumes a paused service.
NET FILE	Displays or manages open files on a server.
NET GROUP	Displays or manages global groups.
NET LOCALGROUP	Displays or manages local group accounts.
NET NAME	Displays or modifies recipients for messenger service messages.
NET PAUSE	Suspends a service.
NET PRINT	Displays or manages print jobs and shared queues.
NET SEND	Sends a messenger service message.
NET SESSION	Lists or disconnects sessions.
NET SHARE	Displays or manages shared printers and directories.

COMMAND	DESCRIPTION
NET START	Lists or starts network services.
NET STATISTICS	Displays workstation and server statistics.
NET STOP	Stops services.
NET TIME	Displays or synchronizes network time.
NET USE	Displays or manages remote connections.
NET USER	Displays or manages local user accounts.
NET VIEW	Displays network resources or computers.
NETSH	Invokes a separate command prompt that allows you to manage the configuration of various network services on local and remote computers.
NETSTAT	Displays the status of network connections.
PATH	Displays or sets a search path for executable files in the current command window.
PATHPING	Traces routes, and provides packet-loss information.
PAUSE	Suspends the processing of a script, and waits for keyboard input.
PING	Determines whether a network connection can be established.
POPD	Changes to the directory stored by PUSHD.
PRINT	Prints a text file.
PROMPT	Modifies the command prompt.
PUSHD	Saves the current directory and then changes to a new directory.
RD/RMDIR	Removes a directory.
RECOVER	Recovers readable information from a bad or defective disk.
REG ADD	Adds a new subkey or entry to the registry.
REG COMPARE	Compares registry subkeys or entries.
REG COPY	Copies a registry entry to a specified key path on a local or remote system.
REG DELETE	Deletes a subkey or entries from the registry.
REG QUERY	Lists the entries under a key and the names of subkeys (if any).
REG RESTORE	Writes saved subkeys and entries back to the registry.

COMMAND	DESCRIPTION
REG SAVE	Saves a copy of specified subkeys, entries, and values to a file.
REGSVR32	Registers and unregisters DLLs.
REM	Adds comments to scripts.
REN	Renames a file.
ROUTE	Manages network routing tables.
SET	Displays or modifies Windows environment variables. Also used to evaluate numeric expressions at the command line.
SETLOCAL	Begins the localization of environment changes in a batch file.
SFC	Scans and verifies protected system files.
SHIFT	Shifts the position of replaceable parameters in scripts.
START	Starts a new command-shell window to run a specified program or command.
SUBST	Maps a path to a drive letter.
TIME	Displays or sets the system time.
TITLE	Sets the title for the command-shell window.
TRACERT	Displays the path between computers.
TYPE	Displays the contents of a text file.
VER	Displays the Windows version.
VERIFY	Tells Windows whether to verify that your files are written correctly to a disk.
VOL	Displays a disk volume label and serial number.

Forcing disk partition removal during installation

During installation, you might be unable to select the hard disk you want to use. This issue can arise if the hard-disk partition contains an invalid byte offset value. To resolve this issue, you need to remove the partitions on the hard disk (which destroys all associated data) and then create the necessary partition by using the advanced options in the Setup program. During installation, on the Where Do You Want To Install Windows page, you can remove unrecognized hard-disk partitions by following these steps:

1. Press Shift+F10 to open a command prompt.
2. At the command prompt, enter **diskpart**. This starts the DiskPart utility.
3. To view a list of disks on the computer, enter **list disk**.
4. Select a disk by entering **select disk *DiskNumber***, where *DiskNumber* is the number of the disk you want to work with.

5. To permanently remove the partitions on the selected disk, enter **clean**.

6. When the cleaning process is finished, enter **exit** to exit the DiskPart utility.

7. Enter **exit** to exit the command prompt.

8. In the Install Windows dialog box, tap or click the back arrow button to return to the previous window.

9. On the Which Type Of Installation Do You Want page, tap or click Custom (Advanced) to start a custom install.

10. On the Where Do You Want To Install Windows page, tap or click the disk you previously cleaned to select it as the installation partition. As necessary, tap or click the Disk Options link to display the Delete, Format, New, and Extend partition configuration options.

11. Tap or click New. In the Size box, set the size of the partition in megabytes, and then tap or click Apply.

Loading disk device drivers during installation

During installation, on the Where Do You Want To Install Windows page, you can use the Load Driver option to load the device drivers for a hard disk drive or a hard disk controller. Typically, you use this option when a disk drive you want to use for installing the operating system isn't available for selection because the device drivers aren't available.

To load the device drivers and make the hard disk available, follow these steps:

1. During installation, on the Where Do You Want To Install Windows page, tap or click Load Driver.

2. When prompted, insert the installation media into a DVD drive or USB flash drive, and then tap or click OK. Setup then searches the computer's removable media drives for the device drivers.

   - If Setup finds multiple device drivers, select the driver to install, and then tap or click Next.

   - If Setup doesn't find the device driver, tap or click Browse to use the Browse For Folder dialog box to select the device driver to load, tap or click OK, and then tap or click Next.

You can tap or click the Rescan button to have Setup rescan the computer's removable media drives for the device drivers. If you are unable to install a device driver successfully, tap or click the back arrow button in the upper-left corner of the Install Windows dialog box to go back to the previous page.

Creating, formatting, deleting, and extending disk partitions during installation

When you are performing a clean installation and have started the computer from the distribution media, the Where Do You Want To Install Windows page has additional options. You can display these options by tapping or clicking Drive Options (Advanced). These additional options are used as follows:

- **New**   Creates a partition. You must then format the partition.

- **Format**   Formats a new partition so that you can use it for installing the operating system.

- **Delete** Deletes a partition that is no longer wanted.
- **Extend** Extends a partition to increase its size.

The sections that follow discuss how to use each of these options. If these options aren't available, you can still work with the computer's disks. On the Where Do You Want To Install Windows page, press Shift+F10 to open a command prompt. At the command prompt, enter **diskpart** to start the DiskPart utility.

CREATING DISK PARTITIONS DURING INSTALLATION

Creating a partition allows you to set the partition's size. Because you can create new partitions only in areas of unallocated space on a disk, you might need to delete existing partitions to be able to create a partition of the size you want. After you create a partition, you can format the partition so that you can use it to install a file system. If you don't format a partition, you can still use it for installing the operating system. In this case, Setup formats the partition when you continue installing the operating system.

You can create a new partition by following these steps:

1. During installation, on the Where Do You Want To Install Windows page, tap or click Drive Options (Advanced) to display the advanced options for working with drives.
2. Tap or click the disk on which you want to create the partition, and then tap or click New.
3. In the Size box, set the size of the partition in megabytes, and then tap or click Apply to have Setup create a partition on the selected disk.

After you create a partition, you need to format the partition to continue with the installation.

FORMATTING DISK PARTITIONS DURING INSTALLATION

Formatting a partition creates a file system on the partition. When formatting is complete, you have a formatted partition on which you can install the operating system. Keep in mind that formatting a partition destroys all data on the partition. You should format existing partitions (rather than ones you just created) only when you want to remove an existing partition and all its contents so that you can start the installation from a freshly formatted partition.

You can format a partition by following these steps:

1. During installation, on the Where Do You Want To Install Windows page, tap or click Drive Options (Advanced) to display the advanced options for working with drives.
2. Tap or click the partition that you want to format.
3. Tap or click Format. When prompted to confirm that you want to format the partition, tap or click OK. Setup then formats the partition.

DELETING DISK PARTITIONS DURING INSTALLATION

Deleting a partition removes a partition you no longer want or need. When Setup finishes deleting the partition, the disk space previously allocated to the partition becomes unallocated space on the disk. Deleting the partition destroys all data on the partition. Typically, you need to delete a partition only when it is in the wrong format or when you want to combine areas of free space on a disk.

You can delete a partition by following these steps:

1. During installation, on the Where Do You Want To Install Windows page, tap or click Drive Options (Advanced) to display the advanced options for working with drives.
2. Tap or click the partition you want to delete.
3. Tap or click Delete. When prompted to confirm that you want to delete the partition, tap or click OK. Setup then deletes the partition.

EXTENDING DISK PARTITIONS DURING INSTALLATION

Windows Server 2012 R2 requires at least 10 GB of disk space for installation, and at least 32 GB of available disk space is recommended. If an existing partition is too small, you won't be able to use it to install the operating system. To resolve this, you can extend a partition to increase its size by using areas of contiguous, unallocated space on the current disk. You can extend a partition with an existing file system only if it is formatted with NTFS 5.2 or later. New partitions created in Setup can be extended also, provided that the disk on which you create the partition has unallocated space.

You can extend a partition by following these steps:

1. During installation, on the Where Do You Want To Install Windows page, tap or click Drive Options (Advanced) to display the advanced options for working with drives.
2. Tap or click the partition you want to extend.
3. Tap or click Extend. In the Size box, set the size of the partition in megabytes, and then tap or click Apply to extend the selected partition.
4. When prompted to confirm that you want to extend the partition, tap or click OK. Setup then extends the partition.

Changing the installation type

Unlike earlier releases of Windows Server, you can change the installation type of any server running Windows Server 2012 R2. This is possible because a key difference between the installation types relates to whether the installation has the following User Interfaces and Infrastructure features:

- Graphical Management Tools And Infrastructure
- Desktop Experience
- Server Graphical Shell

Full-server installations have both the Graphical Management Tools And Infrastructure feature and the Server Graphical Shell feature. They also might have Desktop Experience. Alternatively, minimal-interface installations have only the Graphical Management Tools And Infrastructure feature and Server Core installations have none of these features.

Knowing that Windows also automatically installs or uninstalls dependent features, server roles, and management tools to match the installation type, you can convert from one installation type to another simply by adding or removing the appropriate User Interfaces and Infrastructure features.

Converting full-server and minimal-interface installations

To convert a full-server installation to a minimal-interface installation, you remove the Server Graphical Shell. Although you can use the Remove Roles And Features Wizard to do this, you also can do this at a Windows PowerShell prompt by entering the following command:

```
uninstall-windowsfeature server-gui-shell -restart
```

This command instructs Windows Server to uninstall the Server Graphical Shell and restart the server to finalize the removal. If Desktop Experience also is installed, this feature also will be removed.

> **TIP** As a best practice before you run this or any other command that might have far-reaching effects, you should run the command with the –Whatif parameter. This parameter tells Windows PowerShell to confirm exactly what will happen when a command is run.

To convert a minimal-interface installation to a full-server installation, you add the Server Graphical Shell. You can use the Add Roles And Features Wizard to do this, or you can enter the following command at a Windows PowerShell prompt:

```
install-windowsfeature server-gui-shell -restart
```

This command instructs Windows Server to install the Server Graphical Shell and restart the server to finalize the installation. If you also want to install the Desktop Experience, you can use this command instead:

```
install-windowsfeature server-gui-shell, desktop-experience -restart
```

Converting Server Core installations

To convert a full-server or minimal-interface installation to a Server Core installation, you remove the user interfaces for Graphical Management Tools And Infrastructure. If you remove the WoW64 Support framework, you also convert the server to a Server Core installation. Although you can use the Remove Roles And Features Wizard to remove the user interfaces, you also can do this at a Windows PowerShell prompt by entering the following command:

```
uninstall-windowsfeature server-gui-mgmt-infra -restart
```

This command instructs Windows Server to uninstall the user interfaces for Graphical Management Tools And Infrastructure and restart the server to finalize the removal. Because many dependent roles, role services, and features might be uninstalled along with the user interfaces, run the command with the –Whatif parameter first to get details on what exactly will be uninstalled.

If you installed the server with the user interfaces and converted it to a Server Core installation, you can revert back to a full-server installation with the following command:

```
install-windowsfeature server-gui-mgmt-infra, server-gui-shell -restart
```

As long as the binaries for this feature and any dependent features haven't been removed, the command should succeed. If the binaries were removed, however, or Server Core was the original installation type, you need to specify a source for the required binaries.

You use the –Source parameter to restore required binaries from a Windows Imaging (WIM) format mount point. For example, if your enterprise has a mounted Windows Image for the edition of Windows Server 2012 R2 that you are working with available at the network path \\ImServer18\WinS12EE, you could specify the source as follows:

```
install-windowsfeature server-gui-mgmt-infra, server-gui-shell
-source \\imserver18\wins12ee
```

Though many large enterprises might have standard images that can be mounted by using network paths, you also can mount the Windows Server 2012 R2 distribution media and then use the Windows\WinSXS folder from the installation image as your source. To do this, follow these steps:

1. Insert the installation disc into the server's disk drive, and then create a folder to mount the installation image by entering the following command: **mkdir c:\mountdir**.

2. Locate the index number of the image you want to use by entering the following command at an elevated command prompt, where *e* is the drive designator of the server's disk drive: **dism /get–wiminfo /wimfile:e:\sources \install.wim**.

3. Mount the installation image by entering the following command at an elevated prompt, where *e* is the drive designator of the server's disk drive, *2* is the index of the image to use, and *c:\mountdir* is the mount directory: **dism /mount–wim /wimfile:e:\sources\install.wim /index:2 /mountdir: c:\mountdir /readonly**. Mounting the image might take several minutes.

4. Use Install–WindowsFeature at a Windows PowerShell prompt with the source specified as **c:\mountdir\windows\winsxs**, as shown in this example:

```
install-windowsfeature server-gui-mgmt-infra, server-gui-shell
-source c:\mountdir\windows\winsxs
```

CHAPTER 3

Managing Windows servers

- Managing roles, role services, and features **59**
- Managing system properties **76**

Although you can manage servers running Windows Server 2012 R2 by logging on locally, you'll more typically perform management tasks from a
management computer with management options installed, including the
Remote Server Administration Tools (RSAT). After you've enabled remote management, you can run the Remote Server Administration Tools on your management computer to perform most routine configuration tasks. At times, you
might also need to use Remote Desktop Connection (mstsc.exe) to establish
remote sessions with servers. Remote Desktop Connection allows you to
manage remote systems in much the same way as you would if you were
logged on locally However, remote management options are not enabled by
default. You must enable these options manually as part of your initial server
configuration. You also must ensure that Windows Firewall or any other firewall
that might be between your management computer and the remote server
has exceptions that allow you to work remotely.

Managing roles, role services, and features

When you want to manage server configurations, you'll primarily use Server
Manager to manage roles, role services, and features. Not only can you use
Server Manager to add or remove roles, role services, and features, but you can
also use Server Manager to view the configuration details and status for these
software components.

Performing initial configuration tasks

Server Manager is your central management console for the initial setup and
configuration of roles and features. Not only can Server Manager help you quickly
set up a new server, the console also can help you quickly set up your management
environment.

Normally, Windows Server 2012 R2 automatically starts Server Manager when-ever you log on, and you can access Server Manager on the desktop. If you don't want the console to start each time you log on, tap or click Manage, and then tap or click Server Manager Properties. In the Server Manager Properties dialog box, select Do Not Start Server Manager Automatically At Logon, and then tap or click OK.

NOTE Group Policy also can be used to control automatic start of Server Manager. Enable or disable the Do Not Display Server Manager Automatically At Logon policy setting within Computer Configuration\Administrative Templates\System\Server Manager.

As Figure 3-1 shows, Server Manager's default view is the dashboard. The dash-board has quick links for adding roles and features to local and remote servers, adding servers to manage, and creating server groups. You'll find similar options are on the Manage menu:

- **Add Roles And Features** Starts the Add Roles And Features Wizard, which you can use to install roles, role services, and features on the server.
- **Add Servers** Opens the Add Servers dialog box, which you can use to add servers you want to manage. Added servers are listed when you select the All Servers node. Press and hold or right-click a server in the Servers pane of the All Servers node to display a list of management options, including Restart Server, Manage As, and Remove Server.
- **Create Server Group** Opens the Create Server Group dialog box, which you can use to add servers to server groups for easier management. Server Manager creates role-based groups automatically. For example, domain controllers are listed under AD DS, and you can quickly find information about any domain controllers by selecting the related node.

TIP When you need to connect to a server by using alternate credentials, press and hold or right-click a server in the All Servers node and then click Manage As. In the Windows Security dialog box, enter your alternate credentials, and then tap or click OK. Credentials you provide are cleared when you exit Server Manager. To save the credentials and use them each time you log on, select Remember My Credentials in the Windows Security dialog box. You need to repeat this procedure any time you change the password associated with the alternate credentials.

REAL WORLD When you are working with Server Core installations, you can use Sconfig to configure domain and workgroup membership, the computer's name, remote management, Windows Update, Remote Desktop, network settings, and the date and time. You also can use Sconfig to log off, restart, and shut down the server. To start Sconfig, simply enter **sconfig** at the command prompt. You can then choose menu options and follow the prompts to configure the server.

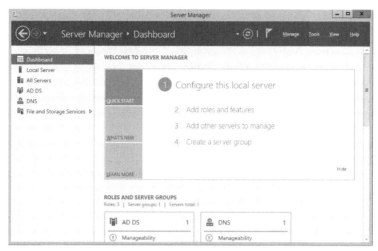

FIGURE 3-1 Use the dashboard for general administration.

In Server Manager's left pane (also referred to as the *console tree*), you'll find options for accessing the dashboard, the local server, all servers added for management, and server groups. When you select Local Server in the console tree, as shown in Figure 3-2, you can manage the basic configuration of the server you are logged on to locally.

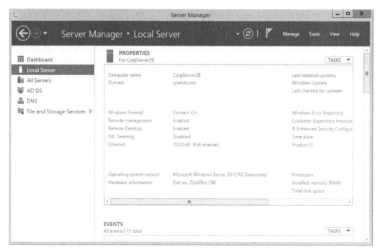

FIGURE 3-2 Manage the properties of the local server.

Information about the local server is organized into several main headings, each with an associated management panel:

- **Best Practices Analyzer** Allows you to run the Best Practices Analyzer on the server and review the results. To start a scan, tap or click Tasks and then tap or click Start BPA Scan.

- **Events** Provides summary information about warning and error events from the server's event logs. Tap or click an event to display more information about the event.

- **Performance** Allows you to configure and view the status of performance alerts for CPU and memory usage. To configure performance alerts, tap or click Tasks and then tap or click Configure Performance Alerts.

- **Properties** Shows the computer name, domain, network IP configuration, time zone, and more. Each property can be clicked to quickly display a related management interface.

- **Roles And Features** Lists the roles and features installed on the server, in the approximate order of installation. To remove a role or feature, press and hold or right-click it and then select Remove Role Or Feature.

- **Services** Lists the services running on the server by name, status, and start type. Press and hold or right-click a service to manage its run status.

The Properties panel is where you perform much of your initial server configuration. Properties available for quick management include the following:

- **Computer Name/Domain** Shows the computer name and domain. Tap or click either of the related links to display the System Properties dialog box with the Computer Name tab selected. You can then change a computer's name and domain information by tapping or clicking Change, providing the computer name and domain information, and then tapping or clicking OK. By default, servers are assigned a randomly generated name and are configured as part of a workgroup called WORKGROUP. In the Small Icons or Large Icons view of Control Panel, you also can display the System Properties dialog box with the Computer Name tab selected by tapping or clicking System, and then tapping or clicking Change Settings under Computer Name, Domain, And Workgroup Settings.

- **Customer Experience Improvement Program** Shows whether the server is participating in the Customer Experience Improvement Program (CEIP). Tap or click the related link to change the participation settings. Participation in CEIP allows Microsoft to collect information about the way you use the server. Microsoft collects this data to help improve future releases of Windows. No data collected as part of CEIP personally identifies you or your company. If you elect to participate, you can also provide information about the number of servers and desktop computers in your organization and in your organization's general industry. If you opt out of CEIP by turning this feature off, you miss the opportunity to help improve Windows.

- **Ethernet** Shows the TCP/IP configuration of wired Ethernet connections. Tap or click the related link to display the Network Connections console. You can then configure network connections by double-tapping or double-clicking the connection you want to work with and then tapping or clicking Properties to open the Properties dialog box. By default, servers are configured to use dynamic addressing for both IPv4 and IPv6. You can also display the Network Connections console by tapping or clicking Change Adapter Settings under Tasks in Network And Sharing Center.

- **IE Enhanced Security Configuration** Shows the status of Internet Explorer Enhanced Security Configuration (IE ESC). Tap or click the related link to enable or disable IE ESC. If you tap or click the link for this option, you can turn this feature on or off for administrators, users, or both. IE ESC is a security feature that reduces the exposure of a server to potential attacks by raising the default security levels in Internet Explorer security zones and changing default Internet Explorer settings. By default, IE ESC is enabled for both administrators and users.

REAL WORLD In most cases, you should enable IE ESC on a server for both users and administrators. However, enabling IE ESC reduces the functionality of Internet Explorer. When IE ESC is enabled, security zones are configured as follows: the Internet zone is set to Medium-High, the Trusted Sites zone is set to Medium, the Local Intranet zone is set to Medium-Low, and the Restricted zone is set to High. When IE ESC is enabled, the following Internet settings are changed: the Enhanced Security Configuration dialog box is on, third-party browser extensions are off, sounds in web pages are off, animations in web pages are off, signature checking for downloaded programs is on, server certificate revocation is on, encrypted pages are not saved, temporary Internet files are deleted when the browser is closed, warnings for secure and nonsecure mode changes are on, and memory protection is on.

- **NIC Teaming** Shows the status and configuration of network interface card (NIC) teaming. Tap or click the related link to add or remove teamed interfaces and to manage related options.

- **Product ID** Shows the product identifier for Windows Server. Tap or click the related link to enter a product key and activate the operating system over the Internet.

- **Remote Desktop** Tap or click the related link to display the System Properties dialog box with the Remote tab selected. You can then configure Remote Desktop by selecting the configuration option you want to use and tapping or clicking OK. By default, no remote connections to a server are allowed. In the Small Icons or Large Icons view of Control Panel, you can display the System Properties dialog box with the Remote tab selected by double-tapping or double-clicking System and then tapping or clicking Remote Settings in the left pane.

- **Remote Management** Shows whether remote management of this server from other servers is enabled. Tap or click the related link to enable or disable remote management.

- **Time Zone** Shows the current time zone for the server. Tap or click the related link to display the Date And Time dialog box. You can then configure the server's time zone by tapping or clicking Change Time Zone, selecting the appropriate time zone, and then tapping or clicking OK twice. You can also display the Date And Time dialog box by pressing and holding or right-clicking the clock on the taskbar and then selecting Adjust Date/Time. Although all servers are configured to synchronize time automatically with an Internet time server, the time synchronization process does not change a computer's time zone.

- **Windows Error Reporting** Shows the status of Windows Error Reporting (WER). Tap or click the related link to change the participation settings for WER. In most cases, you'll want to enable WER for at least the first 60 days following installation of the operating system. With WER enabled, your server sends descriptions of problems to Microsoft, and Windows notifies you of possible solutions to those problems. You can view problem reports and possible solutions by using Action Center. To open Action Center, tap or click the Action Center icon in the notification area of the taskbar, and then click Open Action Center.

- **Windows Firewall** Shows the status of Windows Firewall. If Windows Firewall is active, this property displays the name of the firewall profile that currently applies and the firewall status. Tap or click the related link to display the Windows Firewall utility. By default, Windows Firewall is enabled. In the Small Icons or Large Icons view of Control Panel, you can display Windows Firewall by tapping or clicking the Windows Firewall option.

- **Windows Update** Shows the current configuration of Windows Update. Tap or click the related link to display the Windows Update utility in Control Panel, which you can then use to enable automatic updating (if Windows Update is disabled) or to check for updates (if Windows Update is enabled). In the Small Icons or Large Icons view of Control Panel, you can display Windows Update by selecting the Windows Update option.

NOTE I've provided this summary of options as an introduction and quick reference. I'll discuss the related configuration tasks and technologies in more detail throughout this and other chapters in the book.

Navigating Server Manager essentials and binaries

The Server Manager console is designed to handle core system administration tasks. You'll spend a lot of time working with this tool, and you should get to know every detail. By default, Server Manager is started automatically. If you closed the console or disabled automatic startup, you can open the console by tapping or clicking the related option on the taskbar. Alternatively, another way to do this is by pressing the Windows key, typing **ServerManager.exe** into the Everywhere Search box, and then pressing Enter.

Server Manager's command-line counterpart is the ServerManager module for Windows PowerShell. At a Windows PowerShell prompt, you can obtain a detailed list of a server's current state with regard to roles, role services, and features by entering **get-windowsfeature**. Each installed role, role service, and feature is highlighted and marked as such, and a management naming component in brackets follows the display name of each role, role service, and feature. By using Install–WindowsFeature or Uninstall–WindowsFeature followed by the management name, you can install or uninstall a role, role service, or feature. For example, you can install Network Load Balancing by entering **install-windowsfeature nlb**. You can add **-includeallsubfeature** when installing components to add all subordinate role services or features. Management tools are not included by default. To add the management tools, add **-includemanagementtools** when installing components.

REAL WORLD When you are working with Windows PowerShell 3.0 or later, modules are imported implicitly. Otherwise, you need to import the module before you can use the cmdlets it provides. You import the ServerManager module by entering **Import-Module ServerManager** at the Windows PowerShell prompt. After the module is imported, you can use it with the currently running instance of Windows PowerShell. The next time you start Windows PowerShell, you need to import the module again if you want to use its features.

Binaries needed to install roles and features are referred to as *payloads*. With Windows Server 2012 R2, payloads are stored in subfolders of the %SystemDrive% \Windows\WinSXS folder. Not only can you uninstall a role or feature, but you also can uninstall and remove the payload for a feature or role by using the –Remove parameter of the Uninstall–WindowsFeature cmdlet. Subcomponents of the role or feature are also removed. To also remove management tools, add the **-include-allmanagementtools** parameter.

When you want to install a role or feature, you can install the related components and restore any removed payloads for these components by using the Install–WindowsFeature cmdlet. By default, when you use Install–WindowsFeature, payloads are restored via Windows Update.

In the following example, you restore the Active Directory Services (AD DS) binaries and all related subfeatures via Windows Update:

```
install-windowsfeature -name ad-domain-services -includeallsubfeature
```

You can use the –Source parameter to restore a payload from a Windows Imaging (WIM) format mount point. For example, if your enterprise has a mounted Windows Image for the edition of Windows Server 2012 R2 you are working with available at the network path \\ImServer18\WinS12EE, you could specify the source as follows:

```
install-windowsfeature -name ad-domain-services -includeallsubfeature
-source \\imserver18\wins12ee
```

Keep in mind that the path you specify is used only if required binaries are not found in the Windows Side-By-Side folder on the destination server. Although many large enterprises might have standard images that can be mounted by using network paths, you also can mount the Windows Server 2012 R2 distribution media and use the Windows\WinSXS folder from the installation image as your source. To do this, follow these steps:

1. Insert the installation disc into the server's CD/DVD drive, and then create a folder to mount the Installation image by entering the following command: **mkdir c:\mountdir.**

2. Locate the index number of the image you want to use by entering the following command at an elevated command prompt, where *e:* is the drive designator of the server's disc drive: **dism /get-wiminfo /wimfile:e:\sources\install.wim.**

3. Mount the installation image by entering the following command at an elevated command prompt, where *e:* is the drive designator of the server's disc drive, *2* is the index of the image to use, and *c:\mountdir* is the mount directory: **dism /mount–wim /wimfile:e:\sources\install.wim /index:2 /mountdir:c:\mountdir /readonly**. Mounting the image might take several minutes.

4. Use Install–WindowsFeature at a Windows PowerShell command prompt with the source specified as **c:\mountdir\windows\winsxs**, as shown in this example:

   ```
   install-windowsfeature -name ad-domain-services -includeallsubfeature
   -source c:\mountdir\windows\winsxs
   ```

Group Policy can be used to control whether Windows Update is used to restore payloads and to provide alternate source paths for restoring payloads. The policy you want to work with is Specify Settings For Optional Component Installation And Component Repair, which is under Computer Configuration\Administrative Templates \System. This policy also is used for obtaining payloads needed to repair components.

If you enable this policy (as shown in Figure 3-3), you can do the following:

- Specify the alternate source file path for payloads as a network location. For network shares, enter the UNC path to the share, such as \\CorpServer82 \WinServer2012\. For mounted Windows images, enter the WIM path prefixed with **WIM:** and including the index of the image to use, such as WIM:\\CorpServer82\WinServer2012\install.wim:4.

- Specify that Windows Update should never be used to download payloads. If you enable the policy and use this option, you do not have to specify an alternate path. In this case, payloads cannot be obtained automatically and administrators will need to explicitly specify the alternate source path.

- Specify that Windows Update should be used for repairing components rather than Windows Server Update Services.

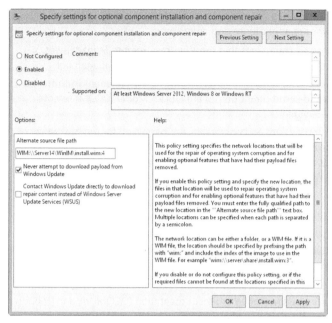

FIGURE 3-3 Control component installation through Group Policy.

Managing your servers remotely

You can use Server Manager and other Microsoft Management Consoles (MMCs) to perform many management tasks on remote computers, as long as the computers are in the same domain or you are working in a workgroup and have added the remote computers in a domain as trusted hosts. You can connect to servers running full-server, minimal-interface, and Server Core installations. On the computer you want to use for managing remote computers, you should be running a current Windows desktop or server operating system, and you need to install the Remote Server Administration Tools.

With Windows Server 2012 R2, the Remote Server Administration Tools are installed as a feature by using the Add Roles And Features Wizard. If the binaries for the tools have been removed, you need to install the tools by specifying a source, as discussed in the "Navigating Server Manager essentials and binaries" section earlier in the chapter.

You can get the Remote Server Administration Tools for Windows 8.1 as a download from the Microsoft Download Center (*http://download.microsoft.com*). Different versions are available for x64 and x86 systems.

By default, remote management is enabled for servers running Windows Server 2012 R2 for two types of applications and commands:

- Applications and commands that use Windows Remote Management (WinRM) and Windows PowerShell remote access for management
- Applications and commands that use Windows Management Instrumentation (WMI) and Distributed Component Object Model (DCOM) remote access for management

These types of applications and commands are permitted for remote management because of exceptions configured in Windows Firewall, which is enabled by default for Windows Server 2012 R2. In Windows Firewall, exceptions for allowed apps that support remote management include the following:

- Windows Management Instrumentation
- Windows Remote Management
- Windows Remote Management (Compatibility)

In Windows Firewall With Advanced Security, there are inbound rules that correspond to the standard firewall allowed apps:

- For WMI, the inbound rules are Windows Management Instrumentation (WMI-In), Windows Management Instrumentation (DCOM-In), and Windows Management Instrumentation (ASync-In).
- For WinRM, the matching inbound rule is Windows Remote Management (HTTP-In).
- For WinRM compatibility, the matching inbound rule is Windows Remote Management - Compatibility Mode (HTTP-In).

You manage these exceptions or rules in either the standard Windows Firewall or the Windows Firewall With Advanced Security, not in both. If you want to allow remote management by using Server Manager, MMCs, and Windows PowerShell, you typically want to permit WMI, WinRM, and WinRM compatibility exceptions in Windows Firewall.

When you are working with Server Manager, you can select Local Server in the console tree to view the status of the remote management property. If you don't want to allow remote management of the local server, click the related link. In the Configure Remote Management dialog box, clear Enable Remote Management Of This Server From Other Computers, and then tap or click OK.

When you clear Enable Remote Management Of This Server From Other Computers and then tap or click OK, Server Manager performs several background tasks that disable Windows Remote Management and Windows PowerShell remote access for management on the local server. One of these tasks is to turn off the related exception that allows apps to communicate through Windows Firewall by using Windows Remote Management. The exceptions for Windows Management Instrumentation and Windows Remote Management (Compatibility) aren't affected.

You must be a member of the Administrators group on computers you want to manage by using Server Manager. For remote connections in a workgroup-to-workgroup or workgroup-to-domain configuration, you should be logged on using the built-in Administrator account, or configure the *LocalAccountTokenFilterPolicy* registry key to allow remote access from your computer. To set this key, enter the following command at an elevated, administrator command prompt:

```
reg add HKLM\SOFTWARE\Microsoft\Windows\CurrentVersion\Policies\System /v
LocalAccountTokenFilterPolicy /t REG_DWORD /d 1 /f
```

> **NOTE** You also can enable remote management by entering **configure-SMRemoting.exe –enable** at an elevated, administrator command prompt.

If you want to make it possible to remotely manage a computer running Windows 8.1 by using the WS-Management protocol, enter **winrm quickconfig** at an elevated command prompt. Then each time you are prompted to make configuration changes, enter **Y**. This will start the Windows Remote Management service, configure WinRM to accept WS-Management requests on any IP address, create a Windows Firewall exception for Windows Remote Management, and configure *LocalAccountTokenFilterPolicy* to grant appropriate administrative rights for remote management.

Many other types of remote management tasks depend on other exceptions for Windows Firewall. Keep the following in mind:

- Remote Desktop is enabled or disabled separately from remote management. To allow someone to connect to the local server by using Remote Desktop, you must allow related connections to the computer and configure access as discussed in Chapter 4, "Monitoring services, processes, and events."

- Remote Service Management must be configured as an allowed app in Windows Firewall to remotely manage a computer's services. In the advanced firewall, several related rules allow management via named pipes (NP) and remote procedure calls (RPC).

- Remote Event Log Management must be configured as an allowed app in Windows Firewall to remotely manage a computer's event logs. In the advanced firewall, there are several related rules that allow management via NP and RPC.

- Remote Volume Management must be configured as an allowed app in Windows Firewall to remotely manage a computer's volumes. In the advanced firewall, there are several related rules that allow management of the Virtual Disk Service and Virtual Disk Service Loader.

- Remote Scheduled Task Management must be configured as an allowed app in Windows Firewall to remotely manage a computer's scheduled tasks. In the advanced firewall, there are several related rules that allow management of scheduled tasks via RPC.

- Only Remote Service Management is enabled by default.

You can configure remote management on a Server Core installation of Windows Server 2012 R2 by using Sconfig. Start the Server Configuration utility by entering **sconfig**.

Connecting to and working with remote servers

Using Server Manager, you can connect to and manage remote servers, provided that you've added the server for management. To add servers one at a time to Server Manager, complete these steps:

1. Open Server Manager. In the left pane, select All Servers to view the servers that have been added for management already. If the server you want to work with isn't listed, select Add Servers on the Manage menu to display the Add Servers dialog box.

2. The Add Servers dialog box has several panels for adding servers:

   - The Active Directory panel, selected by default, allows you to enter the computer name or fully qualified domain name of the remote server that is running Windows Server. After you enter a name, tap or click Find Now.

   - The DNS panel allows you to add servers by computer name or IP address. After you enter the name or IP address, tap or click the Search button.

3. In the Name list, double-tap or double-click the server to add it to the Selected list.

4. Repeat steps 2 and 3 to add others servers, and then tap or click OK.

To add many servers to Server Manager, you can use the Import process and these steps:

1. Create a text file that has one host name, fully qualified domain name, or IP address per line.

2. In Server Manager, select Add Servers on the Manage menu. In the Add Servers dialog box, select the Import panel.

3. Tap or click the options button to the right of the File box, and then use the Open dialog box to locate and open the server list.

4. In the Computer list, double-tap or double-click each server you want to add to the Selected list. Tap or click OK.

After you add a remote computer, the Server Manager console shows the name of the remote computer in the All Servers view. Server Manager always resolves IP addresses to host names. As shown in Figure 3-4, the All Servers view also lists the Manageability status of the server. If a server is listed as Not Accessible, you typically need to log on locally to resolve the problem.

In the All Servers view, the servers you add are listed in the Servers pane so that you can manage them each time you work with Server Manager. Server Manager tracks the services, events, and more for each added server, and each server is added to the appropriate server groups automatically based on the roles and features installed.

Automatically created server groups make it easier to manage the various roles and features that are installed on your servers. If you select the AD DS group, as an example, you get a list of the domain controllers you added for management in addition to any critical or warning events for these servers and the status of services the role depends on.

If you want to group servers by department, geographic location, or otherwise, you can create your own server groups. When you create groups, the servers you want to work with don't have to be added to Server Manager already. You can add servers by searching Active Directory or Domain Name System (DNS), or by importing a list of host names, fully qualified domain names, or IP addresses. Any server you add to a custom group is added automatically for management, too.

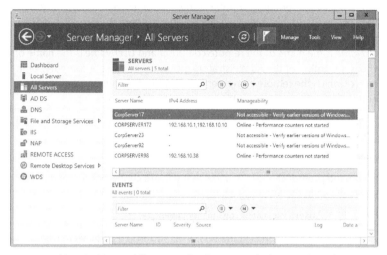

FIGURE 3-4 Note the Manageability status of each server, and take corrective actions as necessary.

To create a server group, complete these steps:

1. Open Server Manager. Select Create Server Group on the Manage menu to display the Create Server Group dialog box.

2. Enter a descriptive name for the group. Use the panels and options provided to add servers to the group. Keep the following in mind:

   ■ The Server Pool panel, selected by default, lists servers that have been added for management already. If a server you want to add to your group is listed here, add it to the group by double-tapping or double-clicking it.

   ■ The Active Directory panel allows you to enter the computer name or fully qualified domain name of the remote server that is running Windows Server. After you enter a name, tap or click Find Now. In the Name list, double-tap or double-click a server to add it to the Selected list.

   ■ The DNS panel allows you to add servers by computer name or IP address. After you enter the name or IP address, tap or click the Search button. In the Name list, double-tap or double-click a server to add it to the Selected list.

   ■ The Import panel allows you to import a list of servers. Tap or click the options button to the right of the File box, and then use the Open dialog box to locate and open the server list. In the Computer list, double-tap or double-click a server to add it to the Selected list.

3. Tap or click OK to create the server group.

When you press and hold or right-click a server name in the Servers pane of a server group or in the All Servers view, you display an extended list of management options. These options perform the corresponding task or open the corresponding management tool with the selected server in focus. For example, if you were to right-click CorpServer172 and then select Computer Management, Computer Management connects to CorpServer172 and then opens.

You can work with a remote computer using an interactive remote Windows PowerShell session. To do this, open an elevated, administrator Windows PowerShell prompt. Type **enter-pssession** *ComputerName* **-credential** *UserName*, where *ComputerName* is the name of the remote computer and *UserName* is the name of a user who is a member of the Administrators group on the remote computer or in the domain of which the remote computer is a member. When prompted to enter the authorized user's password, type the password and then press Enter.

The following example enters an interactive remote session with Server85 using the credentials of Williams:

```
enter-pssession server85 -credential williams
```

The command prompt changes to show that you are connected to the remote computer, as shown in the following example:

```
[Server85]: PS C:\Users\wrstanek.cpandl\Documents>
```

You can now enter commands in the session as you would if you were using Windows PowerShell locally. When you connect to a server in this way, you use the standard PowerShell remoting configuration. You can end the interactive session by using the command **Exit-PSSession** or entering **exit**.

Adding and removing roles, role services, and features

Server Manager automatically creates server groups based on the roles of the servers added for management. As an example, the first time you add a domain controller, Server Manager might create AD DS, DNS, and File And Storage Services groups to help you more easily track the roles of the domain controllers.

When you select a role-based group in the left pane, the Servers pane shows the servers you added for management that have this role. The details for the selected server group provide the following information:

- Summary information about events. Server Manager lists recent warning and error events. If you tap or click an event, you can get more information about the event.

- Summary information about the status of related system services. You can press and hold or right-click a service to manage its run status.

TIP By default, Server Manager refreshes details every 10 minutes. You can refresh the details manually by tapping or clicking the Refresh button on the Tasks toolbar. If you want to set a different default refresh interval, tap or click Manage and then tap or click Server Manager Properties. Next, set the new refresh interval in minutes and then tap or click OK.

You can manage a service by pressing and holding or right-clicking the service and then tapping or clicking Stop Service, Start Service, Pause Service, Resume Service, or Restart Service as appropriate. In many cases, if a service isn't running as you think it should, you can use the Restart option to resolve the issue by stopping and then starting the service. See Chapter 4 for detailed information about working with events and system services.

The Manage menu has two key options for working with roles and features:

- **Add Roles And Features** Starts the Add Roles And Features Wizard, which you can use to install roles and features on a server added for management
- **Remove Roles And Features** Starts the Remove Roles And Features Wizard, which you can use to uninstall roles and features on a server added for management

With Windows Server 2012 R2, you can install roles and features on running servers (whether physical machines or virtual) in addition to virtual hard disks. Servers must be added for management in Server Manager, and they must be online. Virtual hard disks that you want to work with don't have to be online, but they must be selectable when you are browsing for them. Because of this, you might need to map a network drive to access a network share. With this in mind, you can add a server role or feature by following these steps:

1. In Server Manager, click Add Roles And Features on the Manage menu. This starts the Add Roles And Features Wizard. If the wizard displays the Before You Begin page, read the introductory text, and then tap or click Next. You can avoid displaying the Before You Begin page the next time you start this wizard by selecting the Skip This Page By Default check box before tapping or clicking Next.

2. On the Select Installation Type page, Role-Based Or Feature-Based Installation is selected by default. Tap or click Next.

3. On the Select Destination Server page, you can choose to install roles and features on running servers or virtual hard disks. Either select a server from the server pool or select a server from the server pool on which to mount a virtual hard disk (VHD). If you are adding roles and features to a VHD, tap or click Browse, and then use the Browse For Virtual Hard Disks dialog box to locate the VHD. When you are ready to continue, tap or click Next.

   NOTE Only servers running Windows Server 2012 R2 and that have been added for management in Server Manager are listed.

4. On the Select Server Roles page, select the role or roles to install. If additional features are required to install a role, an additional dialog box will be displayed. Tap or click Add Features to close the dialog box and add the required features to the server installation. Tap or click Next to continue.

NOTE Some roles cannot be added at the same time as other roles. You have to install each role separately. Other roles cannot be combined with existing roles, and you'll get warning prompts about this. A server running a Server Core installation can act as a domain controller and can also hold any of the flexible single-master operations (FSMO) roles for Active Directory.

5. On the Select Features page, select the feature or features to install. If additional features are required to install a feature you selected, an additional dialog box will be displayed. Tap or click Add Features to close the dialog box and add the required features to the server installation. When you are ready to continue, tap or click Next.

6. With some roles, an extra wizard page will be displayed, and this provides additional information about using and configuring the role. You might also have the opportunity to install additional role services as part of a role. For example, with Print And Document Services, Web Server Role (IIS), and WSUS, an additional information page and a page for selecting role services to install along with the role will be displayed.

7. On the Confirmation Installations Selections page, tap or click the Export Configuration Settings link to generate an installation report that can be displayed in Internet Explorer.

8. If the server on which you want to install roles or features doesn't have all the required binary source files, the server gets the files via Windows Update by default or from a location specified in Group Policy. You also can specify an alternate path for the source files. To do this, click the Specify An Alternate Source Path link, enter that alternate path in the box provided, and then tap or click OK. For example, if you mounted a Windows image and made it available on the local server as discussed in the section "Navigating Server Manager essentials and binaries" earlier in this chapter, you could enter the alternate path as **c:\mountdir\windows\winsxs**. For network shares, enter the UNC path to the share, such as **\\CorpServer82\WinServer2012**. For mounted Windows images, enter the WIM path prefixed with **WIM:** and including the index of the image to use, such as **WIM:\\CorpServer82\WinServer2012 \install.wim:4**.

9. After you review the installation options and save them as necessary, tap or click Install to begin the installation process. The Installation Progress page tracks the progress of the installation. If you close the wizard, tap or click the Notifications icon in Server Manager, and then tap or click the link provided to reopen the wizard.

10. When the wizard finishes installing the server with the roles and features you selected, the Installation Progress page will be updated to reflect this. Review the installation details to ensure that all phases of the installation were completed successfully.

   Note any additional actions that might be required to complete the installation, such as restarting the server or performing additional installation tasks.

   If any portion of the installation failed, note the reason for the failure. Review the Server Manager entries for installation problems and take corrective actions as appropriate.

You can remove roles and features from a server by following these steps:

1. In Server Manager, click Remove Roles And Features on the Manage menu. This starts the Remove Roles And Features Wizard. If the wizard displays the Before You Begin page, read the introductory text and then tap or click Next. You can avoid displaying the Before You Begin page the next time you start this wizard by selecting the Skip This Page By Default check box before tapping or clicking Next.

2. On the Select Destination Server page, you can choose to remove roles and features from running servers or virtual hard disks (VHDs). Either select a server from the server pool or select a server from the server pool on which to mount a VHD. If you are removing roles and features from a VHD, tap or click Browse, and then use the Browse For Virtual Hard Disks dialog box to locate the VHD. When you are ready to continue, tap or click Next.

3. On the Remove Server Roles page, clear the check box for the role you want to remove. If you try to remove a role that another role or feature depends on, a warning prompt appears stating that you cannot remove the role unless you also remove the other role. If you tap or click the Remove Features button, the wizard also removes the dependent roles and features. Note that if you want to keep related management tools, you should clear the Remove Management Tools check box prior to tapping or clicking the Remove Features button and then click Continue. Tap or click Next.

4. On the Remove Features page, the currently installed features are selected. To remove a feature, clear the related check box. If you try to remove a feature that another feature or role depends on, a warning prompt appears stating that you cannot remove the feature unless you also remove the other feature or role. If you tap or click the Remove Features button, the wizard also removes the dependent roles and features. Note that if you want to keep related management tools, you should clear the Remove Management Tools check box and then click Continue prior to tapping or clicking the Remove Features button. Tap or click Next.

5. On the Confirm Removal Selections page, review the related components that the wizard will remove based on your previous selections, and then tap or click Remove. The Removal Progress page tracks the progress of the removal. If you close the wizard, tap or click the Notifications icon in Server Manager, and then tap or click the link provided to reopen the wizard.

6. When the wizard finishes modifying the server configuration, the Removal Progress page is displayed. Review the modification details to ensure that all phases of the removal process were completed successfully.

   Note any additional actions that might be required to complete the removal, such as restarting the server or performing additional removal tasks.

   If any portion of the removal failed, note the reason for the failure. Review the Server Manager entries for removal problems and take corrective actions as appropriate.

Managing system properties

You use the System console to view system information and perform basic configuration tasks. To access the System console, double-tap or double-click System in Control Panel. As Figure 3-5 shows, the System console is divided into four basic areas that provide links for performing common tasks and a system overview:

- **Windows Edition** Shows the operating system edition and version, and lists any service packs you applied.

- **System** Lists the processor, memory, and type of operating system installed on the computer. The type of operating system is listed as 32-bit or 64-bit.

- **Computer Name, Domain, And Workgroup Settings** Provides the computer name, description, domain, and workgroup details. If you want to change any of this information, tap or click Change Settings, and then tap or click Change in the System Properties dialog box.

- **Windows Activation** Shows whether you have activated the operating system and the product key. If Windows Server 2012 R2 isn't activated yet, tap or click the link provided to start the activation process and then follow the prompts.

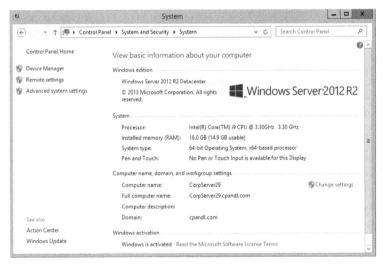

FIGURE 3-5 Use the System console to view and manage system properties.

When you're working in the System console, links in the left pane provide quick access to key support tools, including the following:

- Device Manager
- Remote Settings
- Advanced System Settings

Although volume-licensed versions of Windows Server 2012 R2 might not require activation or product keys, retail versions of Windows Server 2012 R2 require both activation and product keys. If Windows Server 2012 R2 has not been activated, you can activate the operating system by selecting Activate Windows Now under Windows Activation. You can also activate Windows by entering **slmgr -ato** at a command prompt.

You can change the product key provided during installation of Windows Server 2012 R2 to stay in compliance with your licensing plan. At a command prompt, type **slmgr -ipk** followed by the product key you want to use, and then press Enter. When Windows finishes validating the product key, you need to reactivate the operating system.

NOTE The Windows Software Management Licensing tool has many other options, including options for offline activation by using a confirmation identifier. To view this and other options, enter **slmgr** at a command prompt.

Within the System console, you can access the System Properties dialog box and use this dialog box to manage system properties. Tap or click Change Settings under Computer Name, Domain, And Workgroup Settings. The following sections examine key areas of the operating system you can configure by using the System Properties dialog box.

Configuring server name and domain membership

You can display and modify the computer's network identification on the Computer Name tab of the System Properties dialog box. The Computer Name tab displays the full computer name of the system and the domain membership. The full computer name is essentially the DNS name of the computer, which also identifies the computer's place within the Active Directory hierarchy. If a computer is a domain controller or a certificate authority, you can change the computer name only after removing the related role from the computer.

You can join a computer to a domain or workgroup by following these steps:

1. On the Computer Name tab of the System Properties dialog box, tap or click Change. This displays the Computer Name/Domain Changes dialog box.

2. To put the computer in a workgroup, select the Workgroup option and then enter the name of the workgroup to join.

3. To join the computer to a domain, select the Domain option, enter the name of the domain to join, and then tap or click OK.

4. If you changed the computer's domain membership, a Windows Security prompt appears. Enter the name and password of an account with permission to add the computer to the specified domain or to remove the computer from a previously specified domain, and then tap or click OK.

5. When prompted that your computer has joined the workgroup or domain you specified, tap or click OK.

6. A prompt appears stating that you need to restart the computer. Tap or click OK.

7. Tap or click Close, and then tap or click Restart Now to restart the computer.

To change the name of a computer, follow these steps:

1. On the Computer Name tab of the System Properties dialog box, tap or click Change. This displays the Computer Name/Domain Changes dialog box.
2. In the Computer Name box, enter the new name for the computer.
3. A prompt appears stating that you need to restart the computer. Tap or click OK.
4. Tap or click Close, and then tap or click Restart Now to restart the computer.

Configuring driver installation options

The System Properties dialog box's Hardware tab provides access to Device Manager and Driver Installation Settings. To access the Hardware tab, open the System Properties dialog box, and then tap or click the Hardware tab.

For installed devices, you can configure Windows Server to download driver software and realistic icons for devices. By default, Windows Server does not do this. If you want a computer to check for drivers automatically, tap or click the Device Installation Settings button and then select either Yes, Do This Automatically or No, Let Me Choose What To Do. If you want to choose what to do, you can specify the following:

- Always install the best driver software from Windows Update.
- Never install driver software from Windows Update.
- Automatically get the device app and info provided by your device manufacturer.

The first two options do exactly what they say. The final option tells Windows Update that you want to get metadata and companion applications for devices. Tap or click Save Changes, and then tap or click OK to apply your changes.

Configuring memory and performance options

The System Properties dialog box's Advanced tab controls many of the key features of the Windows operating system, including application performance, virtual memory usage, the user profile, environment variables, and startup and recovery. To access the Advanced tab, open the System Properties dialog box, and then tap or click the Advanced tab.

Setting Windows performance

Windows Server has many graphics enhancements that make the UI more visually appealing but use system resources unnecessarily. These enhancements include many visual effects for menus, toolbars, windows, and the taskbar. As part of optimizing server performance, you might want to reduce resource usage to support these graphics enhancements. To do this, follow these steps:

1. Tap or click the Advanced tab in the System Properties dialog box, and then tap or click Settings in the Performance panel to display the Performance Options dialog box.

2. The Visual Effects tab is selected by default. You have the following options for controlling visual effects:

   - **Let Windows Choose What's Best For My Computer**   Use this to enables the operating system to choose the performance options based on the hardware configuration. For a newer computer, this option will probably have the same effect as choosing the Adjust For Best Appearance option. The key distinction, however, is that this option is chosen by Windows based on the available hardware and its performance capabilities.

   - **Adjust For Best Appearance**   When you optimize Windows for best appearance, you enable all visual effects for all graphical interfaces. Menus and the taskbar use transitions and shadows. Screen fonts have smooth edges. List boxes have smooth scrolling. Folders use web views and more.

   - **Adjust For Best Performance**   When you optimize Windows for best performance, you turn off the resource-intensive visual effects, such as slide transitions and smooth edges for fonts, while maintaining a basic set of visual effects.

   - **Custom**   You can customize the visual effects by selecting or clearing the visual effects options in the Performance Options dialog box. If you clear all options, Windows does not use visual effects.

3. Tap or click Apply when you have finished changing visual effects. Tap or click OK twice to close the open dialog boxes.

Setting application performance

Application performance is related to processor-scheduling caching options you set for the Windows Server 2012 R2 system. Processor scheduling determines the responsiveness of applications you are running interactively (as opposed to background applications that might be running on the system as services). You control application performance by following these steps:

1. Access the Advanced tab in the System Properties dialog box, and then display the Performance Options dialog box by tapping or clicking Settings in the Performance panel.

2. In the Performance Options dialog box, tap or click the Advanced tab.

3. In the Processor Scheduling panel, you have the following options:

- **Programs**   Use this option to give the active application the best response time and the greatest share of available resources. Generally, you'll want to use this option only on development servers or when you are using Windows Server 2012 R2 as your desktop operating system.

- **Background Services**   Use this option to give background applications a better response time than the active application. Generally, you'll want to use this option for production servers.

4. Tap or click OK.

Configuring virtual memory

With virtual memory, you can use disk space to extend the amount of memory available on a system by using part of the hard disk as part of system memory. This feature writes RAM to disks by using a process called *paging*. With paging, a set amount of RAM, such as 8192 megabytes (MB), is written to the disk as a paging file. The paging file can be accessed from the disk when needed in place of physical RAM.

An initial paging file is created automatically for the drive containing the operating system. By default, other drives don't have paging files, so you must create these paging files if you want them. When you create a paging file, you set an initial size and a maximum size. Paging files are written to the volume as a file named Pagefile.sys.

REAL WORLD   Current releases of Windows Server automatically manage virtual memory much better than their predecessors. Typically, Windows Server allocates virtual memory in an amount at least as large as the total physical memory installed on the computer. This helps to ensure that paging files don't become fragmented, which can result in poor system performance. If you want to manage virtual memory manually, you can use a fixed virtual memory size in most cases. To do this, set the initial size and the maximum size to the same value. This ensures that the paging file is consistent and can be written to a single contiguous file (if possible, given the amount of space on the volume). In most cases, for computers with 8 gigabytes (GB) of RAM or less, I recommend setting the total paging file size so that it's twice the amount of physical RAM on the system. For instance, on a computer with 8 GB of RAM, you would ensure that the Total Paging File Size For All Drives setting is at least 16,384 MB. On systems with more than 8 GB of RAM, you should follow the hardware manufacturer's guidelines for configuring the paging file. Typically, this means setting the paging file to be the same size as physical memory.

You can configure virtual memory by following these steps:

1. Access the Advanced tab in the System Properties dialog box, and then display the Performance Options dialog box by tapping or clicking Settings in the Performance panel.

2. In the Performance Options dialog box, tap or click the Advanced tab, and then tap or click Change to display the Virtual Memory dialog box, shown in Figure 3-6.

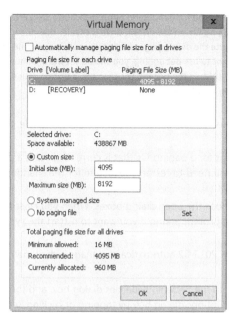

FIGURE 3-6 Virtual memory extends the amount of RAM on a system.

The following information is provided:

- **Paging File Size For Each Drive** Provides information about the currently selected drive, and allows you to set its paging file size. Space Available indicates how much space is available on the drive.

- **Drive [Volume Label] and Paging File Size** Shows how virtual memory is currently configured on the system. Each volume is listed with its associated paging file (if any). The paging file range shows the initial and maximum size values set for the paging file.

- **Total Paging File Size For All Drives** Provides a recommended size for virtual RAM on the system, and tells you the amount currently allocated. If this is the first time you're configuring virtual RAM, notice that the recommended amount has already been given to the system drive (in most instances).

3. By default, Windows Server manages the paging file size for all drives. If you want to configure virtual memory manually, clear the Automatically Manage Paging File Size For All Drives check box.

4. In the Drive list, select the volume you want to work with.

5. Select Custom Size, and then enter values in the Initial Size and Maximum Size boxes.

6. Tap or click Set to save the changes.

7. Repeat steps 4–6 for each volume you want to configure.

NOTE The paging file is also used for debugging purposes when a Stop error occurs on the system. If the paging file on the system drive is smaller than the minimum amount required to write the debugging information to the paging file, this feature is disabled. If you want to use debugging, you should set the minimum size to equal the amount of RAM on the system. For example, a system with 4 GB of RAM would need a paging file of 4 GB on the system drive.

8. Tap or click OK. If prompted to overwrite an existing Pagefile.sys file, tap or click Yes.

9. If you updated the settings for a paging file that is currently in use, a prompt appears indicating that you need to restart the system for the changes to take effect. Tap or click OK.

10. Tap or click OK twice to close the open dialog boxes. When you close the System utility, you'll get a prompt asking if you want to restart the system. Tap or click Restart.

You can have Windows Server 2012 R2 automatically manage virtual memory by following these steps:

1. Access the Advanced tab in the System Properties dialog box, and then display the Performance Options dialog box by tapping or clicking Settings in the Performance panel.

2. Tap or click the Advanced tab, and then tap or click Change to display the Virtual Memory dialog box.

3. Select the Automatically Manage Paging File Size For All Drives check box.

4. Tap or click OK three times to close the open dialog boxes.

NOTE If you updated the settings for the paging file currently in use, a prompt appears indicating that you need to restart the server for the changes to take effect. Tap or click OK. When you close the System Properties dialog box, you'll get a prompt telling you that you need to restart the system for the changes to take effect. On a production server, you should schedule this restart outside normal business hours.

Configuring Data Execution Prevention

Windows Server 2012 R2 requires a processor that includes hardware-based Data Execution Prevention (DEP) support. *DEP* is a memory-protection technology. DEP tells the computer's processor to mark all memory locations in an application as nonexecutable unless the location explicitly contains executable code. If code is executed from a memory page marked as nonexecutable, the processor can raise an exception and prevent the code from executing. This process prevents malicious code such as a virus from inserting itself into most areas of memory, because only specific areas of memory are marked as having executable code.

In Windows Server 2012, memory randomization and other enhancements also prevent malware from inserting itself into startup and running processes. Windows Server 2012 uses address space layout randomization (ASLR) to randomly determine how and where important data is stored in memory, which makes it much more difficult for malware to find the specific locations in memory to attack.

NOTE The 32-bit versions of Windows support DEP as implemented by Advanced Micro Devices, Inc. (AMD) processors that provide the no-execute page-protection (NX) processor feature. Such processors support the related instructions and must be running in physical address extension (PAE) mode. The 64-bit versions of Windows also support the NX processor feature.

USING AND CONFIGURING DEP

You can determine whether a computer supports DEP by using the System utility. If a computer supports DEP, you can also configure it by following these steps:

1. Access the Advanced tab in the System Properties dialog box, and then display the Performance Options dialog box by tapping or clicking Settings in the Performance panel.

2. In the Performance Options dialog box, tap or click the Data Execution Prevention tab. The text at the bottom of this tab indicates whether the computer supports execution protection.

3. If a computer supports execution protection and is configured appropriately, you can configure DEP by using the following options:

   ■ **Turn On DEP For Essential Windows Programs And Services Only** Enables DEP only for operating system services, programs, and components. This is the default and recommended option for computers that support execution protection and are configured appropriately.

   ■ **Turn On DEP For All Programs Except Those I Select** Configures DEP, and allows for exceptions. Select this option, and then tap or click Add to specify programs that should run without execution protection. With this option, execution protection will work for all programs except those you select.

4. Tap or click OK.

ADDING AND REMOVING PROGRAMS AS EXCEPTIONS

If you turned on DEP and allowed exceptions, you can add or remove a program as an exception by following these steps:

1. Access the Advanced tab in the System Properties dialog box, and then display the Performance Options dialog box by tapping or clicking Settings in the Performance panel.

2. In the Performance Options dialog box, tap or click the Data Execution Prevention tab.

3. To add a program as an exception, tap or click Add. Use the Open dialog box to find the executable file for the program you are configuring as an exception, and then tap or click Open.

4. To temporarily disable a program as an exception (this might be necessary for troubleshooting), clear the check box next to the program name.

5. To remove a program as an exception, tap or click the program name, and then tap or click Remove.

6. Tap or click OK to save your settings.

Understanding DEP compatibility

To be compatible with DEP, applications must be able to mark memory explicitly with Execute permission. Applications that cannot do this will not be compatible with the NX processor feature. If you experience memory-related problems running applications, you should determine which applications are having problems and configure them as exceptions rather than disable execution protection completely. This way, you still get the benefits of memory protection and can selectively disable memory protection for programs that aren't running properly with the NX processor feature.

Execution protection is applied to both user-mode and kernel-mode programs. A user-mode execution protection exception results in a STATUS_ACCESS_VIOLATION exception. In most processes, this exception will be an unhandled exception, resulting in termination of the process. This is the behavior you want, because most programs violating these rules, such as a virus or worm, will be malicious in nature.

You cannot selectively enable or disable execution protection for kernel-mode device drivers the way you can with applications. Furthermore, on compliant 32-bit systems, execution protection is applied by default to the memory stack. On compliant 64-bit systems, execution protection is applied by default to the memory stack, the paged pool, and the session pool. A kernel-mode execution protection access violation for a device driver results in an ATTEMPTED_EXECUTE_OF_NOEXECUTE_MEMORY exception.

Configuring system and user environment variables

Windows uses environment variables to track important strings, such as a path where files are located or the logon domain controller host name. Environment variables defined for use by Windows—called *system environment variables*—are the same no matter who is logged on to a particular computer. Environment variables defined for use by users or programs—called *user environment variables*—are different for each user of a particular computer.

You configure system and user environment variables by means of the Environment Variables dialog box, shown in Figure 3-7. To access this dialog box, open the System Properties dialog box, tap or click the Advanced tab, and then tap or click Environment Variables.

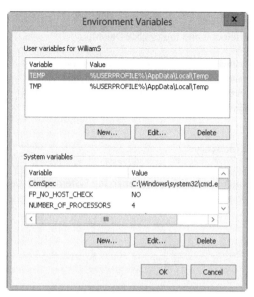

FIGURE 3-7 Configure system and user environment variables in the Environment Variables dialog box.

CREATING AN ENVIRONMENT VARIABLE

You can create an environment variable by following these steps:

1. Tap or click New under User Variables or under System Variables, whichever is appropriate. This opens the New User Variable dialog box or the New System Variable dialog box, respectively.

2. In the Variable Name box, enter the variable name. In the Variable Value box, enter the variable value.

3. Tap or click OK.

EDITING AN ENVIRONMENT VARIABLE

You can edit an environment variable by following these steps:

1. Select the variable in the User Variables or System Variables list.

2. Tap or click Edit under User Variables or under System Variables, whichever is appropriate. The Edit User Variable dialog box or the Edit System Variable dialog box opens.

3. Enter a new value in the Variable Value box, and then tap or click OK.

DELETING AN ENVIRONMENT VARIABLE

To delete an environment variable, select it and tap or click Delete.

NOTE **When you create or modify environment variables, most of the variables are valid immediately after they are created or modified. With system variables, some changes take effect after you restart the computer. With user variables, some changes take effect the next time the user logs on to the system.**

Configuring system startup and recovery

You configure system startup and recovery properties in the Startup And Recovery dialog box, shown in Figure 3-8. To access this dialog box, open the System Properties dialog box, tap or click the Advanced tab, and then tap or click Settings in the Startup And Recovery panel.

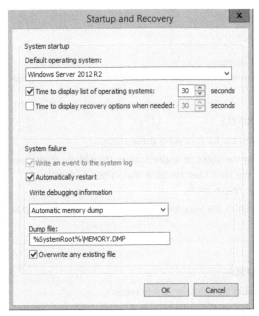

FIGURE 3-8 Configure system startup and recovery properties in the Startup And Recovery dialog box.

SETTING STARTUP OPTIONS

The System Startup area of the Startup And Recovery dialog box controls system startup. To specify the default operating system for a computer with multiple bootable operating systems, select one of the operating systems listed in the Default Operating System list. These options change the configuration settings used by the Windows Boot Manager.

Upon startup of a computer with multiple bootable operating systems, Windows Server displays the startup configuration menu for 30 seconds by default. You can change this by performing either of the following actions:

- Boot immediately to the default operating system by clearing the Time To Display List Of Operating Systems check box.

- Display the available options for a specific amount of time by selecting the Time To Display List Of Operating Systems check box and then setting a time delay in seconds.

On most systems, you'll generally want to use a value of 3 to 5 seconds. This is long enough for you to make a selection, yet short enough to expedite the system startup process.

When the system is in a recovery mode and booting, a list of recovery options might be displayed. As you can with the standard startup options, you can configure recovery startup options in one of two ways. You can set the computer to boot immediately by using the default recovery option by clearing the Time To Display Recovery Options When Needed check box, or you can display the available options for a specific amount of time by selecting Time To Display Recovery Options When Needed and then setting a time delay in seconds.

SETTING RECOVERY OPTIONS

You control system recovery with the System Failure and Write Debugging Information areas of the Startup And Recovery dialog box. Administrators use recovery options to control precisely what happens when the system encounters a nonrecoverable system error (also known as a *Stop error*). The available options for the System Failure area are as follows:

- **Write An Event To The System Log**   This option logs the error in the system log, allowing administrators to review the error later using Event Viewer.

- **Automatically Restart**   Select this option to have the system attempt to reboot when a nonrecoverable system error occurs.

NOTE   Configuring automatic reboots isn't always a good thing. Sometimes you might want the system to halt rather than reboot to ensure that the system gets proper attention. Otherwise, you would know that the system rebooted only when you viewed the system logs or if you happened to be in front of the system's monitor when it rebooted.

You use the Write Debugging Information list to choose the type of debugging information you want to write to a dump file. You can use the dump file to diagnose system failures. The options are as follows:

- **None**   Use this option if you don't want to write debugging information.

- **Small Memory Dump**   Use this option to dump the physical memory segment in which the error occurred. This dump is 256 kilobytes (KB) in size.

- **Kernel Memory Dump** Use this option to dump the physical memory area being used by the Windows kernel. The dump file size depends on the size of the Windows kernel.

- **Complete Memory Dump** Use this option to dump all physical memory. The dump file size depends on the amount of physical memory being used, up to a maximum file size equal to the total physical RAM on the server.

- **Automatic Memory Dump** Use this option to let Windows determine which type of memory dump is best, and then create the dump file accordingly.

If you elect to write to a dump file, you must also set a location for it. The default dump locations are %SystemRoot%\Minidump for small memory dumps and –%SystemRoot%\Memory.dmp for all other memory dumps. You'll also usually want to select Overwrite Any Existing File. Selecting this option ensures that any existing dump files are overwritten if a new Stop error occurs.

BEST PRACTICES You can create the dump file only if the system is properly configured. The system drive must have a sufficiently large memory-paging file (as set for virtual memory on the Advanced tab), and the drive the dump file is written to must have sufficient free space. For example, my server has 8 GB of RAM and requires a paging file on the system drive of the same size—8 GB. In establishing a baseline for kernel memory usage, I found that the server uses between 892 and 1076 MB of kernel memory. Because the same drive is used for the dump file, the drive must have at least 9 GB of free space to create a dump of debugging information. (That's 8 GB for the paging file and about 1 GB for the dump file.)

CHAPTER 4

Monitoring services, processes, and events

- Managing applications, processes, and performance **89**
- Managing system services **103**
- Event logging and viewing **114**

A s an administrator, you need to keep an eye on network systems. The status and usage of system resources can change dramatically over time. Services might stop running. File systems might run out of space. Applications might throw exceptions that, in turn, can cause system problems. Unauthorized users might try to break into the system. The techniques discussed in this chapter can help you identify and resolve these and other system problems.

Managing applications, processes, and performance

Any time you start an application or type a command at the command line, Windows Server 2012 R2 starts one or more processes to handle the related program. Generally, processes you start in this manner are called *interactive processes*—that is, you start the processes interactively with the keyboard or mouse. If the application or program is active and selected, the interactive process has control over the keyboard and mouse until you switch control by terminating the program or selecting a different one. When a process has control, it's said to be running *in the foreground*.

Processes can also run *in the background*. For processes started by users, this means that programs that aren't currently active can continue to operate, but they generally aren't given the same priority as active processes. You can also configure background processes to run independently of the user logon session; the operating system usually starts such processes. An example of this type of background process is a scheduled task run by the operating system. The configuration settings for the task tell the system to execute a command at a specified time.

Getting started with Task Manager

The key tool you use to manage system processes and applications is Task Manager. You can use any of the following techniques to display Task Manager:

- Press Ctrl+Shift+Esc.
- Press Ctrl+Alt+Del, and then tap or click Task Manager.
- Press the Windows logo key, type **taskmgr**, and then press Enter.
- Press and hold or right-click the taskbar, and then tap or click Task Manager on the shortcut menu.

NOTE When you press the Windows logo key and type **taskmgr**, two matches are displayed. One match is the full name, Task Manager. The other match is the command name, taskmgr.

The following sections cover techniques you use to work with Task Manager.

Viewing and working with processes

Task Manager has two general views:

- **Summary**   Shows only applications running in the foreground, which lets you quickly select and work with foreground applications
- **Expanded**   Expands the view, providing additional tabs that you can use to get information about all running processes, system performance, connected users, and configured services

If you are in summary view, you can switch to expanded view by tapping or clicking More Details. If you are in the expanded view, you can switch to summary view by tapping or clicking Fewer Details. When you close and reopen Task Manager, the view that you last used is displayed.

Generally, as an administrator, you'll work with the expanded view. As shown in Figure 4-1, the expanded view has multiple tabs you can select to work with running processes, system performance, connected users, and configured services. The Processes tab, also shown in Figure 4-1, shows the general status of processes. Processes are grouped by type and listed alphabetically within each type by default. There are three general types:

- Apps, which are programs running in the foreground
- Background processes, which are programs running in the background
- Windows processes, which are processes run by the operating system

NOTE The Group By Type option on the View menu controls whether grouping is used. If you clear this option, all processes are listed alphabetically without grouping by type. Note also that you can start a new program from within Task Manager by tapping or clicking Run New Task on the File menu and then entering a command to run the application. Options are included for running the task with Administrator privileges and for browsing to find the executable you want to work with.

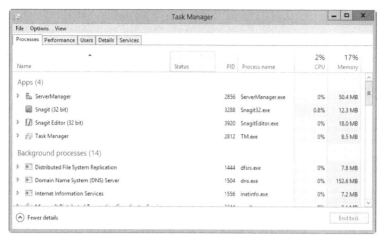

FIGURE 4-1 View the status of processes currently running on the server.

> **REAL WORLD** Many Windows processes also are grouped by the service host they are running under, which can include Local Service, Local System, and Network Service. The number of grouped processes is shown in parentheses, and you can expand the related node to view the actual processes. Select Expand All on the View menu to expand all process groups for easy viewing.

The Status column tells you whether an application is running normally or has stopped responding. A blank status is normal and indicates the process is running normally. Any other status indicates a problem, such as when an application might be frozen and you might want to end the task related to it. However, some applications might not respond to the operating system during certain process-intensive tasks. Because of this, you should be certain the application is really not responding before you end its related task.

You can stop a process by selecting the process and then tapping or clicking End Task. You shouldn't try to stop Windows processes by using this technique. If you try to stop a Windows process or a group of Windows processes, Task Manager displays a warning prompt similar to the one shown in Figure 4-2. This warning states that ending this process will cause Windows to become unusable or to shut down. To proceed, you must select Abandon Unsaved Data And Shut Down, and then tap or click Shut Down. Windows then displays a blue screen with an error code. After collecting error information, Windows will restart.

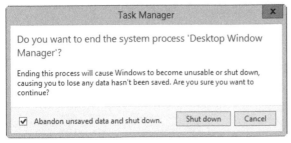

FIGURE 4-2 Stopping processes for essential Windows services causes Windows to become unusable or to shut down.

Other columns on the Processes tab provide a lot of information about running processes. You can use this information to determine which processes are over-consuming system resources, such as CPU time and memory. Although only CPU and Memory columns are displayed by default, other columns can be added by pressing and holding or right-clicking any column header and then selecting check boxes for the additional columns to display. In addition to name and status, the other available columns include the following:

- **CPU** The percentage of CPU utilization for the process (across all cores). The bold value in the column header represents the total CPU utilization for the server (across all cores).
- **Memory** The total physical memory reserved for the process. The bold value in the column header represents the total physical memory utilization for the server.
- **Command Line** The full file path to the executable running the process, and any command-line arguments passed in when the process was started.
- **PID** The numeric identifier for the process.
- **Process Name** The name of the process or executable running the process.
- **Publisher** The publisher of the process, such as Microsoft Corporation.
- **Type** The general process type displayed as app, background process, or Windows process. This information is useful if you cancel the selection for the Group By Type option on the View menu.

Pressing and holding or right-clicking an application's listing in Task Manager displays a shortcut menu that you can use to do the following:

- End the application's task.
- Create a dump file for debugging the process.
- Go to the related process on the Details tab.

- Open the file location for the related executable.
- Open the Properties dialog box for the related executable.

NOTE The Go To Details option is very helpful when you're trying to find the primary process for a particular application. Selecting this option highlights the related process on the Details tab.

Administering processes

Task Manager's Details tab is shown in Figure 4-3. This tab provides detailed information about the processes that are running. The columns displayed by default on the Details tab are similar to those provided on the Processes tab:

- **Name** The name of the process or executable running the process
- **User Name** The name of the user or system service running the process
- **CPU** The percentage of CPU utilization for the process
- **Memory (Private Working Set)** The amount of physical memory reserved by the process
- **Status** The run status of the process
- **Description** A description of the process

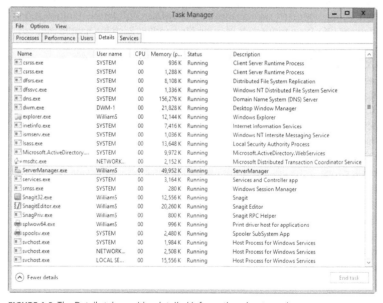

FIGURE 4-3 The Details tab provides detailed information about running processes.

Other columns can be added by pressing and holding or right-clicking any column header and then tapping or clicking Select Columns. When you're trying to troubleshoot system problems by using process information, you might want to add the following columns to the view:

- **Base Priority** Displays how much of the system's resources are allocated to a process. To set the priority for a process, press and hold or right-click the process, choose Set Priority, and then select the new priority from these options: Low, Below Normal, Normal, Above Normal, High, and RealTime. Most processes have a normal priority by default. The highest priority is given to real-time processes.

- **CPU Time** Shows the total amount of CPU cycle time used by a process since it was started. To quickly display the processes that are using the most CPU time, display this column, and then tap or click the column header to sort process entries by CPU time.

- **Data Execution Protection** Specifies whether DEP is enabled or disabled for the process.

- **Elevated** Specifies whether the process is running with elevated, administrator privileges.

- **Handles** Shows the total number of file handles maintained by the process. Use the handle count to gauge how dependent the process is on the file system. Some processes, such as those used by Microsoft Internet Information Services (IIS), have thousands of open file handles. Each file handle requires system memory to be maintained.

- **I/O Reads, I/O Writes** Shows the total number of disk input/output (I/O) reads or writes since the process was started. Together, the number of I/O reads and writes tells you how much disk I/O activity has occurred. If the number of I/O reads and writes is growing disproportionately to actual activity on the server, the process might not be caching files or file caching might not be properly configured. Ideally, file caching reduces the need for I/O reads and writes.

- **Page Faults** Shows whether there are page faults. A *page fault* occurs when a process requests a page in memory and the system can't find it at the requested location. If the requested page is elsewhere in memory, the fault is called a *soft page fault*. If the requested page must be retrieved from disk, the fault is called a *hard page fault*. Most processors can handle large numbers of soft faults. Hard faults, however, can cause significant delays.

- **Paged Pool, NP Pool** Shows the paged pool and nonpaged pool. A *paged pool* is an area of system memory for objects that can be written to disk when they aren't used. *NP pool*, or nonpaged pool, is an area of system memory for objects that can't be written to disk. You should note processes that require a large amount of nonpaged pool memory. If there isn't enough free memory on the server, these processes might be the reason for a high level of page faults.

- **Peak Working Set** Shows the highest amount of memory used by the process. The change, or delta, between current memory usage and peak memory usage is also important to note. Applications that have a high delta between base memory usage and peak memory usage, such as Microsoft SQL Server, might need to be allocated more memory when they start so that they perform better.

- **Platform** Specifies whether the process is running on the 64-bit or 32-bit platform. Windows 64-bit editions support both 64-bit and 32-bit applications by using the Windows on Windows 64 (WoW64) x86 emulation layer. The WoW64 subsystem isolates 32-bit applications from 64-bit applications. This prevents file-system and registry problems. The operating system provides interoperability across the 32-bit/64-bit boundary for the Component Object Model (COM) and for basic operations. However, 32-bit processes cannot load 64-bit dynamic-link libraries (DLLs), and 64-bit processes cannot load 32-bit DLLs.

- **Process ID (PID)** Shows the numeric identifier for the process.

- **Session ID** Shows the identifier for the session under which the process is running.

- **Threads** Shows the current number of threads the process is using. Most server applications are multithreaded. Multithreading allows concurrent execution of process requests. Some applications can dynamically control the number of concurrently executing threads to improve application performance. Too many threads, however, can actually reduce performance, because the operating system has to switch thread contexts too frequently.

- **UAC Virtualization** Indicates whether User Account Control (UAC) virtualization is enabled, disabled, or not allowed in the process. UAC virtualization is needed for legacy applications written for early releases of Windows. When UAC virtualization is enabled for these applications, error notifications and error logging related to virtualized files and registry values are written to the virtualized location rather than to the actual location to which the process was trying to write. If virtualization is required but disabled or not allowed, the process will silently fail when trying to write to protected folders or protected areas of the registry.

If you examine processes running in Task Manager, you'll notice a process called System Idle Process. You can't set the priority of this process. Unlike processes that track resource usage, System Idle Process tracks the percentage of system resources that aren't used. Thus, a 99 in the CPU column of the System Idle Process means that 99 percent of system resources currently aren't being used.

Processes that are waiting to use a resource that is locked by another process are in a wait state and can continue only when the locked resource is released. As part of normal operations, resources are locked for one process or another and then released to be used by another process. Sometimes, though, with poorly architected programs, a process can get stuck waiting for a resource that never gets released.

You can view the wait chain for processes by pressing and holding or right-clicking the process and then tapping or clicking Analyze Wait Chain. If the process is waiting for a resource to be released, the wait chain is displayed for that process (as shown in Figure 4-4). The root node in the wait tree is the process using, or waiting to use, the required resource. A process waiting on another process for a resource might explain why a process doesn't seem as responsive as you might expect.

If you suspect there's a locking problem, you can select one or more processes in the wait chain and then tap or click End Process. Task Manager then stops the processes, which should free the locked resource. However, keep in mind that it is routine and normal for processes to lock resources while those resources are being used and then to free the resources when they are no longer being used. A problem occurs when a process fails to release a resource, as can happen with a poorly architected program.

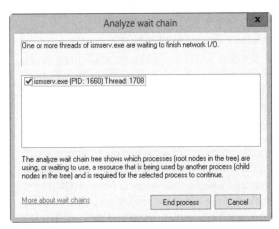

FIGURE 4-4 Analyzing wait chains to identify threads waiting to finish.

As you examine processes, keep in mind that a single application might start multiple processes. Generally, these processes are dependent on a central process. From this main process, a process tree containing dependent processes is formed. You can find the main process for an application by pressing and holding or right-clicking the application on the Processes tab and selecting Go To Details. When you terminate processes, you'll usually want to target the main application process or the application itself rather than dependent processes. This ensures that the application is stopped cleanly.

To stop the main application process and dependent processes, you have several choices:

- Press and hold or right-click the application on the Processes tab, and then tap or click End Task.

- Press and hold or right-click the main application process on the Details tab, and then tap or click End Task.

- Press and hold or right-click the main or a dependent process on the Processes tab, and then tap or click End Process Tree.

Viewing system services

Task Manager's Services tab provides an overview of system services. This tab displays services by name, process ID, description, status, and group. As shown in Figure 4-5, multiple services typically run under the same process ID. You can quickly sort services by their process ID by tapping or clicking the related column heading. You can tap or click the Status column heading to sort services according to their status, Running or Stopped.

The Group column provides additional options about related identities or service host contexts under which a service runs:

- Services running under an identity with a restriction have the restriction listed in the Group column. For example, a service running under the Local Service identity might be listed as LocalServiceNoNetwork to indicate that the service has no network access, or a service might be listed as Local-SystemNetworkRestricted to indicate that the service has restricted access to the network.

- Services that have Svchost.exe list their associated context for the –k parameter. For example, the RemoteRegistry service runs with the command line svchost.exe –k regsvc. An entry of regsvc appears in the Group column for this service.

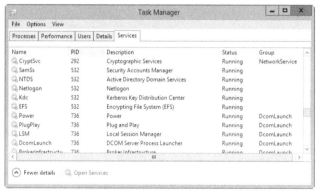

FIGURE 4-5 The Services tab provides a quick overview of the status of system services.

Pressing and holding or right-clicking a service's listing in Task Manager displays a shortcut menu that allows you to do the following:

- Start a stopped service.
- Stop a started service.
- Go to the related process on the Details tab.

Viewing and managing system performance

The Performance tab in Task Manager provides an overview of CPU and memory usage. As shown in Figure 4-6, the tab displays graphs and statistics. This information gives you a quick check of system resource usage. For more detailed information, use Performance Monitor, as explained later in this chapter.

The graphs on the Performance tab provide the following information:

- **CPU**   A graph of CPU usage plotted over time
- **Memory**   A graph of memory usage plotted over time
- **Ethernet**   A graph of network throughput plotted over time

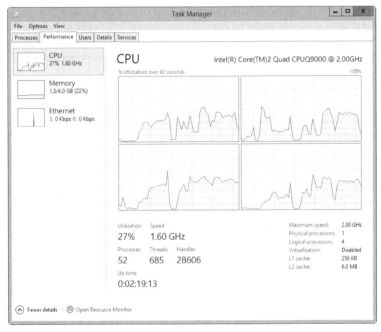

FIGURE 4-6 The Performance tab provides a quick check of system resource usage.

Tap or click a summary graph in the left pane to view detailed information for that graph in the right pane. To view a close-up of any graph, double-tap or double-click the graph. Double-tapping or double-clicking again returns you to normal viewing mode.

The Update Speed option on the View menu allows you to change the speed of graph updating and to pause the graph. Updates occur once every four seconds for Low, once every two seconds for Normal, and twice per second for High.

CPU usage: the basics

When you select CPU, the % Utilization graph shows overall processor utilization for the last 60 seconds. If a system has multiple CPUs, a graph is displayed for each CPU by default. You also can view logical processors or NUMA nodes by pressing and holding or right-clicking a CPU graph, clicking Change Graph To, and then clicking Logical Processors or NUMA Nodes as appropriate.

To view kernel times, press and hold or right-click a CPU graph, and then select Show Kernel Times. Because usage by the kernel is plotted separately, you can more easily track the amount of CPU time used by the operating system kernel.

TIP Tracking the kernel usage can be helpful for troubleshooting. For example, if you are using Microsoft Internet Information Services (IIS) with output caching in kernel mode, you can get a better understanding of how kernel caching might be affecting CPU usage and overall performance by showing kernel times. Kernel usage tracking isn't enabled by default because it adds to the overhead of monitoring a server in Task Manager.

You can use the CPU information provided to quickly determine the up time for the server, the number of physical processors, the number of logical processors, whether hardware virtualization is enabled, and the amount of on-processor cache for each available register (L1, L2, L3). Keep the following in mind:

- **Handles** Shows the number of I/O handles in use; *I/O handles* act as tokens that let programs access resources. I/O throughput and disk performance affect a system more than a consistently high number of I/O handles.

- **Threads** Shows the number of threads in use; *threads* are the basic units of execution within processes.

- **Processes** Shows the number of processes in use; *processes* are running instances of applications or executable files.

- **Up Time** Shows how long the system has been up since it was last started.

If CPU usage is consistently high, even under average usage conditions, you might want to perform more detailed performance monitoring to determine the cause of the problem. Memory is often a source of performance problems, and you should rule it out before upgrading or adding CPUs. For more details, see Chapter 5 "Optimizing system performance."

Memory usage: the basics

When you select Memory, the Memory Usage graph shows overall usage of the private working set for the last 60 seconds. The Memory Composition histogram shows the following:

- **In-Use Memory** The amount of memory being used by processes
- **Modified Memory** The amount of memory whose contents must be written to disk before the memory can be used for another purpose

- **Standby Memory** The amount of memory with cached data and code not actively being used
- **Free Memory** The amount of memory that is not currently allocated for any purpose

NOTE You can use the memory information provided to quickly determine the speed of the memory, the number of memory slots used and available, and the memory form factor.

The total amount of physical RAM configured on the server is listed in the upper-right corner when you are working with the memory graphs. Other memory statistics shown below the memory graphs provide the following information:

- **In Use** Shows the amount of physical RAM that is in use on the server.
- **Available** Shows the amount of physical RAM that is available for use (includes memory marked as *standby* and *free*). If a server has very little physical memory free, you might need to add memory to the system. In general, you want the free memory to be no less than 5 percent of the total physical memory on the server.
- **Committed** Lists the virtual memory currently in use followed by the total amount of virtual memory available. If the current page file usage is consistently within 10 percent of the maximum value (meaning consistent usage of 90 percent or more), you might want to add physical memory, increase the amount of virtual memory, or do both.
- **Cached** Shows the amount of memory used for system caching.
- **Paged Pool** Provides information on noncritical kernel memory used by the operating system kernel.
- **Non-paged Pool** Provides information on critical kernel memory used by the operating system kernel.

Critical portions of kernel memory must operate in RAM and can't be paged to virtual memory. Because of this, this type of kernel memory is listed as being in the nonpaged pool. The rest of kernel memory can be paged to virtual memory and is listed as being in the paged pool.

Network usage: the basics

When you select Ethernet, Task Manager provides an overview of the network adapters used by the system. You can use the information provided to quickly determine the percent utilization, link speed, and operational status of each network adapter configured on a system.

The name of the active network adapter in the Network Connections folder is shown in the upper-right corner. If a system has one network adapter, the summary graph shows details of the network traffic on this adapter over time. If a system has multiple network adapters, the graph displays a composite index of all network connections, which represents all network traffic.

You can view detailed information about link speed, link state, bytes sent, bytes received, and more by pressing and holding or right-clicking the Network Throughput graph and then clicking View Network Details. When working with network details, keep the following in mind:

- **Network Utilization** Percentage of network usage based on the initial connection speed for the interface or the combined speed of teamed interfaces. For example, an adapter with an initial link speed of 10 gigabits per second (Gbps) and current traffic of 100 megabits per second (Mbps) is utilized at 1 percent.

- **Link Speed** Connection speed of the interface as determined by the initial connection speed, such as 1 Gbps or 10 Gbps.

- **State** Operational status of network adapters, such as Connected or Disconnected.

- **Bytes Sent Throughput** Percentage of current connection bandwidth used by traffic sent from the system.

- **Bytes Received Throughput** Percentage of current connection bandwidth used by traffic received by the system.

- **Bytes Throughput** Percentage of current connection bandwidth used for all traffic on the network adapter.

- **Bytes Sent** Cumulative total bytes sent on the connection to date.

- **Bytes Received** Cumulative total bytes received on the connection to date.

- **Bytes** Cumulative total bytes on the connection to date.

REAL WORLD Any time usage is consistently approaching or exceeding 50 percent of total capacity, you should start monitoring the server more closely, and you might want to consider adding network adapters. Plan any upgrade carefully; a lot more planning is required than you might think. Consider the implications not only for that server but also for the network as a whole. You might also have connectivity problems if you exceed the allotted bandwidth of your service provider—it can often take months to obtain additional bandwidth for external connections.

Viewing and managing remote user sessions

Remote users can use Remote Desktop to connect to remote systems. Remote Desktop allows you to manage systems remotely, as if you were sitting at the console. Windows Server 2012 R2 allows up to two active console sessions at a time.

One way to view and manage remote desktop connections is to use Task Manager. To do this, start Task Manager, and then tap or click the Users tab, shown in Figure 4-7. The Users tab shows interactive user sessions for both local and remote users.

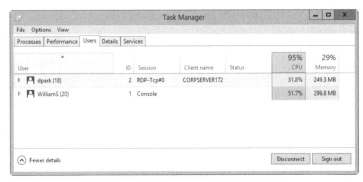

FIGURE 4-7 The Users tab allows you to view and manage user sessions.

Each user connection is listed with user name, status, CPU utilization, and memory usage by default. Other columns can be added by pressing and holding or right-clicking any column header and then tapping or clicking the columns to add. Available columns include:

- **ID** The session ID. The first logon has a session ID of 1. The second logon has an ID of 2.

- **Session** The session type. A user logged on to the local system is listed with Console as the session type. Other users have a session type that indicates the connection type and protocol being used, such as RDP-TCP for a connection that is using the Remote Desktop Protocol (RDP) with TCP as the transport protocol.

- **Client name** For remote connections, lists the name of the originating client computer.

CPU and memory utilization details are convenient for troubleshooting performance issues related to logged-on users. The combined utilization value is listed above the column heading, and individual utilization values for each logged-on user are listed below it.

In the example shown in Figure 4-7, the server's CPU is 95% utilized by the logged-on users. This high usage level could affect the overall performance of the server, and the server might not be as responsive when performing other tasks.

If you press and hold or right-click a user session, you have the following options:

- **Connect** Allows you to connect a remote user session if it's inactive.

- **Disconnect** Allows you to disconnect a local or remote user session, halting all user-started applications without saving application data.

- **Sign Off** Allows you to log off a user by using the normal logoff process. Application data and system state information are saved just as they are during a typical logoff.

- **Send Message** Allows you to send a console message to a logged-on user.

Also new for Windows Server 2012 R2 is the user's name is followed by the number of processes that user is running. If you double-tap or double-click the user's name, an entry for each running process is displayed. Processes are listed by name, CPU usage, and memory usage.

Managing system services

Services provide key functions to workstations and servers. To manage system services on the local server or a remote server, you use the Services panel in Server Manager or the Services node in Computer Management. To work with services on remote servers, remote management and inbound exceptions for Remote Service Management must be enabled. For more information, see "Managing your servers remotely" in Chapter 3, "Managing Windows Servers."

Navigating services in Server Manager

When you are working with Server Manager and select the Local Server node, the All Servers node, or a server group node, the right pane will have a Services panel, like the one shown in Figure 4-8. If you select the server you want to work with in the Servers panel, its services are listed in the Services panel. You can use this panel as follows:

- For a server you are logged on to locally, you can use the Services panel in the Local Server node.

- For a local or remote server, you can use the Services panel in the All Servers node to work with services.

- Automatically created server group nodes are organized by server roles, such as Active Directory Domain Services (AD DS) or Domain Name System (DNS), and you'll be able to manage the services running on servers that role depends on.

- For custom server groups created by you or other administrators, you'll be able to use the related Services panel to manage services on any remote servers that have been added to the group.

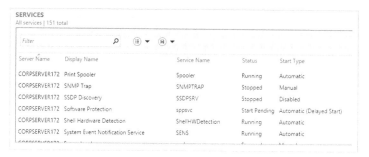

SERVICES
All services | 151 total

Server Name	Display Name	Service Name	Status	Start Type
CORPSERVER172	Print Spooler	Spooler	Running	Automatic
CORPSERVER172	SNMP Trap	SNMPTRAP	Stopped	Manual
CORPSERVER172	SSDP Discovery	SSDPSRV	Stopped	Disabled
CORPSERVER172	Software Protection	sppsvc	Start Pending	Automatic (Delayed Start)
CORPSERVER172	Shell Hardware Detection	ShellHWDetection	Running	Automatic
CORPSERVER172	System Event Notification Service	SENS	Running	Automatic

FIGURE 4-8 Use the Services panels in Server Manager to manage services on local and remote servers.

The columns on the Services panel can be adjusted by pressing and holding or right-clicking any column header and then tapping or clicking the columns to add or remove. The columns you can use include the following:

- **Server Name** The name of the server on which the service is running.
- **FQDN** The fully qualified domain name (FQDN) of the server on which the service is running.
- **Display Name** The descriptive name of the service.
- **Service Name** The internal name of the service.
- **Description** A short description of the service and its purpose.
- **Status** The status of the service as running, paused, or stopped.
- **Start Type** The startup setting for the service. Automatic services are started when the system starts. Users or other services start manual services. Disabled services are turned off and can't be started while they remain disabled.

TIP When you are working with many servers, use the service grouping options to help you more easily manage services. You can group services by server name, FQDN, display name, service name, status, and start type by pressing and holding or right-clicking any column header, selecting Group By, and then clicking your grouping option.

Navigating services in Computer Management

For quick and easy management of any service on a remote server, you can use the Services node in Computer Management. You can open Computer Management and automatically connect to a remote server from Server Manager. To do this, follow these steps:

1. Select All Servers or any server group node in the left pane.
2. On the Servers panel, press and hold or right-click the server to which you want to connect.
3. Tap or click Computer Management.

TIP When you are working with remote servers in Computer Management, many features rely on remote management and appropriate firewall exceptions being enabled, as discussed in Chapter 3. If the user account you are currently using doesn't have the appropriate credentials for working with the remote server, you won't be able to connect to the server in Computer Management. To use alternate credentials, press and hold or right-click the server to which you want to connect, select Manage As, enter your alternate credentials, and then click OK. Optionally, you can select Remember My Credentials before clicking OK to save the credentials for each time you log on and want to work with the server remotely. After you set your credentials, press and hold or right-click the server to which you want to connect and then click Computer Management. Now Computer Management will open and connect to the server using the credentials you specified.

When you are working with Computer Management, you view and work with services by expanding the Services And Applications node and then selecting the Services node, as shown in Figure 4-9. The columns in the Services pane are slightly different from those shown when you are working with the Services node in Computer Management:

- **Name** The name of the service. Only services installed on the system are listed here. Double-tap or double-click an entry to configure its startup options. If a service you need isn't listed, you can install it by installing the related role or feature, as discussed in Chapter 3.

- **Description** A short description of the service and its purpose.

- **Status** The status of the service, indicated as running, paused, or stopped. (Stopped is indicated by a blank entry.)

- **Startup Type** The startup setting for the service. Automatic services are started when the system starts. Users or other services start manual services. Disabled services are turned off and can't be started while they remain disabled.

- **Log On As** The account the service logs on as. The default in most cases is the local system account.

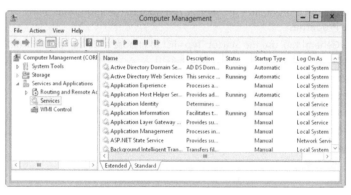

FIGURE 4-9 Use the Services pane to manage services on local and remote computers.

The Services pane has two views: Extended and Standard. To change the view, use the tabs at the bottom of the Services pane. In Extended view, quick links are provided for managing services. Tap or click Start to start a stopped service. Tap or click Restart to stop and then start a service—essentially resetting that service. If you select a service when the Services pane is in Extended view, a description that details the service's purpose is displayed.

NOTE Both the operating system and a user can disable services. Generally, Windows Server 2012 R2 disables a service if a possible conflict with another service exists.

Starting, stopping, and pausing services

As an administrator, you often have to start, stop, or pause services. To start, stop, or pause a service, press and hold or right-click the service you want to manage and then select Start, Stop, or Pause as appropriate. You can also choose Restart to have Windows stop and then start the service after a brief pause. Additionally, if you pause a service, you can use the Resume option to resume normal operation.

> **NOTE** When services that are set to start automatically fail, the status is listed as blank, and you usually receive notification in a pop-up dialog box. Service failures can also be logged to the system's event logs. In Windows Server 2012 R2, you can configure actions to handle service failure automatically. For example, you can have Windows Server 2012 R2 attempt to restart the service for you. For details, see the section "Configuring Service Recovery" later in this chapter.

Configuring service startup

You can set services to start manually or automatically. You can also turn them off permanently by disabling them. You configure service startup in Computer Management by following these steps:

1. Press and hold or right-click the service you want to configure, and then choose Properties.

2. On the General tab, use the Startup Type list to choose a startup option from the following choices, as shown in Figure 4-10:

   - **Automatic** Select Automatic to start services when the system starts.
   - **Automatic (Delayed Start)** Select Automatic (Delayed Start) to delay the start of the service until all nondelayed automatic services have started.
   - **Manual** Select Manual to allow the services to be started manually.
   - **Disabled** Select Disabled to turn off the service.

3. Tap or click OK.

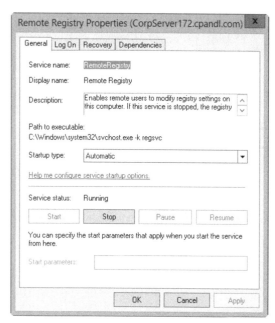

FIGURE 4-10 Configure service startup options by using the General tab's Startup Type list.

Configuring service logon

You can configure services to log on as a system account or as a specific user. To do either, follow these steps:

1. In Computer Management, press and hold or right-click the service you want to configure, and then click Properties.

2. Click the Log On tab, shown in Figure 4-11.

3. Click Local System Account if you want the service to log on by using the system account (the default for most services). If the service provides a user interface that can be manipulated, select Allow Service To Interact With Desktop to allow users to control the service's interface.

4. Click This Account if you want the service to log on by using a specific user account. Be sure to enter an account name and password in the text boxes provided. Use the Browse button to search for a user account if necessary.

5. Tap or click OK.

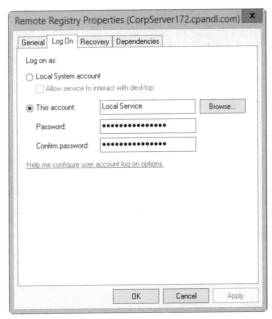

FIGURE 4-11 Use the Log On tab to configure the service logon account.

SECURITY ALERT You should keep track of any accounts that are used with services. These accounts can be the source of security problems if they're not configured properly. Service accounts should have the strictest security settings and as few permissions as possible while allowing the service to perform necessary functions. Typically, accounts used with services don't need many of the permissions you would assign to a typical user account. For example, most service accounts don't need the right to log on locally. Every administrator should know what service accounts are used (so that they can better track the use of these accounts) and should treat the accounts as if they were administrator accounts. This means using secure passwords, carefully monitoring account usage, carefully applying account permissions and privileges, and so on.

Configuring service recovery

You can configure services to take specific actions when a service fails. For example, you can attempt to restart the service or run an application. To configure recovery options for a service, follow these steps:

1. In Computer Management, press and hold or right-click the service you want to configure, and then click Properties.

2. Tap or click the Recovery tab, shown in Figure 4-12.

Remote Registry Properties (CorpServer172.cpandl.com) X

General | Log On | Recovery | Dependencies

Select the computer's response if this service fails. Help me set up recovery actions

First failure: Restart the Service   ▼

Second failure: Restart the Service   ▼

Subsequent failures: Take No Action   ▼

Reset fail count after: 1   days

Restart service after: 1   minutes

☐ Enable actions for stops with errors.   Restart Computer Options...

Run program
Program:
[   ]   Browse...

Command line parameters: [   ]

☐ Append fail count to end of command line (/fail=%1%)

OK   Cancel   Apply

FIGURE 4-12 Use the Recovery tab to specify actions that should be taken in case of service failure.

NOTE Windows Server 2012 R2 automatically configures recovery for critical system services during installation. In most cases, you'll find that critical services are configured to restart automatically if the service fails. Some extremely critical services, such as DCOM Server Process Launcher and Group Policy Client, are configured to restart the computer if the service fails. You cannot change these settings because they are not available.

3. You can now configure recovery options for the first, second, and subsequent recovery attempts. The following options are available:

- **Take No Action** The operating system won't attempt recovery for this failure but might still attempt recovery of previous or subsequent failures.

- **Restart The Service** Stops and then starts the service after a brief pause.

- **Run A Program** Allows you to run a program or a script in case of failure. The script can be a batch program or a Windows script. If you select this option, set the full file path to the program you want to run, and then set any necessary command-line parameters to pass in to the program when it starts.

- **Restart The Computer** Shuts down and then restarts the computer. Before you choose this option, double-check the computer's Startup and Recovery options. You want the system to select defaults quickly and automatically.

BEST PRACTICES When you configure recovery options for critical services, you might want to try to restart the service on the first and second attempts and then restart the server on the third attempt.

4. Configure other options based on your previously selected recovery options. If you elected to run a program as a recovery option, you need to set options in the Run Program panel. If you elected to restart the service, you need to specify the restart delay. After stopping the service, Windows Server waits for the specified delay before trying to start the service. In most cases, a delay of one to two minutes should be sufficient.

5. Tap or click OK.

Disabling unnecessary services

As an administrator, you need to ensure that servers and the network are secure, and unnecessary services are a potential source of security problems. For example, in many organizations that I've reviewed for security problems, I've found servers running Worldwide Web Publishing Service, Simple Mail Transfer Protocol (SMTP), and File Transfer Protocol (FTP) Publishing Service when these services weren't needed. Unfortunately, these services can make it possible for anonymous users to access servers and can also open the server to attack if not properly configured.

If you find unnecessary services, you have several options. With services installed through roles, role services, or features, you can remove the related role, role service, or feature to remove the unnecessary component and its related services. Or you can simply disable the services that aren't being used. Typically, you'll want to start by disabling services rather than uninstalling components. This way, if you disable a service and another administrator or a user says he or she can't perform a particular task anymore, you can enable the related service again if necessary.

To disable a service, follow these steps:

1. In Computer Management, press and hold or right-click the service you want to configure, and then click Properties. On the General tab, click Disabled in the Startup Type list.

2. Disabling a service doesn't stop a running service. It only prevents the service from being started the next time the computer is started, meaning that the security risk still exists. To address this, tap or click Stop on the General tab in the Properties dialog box, and then tap or click OK.

Troubleshooting services

When you think a computer has a problem related to services—their status or configuration, for example—one of the fastest ways to troubleshoot is to use Windows PowerShell. Windows PowerShell provides several cmdlets for working with system services, including:

- **Get-Service** Gets information about the services
- **Stop-Service** Stops one or more running services
- **Start-Service** Starts one or more stopped services
- **Suspend-Service** Suspends (pauses) one or more running services
- **Resume-Service** Resumes one or more suspended (paused) services
- **Restart-Service** Stops and then starts one or more services
- **Set-Service** Changes the properties or status of a service on a local or remote computer
- **New-Service** Creates a new Windows service in the registry and in the services database

To get a list of all services configured on a system, type **get-service** at the command prompt. Optionally, use the –ComputerName parameter to specify a remote computer to work with, as shown in this example:

```
Get-Service -ComputerName CorpServer18
```

If you want to check multiple computers, simply enter the computer name in a comma-separated list:

```
Get-Service -ComputerName Server18, Server24, Server30
```

Regardless of whether you check the local computer or remote computers, the standard output shows the status, name, and display name of each configured service, as shown in the following example:

```
Status   Name            DisplayName
------   ----            -----------
Running  ADWS            Active Directory Web Services
Stopped  AeLookupSvc     Application Experience
Stopped  ALG             Application Layer Gateway Service
Stopped  AllUserInstallA... Windows All-User Install Agent
Stopped  AppIDSvc        Application Identity
Running  Appinfo         Application Information
```

Knowing this, you can display information about a specific service by using its name or display name, such as the following:

```
Get-Service -DisplayName "Application Experience" -ComputerName
CorpServer18
```

To match partial names, you can use wildcard characters. In this example, you want to check the status of key services used by Hyper-V:

```
Get-Service –DisplayName Hyper* –ComputerName CorpServer18
```

As part of troubleshooting, you might also want to locate all services that are disabled or stopped on a computer. To find disabled services, you can enter the following:

```
Get-Service | where {$_.status -eq 'disabled'}
```

To find stopped services, you can enter the following:

```
Get-Service | where {$_.status -eq 'stopped'}
```

A service can start only if the services it depends on also are started. You can use the –RequiredServices parameter to confirm the status of the services that are required for a particular service to start. Alternatively, you can check the status of services that depend on a particular service by using the –DependentServices parameter.

As part of troubleshooting, you might need to determine the start mode of services. If a service isn't configured to start automatically, that would explain why it isn't running. Although Get-Service doesn't display the StartMode of services, you can use Get-WMIObject Win32_Service to get extended information about services, including their start mode.

The syntax for displaying detailed information about a particular service follows:

```
Get-WMIObject Win32_Service -Filter "name='ServiceName'" | Select *
```

Or you could use the following:

```
Get-WMIObject Win32_Service -Filter "displayname='DisplayName'" | Select *
```

In these examples, you use Get-WMIObject Win32_Service to examine all services on a computer and filter the results by either the name or display name of the service. You then use Select-Object (which has Select as an alias) to list all associated properties.

In your troubleshooting, you might want to list the start mode of all enabled services on a computer. The following example shows one way to do this:

```
get-wmiobject win32_service -filter "StartMode <>'disabled'" |
sort StartMode | format-table -GroupBy StartMode
-Property Name,State
```

Here, you list all enabled services on a computer, sorting the output by the start mode, and then alphabetically list services in each group by name and state. The output is similar to the following:

```
StartMode: Auto

Name                                        State
----                                        -----
Netlogon                                    Running
NlaSvc                                      Running
MpsSvc                                      Running
...
    StartMode: Manual

Name                                        State
----                                        -----
AppReadiness                                Stopped
vmicguestinterface                          Stopped
UmRdpService                                Running
...
```

Rather than list all services, you might instead want to quickly identify services that should be running but aren't. To do this, you can use the following command:

```
get-wmiobject win32_service -filter "startmode='auto' AND state<> 'Running'"
 | Select Name,State
```

Here, you use Get-WMIObject Win32_Service to examine all services that have the Auto start mode (which includes services that have a delayed automatic start) but aren't running. You look for services that have a state other than 'Running' to ensure services with any state other than 'Running' are included in the results, as shown in this sample output:

```
name                                        state
----                                        -----
RemoteRegistry                              Stopped
sppsvc                                      Stopped
workfolderssvc                              Stopped
```

To determine whether a service that should have started automatically but didn't start because a required service isn't running, you can enter the following command:

```
get-wmiobject win32_service -filter "startmode='auto' AND state<> 'Running'"
 | get-service -RequiredServices
```

Here, you use Get-WMIObject Win32_Service to examine all services that have the Auto start mode but aren't running. You then display the details regarding services that are required for the stopped service to start. If a required service is stopped, that could explain why a service was stopped. You then typically would begin deeper troubleshooting by trying to determine why the required service didn't start. Otherwise, if required services are running or if there are no required services, you would begin deeper troubleshooting by trying to determining why the original service didn't start.

Event logging and viewing

Event logs provide historical information that can help you track down system and security problems. To work with services on remote servers, remote management and inbound exceptions for Remote Service Management must be enabled.

The Windows Event Log service controls whether events are tracked. When you start this service, you can track user actions and resource usage events through the event logs. Two general types of log files are used:

- **Windows logs**   Logs that the operating system uses to record general system events related to applications, security, setup, and system components
- **Applications and services logs**   Logs that specific applications and services use to record application-specific or service-specific events

Windows logs that are used include:

- **Application**   This log records events logged by applications, such as the failure of SQL Server to access a database. The default location is %SystemRoot% \System32\Winevt\Logs\Application.evtx.
- **Forwarded Events**   When event forwarding is configured, this log records forwarded events from other servers. The default location is %SystemRoot% \System32\Config\ForwardedEvents.evtx.
- **Security**   This log records events you've set for auditing with local or global group policies. The default location is %SystemRoot%\System32 \Winevt\Logs\Security.evtx.

  NOTE   Any user who needs access to the security log must be granted the user right to the following: Manage Auditing and the Security Log. By default, members of the Administrators group have this user right. To learn how to assign user rights, see the section "Configuring user rights policies" in Chapter 9, "Creating user and group accounts."

- **Setup**   This log records events logged by the operating system or its components during setup and installation. The default location is %SystemRoot% \System32\Winevt\Logs\Setup.evtx.
- **System**   This log records events logged by the operating system or its components, such as the failure of a service to start when the system starts. The default location is %SystemRoot%\System32\Winevt\Logs\System.evtx.

Applications and services logs available include the following:

- **DFS Replication** This log records Distributed File System (DFS) replication activities. The default location is %SystemRoot%\System32\Winevt\Logs\Dfs Replication.evtx.

- **Directory Service** This log records events logged by Active Directory Domain Services (AD DS) and its related services. The default location is %SystemRoot%\System32\Winevt\Logs\Directory Service.evtx.

- **DNS Server** This log records DNS queries, responses, and other DNS activities. The default location is %SystemRoot%\System32\Winevt \Logs\DNS Server.evtx.

- **File Replication Service** This log records file replication activities on the system. The default location is %SystemRoot%\System32\Winevt \Logs\File Replication Service.evtx.

- **Hardware Events** When hardware subsystem event reporting is configured, this log records hardware events reported to the operating system. The default location is %SystemRoot%\System32\Config\Hardware.evtx.

- **Microsoft\Windows** This provides logs that track events related to specific Windows services and features. Logs are organized by component type and event category. Operational logs track events generated by the standard operations of the related component. In some cases, supplemental logs are displayed for analysis, debugging, and recording administration-related tasks.

- **Windows PowerShell** This log records activities related to the use of Windows PowerShell. The default location is %SystemRoot%\System32 \Winevt\Logs\Windows PowerShell.evtx.

Accessing events in Server Manager

When you are working with Server Manager and select the Local Server node, the All Servers node, or a server group node, the right pane will have an Events panel, like the one shown in Figure 4-13. When you select the server you want to work with in the Servers panel, its events are listed in the Events panel. You can use this panel as follows:

- For a server you are logged on to locally, you can use the Events panel in the Local Server node or the All Servers node to view recent warning and error events in the application and system logs.

- Automatically created server group nodes are organized by server roles, such as AD DS or DNS, and you'll be able to view recent error and warning events in logs related to the server role, if applicable. Not all roles have associated logs, but some roles, like AD DS, have multiple associated logs.

- For custom server groups created by you or other administrators, you'll be able to use the related Events panel to view recent warning and error events in the application and system logs.

EVENTS
All events | 17 total

Server Name	ID	Severity	Source	Log	Date
CORPSERVER172	5008	Error	DFSR	DFS Replication	5/17,
CORPSERVER172	5014	Warning	DFSR	DFS Replication	5/17,
CORPSERVER172	1308	Warning	Microsoft-Windows-ActiveDirectory_DomainService	Directory Service	5/17,
CORPSERVER172	1308	Warning	Microsoft-Windows-ActiveDirectory_DomainService	Directory Service	5/17,
CORPSERVER172	5002	Error	DFSR	DFS Replication	5/17,
CORPSERVER172	1308	Warning	Microsoft-Windows-ActiveDirectory_DomainService	Directory Service	5/17,

FIGURE 4-13 Use the Events panels in Server Manager to track errors and warnings.

The columns on the Events panel can be adjusted by pressing and holding or right-clicking any column header and then tapping or clicking the columns to add or remove. The columns you can use include:

- **Server Name**   The name of the server on which the service is running
- **FQDN**   The fully qualified domain name of the server on which the service is running
- **ID**   Generally, a numeric identifier for the specific event, which could be helpful when searching knowledge bases
- **Severity**   The event level as an error or warning
- **Source**   The application, service, or component that logged the event
- **Log**   The log in which the event was recorded
- **Date And Time**   The date and time the event was recorded

> **TIP**   When you are working with many servers, use the grouping options to help you more easily manage events. You can group events by server name, FDQN, ID, severity, source, log, and date and time by pressing and holding or right-clicking any column header, clicking Group By, and then selecting your grouping option.

Accessing events in Event Viewer

To work with event logs on remote servers, remote management and inbound exceptions for Remote Event Log Management must be enabled. For more information, see the section "Managing your servers remotely" in Chapter 3.

You access the event logs by following these steps:

1. In Server Manager, select All Servers or any server group node in the left pane.

2. On the Servers panel, press and hold or right-click the server to which you want to connect.

3. Tap or click Computer Management to automatically connect to the selected server.

4. In Computer Management, you view and work with the event logs by expanding the System Tools node and then selecting the Event Viewer node, as shown in Figure 4-14.

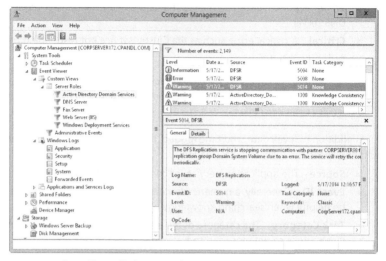

FIGURE 4-14 Event Viewer displays events for the selected log or custom view.

5. Expand the Event Viewer node. You can work with the server's event logs in the following ways:

- To view all errors and warnings for all logs, expand Custom Views, and then select Administrative Events. In the main pane, a list of all warning and error events for the server is displayed.

- To view all errors and warnings for a specific server role, expand Custom Views, expand Server Roles, and then select the role to view. In the main pane, a list of all events for the selected role is displayed.

- To view events in a specific log, expand the Windows Logs node, the Applications And Services Logs node, or both nodes. Select the log you want to view, such as Application or System.

6. Use the information in the Source column to determine which service or process logged a particular event.

As shown in Figure 4-14, entries in the main pane of Event Viewer provide a quick overview of when, where, and how an event occurred. To obtain detailed information about an event, review the details provided on the General tab in the lower portion of the main pane. The event level or keyword precedes the date and time of the event. Event levels include the following:

- **Information** An informational event, which is generally related to a successful action.
- **Audit Success** An event related to the successful execution of an action.

- **Audit Failure** An event related to the failed execution of an action.
- **Warning** A warning. Details for warnings are often useful in preventing future system problems.
- **Error** A noncritical error, such as the failure of a zone transfer request on a DNS server.
- **Critical** A critical error, such as the Cluster service not responding because a quorum was lost.

NOTE Warnings and errors are the two key types of events you'll want to examine closely. Whenever these types of events occur and you're unsure of the cause, review the detailed event description.

In addition to level, date, and time logged, the summary and detailed event entries provide the following information:

- **Source** The application, service, or component that logged the event
- **Event ID** Generally, a numeric identifier for the specific event, which could be helpful when searching knowledge bases
- **Task Category** The category of the event, which is almost always set to None, but is sometimes used to further describe the related action, such as a process or a service
- **User** The user account that was logged on when the event occurred, if applicable
- **Computer** The name of the computer on which the event occurred
- **Description** In the detailed entries, a text description of the event
- **Data** In the detailed entries, any data or error code output by the event

Filtering event logs

Event Viewer creates several filtered views of the event logs for you automatically. Filtered views are listed under the Custom Views node. When you select the Administrative Events node, a list of all errors and warnings for all logs is displayed. When you expand the Server Roles node and then select a role-specific view, a list of all events for the selected role is displayed.

If you want to create a custom view of your own, you can do so in Computer Management by following these steps:

1. In the left pane, press and hold or right-click the Custom Views node, and then tap or click Create Custom View. This opens the dialog box shown in Figure 4-15.

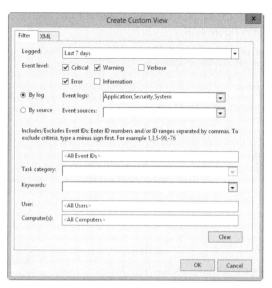

FIGURE 4-15 You can filter logs so that only specific events are displayed.

2. Use the Logged list to select a time frame for logging events. You can choose to include events from the last hour, last 12 hours, last 24 hours, last 7 days, or last 30 days. Alternatively, you can set a custom range.

3. Use the Event Level check boxes to specify the level of events to include. Select Verbose to display additional details for events.

4. Create a custom view for either a specific set of logs or a specific set of event sources:

   ▪ Use the Event Logs list to select event logs to include. You can select multiple event logs by selecting their check boxes. If you select specific event logs, all other event logs are excluded.

   ▪ Use the Event Sources list to select event sources to include. You can select multiple event sources by selecting their check boxes. If you select specific event sources, all other event sources are excluded.

5. Optionally, use the User and Computer(s) boxes to specify users and computers that should be included. If you do not specify users and computers to include, events generated by all users and computers are included.

6. When you tap or click OK, Windows displays the Save Filter To Custom View dialog box, shown in Figure 4-16.

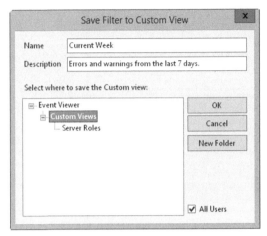

FIGURE 4-16 Save the filtered view.

7. Type a name and description for the custom view.

8. Select where to save the custom view. By default, custom views are saved under the Custom Views node. You can create a new node by tapping or clicking New Folder, entering a name for the folder, and then tapping or clicking OK.

9. Tap or click OK to close the Save Filter To Custom View dialog box, which displays a filtered list of events. Review these events carefully, and take steps to correct any problems that exist.

If you want to review a particular type of event, you can filter the log in Computer Management by following these steps:

1. Expand Windows Logs or Applications And Services Logs as appropriate for the type of log you want to configure to display a list of event logs.

2. Press and hold or right-click the log you want to work with, and then tap or click Filter Current Log. This opens a dialog box similar to the one shown earlier in Figure 4-15.

3. Use the Logged list to select the time frame for logging events. You can choose to include events from the last hour, last 12 hours, last 24 hours, last 7 days, or last 30 days.

4. Use the Event Level check boxes to specify the level of events to include. Select Verbose to get additional details.

5. Use the Event Sources list to select event sources to include. If you select specific event sources, all other event sources are excluded.

6. Optionally, use the User and Computer(s) boxes to specify users and computers that should be included. If you do not specify users and computers, events generated by all users and computers are included.

7. Tap or click OK, which displays a filtered list of events. Review these events carefully, and take steps to correct any problems that exist. To clear the filter and display all events for the log, tap or click Clear Filter in the Actions pane or on the Action menu.

Setting event log options

Log options allow you to control the size of event logs and also how logging is handled. By default, event logs are set with a maximum file size. When a log reaches this limit, events are overwritten to prevent the log from exceeding the maximum file size.

To set log options in Computer Management, follow these steps:

1. Expand Windows Logs or Applications And Services Logs as appropriate for the type of log you want to configure. This displays a list of event logs.

2. Press and hold or right-click the event log whose properties you want to set, and then tap or click Properties on the shortcut menu. This opens the dialog box shown in Figure 4-17.

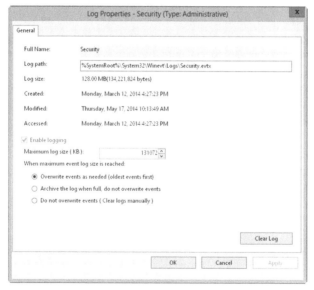

FIGURE 4-17 Configure log settings according to the level of auditing on the system.

3. Type or set a maximum size in kilobytes (KB) in the Maximum Log Size box. Make sure that the drive containing the operating system has enough free space for the maximum log size you specify. Log files are stored in the %SystemRoot%\System32\Winevt\Logs directory by default.

4. Select an event log–wrapping mode. The following options are available:

- **Overwrite Events As Needed (Oldest Events First)** Events in the log are overwritten when the maximum file size is reached. Generally, this is the best option on a low-priority system.

- **Archive The Log When Full, Do Not Overwrite Events** When the maximum file size is reached, Windows archives the events by saving a copy of the current log in the default directory. Windows then creates a new log for storing current events.

- **Do Not Overwrite Events (Clear Logs Manually)** When the maximum file size is reached, the system generates error messages telling you the event log is full.

5. Tap or click OK when you are finished.

NOTE On critical systems where security and event logging is very important, you should use Archive The Log When Full, Do Not Overwrite Events. When you use this method, you ensure that event history is preserved in archives automatically. You might also want to consider a centralized logging solution.

Clearing event logs

When an event log is full, you need to clear it. To do that in Computer Management, follow these steps:

1. Expand Windows Logs or Applications And Services Logs as appropriate for the type of log you want to configure. This displays a list of event logs.

2. Press and hold or right-click the event log whose properties you want to set, and then tap or click Clear Log on the shortcut menu.

3. Click Save And Clear to save a copy of the log before clearing it. Click Clear to continue without saving the log file.

Archiving event logs

On key systems such as domain controllers and application servers, you'll want to keep several months' worth of logs. However, it usually isn't practical to set the maximum log size to accommodate this. Instead, you should allow Windows to periodically archive the event logs, or you should manually archive the event logs.

Archive log file types

Logs can be archived as the following four types of files:

- Event (.evtx) for access in Event Viewer
- Tab-delimited text (.txt) for access in text editors or word processors or to import into spreadsheets and databases
- Comma-delimited text (.csv) for importing into spreadsheets or databases
- XML (.xml) for saving as an XML file

When you export log files to a comma-delimited file, a comma separates each column in the event entry. The event entries look like the following.

```
Information,07/21/14 3:43:24 PM,DNS Server,2,None,The DNS server has
started.
Error,07/21/14 3:40:04 PM,DNS Server,4015,None,The DNS server has
encountered a critical error from the Directory Service (DS). The data is
the error code.
```

The format for the entries is as follows.

```
Level,Date and Time,Source,Event ID,Task Category,Description
```

Creating log archives

Windows creates log archives automatically when you select the event log–wrapping mode named Archive The Log When Full, Do Not Overwrite Events. You can create a log archive manually in Computer Management by following these steps:

1. Expand Windows Logs or Applications And Services Logs as appropriate for the type of log you want to configure. This displays a list of event logs.

2. Press and hold or right-click the event log you want to archive, and then tap or click Save All Events As on the shortcut menu.

3. In the Save As dialog box, select a directory, and then enter a log file name.

4. In the Save As Type list, Event Files (*.evtx) is the default file type. Select the log file type you want to use, and then click Save. Note that you might not be able to use the .evtx file type to save events from a remote computer to a local folder. In this case, you need to save the events to the local computer with a different extension, such as .xml. Otherwise, save the events with the .evtx extension on the remote computer.

5. If you plan to view the log on other computers, you might need to include display information. To save display information, click Display Information For These Languages, choose the language in the list provided, and then tap or click OK. Otherwise, just tap or click OK to save the log without display information.

NOTE If you plan to archive logs regularly, you might want to create an archive directory in which you can easily locate the log archives. You should also name the log file so that you can easily determine the log file type and the period of the archive. For example, if you're archiving the system log file for January 2014, you might want to use the file name **System Log January 2014**.

TIP The best file type to use for archiving is .evtx. Use this extension if you plan to review old logs in Event Viewer. However, if you plan to review logs in other applications, you might need to save the logs in a tab-delimited or comma-delimited format. With the tab-delimited or comma-delimited format, you sometimes need to edit the log file in a text editor for the log to be properly interpreted. If you saved the log with the .evtx extension, you can always save another copy in tab-delimited or comma-delimited format later by doing another Save As after opening the archive in Event Viewer.

Viewing log archives

You can view log archives in text format in any text editor or word processor. You should view log archives in the event log format in Event Viewer. You can view log archives in Event Viewer by following these steps:

1. In Computer Management, select and then press and hold or right-click the Event Viewer node. On the shortcut menu, click Open Saved Log.

2. In the Open Saved Log dialog box, select a directory and a log file name. By default, the Event Logs Files format is selected. This ensures that logs saved as .evtx, .evt, and .etl are listed. You can also filter the list by selecting a specific file type.

3. Tap or click Open. If you are prompted about converting the log to the new event log format, tap or click Yes.

4. Windows displays the Open Saved Log dialog box. Enter a name and description for the saved log.

5. Specify where to save the log. By default, saved logs are listed under Saved Logs. You can create a new node by tapping or clicking New Folder, entering a name for the folder, and then tapping or clicking OK.

6. Tap or click OK to close the Open Saved Log dialog box. This displays the contents of the saved log.

TIP To remove the saved log from Event Viewer, tap or click Delete in the Actions pane or on the Action menu. When prompted to confirm, tap or click Yes. The saved log file still exists in its original location.

Optimizing system performance

M onitoring a server isn't something you should do haphazardly. You need to have a clear plan—a set of goals you hope to achieve. Troubleshooting a performance problem is a key reason for monitoring. For example, users might be having problems connecting to an application running on a server, and you might want to monitor the server to identify the source of the problem.

Another common reason for wanting to monitor a server is to improve server performance. You do this by improving disk I/O, reducing CPU usage, and cutting down the network traffic load on the server. Unfortunately, you often need to make trade-offs when it comes to resource usage. For example, as the number of users accessing a server grows, you might not be able to reduce the network traffic load, but you might be able to improve server performance through load balancing or by distributing key data files on separate drives.

Preparing for monitoring

Before you start monitoring a server, you might want to establish baseline performance metrics for your server. To do this, you measure server performance at various times and under different load conditions. You can then compare the baseline performance with subsequent performance to determine how the server is performing. Performance metrics that are well above the baseline measurements might indicate areas where the server needs to be optimized or reconfigured.

Creating a monitoring plan

After you establish baseline metrics, you should formulate a monitoring plan. A comprehensive monitoring plan includes the following steps:

1. Determine which server events should be monitored to help you accomplish your goal.
2. Set filters to reduce the amount of information collected.
3. Configure performance counters to watch resource usage.
4. Log the event data so that it can be analyzed.
5. Analyze the event data to help find solutions to problems.

These procedures are examined later in this chapter. Although you should usually develop a monitoring plan, sometimes you might not want to go through all these steps to monitor your server. For example, you might want to monitor and analyze activity as it happens rather than log and analyze the data later.

The primary tools you use to monitor your servers include the following:

- **Performance Monitor** Displays resource usage over time via counters that you configure. You can use this information to gauge the performance of the server and determine areas that can be optimized.

- **Reliability Monitor** Tracks changes to the system and compares them to changes in system stability. This gives you a graphical representation of the relationship between changes in the system configuration and changes in system stability.

- **Resource Monitor** Provides detailed information about resource usage on the server. The information provided is similar to that provided by Task Manager (though more extensive).

- **Event logs** Provides information that you can use to troubleshoot system-wide problems, including those from the operating system and configured applications. The primary logs you work with are the system, security, and application event logs, as well as logs for configured server roles.

Using the monitoring consoles

Resource Monitor, Reliability Monitor, and Performance Monitor are the tools of choice for performance tuning. You can access Resource Monitor by pressing Ctrl+Shift+Esc and then tapping or clicking the Open Resource Monitor button on the Performance tab of Task Manager. In Server Manager, you can access Resource Monitor in a stand-alone console by tapping or clicking Tools and then tapping or clicking Resource Monitor.

As shown in Figure 5-1, resource usage statistics are broken down into four categories:

- **CPU usage** The summary details show the current CPU utilization and the maximum CPU frequency (as related to processor idling). Expanding the CPU entry (by tapping or clicking the options button) displays a list of currently running executables by name, process ID, description, status, number of threads used, current CPU utilization, and average CPU utilization.

- **Disk usage** The summary details show the number of kilobytes per second being read from or written to disk, and the highest percentage of usage. Expanding the Disk entry (by tapping or clicking the options button) displays a list of currently running executables that are performing or have performed I/O operations. The list is displayed by name, process ID, file being read or written, average number of bytes being read per second, average number of bytes being written per second, total number of bytes being read and written per second, I/O priority, and the associated disk response time.

- **Network usage** The summary details show the current network band-width utilization in kilobytes and the percentage of total bandwidth utiliza-tion. Expanding the Network entry (by tapping or clicking the options but-ton) displays a list of currently running executables that are transferring or have transferred data on the network. The list is displayed by name, process ID, server or IP address being contacted, average number of bytes being sent per second, average number of bytes received per second, and total bytes sent or received per second.

- **Memory usage** The summary details show the current memory utilization and the number of hard faults occurring per second. Expanding the Memory entry (by tapping or clicking the options button) displays a list of currently running executables by name, process ID, hard faults per second, commit memory in KB, working set memory in KB, shareable memory in KB, and private (nonshareable) memory in KB.

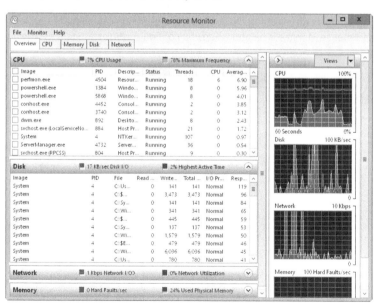

FIGURE 5-1 Review resource usage on the server.

TIP You also can open Resource Monitor by typing **Resource Monitor** in the Everywhere search box and then pressing Enter. As with any locally installed administrative tool, Resource Monitor can only be found in an Everywhere search when you've selected the Show Administrative Tools option. If this option isn't enabled, you can enable it from the Start screen. From the Start screen, press Windows key+C to display the charms and then select Settings. In the Settings panel, select Tiles, and then set Show Administrative Tools to Yes.

Performance Monitor displays statistics graphically for the set of performance parameters you've selected for display. These performance parameters are referred to as *counters*. When you install certain applications on a system, Performance Monitor might be updated with a set of counters for tracking the server's performance. You also can update these counters when you install additional services and add-ons for the application.

In Server Manager, you can access Performance Monitor in a stand-alone console by tapping or clicking Tools and then tapping or clicking Performance Monitor. In Computer Management, you can access the tool as a snap-in in the System Tools node. Expand System Tools\Performance\Monitoring Tools, and then click Performance Monitor.

As Figure 5-2 shows, Performance Monitor creates a graph depicting the counters you're tracking. The update interval for this graph is set to 1 second by default, but it can be configured with a different value. As is apparent when you work with Performance Monitor, the tracking information is most valuable when you record performance information in a log file so that the information can be played back. Also, Performance Monitor is helpful when you configure alerts to send messages when certain events occur.

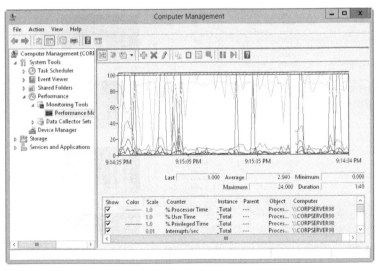

FIGURE 5-2 Review performance measurements for the server.

Windows Server 2012 R2 also includes Reliability Monitor. To access Reliability Monitor, follow these steps:

1. In Control Panel, under System And Security, tap or click Review Your Computer's Status And Resolve Issues.

2. In Action Center, expand the Maintenance panel, and then tap or click View Reliability History.

Alternatively, you can run Reliability Monitor by entering **perfmon /rel** at a command prompt or in the Everywhere search box.

Reliability Monitor tracks changes to the server and compares them to changes in system stability, which provides a graphical representation of the relationship between changes in the system configuration and changes in system stability. Recording software installation, software removal, application failures, hardware failures, Windows failures, and key events regarding the configuration of the server provides a timeline of changes in both the server and its reliability, which you can use to pinpoint changes that are causing problems with stability. For example, if you notice a sudden drop in stability, you can tap or click a data point and then expand the related data set to find the specific event that caused the drop in stability.

Although reliability monitoring is enabled by default for Windows clients, it might be disabled for Windows servers. Opening Reliability Monitor on a server where reliability monitoring is disabled displays an information panel telling you to click here to view how to turn on or reconfigure RACTask. The RACTask is a scheduled task that runs in the background to collect reliability data.

If the RACTask is disabled, you can enable and configure the task by completing the following steps:

1. In Server Manager, on the Tools menu, click Task Scheduler. In Task Scheduler's left pane, expand Task Scheduler Library\Microsoft\Windows, and then click the RAC node.

2. By default, the RACTask runs whenever the system is started, daily at approximately 5:00 P.M. (a random delay of up to 15 minutes is added each scheduled runtime) and when Customer Experience Improvement Program events are logged. Because performing reliability analysis and collection daily at around 5:00 P.M might not be optimal, select RacTask in the main pane and then click Properties on the Actions menu.

3. In the Properties dialog box, on the Triggers tab, select the One Time trigger, and then click Edit. Use the options provided to specify an optimal time to run this task. Cick OK twice to close the open dialog boxes.

4. With RacTask still selected in Task Scheduler, on the Action menu, click Enable. To run the task once now, on the Action menu, click Run.

Choosing counters to monitor

Performance Monitor displays information only for counters you're tracking. Several thousand counters are available, and you'll find counters related to just about every server role you've installed. The easiest way to learn about these counters is to read the explanations available in the Add Counters dialog box. Start Performance Monitor, tap or click Add on the toolbar, and then expand an object in the Available Counters list. Select the Show Description check box, and then scroll through the list of counters for this object.

When Performance Monitor is monitoring a particular object, it can track all instances of all counters for that object. *Instances* are multiple occurrences of a particular counter. For example, when you track counters for the Processor object on a multiprocessor system, you have a choice of tracking all processor instances or specific processor instances. If you think a particular processor is going bad or experiencing other problems, you could monitor just that processor instance.

To select which counters you want to monitor, follow these steps:

1. Performance Monitor has several views and view types. Be sure that current activity is displayed by tapping or clicking View Current Activity on the toolbar or pressing Ctrl+T. You can switch between the view types (Line, Histogram Bar, and Report) by tapping or clicking Change Graph Type or pressing Ctrl+G.

2. To add counters, tap or click Add on the toolbar, or press Ctrl+I. This displays the Add Counters dialog box, shown in Figure 5-3.

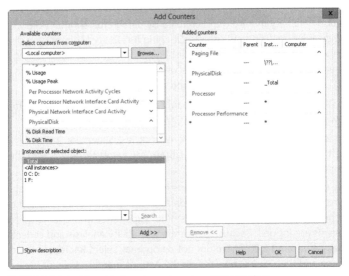

FIGURE 5-3 Select the objects and counters you want to monitor.

3. In the Select Counters From Computer list, enter the Universal Naming Convention (UNC) name of the server you want to work with, such as \\CorpServer84, or choose <Local Computer> to work with the local computer.

NOTE You need to be at least a member of the Performance Monitor Users group in the domain or on the local computer to perform remote monitoring. When you use performance logging, you need to be at least a member of the Performance Log Users group in the domain or on the local computer to work with performance logs on remote computers.

4. In the Available Counters panel, performance objects are listed alphabetically. If you select an object entry by tapping or clicking it, all related counters are selected. Expanding an object entry displays all the related counters, and you can select individual counters by tapping or clicking them. For example, you could expand the entry for the Active Server Pages object and then select the Requests Failed Total, Requests Not Found, Requests Queued, and Requests Total counters.

5. When you select an object or any of its counters, the related instances are displayed. Choose All Instances to select all counter instances for monitoring, or select one or more counter instances to monitor. For example, you could select instances of Anonymous Users/Sec for individual websites or for all websites.

6. When you've selected an object or a group of counters for an object in addition to the object instances, tap or click Add to add the counters to the graph.

7. Repeat steps 4–6 to add other performance parameters.

8. Tap or click OK when you are finished.

TIP Don't try to chart too many counters or counter instances at once. You'll make the display too difficult to read, and you'll use system resources—namely, CPU time and memory—that might affect server responsiveness.

Performance logging

Data collector sets allow you to specify sets of performance objects and counters you want to track. After you create a data collector set, you can easily start or stop monitoring the performance objects and counters included in the set. In a way, this makes data collector sets similar to the performance logs used in early releases of Windows. However, data collector sets are much more sophisticated. You can use a single data set to generate multiple performance counters and trace logs. You can also do the following:

- Assign access controls to manage who can access collected data.
- Create multiple run schedules and stop conditions for monitoring.
- Use data managers to control the size of collected data and reporting.
- Generate reports based on collected data.

In Performance Monitor, you can review currently configured data collector sets and reports under the Data Collector Sets and Reports nodes, respectively. As shown in Figure 5-4, you'll find data sets and reports that are user-defined and system-defined. User-defined data sets are created by users for general monitoring and performance tuning. System-defined data sets are created by the operating system to aid in automated diagnostics.

FIGURE 5-4 Access data collector sets and reports.

Creating and managing data collector sets

To view the currently configured data collector sets, click the Performance Monitor option in the Administrative Tools program group, and then expand the Data Collector Sets node. You can work with data collectors in a variety of ways:

■ You can view currently defined user or system data collector sets by selecting either User Defined or System, as appropriate. When you select a data collector set in the left pane, related data collectors are displayed in the main pane listed by name and type. The Trace type is for data collectors that record performance data whenever related events occur. The Performance Counter type is for data collectors that record data on selected counters when a predetermined interval has elapsed. The Configuration type is for data collectors that record changes to particular registry paths.

- You can view running event traces by selecting Event Trace Sessions. You can then stop a data collector that is running a trace by pressing and holding or right-clicking it and then selecting Stop.

- You can view the enabled or disabled status of event traces configured to run automatically when you start the computer by selecting Startup Event Trace Sessions. You can start a trace by pressing and holding or right-clicking a startup data collector and then selecting Start As Event Trace Session. You can delete a startup data collector by pressing and holding or right-clicking it and then tapping or clicking Delete.

- You can save a data collector as a template that can be used as the basis of other data collectors by pressing and holding or right-clicking the data collector and then selecting Save Template. In the Save As dialog box, select a directory, enter a name for the template, and then tap or click Save. The data collector template is saved as an XML file that can be copied to other systems.

- You can delete a user-defined data collector by pressing and holding or right-clicking it and then selecting Delete. If a data collector is running, you need to stop collecting data first and then delete the collector. Deleting a collector also deletes the related reports.

Collecting performance counter data

Data collectors can be used to record performance data on the selected counters at a specific sampling interval. For example, you could sample performance data for the CPU every 15 minutes.

To collect performance counter data, follow these steps:

1. In Performance Monitor, under the Data Collector Sets node, press and hold or right-click the User Defined node in the left pane, point to New, and then click Data Collector Set.

2. In the Create New Data Collector Set Wizard, enter a name for the data collector, such as **System Performance Monitor** or **Processor Status Monitor**. Note that if you enter an invalid name, such as one with a nonalphanumeric character, you won't be able to continue.

3. Select the Create Manually option, and then tap or click Next.

4. On the What Type Of Data Do You Want To Include page, the Create Data Logs option is selected by default. Select the Performance Counter check box, and then tap or click Next.

5. On the Which Performance Counters Would You Like To Log page, tap or click Add. This displays the Add Counters dialog box, which you can use as previously discussed to select the performance counters to track. When you are finished selecting counters, tap or click OK.

6. On the Which Performance Counters Would You Like To Log page, enter a sampling interval and select a time unit in seconds, minutes, hours, days, or weeks. The sampling interval specifies when new data is collected. For example, if you sample every 15 minutes, the data log is updated every 15 minutes. Tap or click Next when you are ready to continue.

7. On the Where Would You Like The Data To Be Saved page, type the root path to use for logging collected data. Alternatively, tap or click Browse, and then use the Browse For Folder dialog box to select the logging directory. Tap or click Next when you are ready to continue.

BEST PRACTICES The default location for logging is %SystemDrive%\PerfLogs \Admin. Log files can grow in size quickly. If you plan to log data for an extended period, be sure to place the log file on a drive with lots of free space. Remember, the more frequently you update the log file, the greater the drive space and CPU resource usage on the system.

8. On the Create Data Collector Set page, the Run As box lists <Default> to indicate that the log will run under the privileges and permissions of the default system account. To run the log with the privileges and permissions of another user, tap or click Change. Enter the user name and password for the account, and then tap or click OK. User names can be entered in domain \username format, such as cpandl\williams for the Williams account in the Cpandl domain.

9. Click the Open Properties For This Data Collector Set option, and then tap or click Finish. This saves the data collector set, closes the wizard, and then opens the related Properties dialog box.

10. By default, logging is configured to start manually. To configure a logging schedule, tap or click the Schedule tab, and then tap or click Add. You can now set the Active Range, Start Time, and run days for data collection.

11. By default, logging stops only if you set an expiration date as part of the logging schedule. Using the options on the Stop Condition tab, you can configure the log file to stop automatically after a specified period of time, such as seven days, or when the log file is full (if you set a maximum size limit).

12. Tap or click OK when you've finished setting the logging schedule and stop conditions. You can manage the data collector as explained previously.

NOTE You can configure Windows to run a scheduled task when data collection stops. You configure tasks to run on the Tasks tab in the Properties dialog box.

Collecting performance trace data

You can use data collectors to record performance trace data whenever events related to their source providers occur. A source provider is an application or operating system service that has traceable events.

To collect performance trace data, follow these steps:

1. In Performance Monitor, under the Data Collector Sets node, press and hold or right-click the User Defined node in the left pane, point to New, and then click Data Collector Set.

2. In the Create New Data Collector Set Wizard, type a name for the data collector, such as **Logon Trace** or **Disk IO Trace**. Note that if you type an invalid name, such as one with a nonalphanumeric character, you won't be able to continue.

3. Select the Create Manually option, and then tap or click Next.

4. On the What Type Of Data Do You Want To Include page, the Create Data Logs option is selected by default. Select the Event Trace Data check box, and then tap or click Next.

5. On the Which Event Trace Providers Would You Like To Enable page, tap or click Add. Select an event trace provider to track, and then tap or click OK. By selecting individual properties in the Properties list and tapping or clicking Edit, you can track particular property values rather than all values for the provider. Repeat this process to select other event trace providers to track. Tap or click Next when you are ready to continue.

6. Complete steps 7–12 from the procedure in the "Collecting performance counter data" section earlier in this chapter.

Collecting configuration data

You can use data collectors to record changes in registry configuration. To collect configuration data, follow these steps:

1. In Performance Monitor, under the Data Collector Sets node, press and hold or right-click the User Defined node in the left pane, point to New, and then click Data Collector Set.

2. In the Create New Data Collector Set Wizard, enter a name for the data collector, such as **AD Registry** or **Registry Adapter Info**.

3. Select the Create Manually option, and then tap or click Next.

4. On the What Type Of Data Do You Want To Include page, the Create Data Logs option is selected by default. Select the System Configuration Information check box, and then tap or click Next.

5. On the Which Registry Keys Would You Like To Record page, tap or click Add. Type the registry path to track. Repeat this process to add other registry paths to track. Tap or click Next when you are ready to continue.

6. Complete steps 7–12 from the procedure in the "Collecting performance counter data" section earlier in this chapter.

Viewing data collector reports

When you troubleshoot problems, you'll often want to log performance data over an extended period of time and then review the data to analyze the results. For each data collector that has been or is currently active, you'll find related data collector reports. As with data collector sets themselves, data collector reports are organized into two general categories: user-defined and system.

You can view data collector reports in Performance Monitor. Expand the Reports node, and then expand the individual report node for the data collector you want to analyze. Under the data collector's report node, you'll find individual reports for each logging session. A logging session begins when logging starts and ends when logging is stopped.

The most recent log is the one with the highest log number. If a data collector is actively logging, you won't be able to view the most recent log. You can stop collecting data by pressing and holding or right-clicking a data collector set and the clicking Stop. For performance counters, collected data is shown by default · in a graph view from the start of data collection to the end of data collection, as shown in Figure 5-5.

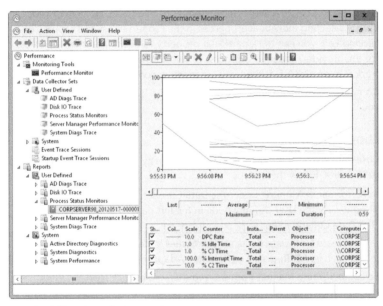

FIGURE 5-5 View data collector reports.

You can modify the report details by using the following process:

1. In the monitor pane, press Ctrl+Q or tap or click the Properties button on the toolbar. This displays the Performance Monitor Properties dialog box.

2. Tap or click the Source tab.

3. Specify data sources to analyze. Under Data Source, tap or click Log Files and then tap or click Add to open the Select Log File dialog box. You can now select additional log files to analyze.

4. Specify the time window you want to analyze. Tap or click Time Range, and then drag the Total Range bar to specify the appropriate starting and ending

times. Drag the left edge to the right to move up the start time. Drag the right edge to the left to make the end time later.

5. Tap or click the Data tab. You can now select counters to view. Select a counter, and then tap or click Remove to remove it from the graph view. Tap or click Add to display the Add Counter dialog box, which you can use to select the counters you want to analyze.

   NOTE Only counters you selected for logging are available. If a counter you want to work with isn't displayed, you need to modify the data collector properties, restart the logging process, and then check the logs at a later date.

6. Tap or click OK. In the monitor pane, tap or click the Change Graph Type button to select the type of graph.

Configuring performance counter alerts

You can configure alerts to notify you when certain events occur or when certain performance thresholds are reached. You can send these alerts as network messages and as events that are logged in the application event log. You can also configure alerts to start applications and performance logs.

To configure an alert, follow these steps:

1. In Performance Monitor, under the Data Collector Sets node, press and hold or right-click the User Defined node in the left pane, point to New, and then click Data Collector Set.

2. In the Create New Data Collector Set Wizard, enter a name for the data collector, such as **Processor Alert** or **Disk IO Alert**.

3. Click the Create Manually option, and then tap or click Next.

4. On the What Type Of Data Do You Want To Include page, click the Performance Counter Alert option, and then tap or click Next.

5. On the Which Performance Counters Would You Like To Monitor page, tap or click Add to display the Add Counters dialog box. This dialog box is identical to the Add Counters dialog box discussed previously. Use the dialog box to add counters that trigger the alert. Tap or click OK when you are finished.

6. In the Performance Counters panel, select the first counter, and then use the Alert When box to set the occasion when an alert for this counter is triggered. Alerts can be triggered when the counter is above or below a specific value. Select Above or Below, and then set the trigger value. The unit of measurement is whatever makes sense for the currently selected counter or counters. For example, to generate an alert if processor time is over 95 percent, select Above, and then enter **95**. Repeat this process to configure other counters you've selected.

7. Complete steps 7–12 from the procedure in the "Collecting performance counter data" section earlier in this chapter.

Tuning system performance

Now that you know how to monitor your system, let's look at how you can tune the operating system and hardware performance. Let's examine the following areas:

- Memory usage and caching
- Processor utilization
- Disk I/O
- Network bandwidth and connectivity

Monitoring and tuning memory usage

Memory is often the source of performance problems, and you should always rule out memory problems before examining other areas of the system. Systems use both physical and virtual memory. To rule out memory problems with a system, you should configure application performance, memory usage, and data throughput settings, and then monitor the server's memory usage to check for problems.

Application performance and memory usage settings determine how system resources are allocated. In most cases, you want to give the operating system and background applications the lion's share of resources. This is especially true for Active Directory, file, print, and network and communications servers. On the other hand, for application, database, and streaming media servers, you should give the programs a server is running the most resources, as discussed in the "Setting application performance" section in Chapter 3, "Managing Windows servers."

Using the monitoring techniques discussed previously in this chapter, you can determine how the system is using memory and check for problems. Table 5-1 provides an overview of counters you'll want to track to uncover memory, caching, and virtual memory (paging) bottlenecks. The table is organized by issue category.

TABLE 5-1 Uncovering Memory-Related Bottlenecks

ISSUE	COUNTERS TO TRACK	DETAILS
Physical and virtual memory usage	Memory\Available Kbytes Memory\Committed Bytes	Memory\Available Kbytes is the amount of physical memory available to processes running on the server. Memory\Committed Bytes is the amount of committed virtual memory. If the server has very little available memory, you might need to add memory to the system. In general, you want the available memory to be no less than 5 percent of the total physical memory on the server. If the server has a high ratio of committed bytes to total physical memory on the system, you might also need to add memory. In general, you want the committed bytes value to be no more than 75 percent of the total physical memory.

ISSUE	COUNTERS TO TRACK	DETAILS
Memory page faults	Memory\Page Faults /sec Memory\Pages Input/sec Memory\Page Reads/sec	A page fault occurs when a process requests a page in memory and the system can't find it at the requested location. If the requested page is elsewhere in memory, the fault is called a soft page fault. If the requested page must be retrieved from disk, the fault is called a hard page fault. Most processors can handle large numbers of soft faults. Hard faults, however, can cause significant delays. Page Faults /sec is the overall rate at which the processor handles all types of page faults. Pages Input /sec is the total number of pages read from disk to resolve hard page faults. Page Reads /sec is the total disk reads needed to resolve hard page faults. Pages Input/sec will be greater than or equal to Page Reads/sec and can give you a good idea of your hard page fault rate. A high number of hard page faults could indicate that you need to increase the amount of memory or reduce the cache size on the server.
Memory paging	Memory\Pool Paged Bytes Memory\Pool Nonpaged Bytes	These counters track the number of bytes in the paged and nonpaged pool. The paged pool is an area of system memory for objects that can be written to disk when they aren't used. The nonpaged pool is an area of system memory for objects that can't be written to disk. If the size of the paged pool is large relative to the total amount of physical memory on the system, you might need to add memory to the system. If the size of the nonpaged pool is large relative to the total amount of virtual memory allocated to the server, you might want to increase the virtual memory size.

IMPORTANT Increasing virtual memory isn't something you should do without careful planning. For detailed guidance on tuning virtual memory, see Chapter 10, "Performance Monitoring and Tuning," in *Windows Server 2012 R2 Inside Out: Configuration, Storage, and Essentials* by William R. Stanek (Microsoft Press, 2014).

Monitoring and tuning processor usage

The CPU does the actual processing of information on your server. As you examine a server's performance, you should focus on the CPU after you eliminate memory bottlenecks. If the server's processors are the performance bottleneck, adding memory, drives, or network connections won't overcome the problem. Instead, you might need to upgrade the processors to faster clock speeds or add processors to increase the server's upper capacity. You could also move processor-intensive applications, such as Microsoft SQL Server, to another server.

Before you make a decision to upgrade CPUs or add CPUs, you should rule out problems with memory and caching. If signs still point to a processor problem, you should monitor the performance counters listed in Table 5-2. Be sure to monitor these counters for each CPU installed on the server.

TABLE 5-2 Uncovering Processor-Related Bottlenecks

ISSUE	COUNTERS TO TRACK	DETAILS
Thread queuing	System\Processor Queue Length	This counter displays the number of threads waiting to be executed. These threads are queued in an area shared by all processors on the system. If this counter has a sustained value of more than 10 threads per processor, you need to upgrade or add processors.
CPU usage	Processor\ % Processor Time	This counter displays the percentage of time the selected CPU is executing a nonidle thread. You should track this counter separately for all processor instances on the server. If the % Processor Time values are high while the network interface and disk I/O throughput rates are relatively low, you need to upgrade or add processors.

Monitoring and tuning disk I/O

With today's high-speed disks, the disk throughput rate is rarely the cause of a bottleneck. That said, accessing memory is much faster than accessing disks. So, if the server has to do a lot of disk reads and writes, a server's overall performance can be degraded. To reduce the amount of disk I/O, you want the server to manage memory efficiently and page to disk only when necessary. You monitor and tune memory usage as discussed in the "Monitoring and tuning memory usage" section earlier in this chapter.

In addition to memory tuning, you can monitor some counters to gauge disk I/O activity. Specifically, you should monitor the counters listed in Table 5-3.

TABLE 5-3 Uncovering Drive-Related Bottlenecks

ISSUE	COUNTERS TO TRACK	DETAILS
Overall drive performance	PhysicalDisk\% Disk Time in conjunction with Processorz \% Processor Time and Network Interface Connection \Bytes Total/sec	If the % Disk Time value is high and the processor and network connection values aren't high, the system's hard disk drives might be creating a bottleneck. Be sure to monitor % Disk Time for all hard disk drives on the server.
Disk I/O	PhysicalDisk\Disk Writes/sec PhysicalDisk\Disk Reads/sec PhysicalDisk\Avg. Disk Write Queue Length PhysicalDisk\Avg. Disk Read Queue Length PhysicalDisk\Current Disk Queue Length	The number of writes and reads per second tell you how much disk I/O activity there is. The write and read queue lengths tell you how many write or read requests are waiting to be processed. In general, you want very few waiting requests. Keep in mind that the request delays are proportional to the length of the queues minus the number of drives in a redundant array of independent disks (RAID) set.

Monitoring and tuning network bandwidth and connectivity

No other factor matters more to the way a user perceives your server's performance than the network that connects your server to the user's computer. The delay, or latency, between when a request is made and the time it's received can make all the difference. With a high degree of latency, it doesn't matter if you have the fastest server on the planet: the user experiences a delay and perceives that your servers are slow.

Generally speaking, the latency experienced by the user is beyond your control. It's a function of the type of connection the user has and the route the request takes to your server. The total capacity of your server to handle requests and the amount of bandwidth available to your servers are factors under your control, however. Network bandwidth availability is a function of your organization's network infrastructure. Network capacity is a function of the network cards and interfaces configured on the servers.

The capacity of your network card can be a limiting factor in some instances. Although 10-Gbps networking is increasingly being used, most servers use 100-Mbps or 1-Gbps network cards, which can be configured in many ways. Someone might have configured a 1-Gbps card for 100 Mbps, or the card might be configured for half duplex instead of full duplex. If you suspect a capacity problem with a network card, you should always check the configuration.

As modern servers often ship with multiple network cards, be sure to check all enabled network adapters. If a server has multiple adapters, you might want to enable and configure NIC teaming to ensure the available bandwidth is used optimally. When NIC teaming is being used, you'll also want to ensure the configuration is optimized for the way the server is currently being used. In Server Manager, you can configure NIC teaming as a Local Server option, which means you must log on locally to the server you want to configure or access the server through a Remote Desktop Connection.

To determine the throughput and current activity on a server's network cards, you can check the following counters:

- Network Adapter\Bytes Received/sec
- Network Adapter\Bytes Sent/sec
- Network Adapter\Bytes Total/sec
- Network Adapter\Current Bandwidth

If the total bytes-per-second value is more than 50 percent of the total capacity under average load conditions, your server might have problems under peak load conditions. You might want to ensure that operations that take a lot of network bandwidth, such as network backups, are performed on a separate interface card. Keep in mind that you should compare these values in conjunction with PhysicalDisk\% Disk Time and Processor\% Processor Time. If the disk time and processor time values are low but the network values are very high, you might have a capacity problem. Solve the problem by optimizing the network card settings or by adding a network card. Remember, planning is everything—it isn't always as simple as inserting a card and plugging it into the network.

CHAPTER 6

Automating administrative tasks, policies, and procedures

- Understanding group policies **146**
- Navigating Group Policy changes **149**
- Managing local group policies **151**
- Managing site, domain, and organizational unit policies **155**
- Maintaining and troubleshooting Group Policy **167**

Performing routine tasks day after day, running around policing systems, and walking users through the basics aren't efficient uses of your time. You'd be much more effective if you could automate these chores and focus on issues that are more important. Support services are all about increasing productivity and allowing you to focus less on mundane matters and more on what's important.

Windows Server 2012 R2 includes many roles, role services, and features that help you support server installations. You can easily install and use some of these components. If you need an administrative tool to manage a role or feature on a remote computer, you can select the tool to install as part of the Remote Server Administration Tools (RSAT) feature. If a server has a wireless adapter, you can install the Wireless LAN Service feature to enable wireless connections. Beyond these and other basic support components, you can use many other support features, including the following:

- **Automatic Updates** Ensures that the operating system is up to date and has the most recent security updates. If you update a server by using Microsoft Update instead of the standard Windows Updates, you can get updates for additional products. By default, Automatic Updates is installed but not enabled on servers running Windows Server 2012 R2. You can configure Automatic Updates by using the Windows Update utility in Control Panel. In Control Panel\System And Security, tap or click Turn Automatic Updating On Or Off.

- **BitLocker Drive Encryption**   Provides an extra layer of security for a server's hard disks. This protects the disks from attackers who have physical access to the server. BitLocker Drive Encryption can be used on servers with or without a Trusted Platform Module (TPM). When you add this feature to a server by using the Add Roles And Features Wizard, you can manage the feature by using the BitLocker Drive Encryption utility in Control Panel. In Control Panel\System And Security, tap or click BitLocker Drive Encryption. Windows Server 2008 R2 and later (such as Windows 7 and later) include BitLocker To Go, which allows you to encrypt USB flash drives. If your server doesn't have BitLocker, run the BitLocker To Go Reader, which is stored in an unencrypted area of the encrypted USB flash drive.

- **Remote Assistance**   Provides an assistance feature that allows an administrator to send a remote assistance invitation to a more senior administrator. The senior administrator can then accept the invitation to view the user's desktop and temporarily take control of the computer to resolve a problem. When you add this feature to a server by using the Add Roles And Features Wizard, you can manage the feature by using options on the Remote tab of the System Properties dialog box. In Control Panel\System And Security, under System, tap or click Allow Remote Access to view the related options.

- **Remote Desktop**   Provides a remote connectivity feature that allows you to connect to and manage a server from another computer. By default, Remote Desktop is installed but not enabled on servers running Windows Server 2012 R2. You can manage the Remote Desktop configuration with the options on the Remote tab of the System Properties dialog box. In Control Panel\System And Security, under System, tap or click Allow Remote Access to view the related options. You can establish remote connections by using the Remote Desktop Connection utility.

- **Task Scheduler**   Allows you to schedule execution of one-time and recurring tasks, such as tasks for performing routine maintenance. Windows Server 2012 R2 makes extensive use of the scheduled task facilities. You can view and work with scheduled tasks in Computer Management. Expand the System Tools, Task Scheduler, and Task Scheduler Library nodes to view configured scheduled tasks.

- **Desktop Experience**   This subfeature of User Interfaces And Infrastructure installs Windows desktop functionality on the server. You can use this feature when you use Windows Server 2012 R2 as your desktop operating system. When you add this feature by using the Add Roles And Features Wizard, the server's desktop functionality is enhanced, and the following programs are also installed: Windows Media Player, Desktop Themes, Video for Windows (AVI support), Disk Cleanup, Sound Recorder, Character Map, and Snipping Tool.

- **Windows Firewall** Helps protect a computer from attack by unauthorized users. Windows Server includes a basic firewall called Windows Firewall and an advanced firewall called Windows Firewall With Advanced Security. By default, the firewalls are not enabled on server installations. To access the basic firewall, tap or click Windows Firewall in Control Panel. To access the advanced firewall, on the Tools menu in Server Manager, click Windows Firewall With Advanced Security.

- **Windows Time** Synchronizes the system time with world time to ensure that the system time is accurate. You can configure computers to synchronize with a specific time server. The way Windows Time works depends on whether a computer is a member of a domain or a workgroup. In a domain, domain controllers are used for time synchronization, and you can manage this feature through Group Policy. In a workgroup, Internet time servers are used for time synchronization, and you can manage this feature through the Date And Time utility.

You can configure and manage these support components in the same way on computers running Windows 8.1 and Windows Server 2012 R2. You'll find extensive coverage of these support components in *Windows 8.1 Pocket Consultant: Essentials & Configuration* by William R. Stanek (Microsoft Press, 2013).

Many other components provide support services. However, you need these additional support services only in specific scenarios. You can use IP Address Management (IPAM) servers when you want to manage your IP address space and track IP address usage trends. You can use Remote Desktop Services when you want to allow users to run applications on a remote server. You can use Windows Deployment Services when you want to enable automated deployment of Windows-based operating systems. The one always-on support service you must master, to succeed with Windows Server 2012 R2, is Group Policy.

REAL WORLD The Start screen charms bar has a search option, which can have Everywhere, Settings, or Files as a focus. When you press the Windows key and then type, the text is entered into the search box. Because the default focus is for an Everywhere search, you can quickly search for installed programs, files, and settings.

Throughout this text, when I refer to entering something in the Everywhere search box, I'm referring to entering search text with Everywhere as a focus. As you enter text, matching results are displayed. When you press Enter, Windows runs the currently selected result. You can also use the Everywhere search to pass in commands with parameters and options. Simply type the command along with its parameters and options as you would at a command prompt.

Want to run Windows PowerShell commands from the Everywhere search box? Simply type **powershell**, and then enter your command.

Understanding group policies

Group policies simplify administration by giving administrators centralized control over privileges, permissions, and capabilities of both users and computers. Through group policies, you can do the following:

- Control access to Windows components, system resources, network resources, Control Panel utilities, the desktop, and the Start screen.
- Create centrally managed directories for special folders, such as a user's Documents folder.
- Define user and computer scripts to run at specified times.
- Configure policies for account lockout and passwords, auditing, user rights assignment, and security. Many of these topics are covered in the "User account setup and organization" section in Chapter 9, "Creating user and group accounts."

The sections that follow explain how you can work with and apply group policies.

Group Policy essentials

You can think of a *policy* as a set of rules that helps you manage users and computers. You can apply group policies to multiple domains, individual domains, subgroups within a domain, or individual systems. Policies that apply to individual systems are referred to as *local group policies* and are stored on the local system only. Other group policies are linked as objects in the Active Directory data store.

To understand group policies, you need to know a bit about the structure of Active Directory. In Active Directory, sites represent the physical structure of your network. A *site* is a group of TCP/IP subnets, with each subnet representing a physical network segment. A domain is a logical grouping of objects for centralized management, and subgroups within a domain are called *organizational units*. Your network might have sites called NewYorkMain, CaliforniaMain, and WashingtonMain. Within the WashingtonMain site, you could have domains called SeattleEast, SeattleWest, SeattleNorth, and SeattleSouth. Within the SeattleEast domain, you could have organizational units called Information Services (IS), Engineering, and Sales.

Group policies apply only to systems running Windows-based operating systems. Group Policy settings are stored in a Group Policy object (GPO). You can think of a GPO as a container for the policies you apply and their settings. You can apply multiple GPOs to a single site, domain, or organizational unit. Because Group Policy is described by using objects, many object-oriented concepts apply. If you know a bit about object-oriented programming, you might expect the concepts of parent-child relationships and inheritance to apply to GPOs—and you'd be right.

A *container* is a top-level object that contains other objects. Through inheritance, a policy applied to a parent container is inherited by a child container. Essentially, this means that a policy setting applied to a parent object is passed down to a child object. For example, if you apply a policy setting in a domain, the setting is inherited by organizational units within the domain. In this case, the GPO for the domain is the parent object, and the GPOs for the organizational units are the child objects.

The order of inheritance is site, domain, organizational unit. This means that the Group Policy settings for a site are passed down to the domains within that site, and the settings for a domain are passed down to the organizational units within that domain.

As you might expect, you can override inheritance. To do this, you specifically assign a policy setting for a child container that is different from the policy setting for the parent. As long as overriding the policy is allowed (that is, overriding isn't blocked), the child container's policy setting will be applied appropriately. To learn more about overriding and blocking GPOs, see the "Blocking, overriding, and disabling policies" section later in this chapter.

In what order are multiple policies applied?

When multiple policies are in place, policies are applied in the following order:

1. Local group policies
2. Site group policies
3. Domain group policies
4. Organizational unit group policies
5. Child organizational unit group policies

If policy settings conflict, the policy settings applied later have precedence and overwrite previously set policy settings. For example, organizational unit policies have precedence over domain group policies. As you might expect, there are exceptions to the precedence rule. These exceptions are discussed in the "Blocking, overriding, and disabling policies" section later in this chapter.

When are group policies applied?

As you'll discover when you start working with group policies, policy settings are divided into two broad categories:

- Those that apply to computers
- Those that apply to users

Computer policies are normally applied during system startup, and user policies are normally applied during logon. The exact sequence of events is often important in troubleshooting system behavior. The events that take place during startup and logon are as follows:

1. The network starts, and then Windows Server applies computer policies. By default, computer policies are applied one at a time in the previously specified order. No user interface is displayed while computer policies are being processed.

2. Windows Server runs startup scripts. By default, startup scripts are executed one at a time, with each completing or timing out before the next one starts. Script execution isn't displayed to the user unless specified.

3. A user logs on. After the user is validated, Windows Server loads the user profile.

4. Windows Server applies user policies. By default, user policies are applied one at a time in the previously specified order. The user interface is displayed while user policies are being processed.

5. Windows Server runs logon scripts. Logon scripts for Group Policy are executed simultaneously by default. Script execution isn't displayed to the user unless specified. Scripts in the Netlogon share run last in a normal command shell window.

6. Windows Server displays the start shell interface configured in Group Policy.

7. By default, Group Policy is refreshed when a user logs off or a computer is restarted automatically within a 90 to 120 minute period. You can change this behavior by setting a Group Policy refresh interval, as discussed in the "Refreshing Group Policy" section later in this chapter. To do this, open a command prompt and enter **gpupdate**.

REAL WORLD   Some user settings, such as Folder Redirection, can't be updated when a user is logged on. The user must log off and then log back on for these settings to be applied. You can enter **gpupdate /logoff** at a command prompt or in the Everywhere search box to log off the user automatically after the refresh. Similarly, some computer settings can be updated only at startup. The computer must be re-started for these settings to be applied. You can enter **gpupdate /boot** at a command prompt or in the Everywhere search box to restart the computer after the refresh.

Group Policy requirements and version compatibility

Group policies apply only to systems running professional and server versions of Windows. As you might expect, each new version of the Windows operating system has brought with it changes to Group Policy. Sometimes these changes have made earlier policies obsolete on newer versions of Windows. In this case, the policy works only on specific versions of Windows, such as only on Windows Vista and Windows Server 2008.

Generally speaking, most policies are forward-compatible. This means that in most cases, policies introduced in a previous release of Windows can be used in the current release of Windows. It also means that policies for Windows 8.1 and Windows Server 2012 R2 usually aren't applicable to earlier releases of Windows. If a policy isn't applicable to a particular version of the Windows operating system, you can't enforce the policy on computers running those versions of Windows.

How will you know if a policy is supported on a particular version of Windows? Easy. The Properties dialog box for each policy setting has a Supported On box. This text-only field lists the policy's compatibility with various versions of Windows. You don't have to open it if you select a policy in any of the Group Policy editors and also have selected the Extended tab (rather than the Standard tab). A Requirements entry is displayed that lists compatibility.

You can also install new policies when you add a service pack, install Windows applications, or add Windows components. This means a wide range of compatibility entries are available.

Navigating Group Policy changes

Microsoft provides the Group Policy Management Console (GPMC) as the central-ized management console called for Group Policy. The GPMC is a feature you can add to any installation of Windows Server 2008 or later by using the Add Roles And Features Wizard. The GPMC is available on Windows desktops when you install the Remote Server Administration Tools (RSAT). After you add the GPMC to a computer, it is available on the Tools menu in Server Manager.

When you want to edit a GPO in the GPMC, the GPMC opens the Group Policy Management Editor, which you use to manage the policy settings. If Microsoft had stopped with these two tools, we'd have a wonderful and easy-to-use policy-management environment. Unfortunately, several other, nearly identical editors also exist:

- **Group Policy Starter GPO Editor**   An editor you can use to create and manage starter policy objects. As the name implies, starter GPOs are meant to provide a starting point for policy objects you'll use throughout your organization. When you create a policy object, you can specify a starter GPO as the source or basis of the object.

- **Local Group Policy Object Editor**   An editor you can use to create and manage policy objects for the local computer. As the name implies, local GPOs are meant to provide policy settings for a specific computer as opposed to settings for a site, domain, or organizational unit.

If you've worked with earlier versions of Windows, you might also be familiar with the Group Policy Object Editor (GPOE). With earlier versions of Windows, the GPOE is the primary editing tool for policy objects. The Group Policy Object Editor, Group Policy Management Editor, Group Policy Starter GPO Editor, and Local Group Policy Object Editor are essentially identical except for the set of policy objects you have access to. For this reason, and because you use these tools to manage individ-ual policy objects in the same way, I won't differentiate between them unless necessary. As a matter of preference, I refer to these tools collectively as *policy editors*. Sometimes, I might use the acronym GPOE to refer to policy editors in general because it is more easily distinguished from the management console, the GPMC.

You can manage policy settings for Windows Vista and later only from comput-ers running Windows Vista or later. The reason for this is that the GPOE and the GPMC for Windows Vista and later releases were updated to work with the XML-based administrative templates format called ADMX.

NOTE   You cannot use early versions of the policy editors with ADMX. You can edit GPOs by using ADMX files only on a computer running Windows Vista or later.

Microsoft had many reasons for going to the ADMX format. The key reasons were to allow greater flexibility and extensibility. Because ADMX files are created by using XML, the files are strictly structured and can be more easily and rapidly parsed during initialization. This can help to improve performance when the operating system processes Group Policy during the startup, logon, logoff, and shutdown phases, in addition to during policy refreshes. Further, the strict structure of ADMX files makes it possible for Microsoft to continue in its internationalization efforts.

ADMX files are divided into language-neutral files ending with the .admx file name extension and language-specific files ending with the .adml extension. The language-neutral files ensure that a GPO has identical core policies. The language-specific files allow policies to be viewed and edited in multiple languages. Because the language-neutral files store a policy's core settings, policies can be edited in any language for which a computer is configured, thus allowing one user to view and edit policies in English and another to view and edit policies in Spanish, for example. The mechanism that determines the language used is the language pack installed on the computer.

Language-neutral ADMX files are installed on computers running Windows Vista or later in the %SystemRoot%\PolicyDefinitions folder. Language-specific ADMX files are installed on computers running Windows 7 and later, and also on computers running Windows Server 2008 R2 and later in the %SystemRoot% \PolicyDefinitions*LanguageCulture* folder. Each subfolder is named by using the corresponding International Organization for Standardization (ISO) language/culture name, such as EN-US for US English.

When you start a policy editor, it automatically reads ADMX files from the policy definitions folders. Because of this, you can copy ADMX files you want to use to an appropriate policy definitions folder to make them available when you are editing GPOs. If the policy editor is running when you copy the file or files, you must restart the policy editor to force it to read the file or files.

In domains, ADMX files can be stored in a central store—the domainwide directory created in the SYSVOL directory (%SystemRoot%\Sysvol\Domain\Policies). When you use a central store, administrative templates are no longer stored with each GPO. Instead, only the current state of the setting is stored in the GPO, and the ADMX files are stored centrally. This reduces the amount of storage space used as the number of GPOs increases and also reduces the amount of data being replicated throughout the enterprise.

When running in Windows Server 2008 or higher domain functional level, servers running Windows Server 2008 or later use Distributed File System (DFS) Replication Service for replicating Group Policy. With DFS replication, only the changes in GPOs are replicated, thereby eliminating the need to replicate an entire GPO after a change.

Current releases of Windows use the Group Policy client service to isolate Group Policy notification and processing from the Windows logon process. Separating Group Policy from the Windows logon process reduces the resources used for background processing of the policy while increasing overall performance and allowing delivery and application of new Group Policy files as part of the update process without requiring a restart.

Computers running Windows Vista or later don't use the trace logging function-ality in Userenv.dll and instead write Group Policy event messages to the System log. Further, the Group Policy operational log replaces previous Userenv logging. When you are troubleshooting Group Policy issues, you use the detailed event messages in the operational log rather than in the Userenv log. In Event Viewer, you can access the operational log under Applications And Services Logs\Microsoft\Windows\GroupPolicy.

Computers running current versions of Windows use Network Location Awareness instead of Internet Control Message Protocol (ICMP, or ping). With Network Location Awareness, a computer is aware of the type of network it is connected to and can be responsive to changes in the system status or network configuration. By using Network Location Awareness, the Group Policy client can determine the computer state, network state, and available network bandwidth for slow-link detection.

Managing local group policies

Computers running current versions of Windows allow the use of multiple local Group Policy objects on a single computer (as long as the computer is not a domain controller). Previously, computers had only one local GPO. Windows allows you to assign a different local GPO to each local user or general user type. This allows the application of policy to be more flexible and supports a wider array of implementation scenarios.

Local Group Policy objects

When computers are being used in a stand-alone configuration rather than a domain configuration, you might find that multiple local GPOs are useful because you no longer have to explicitly disable or remove settings that interfere with your ability to manage a computer before performing administrator tasks. Instead, you can implement one local GPO for administrators and another local GPO for nonadministrators. In a domain configuration, however, you might not want to use multiple local GPOs. In domains, most computers and users already have multiple GPOs applied to them—adding multiple local GPOs to this already varied mix can make managing Group Policy confusing.

Computers running current versions of Windows have three layers of local Group Policy objects:

- **Local Group Policy**   Local Group Policy is the only local Group Policy object that allows both computer configuration and user configuration settings to be applied to all users of the computer.

- **Administrators and Non-Administrators local Group Policy**   Administrators and Non-Administrators Local Group Policy contain only user configuration settings. This policy is applied based on whether the user account being used is a member of the local Administrators group.

- **User-specific local Group Policy**   User-Specific Local Group Policy contains only user configuration settings. This policy is applied to individual users and groups.

These layers of local Group Policy objects are processed in the following order: Local Group Policy, Administrators and Non-Administrators Local Group Policy, User-Specific Local Group Policy.

Because the available user-configuration settings are the same for all local GPOs, a setting in one GPO might conflict with a setting in another GPO. Windows resolves conflicts in settings by overwriting any previous setting with the last-read and most-current settings. The final setting is the one that Windows uses. When Windows resolves conflicts, only the enabled or disabled state of settings matters. A setting set as Not Configured has no effect on the state of the setting from a previous policy application. To simplify domain administration, you can disable processing of local Group Policy objects on computers running Windows Vista or later releases by enabling the Turn Off Local Group Policy Objects Processing policy setting in a domain GPO. In Group Policy, this setting is located under Administrative Templates for Computer Configuration under System\Group Policy.

Accessing the top-level local policy settings

All computers running current releases of Windows have an editable local Group Policy object. Although a domain controller has a local Group Policy object, you shouldn't edit its settings.

The quickest way to access the local GPO on a computer is to enter the following command in the Everywhere search box:

```
gpedit.msc
```

This command starts the GPOE in a Microsoft Management Console (MMC) with its target set to the local computer. To access the top-level local GPO on a remote computer, enter the following in the Everywhere search box:

```
gpedit.msc /gpcomputer:"RemoteComputer"
```

Here *RemoteComputer* is the host name or fully qualified domain name of the remote computer. Note that the double quotation marks are required and that there must not be a space between /gpcomputer: and the remote computer value, as shown in the following example:

```
gpedit.msc /gpcomputer:"corpsvr82"
```

When you are connected to a remote computer, the root node lists the name of the remote computer, as shown in Figure 6-1. Otherwise, the root node label is shown as Local Computer Policy.

FIGURE 6-1 Use the policy editor to manage local policy settings.

You can also manage the top-level local GPO on a computer by following these steps:

1. At a command prompt or in the Everywhere search box, type **mmc**, and then press Enter.

2. In the Microsoft Management Console, tap or click File, and then tap or click Add/Remove Snap-In.

3. In the Add Or Remove Snap-Ins dialog box, tap or click Group Policy Object Editor, and then tap or click Add.

4. In the Select Group Policy Object dialog box, tap or click Finish because the local computer is the default object, and then tap or click OK.

Whether you access the Local GPO directly or by adding GPOE to an MMC, you can now manage local policy settings by using the options provided (see Figure 6-2).

TIP You can use the same MMC snap-in to manage more than one local Group Policy object. In the Add Or Remove Snap-Ins dialog box, you simply add one instance of the Local Group Policy Object Editor for each object you want to work with.

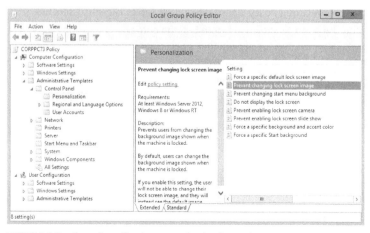

FIGURE 6-2 Use the policy editor to manage local policy settings.

Local Group Policy object settings

Local group policies are stored in the %SystemRoot%\System32\GroupPolicy folder on each computer running Windows Server. In this folder, you'll find the following subfolders:

- **Machine** Stores computer scripts in the Script folder and registry-based policy information for HKEY_LOCAL_MACHINE (HKLM) in the Registry.pol file
- **User** Stores user scripts in the Script folder and registry-based policy information for HKEY_CURRENT_USER (HKCU) in the Registry.pol file

CAUTION You shouldn't edit these folders and files directly. Instead, you should use the appropriate features of one of the Group Policy management tools. By default, these files and folders are hidden. If you want to view hidden files and folders in File Explorer, tap or click the View tab, and then select Hidden Items. You also might want to select File Name Extensions.

Accessing administrator, nonadministrator, and user-specific local Group Policy

By default, the only local policy object that exists on a computer is the Local Group Policy object. You can create and manage other local objects as necessary (except on domain controllers). You can create or access the Administrator Local Group Policy object, the Non-Administrator Local Group Policy Object, or a user-specific local Group Policy object by following these steps:

1. At a command prompt or in the Everywhere search box, type **mmc**, and then press Enter. In the Microsoft Management Console, tap or click File, and then tap or click Add/Remove Snap-In.

2. In the Add Or Remove Snap-Ins dialog box, tap or click Group Policy Object Editor, and then tap or click Add.

3. In the Select Group Policy Object dialog box, tap or click Browse. In the Browse For A Group Policy Object dialog box, tap or click the Users tab.

4. On the Users tab, as shown in Figure 6-3, the entries in the Group Policy Object Exists column specify whether a particular local policy object has been created. Do one of the following:

    - Select Administrators to create or access the Administrators Local Group Policy object.
    - Select Non-Administrators to create or access the Non-Administrators Local Group Policy object.
    - Select the local user whose user-specific local Group Policy object you want to create or access.

5. Tap or click OK. If the selected object doesn't exist, it will be created. Otherwise, the existing object opens for review and editing.

FIGURE 6-3 Select the local user or group to manage.

Policy settings for administrators, nonadministrators, and users are stored in the %SystemRoot%\System32\GroupPolicyUsers folder on each computer running Windows Server. Because these local GPOs apply only to user configuration settings, user-specific policy settings under %SystemRoot%\System32\GroupPolicyUsers have only a User subfolder, and this subfolder stores user scripts in the Script folder and registry-based policy information for HKEY_CURRENT_USER in the Registry.pol file.

Managing site, domain, and organizational unit policies

When you deploy Active Directory Domain Services (AD DS), you can use Active Directory–based Group Policy. Each site, domain, and organizational unit can have one or more group policies. Group policies listed higher in the Group Policy list have higher precedence than policies listed lower in the list. This ensures that policies are applied appropriately throughout the related sites, domains, and organizational units.

Understanding domain and default policies

When you work with Active Directory–based Group Policy, you'll find that each domain in your organization has two default GPOs:

- **Default Domain Controllers Policy GPO**   A default GPO created for and linked to the Domain Controllers organizational unit. This GPO is applicable to all domain controllers in a domain (as long as they aren't moved from this organizational unit). Use it to manage security settings for domain controllers in a domain.

- **Default Domain Policy GPO**   A default GPO created for and linked to the domain itself within Active Directory. Use this GPO to establish baselines for a wide variety of policy settings that apply to all users and computers in a domain.

Typically, the Default Domain Policy GPO is the highest-precedence GPO linked to the domain level, and the Default Domain Controllers Policy GPO is the highest-precedence GPO linked to the Domain Controllers container. You can link additional GPOs to the domain level and to the Domain Controllers container. When you do this, the settings in the highest-precedence GPO override settings in lower-precedence GPOs. These GPOs aren't meant for general management of Group Policy.

The Default Domain Policy GPO is used to manage only the default Account Policies settings and, in particular, three specific areas of Account Policies: password policy, account lockout policy, and Kerberos policy. Several security options are also managed through this GPO. These include Accounts: Rename Administrator Account, Accounts: Administrator Account Status, Accounts: Guest Account Status, Accounts: Rename Guest Account, Network Security: Force Logoff When Logon Hours Expire, Network Security: Do Not Store LAN Manager Hash Value On Next Password Change, and Network Access: Allow Anonymous SID/Name Translation. One way to override these settings is to create a GPO with the overriding settings and link it with a higher precedence to the domain container.

The Default Domain Controllers Policy GPO includes specific User Rights Assignment and Security Options settings that limit the ways domain controllers can be used. One way to override these settings is to create a GPO with the overriding settings and link it with a higher precedence to the Domain Controllers container.

To manage other areas of policy, you should create a GPO and link it to the domain or to an appropriate organizational unit within the domain.

Site, domain, and organizational unit group policies are stored in the %System-Root%\Sysvol\Domain\Policies folder on domain controllers. In this folder, you'll find one subfolder for each policy you defined on the domain controller. The policy folder name is the policy's globally unique identifier (GUID). You can find the policy's GUID on the policy's Properties page on the General tab in the Summary frame. Within these individual policy folders, you'll find the following subfolders:

- **Machine**   Stores computer scripts in the Script folder and registry-based policy information for HKEY_LOCAL_MACHINE (HKLM) in the Registry.pol file
- **User**   Stores user scripts in the Script folder and registry-based policy information for HKEY_CURRENT_USER (HKCU) in the Registry.pol file

CAUTION   Do not edit these folders and files directly. Instead, use the appropriate features of one of the Group Policy management tools.

Using the Group Policy Management Console

You can run the GPMC from the Tools menu in Server Manager. At a prompt or in the Everywhere search box, type **gpmc.msc**, and then press Enter.

As shown in Figure 6-4, the console root node is labeled Group Policy Management, and below this node is the Forest node. The Forest node represents the forest to which you are currently connected and is named after the forest root domain for that forest. If you have appropriate credentials, you can add connections to other forests. To do this, press and hold or right-click the Group Policy Management node, and then tap or click Add Forest. In the Add Forest dialog box, enter the name of the forest root domain in the Domain box, and then tap or click OK.

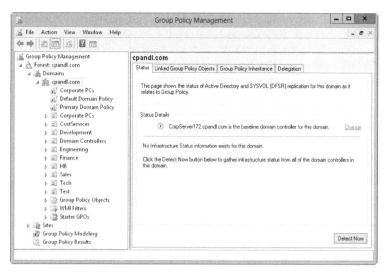

FIGURE 6-4 Use the GPMC to work with GPOs in sites, forests, and domains.

Expanding the Forest node displays the following nodes:

- **Domains** Provides access to the policy settings for domains in the related forest. You are connected to your logon domain by default. If you have appropriate credentials, you can add connections to other domains in the related forest. To do this, press and hold or right-click the Domains node, and then tap or click Show Domains. In the Show Domains dialog box, select the check boxes for the domains you want to add, and then tap or click OK.

- **Sites** Provides access to the policy settings for sites in the related forest. Sites are hidden by default. If you have appropriate credentials, you can add connections for sites. To do this, press and hold or right-click the Sites node, and then tap or click Show Sites. In the Show Sites dialog box, select the check boxes for the sites you want to add, and then tap or click OK.

- **Group Policy Modeling** Provides access to the Group Policy Modeling Wizard, which helps you plan policy deployment and simulate settings for testing purposes. Any saved policy models are also available.

- **Group Policy Results** Provides access to the Group Policy Results Wizard. For each domain you are connected to, all related GPOs and organizational units are available to work with in one location.

GPOs listed under the domain, site, and organizational unit containers in the GPMC are GPO links and not the GPOs themselves. You can access the actual GPOs through the Group Policy objects container of the selected domain. Note that the icons for GPO links have small arrows at the bottom left, similar to shortcut icons, whereas GPOs themselves do not.

When you start the GPMC, the console connects to Active Directory running on the domain controller that is acting as the PDC emulator for your logon domain and obtains a list of all GPOs and organizational units in that domain. It does this by using Lightweight Directory Access Protocol (LDAP) to access the directory store and the Server Message Block (SMB) protocol to access the SYSVOL directory. If the PDC emulator isn't available for some reason, such as when the server is offline, the GPMC displays a prompt so that you can choose to work with policy settings on the domain controller you are currently connected to or on any available domain controller. To change the domain controller you are connected to, press and hold or right-click the domain node for which you want to set the domain controller focus, and then tap or click Change Domain Controller. In the Change Domain Controller dialog box, the domain controller you are currently connected to is listed under Current Domain Controller. Using the Change To options, specify the domain controller to use, and then tap or click OK.

Getting to know the policy editor

With the GPMC, you can edit a GPO by pressing and holding or right-clicking it and then selecting Edit on the shortcut menu. As Figure 6-5 shows, the policy editor has two main nodes:

- **Computer Configuration** Allows you to set policies that should be applied to computers, regardless of who logs on

- **User Configuration** Allows you to set policies that should be applied to users, regardless of which computer they log on to

FIGURE 6-5 The configuration of the policy editor depends on the type of policy you're creating and the add-ons installed.

Under the Computer Configuration and User Configuration nodes, you'll find the Policies and Preferences nodes. Settings for general policies are listed under the Policies node. Settings for general preferences are listed under the Preferences node.

NOTE When I reference settings under the Policies node, I sometimes use a shortcut such as User Configuration\Administrative Templates\Windows Components rather than User Configuration\Policies\Administrative Templates: Policy Definitions\Windows Components. This shortcut tells me that the policy setting being discussed is under User Configuration rather than Computer Configuration and can be found under Administrative Templates\Windows Components.

The exact configuration of Computer Configuration and User Configuration depends on the add-ons installed and which type of policy you're creating. Still, you'll usually find that both Computer Configuration and User Configuration have subnodes for the following:

- **Software Settings** Sets policies for software settings and software installation. When you install software, subnodes might be added to Software Settings.
- **Windows Settings** Sets policies for folder redirection, scripts, and security.
- **Administrative Templates** Sets policies for the operating system, Windows components, and programs. Administrative templates are configured through template files. You can add or remove template files whenever you need to.

NOTE A complete discussion of all the available options is beyond the scope of this book. The sections that follow focus on using administrative templates. Security is covered in chapters later in this book.

Using administrative templates to set policies

Administrative templates provide easy access to registry-based policy settings that you might want to configure. A default set of administrative templates is configured for users and computers in the policy editor. You can also add or remove administrative templates. Any changes you make to policies available through administrative templates are saved in the registry. Computer configurations are saved in HKEY_LOCAL_MACHINE, and user configurations are saved in HKEY_CURRENT_USER.

You can view the currently configured templates in the Administrative Templates node of the policy editor. This node contains policies you can configure for local systems, organizational units, domains, and sites. Different sets of templates are found under Computer Configuration and User Configuration. You can add templates containing new policies in the policy editor when you install new Windows components.

You can use administrative templates to manage the following:

- **Control Panel** Determine the available options and configuration of Control Panel and Control Panel utilities.
- **Desktop** Configure the Windows desktop and the available options from the desktop.

- **Network** Configure networking and network client options for offline files, DNS clients, and network connections.
- **Printers** Configure printer settings, browsing, spooling, and directory options
- **Shared folders** Allow publishing of shared folders and Distributed File System (DFS) roots.
- **Start screen and taskbar** Control the available options and configuration of the Start screen and the taskbar.
- **System** Configure system settings for disk quotas, user profiles, user logon, system restore, error reporting, and so on.
- **Windows components** Determine the available options and configuration of various Windows components, including Event Viewer, Internet Explorer, Task Scheduler, Windows Installer, and Windows Updates.

The best way to get to know which administrative template policies are available is to browse the Administrative Templates nodes. As you browse the templates, you'll find that policies are in one of three states:

- **Not Configured** The policy isn't used, and no settings for it are saved in the registry.
- **Enabled** The policy is actively being enforced, and its settings are saved in the registry.
- **Disabled** The policy is turned off and isn't enforced unless overridden. This setting is saved in the registry.

You can enable, disable, and configure policies by following these steps:

1. In the policy editor, open the Administrative Templates folder in the Computer Configuration or User Configuration node, whichever is appropriate for the type of policy you want to set.

2. In the left pane, select the subfolder containing the policies you want to work with. The related policies are then displayed in the right pane.

3. Double-tap or double-click a policy to display its related Properties dialog box. You can read a description of the policy in the Help pane. The description is available only if one is defined in the related template file.

4. To set the policy's state, select one of the following options:
   - **Not Configured** The policy isn't configured.
   - **Enabled** The policy is enabled.
   - **Disabled** The policy is disabled.

5. If you enable the policy, set any additional parameters, and then tap or click OK.

NOTE Typically, computer policies have precedence in Windows Server. If there's a conflict between a computer policy setting and a user policy setting, the computer policy is enforced.

Creating and linking GPOs

When you work with a policy object, creating an object and linking an object to a specific container within Active Directory are two different actions. You can create a GPO without linking it to any domain, site, or organizational unit. Then, as appropriate, you can link the GPO to a specific domain, site, or organizational unit. You can also create a GPO and link it automatically to a domain, site, or organizational unit. The technique you choose primarily depends on your personal preference and how you plan to work with the GPO. Keep in mind that when you create and link a GPO to a site, domain, or organizational unit, the GPO is applied to the user and computer objects in that site, domain, or organizational unit according to the Active Directory options governing inheritance, the precedence order of GPOs, and other settings.

You can create and then link a GPO to a site, domain, or organizational unit by following these steps:

1. In the GPMC, expand the entry for the forest you want to work with, and then expand the related Domains node by double-tapping or double-clicking each node in turn.

2. Press and hold or right-click Group Policy objects, and then tap or click New. In the New GPO dialog box, enter a descriptive name for the GPO, such as Secure Workstation GPO. If you want to use a starter GPO as the source for the initial settings, select the starter GPO to use in the Source Starter GPO list. When you tap or click OK, the new GPO is added to the Group Policy objects container.

3. Press and hold or right-click the new GPO, and then tap or click Edit. In the policy editor, configure the necessary policy settings, and then close the policy editor.

4. In the GPMC, select the site, domain, or organizational unit. Expand the site node you want to work with. In the right pane, the Linked Group Policy Objects tab shows the GPOs that are currently linked to the selected container (if any).

5. Press and hold or right-click the site, domain, or organizational unit to which you want to link the GPO, and then tap or click Link An Existing GPO. In the Select GPO dialog box, select the GPO you want to link with, and then tap or click OK. When Group Policy is refreshed for computers and users in the applicable site, domain, or organizational unit, the policy settings in the GPO are applied.

You can create and link a GPO as a single operation by following these steps:

1. In the GPMC, press and hold or right-click the site, domain, or organizational unit for which you want to create and link the GPO, and then tap or click Create A GPO In This Domain, And Link It Here.

2. In the New GPO dialog box, enter a descriptive name for the GPO, such as Secure Workstation GPO. If you want to use a starter GPO as the source for the initial settings, select the starter GPO to use in the Source Starter GPO

list. When you tap or click OK, the new GPO is added to the Group Policy Objects container and linked to the previously selected site, domain, or organizational unit.

3. Press and hold or right-click the new GPO, and then tap or click Edit. In the policy editor, configure the necessary policy settings, and then close the policy editor. When Group Policy is refreshed for computers and users in the applicable site, domain, or organizational unit, the policy settings in the GPO are applied.

Creating and using starter GPOs

When you create a GPO in the GPMC, you can base the GPO on a starter GPO. The settings for the starter GPO are then imported into the new GPO, which allows you to use a starter GPO to define the base configuration settings for a new GPO. In a large organization, you should create different categories of starter GPOs based on the users and computers they will be used with or on the required security configuration.

You can create a starter GPO by following these steps:

1. In the GPMC, expand the entry for the forest you want to work with, and then double-tap or double-click the related Domains node to expand it.

2. Press and hold or right-click Starter GPOs, and then tap or click New. In the New Starter GPO dialog box, enter a descriptive name for the GPO, such as **General Management User GPO**. You can also enter comments describing the GPO's purpose. Tap or click OK.

3. Press and hold or right-click the new GPO, and then tap or click Edit. In the policy editor, configure the necessary policy settings, and then close the policy editor.

Delegating privileges for Group Policy management

In Active Directory, all administrators have some level of privileges for performing Group Policy management tasks. Through delegation, other individuals can be granted permissions to perform any or all of the following tasks:

- Create GPOs and manage the GPOs they create.
- View settings, modify settings, delete a GPO, and modify security.
- Manage links to existing GPOs or generate Resultant Set of Policy (RSoP).

In Active Directory, administrators can create GPOs, and anyone who has created a GPO has the right to manage that GPO. In the GPMC, you can determine who can create GPOs in a domain by selecting the Group Policy Objects node for that domain and then tapping or clicking the Delegation tab. On the Delegation tab is a list of groups and users that can create GPOs in the domain. To grant GPO creation permission to a user or group, tap or click Add. In the Select User, Computer, Or Group dialog box, select the user or group, and then tap or click OK.

In the GPMC, you have several ways to determine who has access permissions for Group Policy management. For domain, site, and organizational unit permissions, select the domain, site, or organizational unit you want to work with, and then tap or click the Delegation tab in the right pane, as shown in Figure 6-6. In the Permission list, select the permission you want to check. The options are as follows:

- **Link GPOs**   Lists users and groups that can create and manage links to GPOs in the selected site, domain, or organizational unit
- **Perform Group Policy Modeling Analyses**   Lists users and groups that can determine RSoP for the purposes of planning
- **Read Group Policy Results Data**   Lists users and groups that can determine RSoP that is currently being applied, for the purposes of verification or logging

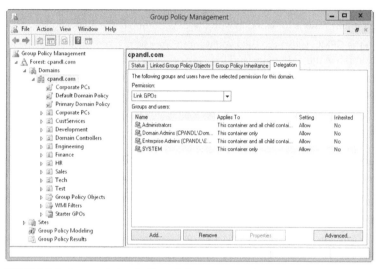

FIGURE 6-6 Review permissions for Group Policy management.

To grant domain, site, or organizational unit permissions, complete the following steps:

1. In the GPMC, select the domain, site, or organizational unit you want to work with, and then tap or click the Delegation tab in the right pane.

2. In the Permission list, select the permission you want to grant. The options are Link GPOs, Perform Group Policy Modeling Analyses, and Read Group Policy Results Data.

3. Tap or click Add. In the Select User, Computer, Or Group dialog box, select the user or group, and then tap or click OK.

4. In the Add Group Or User dialog box, specify how the permission should be applied. To apply the permission to the current container and all child containers, select This Container And All Child Containers. To apply the permission only to the current container, select This Container Only. Tap or click OK.

For individual GPO permissions, select the GPO you want to work with in the GPMC, and then tap or click the Delegation tab in the right pane. One or more of the following permissions are displayed for individual users and groups:

- **Read**   Indicates that the user or group can view the GPO and its settings.

- **Edit Settings**   Indicates that the user or group can view the GPO and change its settings. The user or group cannot delete the GPO or modify security.

- **Edit Settings, Delete, Modify Security**   Indicates that the user or group can view the GPO and change its settings. The user or group can also delete the GPO and modify security.

To grant permissions for working with the GPO, complete the following steps:

1. In the GPMC, select the GPO you want to work with, tap or click the Delegation tab in the right pane, and then tap or click Add.

2. In the Select User, Computer, Or Group dialog box, select the user or group, and then tap or click OK.

3. In the Add Group Or User dialog box, select the permission level, and then tap or click OK.

Blocking, overriding, and disabling policies

Inheritance ensures that every computer and user object in a domain, site, or organizational unit is affected by Group Policy. Most policies have three configuration options: Not Configured, Enabled, or Disabled. Not Configured is the default state for most policy settings. If a policy is enabled, the policy is enforced and is applied directly or through inheritance to all users and computers that are subject to the policy. If a policy is disabled, the policy is not enforced or applied.

You can change the way inheritance works in four key ways:

- Change the link order and precedence.
- Override inheritance (as long as there is no enforcement).
- Block inheritance (to prevent inheritance completely).
- Enforce inheritance (to supersede and prevent overriding or blocking).

For Group Policy, the order of inheritance goes from the site level to the domain level and then to each nested organizational unit level. Keep the following in mind:

- When multiple policy objects are linked to a particular level, the link order determines the order in which policy settings are applied. Linked policy objects are always applied in link-ranking order. Lower-ranking policy objects are processed first, and then higher-ranking policy objects are processed. The policy object processed last has priority, so any policy settings configured in this policy object are final and override those of other policy objects (unless you use inheritance blocking or enforcing).

- When multiple policy objects can be inherited from a higher level, the precedence order shows exactly how policy objects are being processed. As with link order, lower-ranking policy objects are processed before higher-ranking policy objects. The policy object processed last has precedence, so any policy settings configured in this policy object are final and override those of other policy objects (unless you use inheritance blocking or enforcing).

When multiple policy objects are linked at a specific level, you can change the link order (and thus the precedence order) of policy objects by following these steps:

1. In the GPMC, select the container for the site, domain, or organizational unit with which you want to work.

2. In the right pane, select the Linked Group Policy Objects tab (as shown in Figure 6-7). Tap or click the policy object you want to work with.

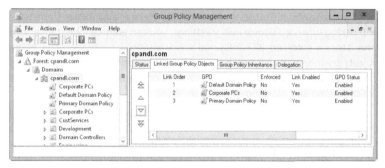

FIGURE 6-7 Change the link order to modify processing order and precedence.

3. Tap or click the Move Link Up or Move Link Down buttons as appropriate to change the link order of the selected policy object.

4. When you are finished changing the link order, confirm that policy objects are being processed in the expected order by checking the precedence order on the Group Policy Inheritance tab.

Overriding inheritance is a basic technique for changing the way inheritance works. When a policy is enabled in a higher-level policy object, you can override inheritance by disabling the policy in a lower-level policy object. When a policy is disabled in a higher-level policy object, you can override inheritance by enabling the policy in a lower-level policy object. As long as a policy is not blocked or enforced, this technique achieves the effects you want.

Sometimes you will want to block inheritance so that no policy settings from higher-level containers are applied to users and computers in a particular container. When inheritance is blocked, only configured policy settings from policy objects linked at that level are applied, and settings from all high-level containers are blocked (as long as there is no policy enforcement).

Domain administrators can use inheritance blocking to block inherited policy settings from the site level. Organizational unit administrators can use inheritance blocking to block inherited policy settings from both the domain and the site level. By using blocking to ensure the autonomy of a domain or organizational unit, you can ensure that domain or organizational unit administrators have full control over the policies that apply to users and computers under their administration.

Using the GPMC, you can block inheritance by pressing and holding or right-clicking the domain or organizational unit that should not inherit settings from higher-level containers, and then selecting Block Inheritance. If Block Inheritance is already selected, selecting it again removes the setting. When you block inheritance in the GPMC, a blue circle with an exclamation point is added to the container's node in the console tree. This notification icon provides a quick way to tell whether any domain or organizational unit has the Block Inheritance setting enabled.

To prevent administrators who have authority over a container from overriding or blocking inherited Group Policy settings, you can enforce inheritance. When inheritance is enforced, all configured policy settings from higher-level policy objects are inherited and applied regardless of the policy settings configured in lower-level policy objects. Thus, enforcement of inheritance is used to supersede the overriding and blocking of policy settings.

Forest administrators can use inheritance enforcement to ensure that configured policy settings from the site level are applied and to prevent the overriding or blocking of policy settings by domain and organizational unit administrators. Domain administrators can use inheritance enforcement to ensure that configured policy settings from the domain level are applied and to prevent the overriding or blocking of policy settings by organizational unit administrators.

Using the GPMC, you can enforce policy inheritance by expanding the top-level container from which to begin enforcement, pressing and holding or right-clicking the link to the GPO, and then tapping or clicking Enforced. For example, if you want to ensure that a domain-level GPO is inherited by all organizational units in the domain, expand the domain container, press and hold or right-click the domain-level GPO, and then tap or click Enforced. If Enforced is already selected, selecting it again removes the enforcement. In the GPMC, you can easily determine which policies are inherited and which policies are enforced. Simply select a policy object anywhere in the GPMC, and then view the related Scope tab in the right pane. If the policy is enforced, the Enforced column under Link Enabled will display Yes, as shown in Figure 6-8.

After you select a policy object, you can press and hold or right-click a location entry on the Scope tab to display a shortcut menu that allows you to manage linking and policy enforcement. Enable or disable links by selecting or clearing the Link Enabled option, respectively. Enable or disable enforcement by selecting or clearing the Enforced option.

Figure 6-8 Enforce policy inheritance to ensure that settings are applied.

Maintaining and troubleshooting Group Policy

Group Policy is a broad area of administration that requires careful management. Like any area of administration, Group Policy must also be carefully maintained to ensure proper operation, and you must diagnose and resolve any problems that occur. To troubleshoot Group Policy, you need a strong understanding of how policy is refreshed and processed. You also need a strong understanding of general maintenance and troubleshooting tasks.

Refreshing Group Policy

When you make changes to a policy, those changes are immediate. However, they aren't propagated automatically. Client computers request policies at the following times:

- When the computer starts
- When a user logs on
- When an application or user requests a refresh
- When a refresh interval is set for Group Policy and the interval has elapsed

Computer configuration settings are applied during startup of the operating system. User configuration settings are applied when a user logs on to a computer. Typically, if there is a conflict between computer and user settings, computer settings have priority and take precedence.

After policy settings are applied, the settings are refreshed automatically to ensure that they are current. The default refresh interval for domain controllers is 5 minutes. For all other computers, the default refresh interval is 90 minutes, with up to a 30-minute variation to avoid overloading the domain controller with numerous concurrent client requests. This means that an effective refresh window for nondomain-controller computers is 90 to 120 minutes.

During a Group Policy refresh, the client computer contacts an available domain controller in its local site. If one or more of the policy objects defined in the domain have changed, the domain controller provides a list of the policy objects that apply to the computer and to the user who is currently logged on, as appropriate. The domain controller does this regardless of whether the version numbers on all the listed policy objects have changed. By default, the computer processes the policy objects only if the version number of at least one of the policy objects has changed. If any one of the related policies has changed, all the policies have to be processed again because of inheritance and the interdependencies between policies.

Security settings are a notable exception to the processing rule. By default, these settings are refreshed every 16 hours (960 minutes) regardless of whether policy objects contain changes. A random offset of up to 30 minutes is added to reduce the impact on domain controllers and the network during updates (making the effective refresh window 960 to 990 minutes). Also, if the client computer detects that it is connecting over a slow network connection, it informs the domain controller, and only the security settings and administrative templates are transferred over the network. This means that by default, only the security settings and administrative templates are applied when a computer is connected over a slow link. You can configure the way slow-link detection works in Group Policy.

You must carefully balance the update frequency with the actual rate of policy change. If policy is changed infrequently, you might want to increase the refresh window to reduce resource usage. For example, you might want to use a refresh interval of 20 minutes on domain controllers and 180 minutes on other computers.

Configuring the refresh interval

You can change the Group Policy refresh interval on a per-policy object basis. To set the refresh interval for domain controllers, follow these steps:

1. In the GPMC, press and hold or right-click the Group Policy object you want to modify, and then tap or click Edit. This GPO should be linked to a container that contains domain controller computer objects.

2. In the Administrative Templates for Computer Configuration under System \Group Policy, double-tap or double-click the Set Group Policy Refresh Interval For Domain Controllers policy. This displays a Properties dialog box for the policy, shown in Figure 6-9.

3. Define the policy by selecting Enabled. Set the base refresh interval in the first Minutes box. You usually want this value to be between 5 and 59 minutes.

4. In the other Minutes box, set the minimum or maximum time variation for the refresh interval. The variation effectively creates a refresh window with the goal of avoiding overload resulting from numerous clients simultaneously requesting a Group Policy refresh. Tap or click OK.

NOTE A faster refresh rate increases the likelihood that a computer has the most current policy configuration. A slower refresh rate reduces the frequency of policy refreshes, which can reduce overhead with regard to resource usage but also increase the likelihood that a computer won't have the most current policy configuration.

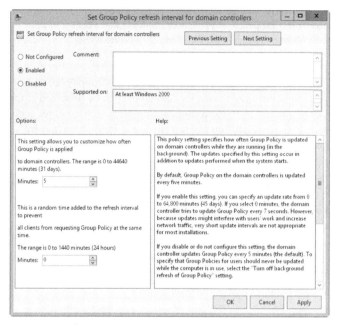

FIGURE 6-9 Configure the refresh interval for Group Policy.

To set the refresh interval for member servers and workstations, follow these steps:

1. In the GPMC, press and hold or right-click the Group Policy object you want to modify, and then tap or click Edit. This GPO should be linked to a container that contains computer objects.

2. In the Administrative Templates for Computer Configuration under System \Group Policy, double-tap or double-click the Set Group Policy Refresh Interval For Computers policy. This displays a dialog box similar to the one in Figure 6-9.

3. Define the policy by selecting Enabled. In the first Minutes box, set the base refresh interval. You usually want this value to be between 60 and 240 minutes.

4. In the other Minutes box, set the minimum or maximum time variation for the refresh interval. The variation effectively creates a refresh window with the goal of avoiding overload resulting from numerous clients simultaneously requesting a Group Policy refresh. Tap or click OK.

You want to be sure that updates don't occur too frequently yet are timely enough to meet expectations or requirements. The more often a policy is refreshed, the more traffic is generated over the network. In a large installation, you typically want to set a refresh rate that is longer than the default to reduce network traffic, particularly if the policy affects hundreds of users or computers. In any installation where users complain about their computers periodically being sluggish, you also might want to increase the policy refresh interval. Consider that a once-a-day or once-a-week update might be all that it takes to keep policies current enough to meet your organization's needs.

As an administrator, you might often need or want to refresh Group Policy manually. For example, you might not want to wait for Group Policy to be refreshed at the automatic interval, or you might be trying to resolve a problem with refreshes and want to force a Group Policy refresh. You can refresh Group Policy manually by using the Gpupdate command-line utility.

You can initiate a refresh in several ways. Entering **gpupdate** at a prompt or in the Everywhere search box refreshes settings in both Computer Configuration and User Configuration on the local computer. Only policy settings that have changed are processed and applied when you run Gpupdate. You can change this behavior by using the /force parameter to force a refresh of all policy settings.

You can refresh user and computer configuration settings separately. To refresh only computer configuration settings, enter **gpupdate /target:computer** at the command prompt. To refresh only user configuration settings, enter **gpupdate /target:user** at the command prompt.

You can also use Gpupdate to log off a user or restart a computer after Group Policy is refreshed. This is useful because some group policies are applied only when a user logs on or when a computer starts. To log off a user after a refresh, add the /Logoff parameter. To restart a computer after a refresh, add the /Boot parameter.

Modeling Group Policy for planning purposes

Modeling Group Policy for planning is useful when you want to test various implementation and configuration scenarios. For example, you might want to model the effect of loopback processing or slow-link detection. You can also model the effect of moving users or computers to another container in Active Directory, or the effect of changing security group membership for users and computers.

All domain and enterprise administrators have permission to model Group Policy for planning, as do those who have been delegated the Perform Group Policy Modeling Analyses permission. To model Group Policy and test various implementation and update scenarios, follow these steps:

1. In the GPMC, press and hold or right-click the Group Policy Modeling node, select Group Policy Modeling Wizard, and then tap or click Next.

2. On the Domain Controller Selection page, select the domain you want to model in the Show Domain Controllers In This Domain list. By default, you will simulate policy on any available domain controller in the selected

domain. If you want to use a specific domain controller, select This Domain Controller, and then tap or click the domain controller to use. Tap or click Next.

3. On the User And Computer Selection page, shown in Figure 6-10, you have the option of simulating policy based on containers or individual accounts. Use one of the following techniques to choose accounts, and then tap or click Next:

   ■ Use containers to simulate changes for entire organizational units or other containers. Under User Information, select Container, and then tap or click Browse to display the Choose User Container dialog box. Use the dialog box to choose any of the available user containers in the selected domain. Under Computer Information, select Container, tap or click Browse to display the Choose Computer Container dialog box, and then choose any of the available computer containers in the selected domain.

   ■ Select specific accounts to simulate changes for a specific user and computer. Under User Information, select User, tap or click Browse to display the Select User dialog box, and then specify a user account. Under Computer Information, select Computer, tap or click Browse to display the Select Computer dialog box, and then specify a computer account.

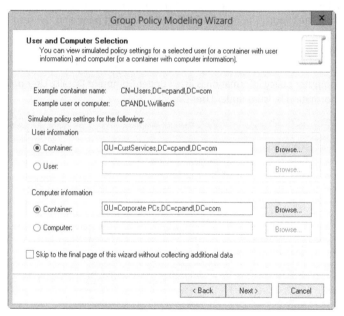

FIGURE 6-10 Select containers or accounts to use in the simulation.

4. On the Advanced Simulation Options page, select any advanced options for Slow Network Connections, Loopback Processing, and Site as necessary, and then tap or click Next.

5. On the User Security Groups page, you can simulate changes to the security group membership of the applicable user or users. Any changes you make to group membership affect the previously selected user or user container. For example, to simulate what happens if a user in the designated user container is a member of the CorpManagers group, add this group to the Security Groups list. Tap or click Next.

6. On the Computer Security Groups page, you can simulate changes to the applicable security group membership for a computer or computers. Any changes you make to group membership affect the previously selected computer or computer container. For example, to simulate what happens if a computer in the designated computer container is a member of the RemoteComputers group, add this group to the Security Groups list. Tap or click Next.

7. You can link Windows Management Instrumentation (WMI) filters to Group Policy objects. By default, the selected users and computers are assumed to meet all the WMI filter requirements, which is what you want in most cases for planning purposes. Tap or click Next twice to accept the default options.

8. Review the selections you made, and then tap or click Next. After the wizard gathers policy information, tap or click Finish. When the wizard finishes generating the report, the report is selected in the left pane and the results are displayed in the right pane.

9. When you select the Details tab in the right pane as shown in Figure 6-11, you can determine the settings that would be applied by browsing the report. Computer policy information is listed under Computer Details. User policy information is listed under User Details.

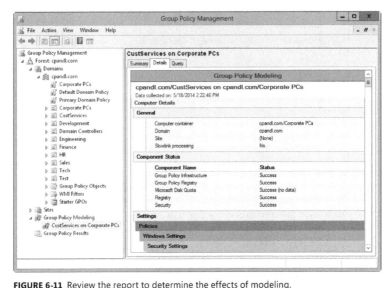

FIGURE 6-11 Review the report to determine the effects of modeling.

Copying, pasting, and importing policy objects

The GPMC features built-in copy, paste, and import operations. Using the copy and paste features is fairly straightforward. The Copy and Paste options are available when you press and hold or right-click a GPO in the GPMC. You can copy a policy object and all its settings in one domain and then browse to the domain into which you want to paste the copy of the policy object. The source and target domains can be any domains you can connect to in the GPMC and for which you have permission to manage related policy objects. In the source domain, you need Read permission to create a copy of a policy object. In the target domain, you need Write permission to write (paste) the copied policy object. Administrators have this privilege, as do those who have been delegated permission to create policy objects.

Copying policy objects between domains works well when you have connectivity between domains and the appropriate permissions. If you are an administrator at a remote office or have been delegated permissions, however, you might not have access to the source domain to create a copy of a policy object. In this case, another administrator can make a backup copy of a policy object for you and then send you the related data. When you receive the related data, you can import the backup copy of the policy object into your domain to create a policy object with the same settings.

Anyone with the Edit Settings Group Policy management privilege can perform an import operation. The import operation overwrites all the settings of the policy object you select. To import a backup copy of a policy object into a domain, follow these steps:

1. In the GPMC, press and hold or right-click Group Policy Objects, and then tap or click New. In the New GPO dialog box, enter a descriptive name for the new GPO, and then tap or click OK.

2. The new GPO is now listed in the Group Policy Objects container. Press and hold or right-click the new policy object, and then tap or click Import Settings. This starts the Import Settings Wizard.

3. Tap or click Next twice to bypass the Backup GPO page. You don't need to create a backup of the GPO at this time because it's new.

4. On the Backup Location page, tap or click Browse. In the Browse For Folder dialog box, select the folder containing the backup copy of the policy object you want to import, and then tap or click OK. Tap or click Next to continue.

5. If multiple backups are stored in the designated backup folder, a list of them will be displayed on the Source GPO page. Tap or click the one you want to use, and then tap or click Next.

6. The Import Settings Wizard scans the policy object for references to security principals and Universal Naming Convention (UNC) paths that might need to be migrated. If any are found, you are given the opportunity to create migration tables or use existing migration tables.

7. Continue through the wizard by tapping or clicking Next, and then tap or click Finish to begin the import process. When importing is complete, tap or click OK.

Backing up and restoring policy objects

As part of your periodic administration tasks, you should back up GPOs to protect them. You can use the GPMC to back up individual policy objects in a domain or all policy objects in a domain by following these steps:

1. In the GPMC, expand and then select the Group Policy Objects node. If you want to back up all policy objects in the domain, press and hold or right-click the Group Policy Objects node, and then tap or click Back Up All. If you want to back up a specific policy object in the domain, press and hold or right-click the policy object, and then select Back Up.

2. In the Back Up Group Policy Object dialog box, tap or click Browse. In the Browse For Folder dialog box, set the location where the GPO backup should be stored.

3. In the Description box, enter a description of the contents of the backup. Tap or click Back Up to start the backup process.

4. The Backup dialog box shows the progress and status of the backup. Tap or click OK when the backup is complete. If a backup fails, check the permissions on the policy and the folder to which you are writing the backup. You need Read permission on a policy and Write permission on the backup folder to create a backup. By default, members of the Domain Admins and Enterprise Admins groups should have these permissions.

Using the GPMC, you can restore a policy object to the state it was in when it was backed up. The GPMC tracks the backup of each policy object separately, even if you back up all policy objects at one time. Because version information is also tracked according to the backup time stamp and description, you can restore the last version of each policy object or a particular version of any policy object.

You can restore a policy object by following these steps:

1. In the GPMC, press and hold or right-click the Group Policy Objects node, and then tap or click Manage Backups. This displays the Manage Backups dialog box.

2. In the Backup Location box, tap or click Browse. In the Browse For Folder dialog box, find the backup folder, and then tap or click OK.

3. All policy object backups in the designated folder are listed under Backed Up GPOs. To show only the latest version of the policy objects according to the time stamp, select Show Only The Latest Version Of Each GPO.

4. Select the GPO you want to restore. If you want to confirm its settings, tap or click View Settings, and then use Internet Explorer to verify that the settings are as expected. When you are ready to continue, tap or click Restore. Confirm that you want to restore the selected policy object by tapping or clicking OK.

5. The Restore dialog box shows the progress and status of the restore operation. If a restore operation fails, check the permissions on the policy object and the folder from which you are reading the backup. To restore a GPO, you need

Edit Settings, Delete, and Modify Security permissions on the policy object and Read permission on the folder containing the backup. By default, members of the Domain Admins and Enterprise Admins groups should have these permissions.

Determining current Group Policy settings and refresh status

You can use Group Policy modeling for logging Resultant Set of Policy (RSoP). When you use Group Policy modeling in this way, you can review all the policy objects that apply to a computer and the last time the applicable policy objects were processed (refreshed). All domain and enterprise administrators have permission to model Group Policy for logging, as do those who have been delegated the permission Read Group Policy Results Data. In the GPMC, you can model Group Policy for the purpose of logging RSoP by pressing and holding or right-clicking the Group Policy Results node, and then clicking Group Policy Results Wizard. When the Group Policy Results Wizard starts, follow the prompts.

Disabling an unused part of Group Policy

Another way to disable a policy is to disable an unused part of the GPO. When you do this, you block computer configuration or user configuration settings, or both, and don't allow them to be applied. When you disable part of a policy that isn't used, the application of GPOs will be faster.

You can enable and disable policies partially or entirely by following these steps:

1. In the GPMC, select the container for the site, domain, or organizational unit with which you want to work.

2. Select the policy object you want to work with, and then tap or click the Details tab in the right pane.

3. Choose one of the following status settings from the GPO Status list, and then tap or click OK when prompted to confirm that you want to change the status of this GPO:

   - **All Settings Disabled**   Disallows processing of the policy object and all its settings.

   - **Computer Configuration Settings Disabled**   Disables processing of computer configuration settings. This means that only user configuration settings are processed.

   - **Enabled**   Allows processing of the policy object and all its settings.

   - **User Configuration Settings Disabled**   Disables processing of user configuration settings. This means that only computer configuration settings are processed.

Changing policy processing preferences

In Group Policy, computer configuration settings are processed when a computer starts and accesses the network. User configuration settings are processed when a user logs on to the network. In the event of a conflict between settings in Computer

Configuration and User Configuration, the computer configuration settings win. It is also important to remember that computer settings are applied from the computer's GPOs, and user settings are applied from the user's GPOs.

In some special situations, you might not want this behavior. On a shared computer, you might want the user settings to be applied from the computer's GPOs, but you might also want to allow user settings from the user's GPOs to be applied. In a secure lab or kiosk environment, you might want the user settings to be applied from the computer's GPOs to ensure compliance with strict security rules or guidelines for the lab. By using loopback processing, you can allow for these types of exceptions and obtain user settings from a computer's GPOs.

To change the way loopback processing works, follow these steps:

1. In the GPMC, press and hold or right-click the Group Policy object you want to modify, and then tap or click Edit.

2. In the Administrative Templates for Computer Configuration under System \Group Policy, double-tap or double-click the Configure User Group Policy Loopback Processing Mode policy. This displays a Properties dialog box for the policy.

3. Define the policy by selecting Enabled, selecting one of the following processing modes from the Mode list, and then tapping or clicking OK:

   - **Replace**   Select the Replace option to ensure that user settings from the computer's GPOs are processed and that user settings in the user's GPOs are not processed. This means that the user settings from the computer's GPOs replace the user settings normally applied to the user.

   - **Merge**   Select the Merge option to ensure that the user settings in the computer's GPOs are processed first, then user settings in the user's GPOs, and then user settings in the computer's GPOs again. This processing technique serves to combine the user settings in both the computer's and the user's GPOs. In the event of a conflict, the user settings in the computer's GPOs take precedence and overwrite the user settings in the user's GPOs.

Configuring slow-link detection

Slow-link detection is used by Group Policy clients to detect increased latency and reduced responsiveness on the network and to take corrective action to reduce the likelihood that processing of Group Policy will further saturate the network. After a slow link is detected, Group Policy clients reduce their network communications and requests, thereby reducing the overall network traffic load by limiting the amount of policy processing they do.

By default, if the connection speed is determined to be less than 500 kilobits per second (which could also be interpreted as high latency/reduced responsiveness on a fast network), the client computer interprets this as a slow network connection and notifies the domain controller. As a result, only security settings and administrative templates in the applicable policy objects are sent by the domain controller during a policy refresh.

You can configure slow-link detection by using the Configure Group Policy Slow Link Detection policy, which is stored in the Administrative Templates for Computer Configuration under System\Group Policy. If you disable this policy or do not configure it, clients use the default value of 500 kilobits per second to determine whether they are on a slow link. If you enable this policy, you can set a specific slow-link value, such as 384 kilobits per second. You also can specify that 3G connections should always be treated as slow links. Alternatively, if you want to disable slow-link detection completely, set the Connection Speed option to 0. This setting effectively tells clients not to detect slow links and to consider all links to be fast.

REAL WORLD Microsoft refers to connections on cellular and broadband as *costed networks*. Several policies are designed to help specify how networking should be used with mobile devices on costed networks. You can:

- Control offline file synchronization on costed networks by using the Enable File Synchronization On Costed Networks policy found under Computer Configuration \Administrative Templates\Network\Offline Files.

- Control background transfers on costed networks by using the Set Default Download Behavior For BITS Jobs On Costed Networks policy found under Computer Configuration\Administrative Templates\Network\Background Intelligent Transfer Services (BITS).

- Specify that costed broadband networks have fixed, variable, or unrestricted usage charges by using the Set Cost policy found under Computer Configuration \Administrative Templates\Network\WLAN Service\WLAN Media Cost.

- Specify that costed cellular networks have fixed, variable, or unrestricted usage charges by using the Set 3G Cost and Set 4G Cost policies found under Computer Configuration \Administrative Templates\Network\WWAN Service\WWAN Media Cost.

You can optimize slow-link detection for various areas of Group Policy processing as necessary. By default, policy areas that are not processed when a slow link is detected include the following:

- Disk Quota Policy Processing
- EFS Recovery Policy Processing
- Folder Redirection Policy Processing
- Scripts Policy Processing
- Software Installation Policy Processing

Security Policy Processing is always enabled automatically for slow links. By default, security policy is refreshed every 16 hours even if security policy has not changed. The only way to stop the forced refresh is to configure security policy processing so that it is not applied during periodic background refreshes. To do this, select the policy setting Do Not Apply During Periodic Background Processing. However, because security policy is so important, the Do Not Apply setting means only that security policy processing is stopped when a user is logged on and using the computer. One of the only reasons you'll want to stop security policy refreshes is applications failing during refresh operations.

You can configure slow-link detection and related policy processing by following these steps:

1. In the GPMC, press and hold or right-click the policy object you want to modify, and then tap or click Edit.

2. In the Administrative Templates for Computer Configuration under System \Group Policy, double-tap or double-click the Configure Group Policy Slow Link Detection policy.

3. Select Enabled to define the policy, as shown in Figure 6-12. In the Connection Speed box, specify the speed that should be used to determine whether a computer is on a slow link. You also can specify that WWAN connections should always be treated as slow links. Tap or click OK.

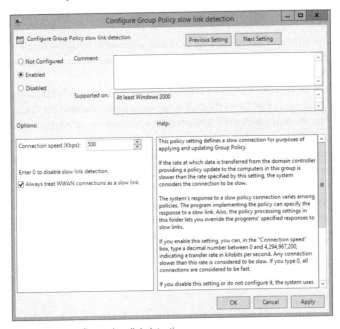

FIGURE 6-12 Configure slow-link detection.

To configure slow-link and background policy processing of key areas of Group Policy, follow these steps:

1. In the GPMC, press and hold or right-click the policy object you want to modify, and then tap or click Edit.

2. Expand Computer Configuration\Administrative Templates\System\Group Policy.

3. Double-tap or double-click the processing policy you want to configure. Click Enabled to define the policy, as shown in Figure 6-13, and then make your configuration selections. The options differ slightly depending on the policy selected and might include the following:

- **Allow Processing Across A Slow Network Connection**   Ensures that the related policy settings are processed even on a slow network

- **Do Not Apply During Periodic Background Processing**   Overrides refresh settings when related policies change after startup or logon

- **Process Even If The Group Policy Objects Have Not Changed**   Forces the client computer to process the related policy settings during a refresh even if the settings haven't changed

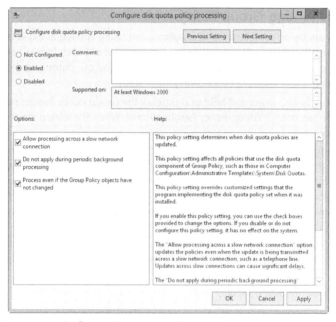

FIGURE 6-13 Configure policy processing for slow links.

4. Tap or click OK to save your settings.

Removing links and deleting GPOs

In the GPMC, you can stop using a linked GPO in two ways:

- Remove a link to a GPO but not the GPO itself.
- Permanently delete the GPO and all links to it.

Removing a link to a GPO stops a site, domain, or organizational unit from using the related policy settings but does not delete the GPO. Because of this, the GPO remains linked to other sites, domains, or organizational units as appropriate. In the GPMC, you can remove a link to a GPO by pressing and holding or right-clicking the GPO link in the container that it is linked to, and then clicking Delete. When prompted to confirm that you want to remove the link, tap or click OK. If you remove all links to the GPO from sites, domains, and organizational units, the GPO continues to exist in the Group Policy Objects container, but its policy settings have no effect in your organization.

Permanently deleting a GPO removes the GPO and all links to it. The GPO will not exist in the Group Policy Objects container and will not be linked to any sites, domains, or organizational units. The only way to recover a deleted GPO is to restore it from a backup (if one is available). In the GPMC, you can remove a GPO and all links to the object from the Group Policy Objects node. Press and hold or right-click the GPO, and then select Delete. When prompted to confirm that you want to remove the GPO and all links to it, tap or click Yes.

Troubleshooting Group Policy

When you are trying to determine why policy is not being applied as expected, one of first things you should do is examine the Resultant Set of Policy for the user and computer experiencing problems with policy settings. You can determine the GPO that a setting is applied from by following these steps:

1. In the GPMC, press and hold or right-click the Group Policy Results node, and then tap or click Group Policy Results Wizard. When the wizard starts, tap or click Next.

2. On the Computer Selection page, select This Computer to view information for the local computer. To view information for a remote computer, select Another Computer, and then tap or click Browse. In the Select Computer dialog box, enter the name of the computer, and then tap or click Check Names. After you select the correct computer account, tap or click OK, and then tap or click Next.

3. On the User Selection page, select the user whose policy information you want to view. You can view policy information for any user who has logged on to the previously selected computer. Tap or click Next.

4. Review the selections you made, and then tap or click Next. After the wizard gathers policy information, tap or click Finish. When the wizard finishes generating the report, the report is selected in the left pane, and the results are displayed in the right pane.

5. To determine the settings that are being applied, browse through the report. Computer and user policy information is listed separately. Computer policy information is listed under Computer Configuration Summary. User policy information is listed under User Configuration Summary.

Using the Gpresult command-line utility, you can also view RSoP. Gpresult provides details about the following:

■ Special settings applied for folder redirection, software installation, disk quota, IPsec, and scripts

■ The last time Group Policy was applied

- The domain controller from which policy was applied, and the security group memberships for the computer and user
- The complete list of GPOs that were applied, and the complete list of GPOs that were not applied because of filters

Gpresult has the following basic syntax:

```
gpresult /s ComputerName /user Domain\UserName
```

Here *ComputerName* is the name of the computer you want to log policy results for, and *Domain\UserName* indicates the user you want to log policy results for. For example, to view the RSoP for CorpPC85 and the user Tedg in the Cpandl domain, you would enter the following command:

```
gpresult /s corppc85 /user cpandl\tedg
```

You can view more detailed output by using one of the two verbose options. The /v parameter turns on verbose output, and results are displayed only for policy settings in effect. The /z parameter turns on verbose output with settings for policy settings in effect and all other GPOs that have the policy set. Because Gpresult output can be fairly long, you should create an HTML report by using the /h parameter, or an XML report by using the /x parameter. The following examples use these parameters:

```
gpresult /s corppc85 /user cpandl\tedg /h gpreport.html
gpresult /s corppc85 /user cpandl\tedg /x gpreport.xml
```

Fixing default Group Policy objects

The Default Domain Policy and Default Domain Controller Policy GPOs are vital to the health of Active Directory Domain Services. If for some reason these policies become corrupted, Group Policy will not function properly. To resolve this, you must use the GPMC to restore a backup of these GPOs. If you are in a disaster-recovery scenario and do not have any backups of the Default Domain Policy or the Default Domain Controller Policy, you can use Dcgpofix to restore the security settings in these policies. The state that Dcgpofix restores these objects to depends on how you modified security and on the security state of the domain controller before you ran Dcgpofix. You must be a member of Domain Admins or Enterprise Admins to run Dcgpofix.

When you run Dcgpofix, both the Default Domain Policy and Default Domain Controller Policy GPOs are restored by default, and you lose any base changes made to these GPOs. Some policy settings are maintained separately and are not lost, including Windows Deployment Services (Windows DS), Security Settings, and Encrypting File System (EFS). Nondefault Security Settings are not maintained, however, which means that other policy changes could also be lost. All other policy settings are restored to their previous values, and any changes you've made are lost.

To run Dcgpofix, log on to a domain controller in the domain in which you want to fix default Group Policy, and then enter **dcgpofix** at an elevated prompt. –Dcgpofix checks the Active Directory schema version number to ensure compatibility between the version of Dcgpofix you are using and the Active Directory schema configuration. If the versions are not compatible, Dcgpofix exits without fixing the default Group Policy objects. By specifying the /ignoreschema parameter, you can enable Dcgpofix to work with different versions of Active Directory. However, default policy objects might not be restored to their original state. Because of this, you should always be sure to use the version of Dcgpofix that is installed with the current operating system.

You also have the option of fixing only the Default Domain Policy or only the Default Domain Controller Policy GPO. If you want to fix only the Default Domain Policy, enter **dcgpofix /target:domain**. If you want to fix only the Default Domain Controller Policy, enter **dcgpofix /target:dc**.

Using Active Directory

Active Directory Domain Services (AD DS) is an extensible and scalable directory service you can use to efficiently manage network resources. As an administrator, you need to be deeply familiar with how Active Directory technology works, and that's exactly what this chapter is about. If you haven't worked with Active Directory technology before, you'll notice immediately that the technology is fairly advanced and has many features.

Introducing Active Directory

For many years now, Active Directory has been the heart of Windows-based domains. Just about every administrative task you perform affects Active Directory in some way. Active Directory technology is based on standard Internet protocols and is designed to help you clearly define your network's structure.

Active Directory and DNS

Active Directory uses Domain Name System (DNS). *DNS* is a standard Internet service that organizes groups of computers into domains. DNS domains are organized into a hierarchical structure. The DNS domain hierarchy is defined on an Internet-wide basis, and the different levels within the hierarchy identify computers, organizational domains, and top-level domains. DNS is also used to map host names to numeric TCP/IP addresses. Through DNS, an Active Directory domain hierarchy can also be defined on an Internet-wide basis, or the domain hierarchy can be separate from the Internet and private.

When you refer to computer resources in a DNS domain, you use a fully qualified domain name (FQDN), such as zeta.microsoft.com. Here, *zeta* represents the name of an individual computer, *microsoft* represents the organizational domain, and *com* is the top-level domain. *Top-level domains (TLDs)* are at the base of the DNS hierarchy. TLDs are organized geographically by using two-letter country codes, such as *CA* for Canada; by organization type, such as *com* for commercial organizations; and by function, such as *mil* for US military installations.

Normal domains, such as microsoft.com, are also referred to as *parent domains* because they're the parents of an organizational structure. You can divide parent domains into subdomains, which you can then use for different offices, divisions, or geographic locations. For example, the FQDN for a computer at the Seattle office for Microsoft could be designated as jacob.seattle.microsoft.com. Here, *jacob* is the computer name, *seattle* is the subdomain, and *microsoft.com* is the parent domain. Another term for a subdomain is a *child domain*.

DNS is an integral part of Active Directory technology—so much so that you must configure DNS on the network before you can install Active Directory. With Windows Server 2012 R2, you install Active Directory in a two-part process. First, you start the process in Server Manager by tapping or clicking Manage and then clicking Add Roles And Features. This runs the Add Roles And Features Wizard, which you use to specify that you want to add the AD DS role to the server. The wizard installs binaries needed for the role, and the progress of this process is shown on the Installation Progress page.

> **REAL WORLD** Binaries needed to install roles and features are referred to as *payloads*. With Windows Server 2012 R2, not only can you uninstall a role or feature, but you also can uninstall and remove the payload for that feature or role by using the –Remove parameter of the Uninstall-WindowsFeature cmdlet.
>
> You can restore a removed payload by using the Install-WindowsFeature cmdlet. By default, payloads are restored via Windows Update. Use the –Source parameter to restore a payload from a WIM mount point. In the following example, you restore the AD DS binaries and all related subfeatures via Windows Update:
>
> ```
> install-windowsfeature -name ad-domain-services
> -includeallsubfeature
> ```

When the installation completes, you start the Active Directory Domain Services Configuration Wizard by tapping or clicking the Promote This Server To A Domain Controller link on the Installation Progress page, and then you use this wizard to configure the role. This wizard replaces Dcpromo.exe, which was used previously for promoting domain controllers. The wizard also will run Adprep.exe to prepare schema as appropriate. If you have not run Adprep.exe separately previously, and you are installing the first domain controller that runs Windows Server 2012 R2 in an existing domain or forest, the wizard will prompt you to supply credentials to run Adprep commands. To prepare a forest, you need to provide credentials for a member of the Enterprise Admins group, the Schema Admins group, and the Domain Admins group in the domain that hosts the schema master. To prepare a domain, you need to provide credentials for a member of the Domain Admins group. If you are installing the first read-only domain controller (RODC) in a forest, you need to provide credentials for a member of the Enterprise Admins group.

If DNS isn't already installed, you are prompted to install it. If no domain exists, the wizard helps you create a domain and configure Active Directory in the new domain. The wizard can also help you add child domains to existing domain structures. To verify that a domain controller is installed correctly, do the following:

- Check the Directory Service event log for errors.
- Ensure that the SYSVOL folder is accessible to clients.
- Verify that name resolution is working through DNS.
- Verify the replication of changes to Active Directory.

NOTE In the rest of this chapter, I'll use the terms *directory* and *domains* to refer to Active Directory and Active Directory domains, respectively, except when I need to distinguish Active Directory structures from DNS or other types of directories.

Keep in mind that when you use Server Manager for Windows Server 2012 R2 and the forest functional level is Windows Server 2003 or higher, any necessary preparations are done automatically when you deploy a domain controller. This means the Configuration Wizard automatically updates the Active Directory schema for the forest and domain so that the schema is compatible with Windows Server 2012 R2 as necessary.

Read-only domain controller deployment

When the domain and forest are operating at the Windows Server 2003 functional level or higher, and your primary domain controller (PDC) emulator for a domain is running Windows Server 2008 or later, you can deploy read-only domain controllers (RODCs). Any domain controller running Windows Server 2008 R2 or later can be configured as an RODC. When you install the DNS Server service on an RODC, the RODC can act as a read-only DNS (RODNS) server. In this configuration, the following conditions are true:

- The RODC replicates the application directory partitions that DNS uses, including the ForestDNSZones and DomainDNSZones partitions. Clients can query an RODNS server for name resolution. However, the RODNS server does not support client updates directly, because the RODNS server does not register resource records for any Active Directory–integrated zone that it hosts.

- When a client attempts to update its DNS records, the server returns a referral. The client can then attempt to update against the DNS server that is provided in the referral. Through replication in the background, the RODNS server then attempts to retrieve the updated record from the DNS server that made the update. This replication request is only for the changed DNS record. The entire list of data changed in the zone or domain is not replicated during this special request.

The first Windows Server 2008 R2 or later domain controller installed in a forest or domain cannot be an RODC. However, you can configure subsequent domain controllers as read-only.

MORE INFO The domain and forest must have the correct schema level to support RODCs and must also be prepared to work with RODCs. Previously, in some cases, this required that you prepare the forest and domain schemas for Windows Server and then update the forest schema again for RODCs. When you use Server Manager for Windows Server 2012 R2, and the Windows Server 2003 or higher forest functional level, any necessary preparations are done automatically as part of domain controller (DC) and RODC deployment.

Features introduced with Windows Server 2008 R2

When you are using Windows Server 2008 R2 and later in your enterprise and have deployed these operating systems on all domain controllers throughout the domains in your Active Directory forest, your domains can operate at the Windows Server 2008 R2 or higher domain functional level, and the forest can operate at the Windows Server 2008 R2 or higher forest functional level. These operating levels allow you to take advantage of the many Active Directory enhancements that improve manageability, performance, and supportability, including the following:

- **Active Directory Recycle Bin** Allows administrators to undo the accidental deletion of Active Directory objects in much the same way as they can recover deleted files from the Windows Recycle Bin. For more information, see the "Using the Active Directory Recycle Bin" section later in this chapter.

- **Managed service accounts** Introduces a special type of domain user account for managed services that reduces service outages and other issues by having Windows manage the account password and related service principal names (SPNs) automatically. For more information, see the "Implementing managed accounts" section in Chapter 9, "Creating user and group accounts."

- **Managed virtual accounts** Introduces a special type of local computer account for managed services that provides the ability to access the network by using a computer identity in a domain environment. For more information, see the "Using virtual accounts" section in Chapter 9.

REAL WORLD Technically, you can use managed service accounts and managed virtual accounts in a mixed-mode domain environment. However, you have to manually manage SPNs for managed service accounts, and the Active Directory schema must be compatible with Windows Server 2008 R2 and higher.

- **Authentication Mechanism Assurance**   Improves the authentication process by allowing administrators to control resource access based on whether a user logs on by using a certificate-based logon method. Thus, an administrator can specify that a user has one set of access permissions when logged on by using a smart card and a different set of access permissions when not logged on by using a smart card.

Other improvements don't require that you raise domain or forest functional levels, but they do require that you use Windows Server 2008 or later. These improvements include the following:

- **Offline domain join**   Allows administrators to preprovision computer accounts in the domain to prepare operating systems for deployment. This allows computers to join a domain without having to contact a domain controller.

- **Active Directory module for Windows PowerShell**   Provides cmdlets for managing Active Directory when you are working with Windows PowerShell.

- **Active Directory Administrative Center**   Provides a task-orientated interface for managing Active Directory. In Server Manager, tap or click Tools, and then tap or click Active Directory Administrative Center.

- **Active Directory Web Services**   Introduces a web service interface for Active Directory domains.

These features are discussed in more detail in Chapter 8, "Core Active Directory administration."

Features introduced with Windows Server 2012

Active Directory Domain Service in Windows Server 2012 has many additional features that give administrators more options for implementing and managing Active Directory. Table 7-1 lists key features. At the least, these features require that you update the Active Directory schema in your forests and domains for Windows Server 2012 or later. You also might need to update the domain, forest, or both functional levels to the Windows Server 2012 or Windows Server 20212 R2 operating level.

TABLE 7-1 Key Active Directory Features for Windows Server 2012

FEATURE	BENEFITS	REQUIREMENTS
Active Directory–based activation	Allows you to use Active Directory to automatically activate clients running Windows 8, Windows 8.1, Windows Server 2012, and Windows Server 2012 R2. Any client connected to the service is activated.	Volume Licensing; Active Directory schema must be updated for at least Windows Server 2012; key is set using Volume Activation server role or command line.
Authentication policies	Allow you to specify access control conditions that restrict the devices that can request Kerberos tickets for user, service, and computer accounts. Applies only to users, computers, managed services accounts, and group managed service accounts.	Accounts must be members of the Protected Users group. Domain controllers must run Windows Server 2012 R2. Windows Server 2012 R2 domain functional level.
Claims-based policy controls	Allow access and audit policies to be defined flexibly.	Claims policy must be enabled for Default Domain Controllers Policy; file servers must run at least Windows Server 2012; domain must have at least one domain controller running Windows Server 2012 or later.
Deferred index creation	Allows deferring of index creation within the directory until UpdateSchemaNow is received or the domain controller is rebooted.	Domain controller must run at least Windows Server 2012.
Enhanced Fine-Grained Password Policy	Allows administrators to use Active Directory Administrative Center for Windows Server 2012 RTM or R2 to create and manage Password Settings objects (PSOs).	Windows Server 2008 or higher domain functional level.

FEATURE	BENEFITS	REQUIREMENTS
Enhanced Recycle Bin	Allows administrators to recover deleted objects by using Active Directory Administrative Center for Windows Server 2012 RTM or R2.	Domain must have Recycle Bin enabled and Windows Server 2008 R2 or higher forest functional level.
Group Managed Service Accounts	Allow multiple services to share a single managed service account.	Active Directory schema must be updated for at least Windows Server 2012; must have at least one domain controller running Windows Server 2012 or later; services must run on Windows Server 2012 RTM or R2.
Kerberos constrained delegation across domains	Allows managed service accounts to act on behalf of users across domains and forests.	Each affected domain must have at least one domain controller running Windows Server 2012 RTM or R2; front-end server must run Windows Server 2012 RTM or R2; back-end server must run Windows Server 2003 or later; and other additional requirements.
Kerberos with Armoring	Improves domain security; allows a domain-joined client and domain controller to communicate over a protected channel.	Domain controllers must be running Windows Server 2012 RTM or Windows Server 2012 R2; Windows Server 2012 RTM or R2 domain functional level; on clients, enable Require FAST policy; on domain controllers, enable Support CBAC And Kerberos Armoring policy.
Off-premises domain join	Allows a computer to be domain-joined over the Internet.	Domain must be Direct Access–enabled, and domain controllers must run Windows Server 2012 RTM or R2.

FEATURE	BENEFITS	REQUIREMENTS
Protected Users security group	Provides additional protections against authentication threats by requiring accounts that are members of this group to use only Kerberos for authentication.	Domain controllers must run Windows Server 2012 R2. Windows Server 2012 R2 domain functional level.
Relative ID (RID) soft ceiling and warnings	Adds warnings as global RID space is used up. Adds a soft ceiling of 900 million RIDs used that prevents RIDs from being issued until administrator overrides.	A domain controller with RID role must run Windows Server 2012 RTM or R2, and domain controllers must run Windows Server 2012 or later.
Server Manager integration	Allows you to perform all the steps required to deploy local and remote domain controllers.	Windows Server 2012 or later; forest functional level of Windows Server 2003 or higher.
Virtual domain controller cloning	Allows you to safely deploy virtualized replicas of domain controllers. Also helps maintain domain controller state.	A domain controller with the PDC emulator role must run Windows Server 2012 or later, and virtual domain controllers must also run Windows Server 2012 or later.

Working with domain structures

Active Directory provides both logical and physical structures for network components. *Logical structures* help you organize directory objects and manage network accounts and shared resources. Logical structures include the following:

- **Organizational units** A subgroup of domains that often mirrors the organization's business or functional structure
- **Domains** A group of computers that share a common directory database
- **Domain trees** One or more domains that share a contiguous namespace
- **Domain forests** One or more domain trees that share common directory information

Physical structures serve to facilitate network communication and to set physical boundaries around network resources. Physical structures that help you map the physical network structure include the following:

- **Subnets** A network group with a specific IP address range and network mask.
- **Sites** One or more subnets. Sites are used to configure directory access and replication.

Understanding domains

An Active Directory domain is simply a group of computers that share a common directory database. Active Directory domain names must be unique. For example, you can't have two microsoft.com domains, but you can have a parent domain microsoft.com, with the child domains seattle.microsoft.com and ny.microsoft.com. If the domain is part of a private network, the name assigned to a new domain must not conflict with any existing domain name on the private network. If the domain is part of the Internet, the name assigned to a new domain must not conflict with any existing domain name throughout the Internet. To ensure uniqueness on the Internet, you must register the parent domain name before using it. You can register a domain through any designated registrar. You can find a current list of designated registrars at InterNIC (*www.internic.net*).

Each domain has its own security policies and trust relationships with other domains. Domains can also span more than one physical location, which means that a domain can consist of multiple sites and those sites can have multiple subnets, as shown in Figure 7-1. Within a domain's directory database, you'll find objects defining accounts for users, groups, computers, and shared resources such as printers and folders.

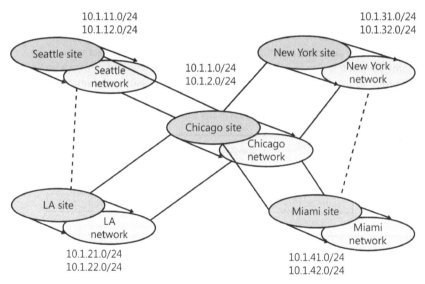

FIGURE 7-1 This network diagram depicts a wide area network (WAN) with multiple sites and subnets.

NOTE User and group accounts are discussed in Chapter 9. Computer accounts and the various types of computers used in Windows Server domains are discussed in the "Working with Active Directory domains" section later in this chapter.

Domain functions are limited and controlled by the domain functional level. Several domain functional levels are available, including the following:

- **Windows Server 2003** Supports domain controllers running Windows Server 2003 and later
- **Windows Server 2008** Supports domain controllers running Windows Server 2008 and later
- **Windows Server 2008 R2** Supports domain controllers running Windows Server 2008 R2 and later
- **Windows Server 2012** Supports domain controllers running Windows Server 2012 and later
- **Windows Server 2012 R2** Supports domain controllers running Windows Server 2012 R2

For further discussion of domain functional levels, see the "Working with domain functional levels" section later in this chapter.

Understanding domain forests and domain trees

Each Active Directory domain has a DNS domain name, such as microsoft.com. One or more domains sharing the same directory data are referred to as a *forest*. The domain names within this forest can be noncontiguous or contiguous in the DNS naming hierarchy.

When domains have a contiguous naming structure, they're said to be in the same *domain tree*. Figure 7-2 shows an example of a domain tree. In this example, the root domain adatum.com has two child domains: seattle.adatumcom and ny.adatum.com. These domains, in turn, have subdomains. All the domains are part of the same tree because they have the same root domain.

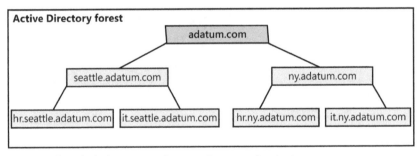

FIGURE 7-2 Domains in the same tree share a contiguous naming structure.

If the domains in a forest have noncontiguous DNS names, they form separate domain trees within the forest. As shown in Figure 7-3, a domain forest can have one or more domain trees. In this example, the adatum.com and microsoft.com domains form the roots of separate domain trees in the same forest.

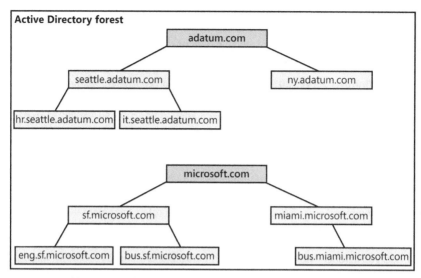

FIGURE 7-3 Multiple trees in a forest with noncontiguous naming structures.

You can access domain structures by using Active Directory Domains And Trusts, shown in Figure 7-4. Active Directory Domains And Trusts is a snap-in for the Microsoft Management Console (MMC). You can also start it from the Tools menu in Server Manager. You'll find separate entries for each root domain. In Figure 7-4, the active domain is cpandl.com.

FIGURE 7-4 Use Active Directory Domains And Trusts to work with domains, domain trees, and domain forests.

Forest functions are limited and controlled by the forest functional level. Several forest functional levels are available, including the ones listed here:

- **Windows Server 2003**   Supports domain controllers running Windows Server 2003 and later
- **Windows Server 2008**   Supports domain controllers running Windows Server 2008 and later

- **Windows Server 2008 R2** Supports domain controllers running Windows Server 2008 R2 and later
- **Windows Server 2012** Supports domain controllers running Windows Server 2012 and later
- **Windows Server 2012 R2** Supports domain controllers running Windows Server 2012 R2

When all domains within a forest are operating in Windows Server 2003 forest functional level, you'll notice improvements over earlier implementations in global catalog replication and replication efficiency. Because link values are replicated, you might also notice improved intersite replication. You can deactivate schema class objects and attributes; use dynamic auxiliary classes; rename domains; and create one-way, two-way, and transitive forest trusts.

The Windows Server 2008 forest functional level offers incremental improve-ments over the Windows Server 2003 forest functional level in Active Directory performance and features. When all domains within a forest are operating in this mode, you'll notice improvements in both intersite and intrasite replication through-out the organization. Domain controllers can also use Distributed File System (DFS) replication rather than file replication service (FRS) replication. In addition, Windows Server 2008 security principals are not created until the PDC emulator operations master in the forest root domain is running Windows Server 2008.

The Windows Server 2008 R2 forest functional level has several additional features. These features include the Active Directory Recycle Bin, managed service accounts, and Authentication Mechanism Assurance.

Although Active Directory for Windows Server 2012 has many enhancements, most of these enhancements require using only Windows Server 2012 domain controllers and schema. The main exception is for Kerberos with Armoring, which requires the Windows Server 2012 domain functional level. Because the key Active Directory enhancements introduced with Windows Server 2012 R2 require the Windows Server 2012 R2 domain functional level, you'll need to use only Windows Server 2012 R2 domain controllers and schema if you want to take advantage of authentication policies and protected users.

Generally, you cannot lower the forest functional level after you raise it. However, when you raise the forest functional level to Windows Server 2012 or higher, you can lower it. If you are using Windows Server 2012 forest functional level, you can lower it to Windows Server 2008 R2. If you are using Windows Server 2012 R2 forest functional level, you can lower it to Windows Server 2012 or Windows Server 2008 R2. Additionally, with either scenario, if Active Directory Recycle Bin has not been enabled, you can lower the forest functional level to Windows Server 2008. You cannot roll the domain functional level back to Windows Server 2003 or lower.

Understanding organizational units

Organizational units (OUs) are subgroups within domains that often mirror an organ-ization's functional or business structure. You can also think of OUs as logical containers into which you place accounts, shared resources, and other OUs. For example, you could create OUs named HumanResources, IT, Engineering, and Marketing for the microsoft.com domain. You could later expand this scheme to include child units. Child OUs for Marketing could include OnlineSales, ChannelSales, and PrintSales.

Objects placed in an OU can come only from the parent domain. For example, OUs associated with seattle.microsoft.com can contain objects for this domain only. You can't add objects from ny.microsoft.com to these containers, but you could create separate OUs to mirror the business structure of seattle.microsoft.com.

OUs are helpful in organizing objects to reflect a business or functional structure. Still, this isn't the only reason to use OUs. Other reasons include the following:

- OUs allow you to assign group policies to a small set of resources in a domain without applying the policies to the entire domain. This helps you set and manage group policies at the appropriate level in the enterprise.

- OUs create smaller, more manageable views of directory objects in a domain. This helps you manage resources more efficiently.

- OUs allow you to delegate authority and to easily control administrative access to domain resources. This helps you control the scope of administrator privileges in the domain. You could grant user A administrative authority for one OU and not for others. Meanwhile, you could grant user B administrative authority for all OUs in the domain.

OUs are represented as folders in Active Directory Users And Computers, as shown in Figure 7-5. This utility is a snap-in for the MMC, and you can also start it from the Tools menu in Server Manager.

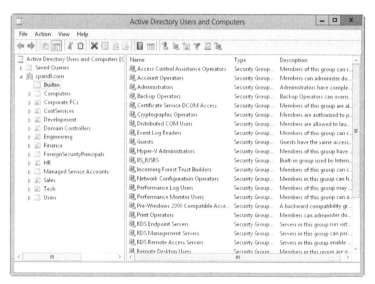

FIGURE 7-5 Use Active Directory Users And Computers to manage users, groups, computers, and organizational units.

Understanding sites and subnets

A *site* is a group of computers in one or more IP subnets. You use sites to map your network's physical structure. Site mappings are independent of logical domain structures, so there's no necessary relationship between a network's physical structure and its logical domain structure. With Active Directory, you can create multiple sites within a single domain or create a single site that serves multiple domains. The IP address ranges used by a site and the domain namespace also have no connection.

You can think of a subnet as a group of network addresses. Unlike sites, which can have multiple IP address ranges, subnets have a specific IP address range and network mask. Subnet names are shown in the form *network/bits-masked*, such as 192.168.19.0/24. In this case, the network address 192.168.19.9 and network mask 255.255.255.0 are combined to create the subnet name 192.168.19.0/24.

> **NOTE** Don't worry—you don't need to know how to create a subnet name. In most cases, you enter the network address and the network mask, and then Windows Server generates the subnet name for you.

Computers are assigned to sites based on their location in a subnet or a set of subnets. If computers in subnets can communicate efficiently with one another over the network, they're said to be *well connected*. Ideally, sites consist of subnets and computers that are all well connected. If the subnets and computers aren't well connected, you might need to set up multiple sites. Being well connected gives sites several advantages:

- When clients log on to a domain, the authentication process first searches for domain controllers that are in the same site as the client. This means that local domain controllers are used first, if possible, which localizes network traffic and can speed up the authentication process.

- Directory information is replicated more frequently within sites than between sites. This reduces the network traffic load caused by replication while ensuring that local domain controllers get up-to-date information quickly. You can also use site links to customize how directory information is replicated between sites. A domain controller that is designated to perform intersite replication is called a *bridgehead server*. By designating a bridgehead server to handle replication between sites, you place the bulk of the intersite replication burden on a specific server rather than on any available server in a site.

You access sites and subnets through Active Directory Sites And Services, shown in Figure 7-6. Because this is a snap-in for the MMC, you can add it to any update-able console. You can also open Active Directory Sites And Services from the Tools menu in Server Manager.

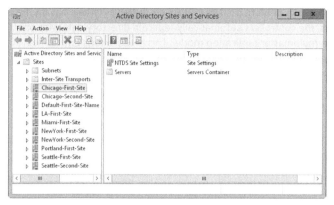

FIGURE 7-6 Use Active Directory Sites And Services to manage sites and subnets.

Working with Active Directory domains

Although you must configure both Active Directory and DNS on a Windows Server network, Active Directory domains and DNS domains have different purposes. Active Directory domains help you manage accounts, resources, and security. DNS domains establish a domain hierarchy that is primarily used for name resolution. Windows Server uses DNS to map host names, such as zeta.microsoft.com, to numeric TCP/IP addresses, such as 172.16.18.8.

Using computers with Active Directory

User computers running professional or business editions of Windows can make full use of Active Directory. These computers access the network as Active Directory clients and have full use of Active Directory features. As clients, these systems can use transitive trust relationships that exist within the domain tree or forest. A transitive trust is one that isn't established explicitly. Rather, the trust is established automatically based on the forest structure and permissions set in the forest. These relationships allow authorized users to access resources in any domain in the forest.

Server computers provide services to other systems and can act as domain controllers or member servers. A domain controller is distinguished from a member server because it runs Active Directory Domain Services. You promote member servers to domain controllers by installing Active Directory Domain Services. You demote domain controllers to member servers by uninstalling Active Directory Domain Services. You use the Add Role And Features and Remove Role And Features wizards to add or remove Active Directory Domain Services. You promote or demote a server through the Active Directory Installation Wizard (Dcpromo.exe).

Domains can have one or more domain controllers. When a domain has multiple domain controllers, the controllers automatically replicate directory data with one another by using a multimaster replication model. This model allows any domain controller to process directory changes and then replicate those changes to other domain controllers.

Because of the multimaster domain structure, all domain controllers have equal responsibility by default. You can, however, give some domain controllers precedence over others for certain tasks, such as specifying a bridgehead server that has priority in replicating directory information to other sites. In addition, some tasks are best performed by a single server. A server that handles this type of task is called an *operations master*. There are five flexible single master operations (FSMO) roles, and you can assign each to a different domain controller. For more information, see the "Understanding operations master roles" section later in this chapter.

Every Windows-based computer that joins a domain has a computer account. Like other resources, computer accounts are stored in Active Directory as objects. You use computer accounts to control access to the network and its resources. A computer accesses a domain by using its account, which is authenticated before the computer can access the network.

REAL WORLD Domain controllers use Active Directory's global catalog to authenticate both computer and user logons. If the global catalog is unavailable, only members of the Domain Admins group can log on to the domain because the universal group membership information is stored in the global catalog, and this information is required for authentication. In Windows Server 2003 and later servers, you have the option of caching universal group membership locally, which solves this problem. For more information, see the "Understanding the directory structure" section later in this chapter.

Working with domain functional levels

To support domain structures, Active Directory includes support for the following domain functional levels:

- **Windows Server 2003 mode**   When the domain is operating in Windows Server 2003 mode, the directory supports domain controllers running Windows Server 2003 or later. A domain operating in Windows Server 2003 mode can use universal groups, group nesting, group type conversion, easy domain controller renaming, update logon time stamps, and Kerberos KDC key version numbers.

- **Windows Server 2008 mode**   When the domain is operating in Windows Server 2008 mode, the directory supports domain controllers running Windows Server 2008 or later. Domain controllers running Windows Server 2003 are no longer supported. A domain operating in Windows Server 2008 mode can use additional Active Directory features, including the DFS replication service for enhanced intersite and intrasite replication.

- **Windows Server 2008 R2 mode**   When the domain is operating in Windows Server 2008 R2 mode, the directory supports domain controllers running Windows Server 2008 R2 or later. Domain controllers running Windows Server 2003 and Windows Server 2008 are no longer supported. A domain operating in Windows Server 2008 R2 mode can use Active Directory Recycle Bin, managed service accounts, Authentication Mechanism Assurance, and other important Active Directory enhancements.

- **Windows Server 2012 mode**   When the domain is operating in Windows Server 2012 mode, the directory supports domain controllers running Windows Server 2012 or later. Domain controllers running Windows Server 2003, Windows Server 2008, and Windows Server 2008 R2 are no longer supported. Active Directory schema for Windows Server 2012 includes many enhancements, but only the Kerberos with Armoring feature requires this mode.

- **Windows Server 2012 R2 mode**   When the domain is operating in Windows Server 2012 R2 mode, the directory supports domain controllers running Windows Server 2012 R2. Domain controllers running Windows Server 2003, Windows Server 2008, Windows Server 2008 R2, and Windows Server 2012 are no longer supported. Active Directory schema for Windows Server 2012 R2 includes enhancements, but only authentication policies and protected users require this mode.

Generally, you cannot lower the domain functional level after you raise it. However, when you raise the domain functional level to Windows Server 2008 R2 or higher, and the forest functional level is Windows Server 2008 or lower, you have the option of rolling the domain functional level back to Windows Server 2008 or Windows Server 2008 R2. You cannot roll the domain functional level back to Windows Server 2003 or lower.

Using the Windows Server 2003 functional level

Every domain in your enterprise should be operating at the Windows Server 2003 functional level or higher, if possible, which will ensure computers in your domains can take advantage of many of the most recent enhancements to Active Directory. After you decommission Windows NT structures and upgrade the Windows 2000 structures in your organization, you can change the functional level to Windows Server 2003 mode operations.

Before updating Windows 2000 domain controllers, you should prepare the domain for upgrade. To do this, you need to update the forest and the domain schema so that they are compatible with Windows Server 2003 domains. A tool called Adprep.exe is provided to automatically perform the update for you. All you need to do is run the tool on the schema operations master in the forest and then on the infrastructure operations master for each domain in the forest. As always, you should test any procedure in a lab before performing it in a production environment.

On the Windows Server 2003 installation media, you'll find Adprep and related files in the i386 subfolder. Follow these steps to perform the upgrade:

1. On the schema operations master in the forest, run **<cdrom>:\support\adprep\adprep.exe /forestprep**. You need to use an administrator account that is a member of Enterprise Admins, Schema Admins, or Domain Admins in the forest root domain.

2. On the infrastructure operations master for each domain in the forest, run **<cdrom>:\support\adprep\adprep.exe /domainprep**. You need to use an account that is a member of the Domain Admins group in an applicable domain.

NOTE To determine which server is the current schema operations master for the domain, open a command prompt and enter **dsquery server -hasfsmo schema**. A directory service path string is returned containing the name of the server, such as "CN =CORPSERVER01,CN=Servers,CN=Default-First-Site-Name,CN=Sites, CN=Configuration,DC=microsoft,DC=com." This string tells you that the schema operations master is CORPSERVER01 in the microsoft.com domain.

NOTE To determine which server is the current infrastructure operations master for the domain, start a command prompt and enter **dsquery server -hasfsmo infr**.

REAL WORLD Generally, anything you can enter at a command prompt can be entered at the Windows PowerShell prompt, too. This is possible because Windows PowerShell looks for external commands and utilities as part of its normal processing. As long as the external command or utility is found in a directory specified by the PATH environment variable, the command or utility is run as appropriate. However, keep in mind that the Windows PowerShell execution order could affect whether a command runs as expected. For Windows PowerShell, the execution order is 1) alternate built-in or profile-defined aliases, 2) built-in or profile-defined functions, 3) cmdlets or language keywords, 4) scripts with the .ps1 extension, and 5) external commands, utilities, and files. Thus, if any element in steps 1 through 4 of the execution order has the same name as a command, that element will run instead of the expected command.

After upgrading your servers, you can raise the domain and forest functionality to take advantage of the additional Active Directory features of the Windows Server 2003 functional level. Keep in mind that after you upgrade, you can use only Windows Server 2003 and later resources in the domain, and you can't go back to any other mode. You should use Windows Server 2003 mode only when you're certain that you don't need Windows NT domain structures, backup domain controllers (BDCs) running Windows NT, or Windows 2000 domain structures.

Using the Windows Server 2008 functional level

After you upgrade the Windows 2000 and Windows Server 2003 structures in your organization, you can change the functional level to Windows Server 2008 mode operations.

Before updating Windows Server 2003 domain controllers, you should prepare the domain for Windows Server 2008. To do this, you need to use Adprep.exe to update the forest and the domain schema so that they are compatible with Windows Server 2008 domains. Follow these steps:

1. On the schema operations master in the forest, copy the contents of the Sources\Adprep folder from the Windows Server 2008 installation media to a local folder, and then run **adprep /forestprep**. If you plan to install any read-only domain controllers, you should also run **adprep /rodcprep**. You need to use an administrator account that is a member of Enterprise Admins, Schema Admins, or Domain Admins in the forest root domain.

2. On the infrastructure operations master for each domain in the forest, copy the contents of the Sources\Adprep folder from the Windows Server 2008 installation media to a local folder, and then run **adprep /domainprep**. You need to use an account that is a member of the Domain Admins group in an applicable domain.

3. If you haven't previously run adprep /domainprep /gpprep in each domain, you need to manually perform this task. Server Manager for Windows Server 2012 R2 will not prepare Group Policy for you. Note that Group Policy needs to be prepared only the first time you deploy domain controllers running Windows Server 2003 SP1 or later. Running adprep /gpprep modifies the access control entries (ACEs) for all Group Policy Object (GPO) folders in the SYSVOL directory to grant read access to all enterprise domain controllers. This level of access is required to support Resultant Set of Policy (RSoP) for site-based policy and causes the NT File Replication Service (NTFRS) to resend all GPOs to all domain controllers.

As always, you should test any procedure in a lab before performing it in a production environment.

> **NOTE** To determine which server is the current schema operations master for the domain, start a command prompt and enter **dsquery server -hasfsmo schema**. To determine which server is the current infrastructure operations master for the domain, start a command prompt and enter **dsquery server -hasfsmo infr**.

After upgrading all domain controllers to Windows Server 2008, you can raise the domain and forest level functionality to take advantage of additional Active Directory features. If you do this, you can use only Windows Server 2008 or later resources in the domain and you can't go back to any other mode. You should use Windows Server 2008 mode only when you're certain that you don't need Windows NT domain structures, Windows NT BDCs, or Windows 2000 or Windows Server 2003 domain structures.

Using the Windows Server 2008 R2 functional level

Windows Server 2008 R2 and later run only on 64-bit hardware. You'll likely need to install Windows Server 2008 R2 and later on new hardware rather than hardware designed for earlier releases of Windows Server.

Before updating domain controllers running Windows Server 2008, you should prepare the domain for Windows Server 2008 R2. To do this, you need to use Adprep.exe to update the forest and the domain schema so that they are compatible with Windows Server 2008 R2 domains. Follow these steps:

1. On the schema operations master in the forest, copy the contents of the Support\Adprep folder from the Windows Server 2008 R2 installation media to a local folder, and then run **adprep /forestprep**. If you plan to install any read-only domain controllers, you should also run **adprep /rodcprep**. You need to use an administrator account that is a member of Enterprise Admins, Schema Admins, or Domain Admins in the forest root domain.

2. On the infrastructure operations master for each domain in the forest, copy the contents of the Support\Adprep folder from the Windows Server 2008 R2 installation media to a local folder, and then run **adprep /domainprep**. You need to use an account that is a member of the Domain Admins group in an applicable domain.

As always, you should test any procedure in a lab before performing it in a production environment.

NOTE To determine which server is the current schema operations master for the domain, start a command prompt and enter **dsquery server -hasfsmo schema**. To determine which server is the current infrastructure operations master for the domain, start a command prompt and enter **dsquery server -hasfsmo infr**.

After upgrading all domain controllers to Windows Server 2008 R2, you can raise the domain and forest level functionality to take advantage of the latest Active Directory features. If you do this, you can use only Windows Server 2008 R2 resources in the domain. You should use Windows Server 2008 R2 mode only when you're certain that you don't need old Windows NT domain structures; Windows NT BDCs; or Windows 2000, Windows Server 2003, or Windows Server 2008 domain structures.

Using the Windows Server 2012 functional level

Windows Server 2012 runs only on 64-bit hardware. Unlike earlier releases of Windows Server, the domain and forest preparations required for updating Active Directory schema don't need to be performed manually. Instead, when you use Server Manager for Windows Server 2012, and the forest functional level is Windows Server 2003 or higher, any necessary preparations are done automatically when you deploy a domain controller running Windows Server 2012. This means the Configuration Wizard automatically updates forest and domain schema.

You also have the option of manually preparing for Windows Server 2012. To do this, you can use Adprep.exe to update the forest and the domain schema so that they are compatible with Windows Server 2012 domains. The steps are similar to those discussed in the previous section.

After upgrading all domain controllers to Windows Server 2012, you can raise the domain and forest level functionality to take advantage of the latest Active Directory features. If you do this, you can use only Windows Server 2012 resources in the domain.

Using the Windows Server 2012 R2 functional level

Windows Server 2012 R2 runs only on 64-bit hardware. As with Windows Server 2012 RTM, the domain and forest preparations required for updating Active Directory schema don't need to be performed manually. Instead, when you use Server Manager for Windows Server 2012 R2, and the forest functional level is Windows Server 2003 or higher, any necessary preparations are done automatically when you deploy a domain controller running Windows Server 2012 R2. This means the Configuration Wizard automatically updates forest and domain schema.

As with Windows Server 2012 RTM, you also have the option of manually preparing for Windows Server 2012 R2. After upgrading all domain controllers to Windows Server 2012 R2, you can raise the domain and forest level functionality to take advantage of the latest Active Directory features. If you do this, you can use only Windows Server 2012 R2 resources in the domain.

Raising or lowering domain and forest functionality

Domains operating in a Windows Server 2003 or higher functional level can use universal groups, group nesting, group type conversion, update logon time stamps, and Kerberos KDC key version numbers. In this mode or higher, administrators can do the following:

- Rename domain controllers without having to demote them first.
- Rename domains running on Windows Server 2003 or higher domain controllers.
- Create extended two-way trusts between two forests.
- Restructure domains in the domain hierarchy by renaming them and putting them at different levels.
- Take advantage of replication enhancements for individual group members and global catalogs.

As compared to earlier implementations, forests operating in a Windows Server 2003 or higher functional level have better global catalog replication and intrasite and intersite replication efficiency, in addition to the ability to establish one-way, two-way, and transitive forest trusts.

REAL WORLD The domain and forest upgrade process can generate a lot of network traffic while information is being replicated around the network. Sometimes the entire upgrade process can take 15 minutes or longer. During this time, you might experience delayed responsiveness when communicating with servers and higher latency on the network, so you might want to schedule the upgrade outside normal business hours. It's also a good idea to thoroughly test compatibility with existing applications (especially legacy applications) before performing this operation.

You can raise the domain level functionality by following these steps:

1. Open Active Directory Domains And Trusts. In the console tree, press and hold or right-click the domain you want to work with, and then tap or click Raise Domain Functional Level. The current domain name and functional level are displayed in the Raise Domain Functional Level dialog box.

2. To change the domain functionality, select the new domain functional level from the list provided, and then tap or click Raise.

3. Tap or click OK. The new domain functional level is replicated to each domain controller in the domain. This operation can take some time in a large organization.

You can raise the forest level functionality by following these steps:

1. Open Active Directory Domains And Trusts. In the console tree, press and hold or right-click the Active Directory Domains And Trusts node, and then tap or click Raise Forest Functional Level. The current forest name and functional level are displayed in the Raise Forest Functional Level dialog box.

2. To change the forest functionality, select the new forest functional level by using the list provided, and then tap or click Raise.

3. Tap or click OK. The new forest functional level is replicated to each domain controller in each domain in the forest. This operation can take some time in a large organization.

Another way to raise domain or forest functional level is to use Active Directory Administrative Center. This tool is available as an option on the Tools menu in Server Manager. Follow these steps to raise the domain functional level:

1. In Active Directory Administrative Center, the local domain is opened for management by default. If you want to work with a different domain, tap or click Manage, and then tap or click Add Navigation Nodes. In the Add Navigation Nodes dialog box, select the domain you want to work with, and then tap or click OK.

2. Select the domain you want to work with by tapping or clicking it in the left pane. In the Tasks pane, tap or click Raise The Domain Functional Level. The current domain name and functional level are displayed in the Raise Domain Functional Level dialog box.

3. To change the domain functionality, select the new domain functional level by using the list provided, and then tap or click Raise.

4. Tap or click OK. The new domain functional level is replicated to each domain controller in the domain. This operation can take some time in a large organization.

Follow these steps to raise the forest functional level:

1. In Active Directory Administrative Center, select the domain you want to work with by tapping or clicking it in the left pane. In the Tasks pane, tap or click Raise The Forest Functional Level. The current forest name and functional level are displayed in the Raise Forest Functional Level dialog box.

2. To change the forest functionality, select the new forest functional level by using the list provided, and then tap or click Raise.

3. Tap or click OK. The new forest functional level is replicated to each domain controller in each domain in the forest. This operation can take some time in a large organization.

Generally, you cannot lower the forest or domain functional level after you raise it. However, there are specific exceptions as discussed previously in this chapter. Keep in mind that if you enabled the Active Directory Recycle Bin, you won't be able to lower the forest functional level.

Understanding the directory structure

Active Directory has many components and is built on many technologies. Directory data is made available to users and computers through data stores and global catalogs. Although most Active Directory tasks affect the data store, global catalogs are equally important because they're used during logon and for information searches. In fact, if the global catalog is unavailable, standard users can't log on to the domain. The only way to change this behavior is to cache universal group membership locally. As you might expect, caching universal group membership has advantages and disadvantages, which I'll discuss in a moment.

You access and distribute Active Directory data by using directory access protocols and replication. *Directory access protocols* allow clients to communicate with computers running Active Directory. *Replication* is necessary to ensure that updates to data are distributed to domain controllers. Although multimaster replication is the primary technique you use to distribute updates, some changes to data can be handled only by individual domain controllers called *operations masters*. A feature of Windows Server 2008 or later called *application directory partitions* also changes the way multimaster replication works.

With application directory partitions, enterprise administrators (those belonging to the Enterprise Admins group) can create replication partitions in the domain forest. These partitions are logical structures used to control the replication of data within a domain forest. For example, you could create a partition to strictly control the replication of DNS information within a domain, thereby preventing other systems in the domain from replicating DNS information.

An application directory partition can appear as a child of a domain, a child of another application partition, or a new tree in the domain forest. Replicas of the application directory partition can be made available on any Active Directory domain controller running Windows Server 2008 or later, including global catalog servers. Although application directory partitions are useful in large domains and forests, they add overhead in terms of planning, administration, and maintenance.

Exploring the data store

The data store contains information about objects, such as accounts, shared resources, OUs, and group policies. Another name for the data store is the *directory*, which refers to Active Directory itself.

Domain controllers store the directory in a file called Ntds.dit. This file's location is set when Active Directory is installed, and it should be on an NTFS file system drive formatted for use with Windows Server 2008 or later. You can also save directory data separately from the main data store. This is true for group policies, scripts, and other types of public information stored on the shared system volume (SYSVOL).

Sharing directory information is called *publishing*. For example, you publish information about a printer by sharing the printer over the network. Similarly, you publish information about a folder by sharing the folder over the network.

Domain controllers replicate most changes to the data store in multimaster fashion. Administrators for small or medium-size organizations rarely need to manage replication of the data store. Replication is handled automatically, but you can customize it to meet the needs of large organizations or organizations with special requirements.

Not all directory data is replicated. Instead, only public information that falls into one of the following three categories is replicated:

- **Domain data**   Contains information about objects within a domain. This includes objects for accounts, shared resources, organizational units, and group policies.
- **Configuration data**   Describes the directory's topology. This includes a list of all domains, domain trees, and forests, and also the locations of the domain controllers and global catalog servers.
- **Schema data**   Describes all objects and data types that can be stored in the directory. The default schema provided with Windows Server describes account objects, shared resource objects, and more. You can extend the default schema by defining new objects and attributes or by adding attributes to existing objects.

Exploring global catalogs

When universal group membership isn't cached locally, global catalogs enable network logon by providing universal group membership information when a logon process is initiated. Global catalogs also enable directory searches throughout the domains in a forest. A domain controller designated as a global catalog stores a full replica of all objects in the directory for its host domain and a partial replica for all other domains in the domain forest.

NOTE   Partial replicas are used because only certain object properties are needed for logon and search operations. Partial replication also means that less information needs to be circulated on the network, reducing the amount of network traffic.

By default, the first domain controller installed on a domain is designated as the global catalog. If only one domain controller is in the domain, the domain controller and the global catalog are the same server. Otherwise, the global catalog is on the domain controller you've configured as such. You can also add global catalogs to a domain to help improve response time for logon and search requests. The recommended technique is to have one global catalog per site within a domain.

Domain controllers hosting the global catalog should be well connected to domain controllers acting as infrastructure masters. The role of infrastructure master is one of the five operations master roles you can assign to a domain controller. In a domain, the infrastructure master is responsible for updating object references. The infrastructure master does this by comparing its data with that of a global catalog. If the infrastructure master finds outdated data, it requests updated data from a global catalog. The infrastructure master then replicates the changes to the other domain controllers in the domain. For more information about operations master roles, see the "Understanding operations master roles" section later in this chapter.

When only one domain controller is in a domain, you can assign the infrastructure master role and the global catalog to the same domain controller. When two or more domain controllers are in the domain, however, the global catalog and the infrastructure master must be on separate domain controllers. If they aren't, the infrastructure master won't find out-of-date data and will never replicate changes. The only exception is when all domain controllers in the domain host the global catalog. In this case, it doesn't matter which domain controller serves as the infrastructure master.

One of the key reasons to configure additional global catalogs in a domain is to ensure that a catalog is available to service logon and directory search requests. Again, if the domain has only one global catalog and the catalog isn't available, and there's no local caching of universal group membership, standard users can't log on, and those who are logged on can't search the directory. In this scenario, the only users who can log on to the domain when the global catalog is unavailable are members of the Domain Admins group.

Searches in the global catalog are very efficient. The catalog contains information about objects in all domains in the forest. This allows directory search requests to be resolved in a local domain rather than in a domain in another part of the network. Resolving queries locally reduces the network load and allows for quicker responses in most cases.

TIP If you notice slow logon or query response times, you might want to configure additional global catalogs. But more global catalogs usually means more replication data being transferred over the network.

Universal group membership caching

In a large organization, having global catalogs at every office location might not be practical. Not having global catalogs at every office location presents a problem, however, if a remote office loses connectivity with the main office or a designated branch office where global catalog servers reside. If this occurs, standard users won't be able to log on; only members of Domain Admins will be able to log on. This happens because logon requests must be routed over the network to a global catalog server at a different office, and this isn't possible with no connectivity.

As you might expect, you can resolve this problem in many ways. You can make one of the domain controllers at the remote office a global catalog server by following the procedure discussed in the "Configuring global catalogs" section in Chapter 8. The disadvantage of this approach is that the designated server or servers will have an additional burden placed on them and might require additional resources. You also have to manage more carefully the up time of the global catalog server.

Another way to resolve this problem is to cache universal group membership locally. Here, any domain controller can resolve logon requests locally without having to go through a global catalog server. This allows for faster logons and makes managing server outages much easier because your domain isn't relying on a single server or a group of servers for logons. This solution also reduces replication traffic. Instead of replicating the entire global catalog periodically over the network, only the universal group membership information in the cache is refreshed. By default, a refresh occurs every eight hours on each domain controller that's caching membership locally.

Universal group membership caching is site-specific. Remember, a site is a physical directory structure consisting of one or more subnets with a specific IP address range and network mask. The domain controllers running Windows Server and the global catalog they're contacting must be in the same site. If you have multiple sites, you need to configure local caching in each site. Additionally, users in the site must be part of a Windows domain running in a Windows Server 2003 or higher functional mode. To learn how to configure caching, see the "Configuring universal group membership caching" section in Chapter 8.

Replication and Active Directory

Regardless of whether you use FRS or DFS replication, the three types of information stored in the directory are domain data, schema data, and configuration data.

Domain data is replicated to all domain controllers within a particular domain. Schema and configuration data are replicated to all domains in the domain tree or forest. In addition, all objects in an individual domain and a subset of object properties in the domain forest are replicated to global catalogs.

This means that domain controllers store and replicate the following:

- Schema information for the domain tree or forest
- Configuration information for all domains in the domain tree or forest
- All directory objects and properties for their respective domains

However, domain controllers hosting a global catalog store and replicate schema information for the forest and configuration information for all domains in the forest. They also store and replicate a subset of the properties for all directory objects in the forest that's replicated only between servers hosting global catalogs and all directory objects and properties for their respective domain:

- Schema information for the forest
- Configuration information for all domains in the forest
- A subset of the properties between global catalogs
- All directory objects and properties for their domain

To get a better understanding of replication, consider the following scenario, in which you're installing a new network:

1. Start by installing the first domain controller in domain A. The server is the only domain controller and also hosts the global catalog. No replication occurs because no other domain controllers are on the network.

2. Install a second domain controller in domain A. Because there are now two domain controllers, replication begins. To make sure that data is replicated properly, assign one domain controller as the infrastructure master and the other as the global catalog. The infrastructure master watches for updates to the global catalog and requests updates to changed objects. The two domain controllers also replicate schema and configuration data.

3. Install a third domain controller in domain A. This server isn't a global catalog. The infrastructure master watches for updates to the global catalog, requests updates to changed objects, and then replicates those changes to the third domain controller. The three domain controllers also replicate schema and configuration data.

4. Install a new domain, domain B, and add domain controllers to it. The global catalog hosts in domain A and domain B begin replicating all schema and configuration data in addition to a subset of the domain data in each domain. Replication within domain A continues as previously described. Replication within domain B begins.

Active Directory and LDAP

The *Lightweight Directory Access Protocol (LDAP)* is a standard Internet communications protocol for TCP/IP networks. LDAP is designed specifically for accessing directory services with the least amount of overhead. LDAP also defines operations that can be used to query and modify directory information.

Active Directory clients use LDAP to communicate with computers running Active Directory whenever they log on to the network or search for shared resources. You can also use LDAP to manage Active Directory.

LDAP is an open standard that many other directory services use. This makes interdirectory communications easier and provides a clearer migration path from other directory services to Active Directory. You can also use Active Directory Service Interfaces (ADSI) to enhance interoperability. ADSI supports the standard application programming interfaces (APIs) for LDAP that are specified in Internet standard Request for Comments (RFC) 1823. You can use ADSI with Windows Script Host to create and manage objects in Active Directory.

Understanding operations master roles

Operations master roles accomplish tasks that are impractical to perform in multi-master fashion. Five operations master roles are defined, and you can assign these roles to one or more domain controllers. Although certain roles can be assigned only once in a domain forest, other roles must be defined once in each domain.

Every Active Directory forest must have the following roles:

- **Schema master**   Controls updates and modifications to directory schema. To update directory schema, you must have access to the schema master. To determine which server is the current schema master for the domain, start a command prompt and enter **dsquery server -hasfsmo schema**.

- **Domain naming master**   Controls the addition or removal of domains in the forest. To add or remove domains, you must have access to the domain naming master. To determine which server is the current domain naming master for the domain, start a command prompt and enter **dsquery server -hasfsmo name**.

These forestwide roles must be unique in the forest. This means that you can assign only one schema master and one domain naming master in a forest.

Every Active Directory domain must have the following roles:

- **Relative ID master**   Allocates relative IDs to domain controllers. Whenever you create a user, group, or computer object, domain controllers assign a unique security ID to the related object. The security ID consists of the domain's security ID prefix and a unique relative ID allocated by the relative ID (RID) master. To determine which server is the current relative ID master for the domain, start a command prompt and enter **dsquery server -hasfsmo rid**.

- **PDC emulator**   When you use mixed-mode or interim-mode operations, the PDC emulator acts as a Windows NT PDC. Its job is to authenticate Windows NT logons, process password changes, and replicate updates to BDCs. The PDC emulator is the default time server and, as such, also performs time synchronization in a domain. To determine which server is the current PDC emulator for the domain, start a command prompt and enter **dsquery server -hasfsmo pdc**.

- **Infrastructure master**   Updates object references by comparing its directory data with that of a global catalog. If the data is outdated, the infrastructure master requests updated data from a global catalog and then replicates the changes to the other domain controllers in the domain. To determine which server is the current infrastructure operations master for the domain, start a command prompt and enter **dsquery server -hasfsmo infr**.

These domainwide roles must be unique in each domain. This means that you can assign only one relative ID master, one PDC emulator, and one infrastructure master in each domain.

Operations master roles are usually assigned automatically, but you can reassign them. When you install a new network, the first domain controller in the first domain is assigned all the operations master roles. If you later create a child domain or a root domain in a new tree, the first domain controller in the new domain is automatically assigned operations master roles, too. In a new domain forest, the domain controller is assigned all operations master roles. If the new domain is in the same forest, the assigned roles are relative ID master, PDC emulator, and infrastructure master. The schema master and domain naming master roles remain in the first domain in the forest.

When a domain has only one domain controller, that computer handles all the operations master roles. If you're working with a single site, the default operations master locations should be sufficient. As you add domain controllers and domains, however, you'll probably want to move the operations master roles to other domain controllers.

When a domain has two or more domain controllers, you should configure two domain controllers to handle operations master roles. In this case, you make one domain controller the operations master and designate the second as your standby operations master. The standby operations master can then be used if the primary one fails. Be sure that the domain controllers are direct replication partners and are well connected.

As the domain structure grows, you might want to split up the operations master roles and place them on separate domain controllers. This can improve the responsiveness of the operations masters. Pay particular attention to the current responsibilities of the domain controller you plan to use.

BEST PRACTICES Two roles you should not separate are schema master and domain naming master. Always assign these roles to the same server. For the most efficient operations, you also usually want the RID master and PDC emulator to be on the same server. But you can separate these roles if necessary. For example, on a large network where peak loads are causing performance problems, you probably want to place the RID master and PDC emulator on separate domain controllers. Additionally, you usually shouldn't place the infrastructure master on a domain controller hosting a global catalog. See the "Exploring global catalogs" section earlier in this chapter for details.

Using the Active Directory Recycle Bin

When your Active Directory forest is operating in the Windows Server 2008 R2 or higher mode, you can use the Active Directory Recycle Bin. The Active Directory Recycle Bin adds an easy-to-use recovery feature for Active Directory objects. When you enable this feature, all link-valued and nonlink-valued attributes of a deleted object are preserved, allowing you to restore the object to the same state it was in before it was deleted. You can also recover objects from the recycle bin without having to initiate an authoritative restore. This differs substantially from the previously available technique, which used an authoritative restore to recover deleted objects from the Deleted Objects container. Previously, when you deleted an object, most of its non-link-valued attributes were cleared and all of its link-valued attributes were removed, which meant that although you could recover a deleted object, the object was not restored to its previous state.

Preparing schema for the Recycle Bin

Before you can make the Recycle Bin available, you must update Active Directory schema with the required Recycle Bin attributes. You do this by preparing the forest and domain for the Windows Server 2008 R2 functional level or higher. When you do this, the schema is updated, and then every object in the forest is also updated with the Recycle Bin attributes. This process is irreversible after it is started.

After you prepare Active Directory, you need to upgrade all domain controllers in your Active Directory forest to Windows Server 2008 R2 or higher and then raise the domain and forest functional levels to the Windows Server 2008 R2 level or higher. Optionally, you can update Active Directory schema in your forests and domains for Windows Server 2012 or later to enable the enhanced Recycle Bin.

After these operations, you can enable and access the Recycle Bin. When Recycle Bin has been enabled, it cannot be disabled. Now when an Active Directory object is deleted, the object is put in a state referred to as *logically deleted* and moved to the Deleted Objects container, shown in Figure 7-7. Also, its distinguished name is altered. A deleted object remains in the Deleted Objects container for the period of time set in the deleted object lifetime value, which is 180 days by default.

REAL WORLD The msDS-deletedObjectLifetime attribute replaces the tombstone-Lifetime attribute. However, when msDS-deletedObjectLifetime is set to $null, the lifetime value comes from the tombstoneLifetime. If the tombstoneLifetime is also set to $null, the default value is 180 days.

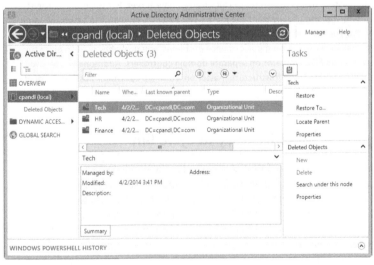

FIGURE 7-7 Deleted objects remain in the Deleted Objects container for the deleted object lifetime value.

Recovering deleted objects

If you elect not to use the Recycle Bin, you can still recover deleted objects from the Deleted Objects container by using an authoritative restore and other techniques I'll discuss in this section. The procedure has not changed from previous releases of Windows Server. What has changed, however, is that the objects are restored to their previous state with all link-valued and non-link-valued attributes preserved. To perform an authoritative restore, the domain controller must be in Directory Services Restore Mode.

Rather than using an authoritative restore and taking a domain controller offline, you can recover deleted objects by using the Ldp.exe administration tool or the Active Directory cmdlets for Windows PowerShell. If you updated the Active Directory schema in your forests and domains for Windows Server 2012 or later, you also can enable the enhanced Recycle Bin, which allows you to recover deleted objects by using Active Directory Administrative Center.

Keep in mind that Active Directory blocks access to an object for a short while after the object is deleted. During this time, Active Directory processes the object's link-value table to maintain referential integrity on the linked attribute's values. Active Directory then permits access to the deleted object.

Using Ldp.exe for basic recovery

You can use Ldp.exe to display the Deleted Objects container and recover a deleted object by following these steps:

1. Type **Ldp.exe** in the Everywhere search box, and then press Enter.

2. On the Options menu, tap or click Controls. In the Controls dialog box, select Return Deleted Objects in the Load Predefined list, and then tap or click OK.

3. Bind to the server that hosts the forest root domain by choosing Bind from the Connection menu. Select the Bind type, and then tap or click OK.

4. On the View menu, tap or click Tree. In the Tree View dialog box, use the BaseDN list to select the appropriate forest root domain name, such as DC=Cpandl,DC=Com, and then tap or click OK.

5. In the console tree, double-tap or double-click the root distinguished name, and then locate the CN=Deleted Objects container.

6. Locate and press and hold or right-click the Active Directory object you want to restore, and then tap or click Modify. This displays the Modify dialog box.

7. In the Edit Entry Attribute box, type **isDeleted**. Do not enter anything in the Values box.

8. Under Operation, tap or click Delete, and then tap or click Enter.

9. In the Edit Entry Attribute box, type **distinguishedName**. In Values, type the original distinguished name of this Active Directory object.

10. Under Operation, tap or click Replace. Select the Extended check box, tap or click Enter, and then tap or click Run.

Using Windows PowerShell for basic and advanced recovery

The Active Directory cmdlets for Windows PowerShell allow you to recover deleted objects by using scripts or by entering commands at a Windows PowerShell prompt. You use Get-ADObject to retrieve the object or objects you want to restore, pass that object or objects to Restore-ADObject, and then Restore-ADObject restores the object or objects to the directory database.

To use the Active Directory cmdlets for recovery, you need to open an elevated, administrator Windows PowerShell prompt by pressing and holding or right-clicking the Windows PowerShell entry on the menu, and then tapping or clicking Run As Administrator. The basic syntax for recovering an object is as follows:

```
Get-ADObject -Filter {ObjectId} -IncludeDeletedObjects | Restore-ADObject
```

ObjectId is a filter value that identifies the object you want to restore. For example, you could restore a deleted user account by display name or SAM account name, as shown in these examples:

```
Get-ADObject -Filter {DisplayName -eq "Rich Tuppy"}
-IncludeDeletedObjects | Restore-ADObject
```

```
Get-ADObject -Filter {SamAccountName -eq "richt"} -IncludeDeletedObjects
| Restore-ADObject
```

Note that nested objects must be recovered from the highest level of the deleted hierarchy to a live parent container. For example, if you accidentally deleted an OU and all its related accounts, you need to restore the OU before you can restore the related accounts.

The basic syntax for restoring container objects such as an OU is as follows:

```
Get-ADObject -ldapFilter:"(msDS-LastKnownRDN=ContainerID)"
-IncludeDeletedObjects | Restore-ADObject
```

ContainerID is a filter value that identifies the container object you want to restore. For example, you could restore the Corporate Services OU, as shown in this example:

```
Get-ADObject -ldapFilter:"(msDS-LastKnownRDN=Corporate_Services)"
-IncludeDeletedObjects | Restore-ADObject
```

If the OU contains accounts you also want to restore, you can now restore the accounts by using the technique discussed previously, or you can restore all accounts at the same time. The basic syntax requires that you establish a search base and associate the accounts with their last known parent, as shown here:

```
Get-ADObject -SearchBase "CN=Deleted Objects,ForestRootDN" -Filter
{lastKnownParent -eq "ContainerCN,ForestRootDN"} -IncludeDeletedObjects |
Restore-ADObject
```

ForestRootDN is the distinguished name of the forest root domain, such as DC=Cpandl,DC=Com, and *ContainerCN* is the common name of the container, such as OU=Corporate_Services or CN=Users. The following example restores all the accounts that were in the Corporate Services OU when it was deleted:

```
Get-ADObject -SearchBase "CN=Deleted Objects,DC=Cpandl,DC=com" -Filter
{lastKnownParent -eq "OU=Corporate_Services,DC=Cpandl,DC=com"}
-IncludeDeletedObjects | Restore-ADObject
```

Using the enhanced Recycle Bin for recovery

The enhanced Recycle Bin makes recovering deleted objects as easy as pointing and clicking or tapping and holding. After you updated the Active Directory schema in your forests and domains for Windows Server 2012 or later, you enable the enhanced Recycle Bin for use by following these steps:

1. In Active Directory Administrative Center, the local domain is opened for management by default. If you want to work with a different domain, tap or click Manage, and then tap or click Add Navigation Nodes. In the Add Navigation Nodes dialog box, select the domain you want to work with, and then tap or click OK.

2. Select the domain you want to work with by tapping or clicking it in the left pane. In the Tasks pane, tap or click Enable Recycle Bin, and then tap or click OK in the confirmation dialog box.

3. Active Directory will begin replicating the change to all domain controllers in the forest. After the change is replicated, the enhanced Recycle Bin will be available for use. If you then tap or click Refresh in Active Directory Administrative Center, you'll notice that a Deleted Object container is now available for domains that use the enhanced Recycle Bin.

Keep in mind that the enhanced Recycle Bin is a forestwide option. When you enable this option in one domain of a forest, Active Directory replicates the change to all domain controllers in all domains of the forest.

With the enhanced Recycle Bin enabled, you can recover deleted objects with ease. In Active Directory Administrative Center, domains using the enhanced Recycle Bin will have a Deleted Object container. In this container, a list of deleted objects is displayed. As discussed previously, deleted objects remain in this container for the deleted object lifetime value, which is 180 days by default.

Each deleted object is listed by name, when it was deleted, the last known parent, and the type. When you select a deleted object by tapping or clicking it, you can use the options in the Tasks pane to work with it. The Restore option restores the object to its original container. For example, if the object was deleted from the Users container, it is restored to this container.

The Restore To option restores the object to an alternate container within its original domain or to a different domain within the current forest. Specify the alternate container in the Restore To dialog box. For example, if the object was deleted from the Users container in the tech.cpandl.com domain, you could restore it to the Devs OU in the eng.cpandl.com domain.

Core Active Directory administration

Core Active Directory administration focuses on key tasks you perform routinely with Active Directory Domain Services (AD DS), such as creating computer accounts or joining computers to a domain. In this chapter, you'll learn about the tools you can use to manage Active Directory and about specific techniques for managing computers, domain controllers, and organizational units (OUs).

Tools for managing Active Directory

Several sets of tools are available for managing Active Directory, including graphical administration tools, command-line tools, support tools, and Windows PowerShell cmdlets.

Active Directory administration tools

Active Directory administration tools are provided as snap-ins for the Microsoft Management Console (MMC). You use the following key tools to manage Active Directory:

- **Active Directory Administrative Center**   For performing management tasks.

- **Active Directory Domains And Trusts**   For working with domains, domain trees, and domain forests.

- **Active Directory Module For Windows PowerShell** For managing Active Directory when you are working with Windows PowerShell.
- **Active Directory Sites And Services** For managing sites and subnets.
- **Active Directory Users And Computers** For managing users, groups, computers, and organizational units.
- **Group Policy Management** For managing the way Group Policy is used in the organization. It provides access to Resultant Set of Policy (RSoP) for modeling and logging.

SECURITY ALERT Windows Firewall can affect remote administration with some MMC snap-ins. If Windows Firewall is enabled on a remote computer and you receive an error message stating that you don't have appropriate rights, the network path isn't found, or access is denied, you might need to configure an exception on the remote computer for incoming TCP port 445. To resolve this problem, you can enable the Windows Firewall: Allow Inbound Remote Administration Exception policy setting within Computer Configuration\Policies\Administrative Templates \Network\Network Connections\Windows Firewall\Domain Profile. Alternatively, enter the following at a command prompt on the remote computer: **netsh firewall set portopening tcp 445 smb enable**. See Microsoft Knowledge Base Article 840634 for more details (*support.microsoft.com/default.aspx?scid=kb;en-us;840634*).

You can access the Active Directory administration tools from the Tools menu in Server Manager, or add them to any updateable MMC. If you're using another computer with access to a Windows Server domain, the tools won't be available until you install them. One technique for installing these tools is to use the Add Roles And Features Wizard to add the Remote Server Administration Tools feature for AD DS.

Active Directory command-line tools

Several tools are provided to let you manage Active Directory from the command line:

- **Adprep** Allows you to manually prepare a Windows forest or domain for installation of Windows domain controllers (DCs). To prepare a forest or a domain, use adprep /forestprep and adprep /domainprep, respectively. If you plan to install any read-only domain controllers, you should also run adprep /rodcprep for the forest.

REAL WORLD As discussed in Chapter 7, "Using Active Directory," Server Manager for Windows Server 2012 R2 automatically prepares forests and domains for you. However, you must use an account with appropriate permissions. For forest and RODC prep to succeed, you need to use an administrator account that is a member of Enterprise Admins, Schema Admins, or Domain Admins in the forest root domain. For domain prep to succeed, you need to use an account that is a member of the Domain Admins group in an applicable domain.

You can run Adprep on any server running a 64-bit version of Windows Server 2008 R2 or later. The server needs network connectivity to the schema master for the forest and the infrastructure master of the domain where you want to add the domain controller. The server from which you are running Adprep should be domain joined.

- **Dsadd** Adds computers, contacts, groups, organizational units, and users to Active Directory. Enter **dsadd objectname /?** at a command prompt to display Help information about using the command, such as dsadd computer /?.

- **Dsget** Displays properties of computers, contacts, groups, organizational units, users, sites, subnets, and servers registered in Active Directory. Enter **dsget objectname /?** at a command prompt to display Help information about using the command, such as dsget subnet /?.

- **Dsmod** Modifies properties of computers, contacts, groups, organizational units, users, and servers that exist in Active Directory. Enter **dsmod objectname /?** at a command prompt to display Help information about using the command, such as dsmod server /?.

- **Dsmove** Moves a single object to a new location within a single domain or renames the object without moving it. Enter **dsmove /?** at a command prompt to display Help information about using the command.

- **Dsquery** Uses search criteria to find computers, contacts, groups, organizational units, users, sites, subnets, and servers in Active Directory. Enter **dsquery /?** at a command prompt to display Help information about using the command.

- **Dsrm** Removes objects from Active Directory. Enter **dsrm /?** at a command prompt to display Help information about using the command.

- **Ntdsutil** Allows the user to view site, domain, and server information; manage operations masters; and perform database maintenance of Active Directory. Enter **ntdsutil /?** at a command prompt to display Help information about using the command.

Whereas Adprep is located in the \support\adprep folder on the Windows Server 2012 R2 installation media, the other tools become available when you install the Remote Server Management Tools for AD DS.

Active Directory support tools

Many support tools for Active Directory are included in the management tools for AD DS. Table 8-1 lists some of the most useful support tools for configuring, managing, and troubleshooting Active Directory.

TABLE 8-1 Quick Reference for Active Directory Support Tools

SUPPORT TOOL	EXECUTABLE NAME	DESCRIPTION
ADSI Edit	Adsiedit.msc	Opens and edits the Active Directory Services Interface for domain, schema, and configuration containers
Active Directory Administration Tool	Ldp.exe	Performs Lightweight Directory Access Protocol (LDAP) operations on Active Directory
Directory Services Access Control Lists Utility	Dsacls.exe	Manages access control lists (ACLs) for objects in Active Directory
Distributed File System Utility	Dfsutil.exe	Manages the Distributed File System (DFS) and displays DFS information
DNS Server Troubleshooting Tool	Dnscmd.exe	Manages properties of Domain Name System (DNS) servers, zones, and resource records
Replication Diagnostics Tool	Repadmin.exe	Manages and monitors replication by using the command line
Windows Domain Manager	Netdom.exe	Allows domain and trust relationships management from the command line

Using Active Directory Users And Computers

Active Directory Users And Computers is one of the primary administration tools you use to manage Active Directory. With this utility, you can handle all user, group, and computer-related tasks, and manage organizational units.

You can start Active Directory Users And Computers by selecting its related option on the Tools menu in Server Manager. You can also add Active Directory Users And Computers as a snap-in to any console that can be updated. By default, Active Directory Users And Computers works with the domain to which your computer is currently connected. You can access computer and user objects in this domain through the console tree, as shown in Figure 8-1. If you can't find a domain controller, or if the domain you want to work with isn't shown, you might need to connect to a domain controller in the current domain or to a domain controller in a different domain. Other high-level tasks you might want to perform with Active Directory Users And Computers are viewing advanced options or searching for objects.

When you access a domain in Active Directory Users And Computers, the following standard set of folders is displayed:

- **Builtin** The list of built-in user accounts and groups.
- **Computers** The default container for computer accounts.

- **Domain Controllers** The default container for domain controllers.
- **ForeignSecurityPrincipals** Information about objects from a trusted external domain. Normally, these objects are created when an object from an external domain is added to a group in the current domain.
- **Managed Service Accounts** The default container for managed service accounts.
- **Microsoft Exchange Security Groups** The default container for groups used by Microsoft Exchange Server. This folder is listed only if Exchange Server is running in the environment.
- **Saved Queries** Contains saved search criteria so that you can quickly perform previously run Active Directory searches.
- **Users** The default container for users.

Active Directory Users And Computers has advanced options that aren't displayed by default. To access these options and display the following additional folders, tap or click View, and then select Advanced Features:

- **LostAndFound** Contains objects that have been orphaned. You can delete or recover them.
- **NTDS Quotas** Contains directory service quota data.
- **Program Data** Contains stored Active Directory data for Microsoft applications.
- **System** Contains built-in system settings.
- **TPM Devices** Lists devices with Trusted Platform Module (TPM) owner information stored in Active Directory.

You can also add folders for organizational units. In Figure 8-1, there are multiple administrator-created organizational units in the cpandl.com domain. These include Corporate PCs, CustServices, Development, Engineering, and Finance.

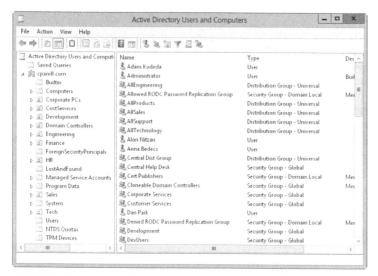

FIGURE 8-1 When you're working with Active Directory Users And Computers, you can access computer and user objects through the console tree.

By default, you are connected to the local domain and to the first domain controller that responds to your request. You can work with any domain in the forest provided that you have the proper access permissions. To do this, you simply connect to the domain by following these steps:

1. In the console tree, press and hold or right-click Active Directory Users And Computers, and then tap or click Change Domain.

2. The Change Domain dialog box displays the current (or default) domain. Enter a new domain name, or tap or click Browse, select a domain in the Browse For Domain dialog box, and then tap or click OK.

3. If you always want to use this domain when working with Active Directory Users And Computers, select the Save This Domain Setting For The Current Console check box, and then tap or click OK. Otherwise, just tap or click OK.

If you start Active Directory Users And Computers and no objects are available, it might be because you are not connected to a domain, or a domain controller could not be located. You need to connect to a domain controller to access user, group, and computer objects. To connect to a domain controller, follow these steps:

1. In the console tree, press and hold or right-click Active Directory Users And Computers, and then tap or click Change Domain Controller.

    The current domain and domain controller you're working with in the Change Directory Server dialog box are displayed.

2. The Change To list displays the available controllers in the domain. The default selection is Any Writable Domain Controller. If you select this option, you'll be connected to the domain controller that responds to your request first. Otherwise, choose a specific domain controller to which you want to connect.

3. If you always want to use this domain controller when working with Active Directory Users And Computers, select the Save This Setting For The Current Console check box, and then tap or click OK. Otherwise, just tap or click OK.

NOTE The Change Directory Server dialog box also shows you the site associated with domain controllers in addition to the domain controller type, version, and status. If the domain controller type is listed as GC, the domain controller is also hosting a global catalog.

You might also want to connect to a specific domain controller for troubleshooting. For example, if you suspect that replication isn't working properly, you might want to inspect the objects on a specific controller. After you're connected, you can look for discrepancies in recently updated objects.

Active Directory Users And Computers has a built-in search feature you can use to find accounts, shared resources, and other directory objects. You can easily search the current domain, a specific domain, or the entire directory.

You search for directory objects by following these steps:

1. In the console tree, press and hold or right-click the current domain or a specific container that you want to search, and then tap or click Find. This opens a Find dialog box similar to the one shown in Figure 8-2.

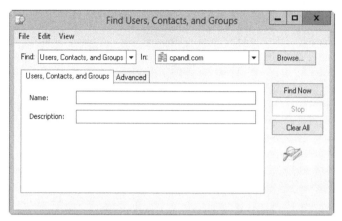

FIGURE 8-2 In the Find dialog box, you can search for resources in Active Directory.

2. In the Find list, choose the type of search you want. The options include the following:

   - **Users, Contacts, And Groups**   Search for user and group accounts, and also contacts listed in the directory service.
   - **Computers**   Search for computer accounts by type, name, and owner.
   - **Printers**   Search for printers by name, model, and features.
   - **Shared Folders**   Search for shared folders by name or keyword.
   - **Organizational Units**   Search for organizational units by name.
   - **Custom Search**   Perform an advanced search or LDAP query.
   - **Common Queries**   Search quickly for account names, account descriptions, disabled accounts, nonexpiring passwords, and days since the last logon.

3. Using the In list, select the location you want to search. If you chose a container to search in step 2, such as Computers, this container is selected by default. To search all objects in the directory, tap or click Entire Directory.

4. Enter your search parameters, and then tap or click Find Now. As shown in Figure 8-3, any matching entries are displayed in the search results. Double-tap or double-click an object to view or modify its property settings. Press and hold or right-click the object to display a shortcut menu of options for managing the object.

NOTE The search type determines which text boxes and tabs are available in the Find dialog box. In most cases, you'll simply want to enter the name of the object you're looking for in the Name box, but other search options are available. For example, with printers, you can search for a color printer, a printer that can print on both sides of the paper, a printer that can staple, and more.

FIGURE 8-3 Objects that match search criteria are displayed in the search results; you can manage them by pressing and holding or right-clicking their entries.

Active Directory Administrative Center and Windows PowerShell

Active Directory Administrative Center, shown in Figure 8-4, provides a task-orientated interface for managing Active Directory. To start this tool, select the related option from the Tools menu in Server Manager. You can use this tool to perform many common tasks, including the following ones:

- Connect to one or more domains.
- Create and manage user accounts, groups, and organizational units.
- Create and manage password settings objects.
- Create and manage authentication policy objects.
- Perform global searches of Active Directory.
- Raise forest and domain functional levels.
- Recover deleted objects from the Active Directory Recycle Bin.

Active Directory Administrative Center is installed by default on Windows Server 2012 R2 and is available on client computers when you install the Remote Server

Administration Tools (RSAT). This tool uses Windows PowerShell to perform administration tasks and relies on the Microsoft .NET Framework. Both of these features must be installed and properly configured for you to use Active Directory Administrative Center.

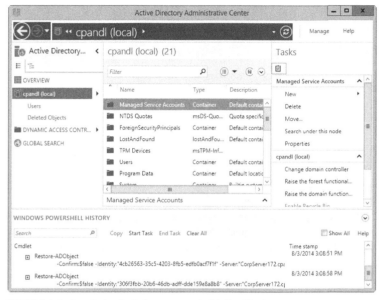

FIGURE 8-4 Perform task-oriented management of Active Directory.

In Active Directory Administrative Center, the local domain is opened for management by default. If you want to work with a different domain, tap or click Manage, and then tap or click Add Navigation Nodes. In the Add Navigation Nodes dialog box, select the domain you want to work with, and then tap or click OK. Afterward, you can select the domain by tapping or clicking it in the left pane.

By default, you are connected to the first domain controller that responds to your request. For troubleshooting replication, you might want to connect to a specific domain controller. After you're connected, you can inspect the objects on that controller and look for discrepancies in recently updated objects. To connect to a specific domain controller, tap or click the domain node in the left pane, and then tap or click Change Domain Controller.

Displayed in the Change Domain Controller dialog box are the current domain and domain controller you're working with, as shown in Figure 8-5. Select a domain controller to use, and then tap or click Change.

Like Active Directory Users And Computers, Active Directory Administrative Center has built-in search features that you can use to find directory objects. The most basic of these is the search filter, which is available when you select a directory container in the left pane.

FIGURE 8-5 Change the domain controller.

Using the search filter, you can quickly find container-level objects within a domain or child OUs within a selected OU. When you select a domain node in the left pane, you can use the filter to quickly find top-level organizational units or built-in containers that start with the letters or words you enter as the filter. For example, you could select the domain node in the left pane and then enter **sa** in the Filter box to find top-level organizational units that begin with the letters "sa," such as *Sales*. As such, a search doesn't include child OUs or subcontainers; it wouldn't include the SalesVT or SalesCA organizational units that were child OUs of Sales.

When you select a specific container, you can search within that container by using the same filtering technique. When you select the Global Search node, you can search the names of all container-level objects and also users, groups, computers, and so on for the currently selected container node.

With global searches, you can change the associated container node by tapping or clicking Scope and then selecting a node to use. Select Global Catalog Search as the node to search nonstandard objects, such as attribute schemas, display specifiers, intersite transports, or class schemas.

> **REAL WORLD** Technically, the filter is based on the start string of any name part of an object. For groups, this means the group name and group Security Accounts Manager (SAM) account name are included. For users, this means the first name, last name, full name, user principal name (UPN), and group SAM account name are included.

Additionally, Active Directory Administrative Center makes use of the web services provided by Active Directory Web Services (ADWS). At least one domain controller in each Active Directory domain you want to manage must have ADWS installed and have the related services running. Connections are made over TCP port 9389 by default, and firewall policies must enable an exception on this port for ADWS.

You can also work with Active Directory by using the Active Directory module for Windows PowerShell. The module is automatically imported when you select the related option on the Tools menu in Server Manager and when you are working with Windows PowerShell 3.0 or later on computers where the Remote Server Administration Tools are installed. Otherwise, this module is not imported into Windows PowerShell by default, and you need to import it before you can work with any Active Directory cmdlets.

At the Windows PowerShell prompt, you can import the Active Directory module by entering **Import-Module ActiveDirectory**. After the module is imported, you can use it with the currently running instance of Windows PowerShell. The next time you start Windows PowerShell, you need to import the module again if you want to use its features. Alternatively, you can select the Active Directory Module For Windows PowerShell option on the Tools menu in Server Manager to import the module when Windows PowerShell starts.

At the Windows PowerShell prompt, you can list all available cmdlets by entering **get-command**. Use Get-Help to get more information about how cmdlets are used. If you enter **get-help *-***, you get a list of all cmdlets that includes a synopsis of the purpose of each cmdlet. To get Help documentation about a specific cmdlet, enter **get-help** followed by the cmdlet name. Several dozen Active Directory cmdlets are available, and you can get a list of the ones you'll use the most by entering **get-help *-ad*** at the Windows PowerShell prompt.

NOTE The Active Directory module for Windows PowerShell is installed by default on Windows Server 2012 R2, and it's available on client computers when you install the Remote Server Administration Tools and select the related options. Windows PowerShell relies on the .NET Framework and Windows Remote Management (WinRM) to perform administrative tasks.

Managing computer accounts

Computer accounts are stored in Active Directory as objects. You use them to control access to the network and its resources. You can add computer accounts to any standard container displayed in Active Directory Users And Computers. The best folders to use are Computers, Domain Controllers, and any organizational units you've created.

Creating computer accounts on a workstation or server

The easiest way to create a computer account is to log on to the computer you want to configure and then join a domain, as described in the "Joining a computer to a domain or workgroup" section later in this chapter. When you do this, the necessary computer account is created automatically and placed in the Computers folder or the Domain Controllers folder, as appropriate. You can also create a computer account in either Active Directory Users And Computers or Active Directory Administrative Center before you try to install the computer.

Creating computer accounts in Active Directory Administrative Center

Using Active Directory Administrative Center, you can create a standard computer account, add the account as a member of specific groups, and set properties about the manager of the computer. To do this, follow these steps:

1. In the Active Directory Administrative Center console tree, press and hold or right-click the container in which you want to place the computer account, tap or click New, and then tap or click Computer. This opens the Create Computer dialog box shown in Figure 8-6.

FIGURE 8-6 Create new computer accounts, and set their managed by and member of properties.

2. Enter the computer name.

3. By default, only members of Domain Admins can join this computer to the domain. To allow a different user or group to join the computer to the domain, tap or click Change, and then select a user or group account in the Select User Or Group dialog box.

    NOTE You can select any existing user or group account. This allows you to delegate the authority to join this computer account to the domain.

4. If this account will be used with applications written for legacy operating systems, select Assign This Computer Account As A Pre–Windows 2000 Computer.

5. Optionally, select Protect From Accidental Deletion to mark the account as protected in Active Directory. Protected accounts can be deleted only if you remove the Protect flag prior to attempting to delete the account.

6. Optionally, assign a security principal as the manager of the computer by tapping or clicking Edit under Managed By, and then selecting a user or group to designate as the manager in the Select User Or Group dialog box. Who you assign as a computer's manager depends on corporate policy and can include the primary user of the computer, a branch manager at a particular office, or a support contact.

7. The computer account is added to the appropriate default computer group automatically. Typically, this is Domain Computers. You can add the computer account to other groups by tapping or clicking Add under Member Of and then using the Select Groups dialog box to specify groups that have accounts to which the computer account should belong.

8. Tap or click OK to create the computer account.

Creating computer accounts in Active Directory Users And Computers

You can create two types of computer accounts: standard computer accounts and managed computer accounts. Managed computer accounts are available when you've installed Windows Deployment Services in your domain.

Using Active Directory Users And Computers, you can create a standard computer account by following these steps:

1. In the Active Directory Users And Computers console tree, press and hold or right-click the container in which you want to place the computer account, tap or click New, and then tap or click Computer. This starts the New Object - Computer Wizard shown in Figure 8-7.

2. Enter the computer name.

3. By default, only members of Domain Admins can join this computer to the domain. To allow a different user or group to join the computer to the domain, tap or click Change, and then select a user or group account in the Select User Or Group dialog box.

   NOTE You can select any existing user or group account. This allows you to delegate the authority to join this computer account to the domain.

4. If this account will be used with applications written for legacy operating systems, select Assign This Computer Account As A Pre–Windows 2000 Computer.

5. If Windows Deployment Services are not installed, tap or click OK to create the computer account. Otherwise, tap or click Next twice, and then tap or click Finish.

FIGURE 8-7 Create new computer accounts by using the New Object - Computer Wizard.

When you are working with Windows Deployment Services, managed computer accounts are used to prestage computer accounts so that a computer can be automatically installed. Using Active Directory Users And Computers, you can create a managed computer account by following these steps:

1. Complete steps 1–4 in the previous procedure. Tap or click Next to display the Managed page.

2. Select the This Is A Managed Computer check box, and then enter the computer's globally unique identifier/universally unique identifier (GUID/ UUID). Tap or click Next.

3. On the Host Server page, you have the option to specify which host server to use or to allow any available host server to be used for remote installation. To select a host server, select The Following Remote Installation Server. In the Find dialog box, tap or click Find Now to display a list of all remote installation servers in the organization. Tap or click the host server you want to use, and then tap or click OK to close the Find dialog box.

4. Tap or click Next, and then tap or click Finish.

REAL WORLD You can find the GUID/UUID in the system BIOS or displayed on the computer case. If Windows PowerShell is installed, you can collect the GUID/UUID by using the Win32_ComputerSystemProduct class of the Windows Management Instrumentation (WMI) interface. The following example returns the universally unique identifier (UUID) of the computer you are logged on to:

```
get-wmiobject -class win32_computersystemproduct | fl uuid
```

Here, you return the UUID of a remote computer:

```
get-wmiobject -class win32_computersystemproduct -computername
engpc24 | format-list pscomputername, uuid
```

After you create a standard or manager computer account in Active Directory Users And Computers, you might want to mark the account as protected. Protected accounts can be deleted only if you remove the Protect flag prior to attempting to delete the account.

To mark a computer account as protected, follow these steps:

1. In Active Directory Users And Computers, ensure that Advanced Features is selected on the View menu.

2. Double-tap or double-click the computer account to open its Properties dialog box.

3. On the Object tab, select Protect Object From Accidental Deletion, and then tap or click OK.

Viewing and editing computer account properties

Using Active Directory Users And Computers or Active Directory Administrative Center, you can view and edit computer account properties by following these steps:

1. In the console tree, expand the domain node.

2. Select the container or organizational unit in which the computer account is located.

3. Double-tap or double-click the account. This displays a Properties dialog box that allows you to view and edit settings.

In Active Directory Users And Computers, advanced tabs and settings are available only when the Advanced Features option is selected on the View menu. In Active Directory Administrative Center, most advanced options are available via tabs on the Extensions panel.

Deleting, disabling, and enabling computer accounts

If you no longer need a computer account, you can delete it permanently from Active Directory. You can also temporarily disable the account and later enable it to be used again.

To delete, disable, or enable computer accounts, follow these steps:

1. Open Active Directory Users And Computers or Active Directory Administrative Center. In the console tree, select the container in which the computer account is located.

2. Press and hold or right-click the computer account, and then do one of the following:

   - Tap or click Delete to delete the account permanently. Tap or click Yes to confirm the deletion.

   - Tap or click Disable Account to temporarily disable the account, and tap or click Yes to confirm the action. A red circle with an X indicates that the account is disabled.

   - Tap or click Enable Account to enable the account so that it can be used again.

If the account is protected, you need to clear the Protect flag before you can delete the account. Double-tap or double-click the account to open its Properties dialog box. Clear the Protect Object From Accidental Deletion check box, and then tap or click OK. In Properties dialog boxes for Active Directory Users And Computers, this check box is on the Object tab. In Active Directory Administrative Center, this check box is on the Computer panel.

> **TIP** If an account is currently in use, you might not be able to disable it. Try shutting down the computer or disconnecting the computer session in the Sessions folder of Computer Management.

Resetting locked computer accounts

Computer accounts have passwords, just like user accounts. Unlike user accounts, however, computer account passwords are managed and maintained automatically. To perform this automated management, computers in the domain store a computer account password, which is changed every 30 days by default, and a secure channel password for establishing secure communications with domain controllers. The secure channel password is also updated by default every 30 days, and both passwords must be synchronized. If the secure channel password and the computer account password get out of sync, the computer won't be allowed to log on to the domain, and a domain authentication error message will be logged for the Netlogon service with an event ID of 3210 or 5722.

If this happens, you need to reset the computer account password. One way to do this is to press and hold or right-click the computer account in Active Directory Users And Computers, and then select Reset Account. You then need to remove the computer from the domain (by making the computer a member of a workgroup or another domain) and then rejoin the computer to the domain.

REAL WORLD Several other ways to reset the computer account password in the same way are available. In Active Directory Administrative Center, you press and hold or right-click the computer account, and then select Reset Account. At the command prompt, you can use Dsmod Computer -Reset to reset a computer account password. In Windows PowerShell, you can use Reset-ComputerMachinePassword and also Set-ADAccountPassword with the –Reset option to reset a computer account password. The following command runs Reset-ComputerMachinePassword on a remote computer:

```
Invoke-Command -ComputerName EngPC84 -ScriptBlock
{Reset-ComputerMachinePassword}
```

All of these options might require the additional steps of removing the computer from the domain (by making the computer a member of a workgroup or another domain) and then rejoining the computer to the domain. The additional steps might be required because the password must be synchronized between the local computer and the domain.

Several tools allow you to reset a computer's password and sync the changes in the domain. On computers where Windows PowerShell is installed, you can use Test-ComputerSecureChannel to test the secure connection between a local computer and a domain. You'll want to log on locally to the computer, open a Windows PowerShell prompt, and then enter the command:

```
test-computersecurechannel
```

You can use the –Server option to test the communications channel with a specific domain controller. If the command returns False, there is a communications problem, and you can use the –Repair option to reset the account password on the local computer and write this change to the related Computer object on a domain controller in the domain. The password change is then replicated to other domain controllers.

Another tool for resetting a computer's password and syncing changes is the Netdom command-line utility. See Microsoft Knowledge Base Article 325850 for more details (*support.microsoft.com/default.aspx?scid=kb;en-us;325850*).

You can use Netdom Verify to test the secure connection between a local computer and a domain. You can use Netdom Resetpwd to reset the account password on the local computer and write this change to the related Computer object on a domain controller in the domain, which in turn ensures that the password change is replicated to other domain controllers.

For a member server, you can reset the computer account password by following these steps:

1. Log on locally to the computer. At a command prompt, enter **netdom resetpwd /s:ServerName /ud:domain\UserName /pd:***, where *Server-Name* is the name of the domain controller to use to set the password, *domain\UserName* specifies an administrator account with the authority to change the password, and * indicates that Netdom should prompt you for the account password before continuing.

2. Enter your password when prompted. Netdom changes the computer account password locally and on the domain controller. The domain controller distributes the password change to other domain controllers in the domain.

3. Restart the computer.

For domain controllers, you must perform additional steps. After you log on locally, you must stop the Kerberos Key Distribution Center service and set its startup type to Manual. After you restart the computer and verify that the password has been successfully reset, you can restart the Kerberos Key Distribution Center service and set its startup type back to Automatic.

Moving computer accounts

Computer accounts are normally placed in the Computers or Domain Controllers containers, or in customized organizational unit containers. You can move an account to a different container by selecting the computer account in Active Direc-tory Users And Computers and then dragging the account to the new location. You can't click and drag accounts in Active Directory Administrative Center.

Using either tool, you can also use the following technique to move computer accounts:

1. In the console tree, select the container in which the computer account is located.

2. Press and hold or right-click the computer account you want to move, and then tap or click Move. This displays the Move dialog box, shown in Figure 8-8.

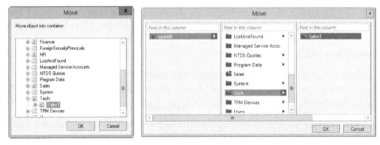

FIGURE 8-8 In the Move dialog box, you can move computer accounts to different containers. (The dialog box in Active Directory Users And Computers is on the left, and the dialog box in Active Directory Administrative Center is on the right.)

3. In the Move dialog box, use the options provided to select the container to which you want to move the computer. Browse to subcontainers or child OUs as necessary, and then tap or click OK.

Managing computers

As its name indicates, Computer Management is used to manage computers. Whether you're working with Active Directory Users And Computers or Active Directory Administrative Center, you can open Computer Management and connect to a specific computer by pressing and holding or right-clicking the computer entry and then selecting Manage from the shortcut menu. This starts Computer Management and automatically connects to the selected computer.

Joining a computer to a domain or workgroup

A computer joined to a domain or workgroup can log on and access the network. Before you get started, make sure that networking components are properly installed on the computer. These should have been installed during the setup of the operating system. TCP/IP settings must be correct and permit communications between the computer you're configuring and a controller in the domain. If Dynamic Host Configuration Protocol (DHCP), Windows Internet Name Service (WINS), and DNS are properly installed on the network, workstations don't need to be assigned a static IP address or have a special configuration. The only requirements are a computer name and a domain name, which you can specify when joining the computer to the domain.

> **REAL WORLD**   Windows Server 2012 R2 automatically grants the Add Workstations To The Domain user right to the implicit group Authenticated Users. This means that any user who logs on to the domain as a User and is authenticated can add workstations to the domain without needing administration privileges. However, as a security precaution, the number of workstations any such user can add to the domain is limited to 10. If an authenticated user exceeds this limit, an error message is displayed.
>
> Although you can use the Ldp.exe tool from the Windows Server 2012 R2 Support Tools to override the default limit on the number of computers an authenticated user can join to a domain (as set by the ms-DS-MachineAccountQuota attribute), this isn't a good security practice. A better technique, and a more appropriate technique where security is a concern, is to create the necessary computer account in a specific OU beforehand or to grant the user the advanced security privilege Create Account Objects for the Computers container. You also might want to grant certain users the Delete Account Objects privilege for the Computers container so that designated users can remove computer accounts from the domain.

During installation of the operating system, a network connection was probably configured for the computer, or you might have previously joined the computer to a domain or a workgroup. If so, you can join the computer to a new domain or workgroup. For joining a computer running Windows Vista or later, and Windows Server 2008 or later, to a domain, see the "Configuring server name and domain membership" section in Chapter 3, "Managing Windows servers."

If the name change is unsuccessful, a message is displayed informing you that the change was unsuccessful or that the account credentials already exist. This problem can occur when you're changing the name of a computer that's already connected to a domain and when the computer has active sessions in that domain. Exit applications that might be connected to the domain, such as File Explorer accessing a shared folder over the network. Then repeat the process for changing the computer's name.

If you have other problems joining a domain, be sure that the computer you're configuring has the proper networking configuration. The computer must have Networking Services installed, and TCP/IP properties must have the correct DNS server settings.

All authenticated users have the Add Workstations To The Domain user right by default and can create up to 10 computer accounts when joining computers to a domain. Users who have the Create Account Objects privilege for the Computers container aren't restricted in this way; they can create an unlimited number of computer accounts in the domain. However, computer accounts created by authenticated users have Domain Admins as the account owner, whereas computer accounts created by users with the Create Account Objects privilege have the creator as the owner. If you grant the Create Account Objects privilege, you also might want to grant the Delete Account Objects privilege so that certain users can remove computer accounts from the domain.

You grant the Create Account Objects, the Delete Account Objects privilege, or both privileges for the Computers container by following these steps:

1. Open Active Directory Users And Computers or Active Directory Administrative Center. In Active Directory Users And Computers, ensure that Advanced Features is enabled on the View menu.

2. Press and hold or right-click the Computers container, and then tap or click Properties.

3. On the Security tab, tap or click Advanced. In the Advanced Security Settings For Computers dialog box, tap or click Add to open the Permission Entry For Computers dialog box.

4. Tap or click Select A Principal. In the Select User, Computer, Service Account, Or Group dialog box, enter the name of the user or group to whom you want to grant privileges, and then tap or click OK. Click OK again.

Using offline domain join

Computers running editions of Windows 7 and later designed for workplaces support offline domain join, as do servers running Windows Server 2008 R2 or later. The related utility, Djoin.exe, is included with these editions of Windows. Any member of Domain Admins can perform offline domain joins (as can anyone who is granted the appropriate user rights).

The basic steps for performing an offline domain join operation follow:

1. Create the computer account in Active Directory, and then force replication of the shared secrets of the computer that is to join the domain.

2. Write the relevant state information that the computer needs to join the domain to a text file, and then make the state information available to the computer.

3. When the computer starts, Windows reads the provisioning data, and the computer is joined to the domain.

NOTE Client computers must be connected to the corporate network to join a domain or receive domain settings. With the remote domain join feature, Windows Server 2012 R2 provides the capability for computers running Windows 8 or later to join a domain and receive domain settings remotely from the Internet.

You run Djoin.exe at an elevated, administrator command prompt to provision the computer account metadata. The computer account metadata is written to a .txt file. After provisioning the computer, you can run Djoin.exe again to request the computer account metadata and insert it into the Windows directory of the destination computer. Alternatively, you can save the computer account metadata in an Unattend.xml file and then specify the Unattend.xml file during an unattended operating system installation.

You can use a .txt file for provisioning by following these steps:

1. Using an account that is allowed to join computers to the domain, log on to a computer that is a member of the domain.

2. Use Djoin.exe to create a text file that contains the computer account metadata. To do this, at an elevated, administrator command prompt, enter **djoin /provision /domain *DomainName* /machine *MachineName* /savefile *FileName***, where *DomainName* is the name of the domain to join, *MachineName* is the computer name, and *FileName* is name of the .txt file where the metadata should be saved, such as:

   ```
   djoin /provision /domain cpandl /machine HrComputer15 /savefile
   Hrcomputer15.txt
   ```

   TIP By default, computer accounts are created in the Computers container. If you want to use a different container, you can add the /Machineou parameter and then specify the container to use. If the computer account object is already created, you can still generate the required metadata by adding the /reuse parameter. If your domain controller is not yet running Windows Server 2008 R2 or Windows Server 2012 R2, add the /downlevel command.

3. On the new computer, use Djoin.exe to import the .txt file. At an elevated, administrator command prompt, enter **djoin /requestODJ /loadfile** **FileName /windowspath %SystemRoot% /localos**, where *FileName* is the name of the metadata file, such as:

```
djoin /requestODJ /loadfile HrComputer15.txt /windowspath
%SystemRoot% /localos
```

4. Ensure that the new computer is connected to the network, and then restart it. During startup, the computer will be joined to the domain.

You can use an Unattend.xml file for provisioning by creating a section in the Unattend.xml file and then adding the contents of the metadata .txt file to the –AccountData element, as shown in this example:

```
<Component>
<Component name=Microsoft-Windows-UnattendedJoin>
    <Identification>
        <Provisioning>
            <AccountData> Insert metadata here! </AccountData>
        </Provisioning>
    </Identification>
</Component>
```

After you create the Unattend.xml file, start the new computer in safe mode or start the computer in the Windows Preinstallation Environment (Windows PE), and then run the Setup command with an answer file, as shown in the following example:

```
setup /unattend: FullPathToAnswerFile
```

Here, *FullPathToAnswerFile* is the full file path to the Unattend.xml file.

Managing domain controllers, roles, and catalogs

Domain controllers perform many important tasks in Active Directory domains. Many of these tasks are discussed in Chapter 7.

Installing and demoting domain controllers

You install a domain controller by configuring Active Directory Domain Services on a server. Later, if you don't want the server to handle controller tasks, you can demote the server. It will then act as a member server again. You follow a similar procedure to install or demote servers, but before you do, you should consider the impact on the network and read the "Understanding the directory structure" section in Chapter 7.

As that section explains, when you install a domain controller, you might need to transfer operations master roles and reconfigure the global catalog structure. Also, before you can install Active Directory Domain Services, DNS must be working on the network. When you install AD DS, you can include DNS server installation, if it is needed. When you create a new domain, a DNS delegation is created automatically during the installation process, and to do this requires credentials that have permissions to update the parent DNS zones.

To add the first domain controller that runs Windows Server 2012 R2 to an existing Active Directory infrastructure, the Active Directory Installation Wizard automatically runs Adprep.exe as needed for the forest and domain. Preparing the forest and domain includes updating the Active Directory schema as needed, creating new objects and containers as needed, and modifying security descriptors and access control lists as needed. For forest prep, the account you use must be a member of the Schema Admins group, the Enterprise Admins group, and the Domain Admins group of the domain that hosts the schema master, which is, by default, the forest root domain. For domain prep, you use an account that can log on to the infrastructure master and is a member of the Domain Admins group. For RODC prep, you must use an account that is a member of the Enterprise Admins group.

Before you demote a domain controller, you should shift any key responsibilities to other domain controllers. This means moving the global catalog off the server and transferring any operations master roles, if necessary. You must also remove any application directory partitions that are on the server.

REAL WORLD Note that with Windows Server 2012 R2 and later, all AD DS installation and configuration tasks are performed via Server Manager. You no longer have to run an installation wizard and a separate command-line promotion task. You also might not need to manually prepare Active Directory for Windows Server 2012 R2.

Also note that you don't have to demote a domain controller to rename it. You can rename a domain controller at any time. The only problem is that the server is unavailable to users during the renaming process, and you might need to force a directory refresh to reestablish proper communications with the server. You can't, however, move a domain controller to a different domain. You must demote the domain controller, update the domain settings for the server and its computer account, and then promote the server to be a domain controller once more.

To install a domain controller, follow these steps:

1. In Server Manager, the local server is added automatically for management. If you want to install AD DS on another server, you need to add the server for management by using the Add Servers option. Using Server Manager for remote management requires the configuration discussed in Chapter 3 and a minimum set of permissions. Typically, you must have Domain Admin or other explicit permissions to add a server and remotely manage it. To install a new Active Directory forest, you must be logged on as the local Administrator for the computer. To install a new child domain or new domain tree, you must be logged on as a member of the Enterprise Admins group. To install an additional domain controller in an existing domain, you must be logged on as a member of the Domain Admins group.

2. In Server Manager, tap or click Manage, and then tap or click Add Roles And Features. This starts the Add Roles And Features Wizard. If the wizard displays the Before You Begin page, read the Welcome message, and then tap or click Next.

3. On the Select Installation Type page, select Role-Based Or Feature-Based Installation, and then tap or click Next.

4. On the Select Destination Server page, the server pool shows servers you've added for management. Tap or click the server you are configuring, and then tap or click Next.

5. On the Select Server Roles page, select Active Directory Domain Services, and then tap or click Next twice. Tap or click Install. This runs the Active Directory Domain Services Installation Wizard.

6. When the initial installation task completes, you need to tap or click Promote This Server To A Domain Controller to start the Active Directory Domain Services Configuration Wizard. If you closed the Add Roles And Features Wizard window, you need to tap or click the Notifications icon, and then tap or click Promote This Server To A Domain Controller.

MORE INFO If the installation fails, note the error and take appropriate corrective action before restarting this procedure. Typical installation errors will relate to permissions, such as those required for preparing the forest or domain for first use of Windows Server. Here, log off and then log back on with an account that has the appropriate permissions.

7. If the computer is currently a member server, the wizard takes you through the steps needed to install Active Directory, which might include automatically preparing the directory schema in the forest and domain for Windows Server 2012 R2. You need to specify whether this is a domain controller for a new domain or an additional domain controller for an existing domain. To verify that a domain controller is installed correctly, you should do the following: check the Directory Service event log for errors, ensure that the SYSVOL folder is accessible to clients, verify that name resolution is working through DNS, and verify replication of changes to Active Directory.

To demote a domain controller, follow these steps:

1. In Server Manager, tap or click Manage, and then tap or click Remove Roles And Features. This starts the Remove Roles And Features Wizard. If the wizard displays the Before You Begin page, read the Welcome message, and then tap or click Next.

2. On the Select Destination Server page, the server pool shows servers you've added for management. Tap or click the server you are configuring, and then tap or click Next.

3. On the Remove Server Roles page, clear the check box for Active Directory Domain Services to specify that this is the role you want to remove.

4. A new dialog box opens. Here, you might want to clear the Remove Management Tools check box to ensure that the AD DS management tools aren't uninstalled and then click Continue. Otherwise, click Remove Features. Click Next twice.

5. On the Credentials page, note your current logon account. If necessary, provide alternate credentials with permissions to remove the domain controller. Click Next.

6. If the Warnings page is displayed, note the warnings, select Proceed With Removal, and then click Next.

7. Enter and then confirm a new password for the server's local Administrator account. The passwords must match. Click Next.

8. On the Confirm Removal Selections page, you have the option of selecting the Restart The Destination Server Automatically If Required check box. Because a restart of the server is required to complete the removal, you might want to choose this option and then confirm it by tapping or clicking Yes. When you are ready to proceed, and then click Remove.

CAUTION Demoting a server gracefully transfers any roles held by the server. However, if previous attempts to demote the domain controller have failed, you can repeat this procedure and then select the Force The Removal Of This Domain Controller check box as part of the removal process. Here, the flexible single master operations (FSMO) roles of the domain controller might be left in an invalid state until they are reassigned by an administrator. The domain data also might be left in an inconsistent state.

REAL WORLD An alternative technique for installing domain controllers is to use backup media. To install a domain controller from backup media, create a backup of the system state data of a domain controller, and then restore it on a different server. When you create a domain controller from backup media, you eliminate the need to replicate the entire directory database over the network to the new domain controller. This can really save the day when you have bandwidth limitations or the directory database has thousands of entries.

Viewing and transferring domainwide roles

You can use Active Directory Users And Computers to view or change the location of domainwide operations master roles. At the domain level, you can work with roles for relative ID (RID) masters, primary domain controller (PDC) emulator masters, and infrastructure masters.

NOTE Operations master roles are discussed in the "Understanding operations master roles" section in Chapter 7. You use Active Directory Domains And Trusts to set the domain naming master role and Active Directory Schema to change the schema master role. The fastest way to determine the current FSMO for all roles is to enter **netdom query fsmo** at a command prompt.

You can view the current operations master roles by following these steps:

1. In Active Directory Users And Computers, press and hold or right-click Active Directory Users And Computers in the console tree. On the shortcut menu, point to All Tasks, and then tap or click Operations Masters. This opens the Operations Masters dialog box, shown in Figure 8-9.

2. The Operations Masters dialog box has three tabs. The RID tab shows the location of the current RID master. The PDC tab shows the location of the current PDC emulator master. The Infrastructure tab shows the location of the current infrastructure master.

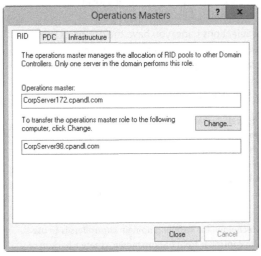

FIGURE 8-9 In the Operations Masters dialog box, transfer operations masters to new locations or simply view their current locations.

You can transfer the current operations master roles by following these steps:

1. Start Active Directory Users And Computers. In the console tree, press and hold or right-click Active Directory Users And Computers, and then tap or click Change Domain Controller.

2. In the Change Directory Server dialog box, tap or click This Domain Controller Or AD LDS Instance, select the domain controller to which you want to transfer an operations master role, and then tap or click OK.

3. In the console tree, press and hold or right-click Active Directory Users And Computers. On the shortcut menu, point to All Tasks, and then tap or click Operations Masters.

4. In the Operations Masters dialog box, tap or click the RID, PDC, or Infrastructure tab as appropriate for the type of role you want to transfer.

5. Tap or click Change to transfer the role to the previously selected domain controller, and then tap or click OK.

Viewing and transferring the domain naming master role

You can use Active Directory Domains And Trusts to view or change the location of the domain naming master in the domain forest. In Active Directory Domains And Trusts, the root level of the control tree shows the currently selected domain.

> **TIP** If you need to connect to a different domain, connect to a domain controller by following steps similar to those described in the "Using Active Directory Users And Computers" section earlier in this chapter. The only difference is that you press and hold or right-click Active Directory Domains And Trusts in the console tree.

To transfer the domain naming master role, follow these steps:

1. Start Active Directory Domains And Trusts. In the console tree, press and hold or right-click Active Directory Domains And Trusts and then tap or click Change Active Directory Domain Controller.

2. In the Change Directory Server dialog box, select the This Domain Controller Or AD LDS Instance option, select the domain controller to which you want to transfer the domain naming master role, and then tap or click OK.

3. In the console tree, press and hold or right-click Active Directory Domains And Trusts, and then tap or click Operations Master. This opens the Operations Master dialog box.

4. The Domain Naming Operations Master box displays the current domain naming master. Tap or click Change to transfer this role to the previously selected domain controller.

5. Tap or click Close.

Viewing and transferring schema master roles

You use Active Directory Schema to view or change the schema master's location. Enter **regsvr32 schmmgmt.dll** at an elevated, administrator command prompt to register Active Directory Schema. You can then transfer the schema master role by following these steps:

1. Add the Active Directory Schema snap-in to an MMC.

2. In the console tree, press and hold or right-click Active Directory Schema, and then tap or click Change Active Directory Domain Controller.

3. Select Any Writable Domain Controller to let Active Directory select the new schema master, or select This Domain Controller Or AD LDS Instance and then select the new schema master.

4. Tap or click OK. In the console tree, press and hold or right-click Active Directory Schema, and then tap or click Operations Master.

5. Tap or click Change in the Change Schema Master dialog box. Tap or click OK, and then tap or click Close.

Transferring roles by using the command line

Another way to transfer roles is to use Netdom to list current FSMO role holders and then Ntdsutil.exe to transfer roles. Ntdsutil is a command-line tool for managing Active Directory. Follow these steps to transfer roles at the command line:

1. Get a list of the current FSMO role holders by entering **netdom query fsmo** at a command prompt.

2. It is recommended (but not required) that you log on to the console of the server you want to assign as the new operations master. You can log on to the console locally or use Remote Desktop Connection.

3. Open a command prompt. One way to do this is by pressing the Windows key, typing **cmd.exe**, and then pressing Enter.

4. At the command prompt, enter **ntdsutil**. This starts the Directory Services Management Tool.

5. At the ntdsutil prompt, enter **roles**. This puts the utility in Operations Master Maintenance mode.

6. At the fsmo maintenance prompt, enter **connections**. At the server connections prompt, enter **connect to server** followed by the fully qualified domain name of the domain controller to which you want to assign the FSMO role, such as:

```
connect to server engdc01.technology.adatum.com
```

7. After you've established a successful connection, enter **quit** to exit the server connections prompt. At the fsmo maintenance prompt, type **transfer**, type the identifier for the role to transfer, and then press Enter. The identifiers are as follows:

   - **pdc** For the PDC emulator role
   - **rid master** For the RID master role
   - **infrastructure master** For the infrastructure master role
   - **schema master** For the schema master role
   - **domain naming master** For the domain naming master role

8. Enter **quit** at the fsmo maintenance prompt, and then enter **quit** at the −ntdsutil prompt.

Seizing roles by using the command line

Occasionally, you might find yourself in a situation where you can't gracefully transfer server roles. For example, a domain controller acting as the RID master might have a drive failure that takes down the entire server. If you're unable to get the server back online, you might need to seize the RID master role and assign this role to another domain controller.

Don't seize a role without first determining how up to date the domain controller that will take over the role is with respect to the previous role owner. Active Directory tracks replication changes by using update sequence numbers (USNs). Because replication takes time, not all domain controllers will necessarily be up to date. If you compare a domain controller's USN to that of other servers in the domain, you can determine whether the domain controller is the most up to date with respect to changes from the previous role owner. If the domain controller is up to date, you can transfer the role safely. If the domain controller isn't up to date, you can wait for replication to occur and then transfer the role to the domain controller.

Windows Server 2012 R2 includes several tools for working with Active Directory replication. One tool you can use is Repadmin. You can display the status of the last inbound replication for a domain controller by using Repadmin /Showrepl. The syntax is:

```
repadmin /showrepl DomainControllerName NamingContext
```

Here, *DomainControllerName* is the fully qualified domain name of the domain controller, and *NamingContext* is the distinguished name of the domain in which the server is located. In this example, you examine the default partition for Server252 in the Cpandl.com domain:

```
repadmin /showrepl server252.cpandl.com dc=cpandl,dc=com
```

To display the highest sequence number for a specified naming context on each replication partner of a designated domain controller, enter the following at a command prompt:

```
repadmin /showutdvec DomainControllerName NamingContext
```

In this example, you display the highest sequence number for the default configuration partition on Server252 in the Cpandl.com domain:

```
repadmin /showutdvec server252.cpandl.com dc=cpandl,dc=com
```

The output shows the highest USN on replication partners for the default configuration partition:

```
Default-First-Site-Name\SERVER252 @ USN    45164 @ Time 2014-03-30 11:35:24

Default-First-Site-Name\SERVER147 @ USN    45414 @ Time 2014-03-30 11:42:16
```

If Server252 was the previous role owner, and the domain controller you are examining has an equal or larger USN for Server252, the domain controller is up to date. However, if Server252 was the previous role owner, and the domain controller you are examining has a lower USN for Server252, the controller is not up to date and you should wait for replication to occur before seizing the role. You can also use Repadmin /Syncall to force the domain controller that is the most up to date with respect to the previous role owner to replicate with all of its replication partners.

In Windows PowerShell, you can use replication management cmdlets to view and troubleshoot Active Directory replication. Related cmdlets include the following:

- **Get-ADReplicationAttributeMetadata** Gets the replication metadata for the attributes of the distinguished name specified
- **Get-ADReplicationFailure** Gets information about replication failure for a specified server, site, domain, or forest, if applicable
- **Get-ADReplicationPartnerMetadata** Gets replication metadata for a specified server, site, domain, or forest
- **Get-ADReplicationQueueOperation** Gets pending operations in a server's replication queue
- **Get-ADReplicationUpToDatenessVectorTable** Gets the highest USN for the specified server, site, domain, or forest
- **Sync-ADObject** Replicates the specified directory object

Use Get-ADReplicationPartnerMetadata to get information about inbound replications for a server with the following syntax:

```
Get-ADReplicationPartnerMetadata -Target Object
[-Scope Server|Site|Domain|Forest] [-Partition
Domain|Schema|Configuration|*]
```

Here, –Target sets the name of the server, site, domain, or forest to work with. Setting the scope is required when you are working with objects other than servers. Setting the partition is required when you want to work with partitions other than the default. In this example, you examine the default partition on CorpServer98:

```
get-adreplicationpartnermetadata -target corpserver98
```

You also can examine all partitions on the server by using the following syntax:

```
get-adreplicationpartnermetadata -target corpserver98 -partition *
```

Like Repadmin /Showutdvec, Get-ADReplicationUpToDatenessVectorTable displays the highest sequence numbers for partitions being replicated and can help you troubleshoot replication issues. Here is the basic syntax:

```
Get-ADReplicationUpToDatenessVectorTable -Target Object
[-Scope Server|Site|Domain|Forest] [-Partition
Domain|Schema|Configuration|*]
```

In this example, you display the highest sequence number for the default partition (the domain configuration partition) on CorpServer98:

```
get-adreplicationuptodatenessvectortable -target corpserver98
```

The output shows the highest USN on replication partners for the default configuration partition:

```
LastReplicationSuccess : 3/30/2014 1:45:57 PM
Partition              : DC=cpandl,DC=com
PartitionGuid          : c39cfdbd-e1a1-4c4c-9355-85d7ea05c10a
Partner                : CN=NTDS Settings,CN=CORPSERVER172,CN=Servers,
CN=Default-First-Site-Name,CN=Sites,CN=Configuration,DC=cpandl,DC=com
PartnerInvocationId    : fb32931c-e319-473a-8069-d781f980057b
Server                 : CorpServer98.cpandl.com
UsnFilter              : 82656

LastReplicationSuccess : 3/30/2014 1:48:44 PM
Partition              : DC=cpandl,DC=com
PartitionGuid          : c39cfdbd-e1a1-4c4c-9355-85d7ea05c10a
Partner                : CN=NTDS Settings,CN=CORPSERVER98,CN=Servers,
CN=Default-First-Site-Name,CN=Sites,CN=Configuration,DC=cpandl,DC=com
PartnerInvocationId    : d8bf2da2-b08d-4d36-bc53-1b7f62643437
Server                 : CorpServer98.cpandl.com
UsnFilter              : 12593
```

You interpret the output much like you would interpret output from Repadmin /Showutdvec. If you suspect a problem, you can use Get-ADReplicationFailure to examine replication issues. Here is the basic syntax:

```
Get-ADReplicationFailure -Target Object [-Scope Server|Site|Domain|Forest]
```

Knowing this, you can display information about all replication failures in the Cpandl.com domain by entering the following:

```
get-adreplicationfailure -Target "cpandl.com" -Scope Domain
```

You can display information for a specific site by entering the following:

```
get-adreplicationfailure -Target "NewYork-FirstSite" -Scope Site
```

Or you can display information for a specific server by entering the following:

```
get-adreplicationfailure -Target CorpServer172
```

Follow these steps to seize a server role:

1. Enter **netdom query fsmo** at a command prompt to get a list of the current FSMO role holders.

2. Ensure that the current domain controller with the role you want to seize is permanently offline. If the server can be brought back online, don't perform this procedure unless you intend to completely reinstall this server.

3. It is recommended that you log on to the console of the server you want to assign as the new operations master. You can log on to the console locally or use Remote Desktop Connection.

4. Open a Command Prompt.

5. At the command prompt, enter **ntdsutil**. This starts the Directory Services Management Tool.

6. At the ntdsutil prompt, enter **roles**. This puts the utility in Operations Master Maintenance mode.

7. At the fsmo maintenance prompt, enter **connections**. At the server connections prompt, enter **connect to server** followed by the fully qualified domain name of the domain controller to which you want to assign the FSMO role, such as:

```
connect to server engdc01.technology.adatum.com
```

8. After you've established a successful connection, enter **quit** to exit the server connections prompt. At the fsmo maintenance prompt, type **seize**, type the identifier for the role to seize, and then press Enter. The identifiers are as follows:

   - **pdc**   For the PDC emulator role
   - **rid master**   For the RID master role
   - **infrastructure master**   For the infrastructure master role
   - **schema master**   For the schema master role
   - **domain naming master**   For the domain naming master role

9. Enter **quit** at the fsmo maintenance prompt, and then enter **quit** at the ntdsutil prompt.

Configuring global catalogs

Global catalogs have an important role on the network. This role is discussed in the "Understanding the directory structure" section in Chapter 7. You configure additional global catalogs by enabling domain controllers to host the global catalog. In addition, if you have two or more global catalogs within a site, you might want a domain controller to stop hosting the global catalog. You do this by disabling the global catalog on the domain controller.

You enable or disable a global catalog by following these steps:

1. In Active Directory Sites And Services, expand the site you want to work with in the console tree.

2. Expand the Servers folder for the site, and then select the server you want to configure to host the global catalog.

3. In the details pane, press and hold or right-click NTDS Settings, and then tap or click Properties.

4. To enable the server to host the global catalog, select the Global Catalog check box on the General tab.

5. To disable the global catalog, clear the Global Catalog check box on the General tab.

CAUTION Don't enable or disable global catalogs without proper planning and analysis of the impact on the network. In a large enterprise environment, designating a domain controller as a global catalog can cause data related to thousands of Active Directory objects to be replicated across the network.

Configuring universal group membership caching

Universal membership caching eliminates the dependency on the availability of a global catalog server during logons. When you enable this feature on a domain operating at the Windows Server 2003 or higher functional level, any domain controller can resolve logon requests locally without having to go through the global catalog server. As discussed in the "Universal group membership caching" section in Chapter 7, this has advantages and disadvantages.

You can enable or disable universal group membership caching by following these steps:

1. In Active Directory Sites And Services, expand and then select the site you want to work with.

2. In the details pane, press and hold or right-click NTDS Site Settings, and then tap or click Properties.

3. To enable universal group membership caching, select the Enable Universal Group Membership Caching check box on the Site Settings tab. Then, in the Refresh Cache From list, choose a site from which to cache universal group memberships. The selected site must have a working global catalog server.

4. To disable universal group membership caching, clear the Enable Universal Group Membership Caching check box on the Site Settings tab.

5. Tap or click OK.

Managing organizational units

As discussed in Chapter 7, organizational units help you organize objects, set Group Policy with a limited scope, and more. In this section, you'll learn how to create and manage organizational units.

Creating organizational units

You usually create organizational units to mirror your organization's business or functional structure. You might also want to create units for administrative reasons, such as if you want to delegate rights to users or administrators. You can create organizational units as subgroups of a domain or as child units within an existing organizational unit.

To create an organizational unit, follow these steps:

1. In Active Directory Users And Computers or Active Directory Administrative Center, press and hold or right-click the domain node or existing organizational unit folder in which you want to add an organizational unit. Tap or click New on the shortcut menu, and then tap or click Organizational Unit.

2. Enter the name of the organizational unit, and then tap or click OK.

3. You can now move accounts and shared resources to the organizational unit. See the "Moving computer accounts" section earlier in this chapter for an example.

Viewing and editing organizational unit properties

You can view and edit organizational unit properties by following these steps:

1. Open Active Directory Users And Computers or Active Directory Administrative Center.

2. Press and hold or right-click the organizational unit you want to work with, and then tap or click Properties. This displays a Properties dialog box that lets you view and edit settings.

Renaming and deleting organizational units

You can rename or delete an organizational unit by following these steps:

1. In Active Directory Users And Computers, press and hold or right-click the organizational unit folder you want to work with.

2. To delete the organizational unit, tap or click Delete. Then confirm the action by tapping or clicking Yes.

3. To rename the organizational unit, tap or click Rename. Type a new name for the organizational unit, and then press Enter.

In Active Directory Administrative Center, you delete organizational units in the same way, but to rename an organizational unit, you open its Properties dialog box, type the new name, and then tap or click OK.

Moving organizational units

You can move organizational units to different locations within a domain at any time. In Active Directory Users And Computers, simply select the organizational unit and then drag it to the desired location.

Using either Active Directory Users And Computers or Active Directory Administrative Center, you can also follow these steps to move organizational units:

1. Press and hold or right-click the organizational unit folder you want to move, and then tap or click Move.

2. In the Move dialog box, expand the domain, select the container to which you want to move the organizational unit, and then tap or click OK.

Managing sites

The Active Directory Domain Services Installation Wizard creates a default site and a default site link when you install Active Directory Domain Services on the first domain controller in a site. The default site is named Default-First-Site-Name, and the default site link is called DEFAULTIPSITELINK. You can rename the default site and site link as necessary. You must create subsequent sites and site links manually.

Configuring a site is a multipart process that includes the following steps:

1. Creating the site
2. Creating one or more subnets and associating them with the site
3. Associating a domain controller with the site
4. Linking the site to other sites by using site links and, if necessary, creating site link bridges

I discuss these tasks in the sections that follow.

Creating sites

Any administrator who is a member of Domain Admins or Enterprise Admins can create sites. You can create a site by following these steps:

1. In Active Directory Sites And Services, press and hold or right-click the Sites container in the console root, and then tap or click New Site.
2. In the New Object - Site dialog box, shown in Figure 8-10, enter a name for the site, such as Chicago-First-Site. Site names cannot contain spaces or any special characters other than a dash.

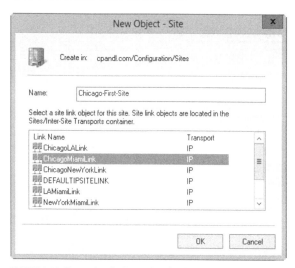

FIGURE 8-10 Create the site by setting the site name and a related site link.

3. Tap or click the site link that you will use to connect this site to other sites. If the site link you want to use doesn't exist, select the default site link and change the site link settings later.

4. Tap or click OK. A prompt is displayed detailing the steps you must complete to finish site configuration. Tap or click OK again.

5. To complete site configuration, complete the remaining configuration tasks.

TIP You can rename a site at any time. In Active Directory Sites And Services, press and hold or right-click the site, and then select Rename. Type the new name for the site, and then press Enter.

Creating subnets

Each site you define must have associated subnets that detail the network segments that belong to the site. Any computer with an IP address on a network segment associated with a site is considered to be located in the site. Although a single site can have multiple subnets associated with it, a subnet can be associated with only one site.

To create a subnet and associate it with a site, follow these steps:

1. In Active Directory Sites And Services, press and hold or right-click the Subnets container in the console tree, and then tap or click New Subnet. This displays the New Object - Subnet dialog box, shown in Figure 8-11.

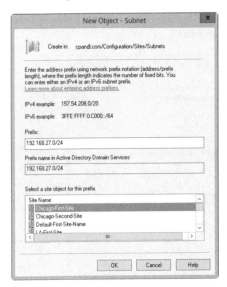

FIGURE 8-11 Create the subnet by entering the network prefix and selecting an associated site.

2. In the Prefix box, enter the IPv4 or IPv6 network address prefix by using the network prefix notation. In network prefix notation, you enter the network ID and then a forward slash, and then you specify which bits are used for the network ID. For example, if the network ID is 192.168.27.0 and the first 24 bits identify the network ID, you enter **192.168.27.0/24** as the network prefix notation.

3. Select the site with which the subnet should be associated, and then tap or click OK.

TIP You can change the site association for a subnet at any time. In Active Directory Sites And Services, double-tap or double-click the subnet in the Subnets folder, and then on the General tab, change the site association in the Site list.

Associating domain controllers with sites

Every site should have at least one domain controller associated with it. By adding a second domain controller to a site, you provide fault tolerance and redundancy. If at least one domain controller in the site is also a global catalog server, you can ensure that directory searches and authentication traffic are isolated to the site.

You can add domain controllers to sites automatically or manually. When you associate subnets with a site, any new domain controllers you install are placed in the site automatically if the domain controller's IP address is within the valid range of IP addresses for the subnet. Existing domain controllers are not automatically associated with sites, however. You must manually associate any existing domain controllers with a new site by moving the domain controller object into the site.

Before you can move a domain controller from one site to another, you must determine in which site the domain controller is currently located. A quick way to do that is to enter the following command at a command prompt:

```
dsquery server -s DomainControllerName | dsget server -site
```

Here, *DomainControllerName* is the fully qualified domain name of the domain controller, such as:

```
dsquery server -s server241.cpandl.com | dsget server -site
```

The output of this command is the name of the site in which the designated domain controller is located.

To move a domain controller from one site to another site, follow these steps:

1. In Active Directory Sites And Services, any domain controllers associated with a site are listed in the site's Servers node. Select the site that the domain controller is currently associated with.

2. Press and hold or right-click the domain controller, and then tap or click Move. In the Move Server dialog box, tap or click the site that should contain the server, and then tap or click OK.

Configuring site links

Sites are groups of IP subnets that are connected by reliable, high-speed links. Most of the time, all subnets on the same local network are part of the same site. Networks with multiple sites are connected via site links. *Site links* are logical, transitive connections between two or more sites. Each site link has a replication schedule, a replication interval, a link cost, and a replication transport.

Because site links are used over wide area network links, bandwidth availability and usage are important considerations when configuring site links. By default, site links are scheduled to replicate data 24 hours a day, seven days a week at an interval of at least 180 minutes. If you know a link has bandwidth limitations, you might need to alter the schedule to allow user traffic to have priority during peak usage times.

When you have multiple links between sites, you need to consider the relative priority of each link. You assign priority based on the availability and reliability of the connection. The default link cost is set to 100. If there are multiple possible routes to a site, the route with the lowest site link cost is used first. Therefore, the most reliable paths with the most bandwidth between sites should be configured in most cases to have the lowest site link cost.

You can configure site links to use either remote procedure call (RPC) over IP or Simple Mail Transfer Protocol (SMTP) as the transport protocol. With IP as the transport, domain controllers establish an RPC over IP connection with a single replication partner at a time and replicate Active Directory changes synchronously. Because RPC over IP is synchronous, both replication partners must be available at the time the connection is established. You should use RPC over IP when there are reliable, dedicated connections between sites.

With SMTP as the transport, domain controllers convert all replication traffic to email messages that are sent between the sites asynchronously. Because SMTP replication is asynchronous, both replication partners do not have to be available at the time the connection is established, and replication transactions can be stored until a destination server is available. You should use SMTP when links are unreliable or not always available.

NOTE If you plan to use SMTP, you must set up a certificate authority (CA). Certificates from the CA are used to digitally sign and encrypt the SMTP messages sent between the sites. With IP, CAs are not required by default.

You can create a site link between two or more sites by following these steps:

1. In Active Directory Sites And Services, expand the Sites container, and then expand the Inter-Site Transports container.
2. Press and hold or right-click the container for the transport protocol you want to use (either IP or SMTP), and then tap or click New Site Link.

3. In the New Object - Site Link dialog box, shown in Figure 8-12, enter a name for the site link, such as ChicagotoSeattleLink. Site link names cannot contain spaces or special characters other than a dash.

4. In the Sites Not In This Site Link list, tap or click the first site that should be included in the link, and then tap or click Add to add the site to the Sites In This Site Link list. Repeat this process for each site you want to add to the link. You must include at least two sites. Tap or click OK.

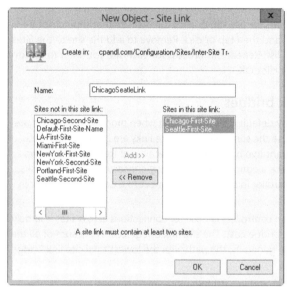

FIGURE 8-12 Create the site link by entering a name for the link and then selecting the associated sites.

When you finish creating the site link, you should configure the link's properties. This allows you to specify the link cost, replication schedule, and replication interval. To configure site link properties, follow these steps:

1. In Active Directory Sites And Services, press and hold or right-click the site link in the details pane, and then tap or click Properties.

2. In the Properties dialog box, the General tab is selected by default. In the Cost box, set the relative cost of the link. The default cost is 100.

3. In the Replicate Every box, set the replication interval. The default interval is 180 minutes.

4. The default replication schedule is 24 hours a day, seven days a week. To set a different schedule, tap or click Change Schedule, set the replication schedule in the Schedule For dialog box, and then tap or click OK.

You can change the sites associated with a site link at any time by following these steps:

1. In Active Directory Sites And Services, press and hold or right-click the site link in the details pane, and then tap or click Properties.

2. In the Properties dialog box, the General tab is selected by default. In the Sites Not In This Site Link list, tap or click the first site that should be included in the link, and then tap or click Add to add the site to the Sites In This Site Link list. Repeat this process for each site you want to add to the link.

3. In the Sites In This Site Link list, tap or click the first site that should not be included in the link, and then tap or click Remove to add the site to the Sites Not In This Site Link list. Repeat this process for each site you want to remove from the link. Tap or click OK.

Configuring site link bridges

All site links are transitive by default. This means that when more than two sites are linked for replication and use the same transport, site links are bridged automatically, allowing links to be transitive between sites. Because of transitivity, any two domain controllers can make a connection across any consecutive series of links. For example, a domain controller in site A could connect to a domain controller in site C through site B.

The link path that domain controllers choose for connections across sites is largely determined by the site link bridge cost. The site link bridge cost is the sum of all the links included in the bridge; generally, the path with the lowest total site link bridge cost is used.

Knowing the costs of links and link bridges, you can calculate the effects of a network link failure and determine the paths that will be used when a connection is down. For example, a domain controller in site A would normally connect to a domain controller in site C through site B. However, if the connection to site B is down, the two domain controllers would choose an alternate path automatically if one is available, such as going through site D and site E to establish a connection.

Intersite replication topology is optimized for a maximum of three hops by default. In large-site configurations, this can have unintended consequences, such as the same replication traffic going over the same link several times. In this case, you should disable automatic site link bridging and manually configure site link bridges. Otherwise, you typically do not want to disable automatic site link bridging.

Within an Active Directory forest, you can enable or disable site link transitivity on a per-transport protocol basis. This means all site links that use a particular transport either use site link transitivity or don't use it. You can configure transitivity for a transport protocol by following these steps:

1. In Active Directory Sites And Services, expand the Sites container, and then expand the Inter-Site Transports container.

2. Press and hold or right-click the container for the transport protocol you want to work with (either IP or SMTP), and then tap or click Properties.

3. To enable site link transitivity, select Bridge All Site Links, and then tap or click OK. When site link transitivity is enabled, any site link bridges you've created for a particular transport protocol are ignored.

4. To disable site link transitivity, clear the Bridge All Site Links check box, and then tap or click OK. When site link transitivity is disabled, you must configure site link bridges for the affected protocol.

After you've disabled transitive links, you can manually create a site link bridge between two or more sites by following these steps:

1. In Active Directory Sites And Services, expand the Sites container, and then expand the Inter-Site Transports container.

2. Press and hold or right-click the container for the transport protocol you want to work with (either IP or SMTP), and then tap or click New Site Link Bridge.

3. In the New Object—Site Link Bridge dialog box, enter a name for the site link bridge. Bridge names cannot contain spaces or special characters other than a dash.

4. In the Site Links Not In This Site Link Bridge list, select a site link that should be included in the bridge, and then tap or click Add to add the site link to the Site Links In This Site Link Bridge list. Repeat this process for each site link you want to add to the bridge. A bridge must include at least two site links. Tap or click OK.

You can change the site links associated with a site link bridge at any time by following these steps:

1. In Active Directory Sites And Services, select the container for the transport protocol you want to work with, press and hold or right-click the site link bridge you want to work with, and then tap or click Properties.

2. In the Properties dialog box, the General tab is selected by default. In the Site Links Not In This Site Link Bridge list, tap or click the first site link that should be included in the bridge, and then tap or click Add to add the site link to the Site Links In This Site Link Bridge list. Repeat this process for each site link you want to add to the bridge.

3. In the Site Links In This Site Link Bridge list, tap or click the first site link that should not be included in the bridge, and then tap or click Remove to add the site link to the Site Links Not In This Site Link Bridge list. Repeat this process for each site link you want to remove from the bridge. Tap or click OK.

Maintaining Active Directory

To ensure proper operations of Active Directory, you need to perform periodic monitoring and maintenance. In your monitoring and maintenance efforts, you'll find that some tools are instrumental to your success. In this section, I'll introduce these tools and some general maintenance tasks.

Using ADSI Edit

When you are diagnosing problems and troubleshooting, the Active Directory administration tool you should use is Active Directory Service Interfaces Editor (ADSI Edit). You can use ADSI Edit to manage the definitions of object classes and their attributes in the schema and to work with other naming contexts, including the default naming context, the Configuration naming context, and the RootDSE naming context. If you want to create custom attributes for users or groups, use ADSI Edit, which you can start by using the related option on the Tools menu in Server Manager.

You can use the ADSI Edit snap-in to connect to a naming context by following these steps:

1. Press and hold or right-click the ADSI Edit node in the console tree, and then select Connect To. This displays the Connection Settings dialog box, shown in Figure 8-13.

FIGURE 8-13 Connect to a naming context in ADSI Edit.

2. In the Connection Settings dialog box, the Select A Well Known Naming Context list is enabled by default. Choose the naming context you want to work with.

3. When you tap or click OK, you are connected to any available domain controller in your logon domain. To connect to a different domain or server, choose Select Or Type A Domain Or Server, and then choose the server or domain you want to work with along with an optional port number for the connection, such as FileServer252.cpandl.com:389. Port 389 is the default port for LDAP.

After you select a naming context, domain, and server, you are connected to and can work with the naming context. As Figure 8-14 shows, when you connect to multiple naming contexts, you have separate nodes for managing each context. For troubleshooting, you can also connect to the same naming context on different servers in the same domain. By comparing the values associated with properties on one server with those on another, you can identify a replication problem.

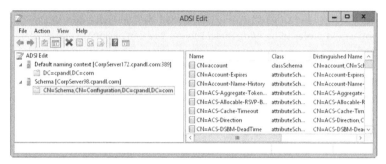

FIGURE 8-14 Browse the naming contexts to examine related containers and properties.

Examining intersite topology

The intersite topology generator (ISTG) on a site is responsible for generating the intersite replication topology. When calculating the replication topology, the ISTG can use considerable processing power, especially as the size of the network grows. Because of this, you should closely monitor the ISTGs in each site to ensure that they are not overloaded.

You can determine which domain controller is the ISTG by following these steps:

1. In Active Directory Sites And Services, expand the Sites container, and then expand the site for the ISTG you want to locate in the console tree.

2. In the details pane, double-tap or double-click NTDS Site Settings. In the NTDS Site Settings dialog box, the current ISTG is listed in the Inter-Site Topology Generator panel.

Replication between sites normally is performed by *bridgehead servers*. A bridgehead server is a domain controller designated by the ISTG to perform intersite replication. The ISTG configures a bridgehead server for each Active Directory partition that needs to be replicated and maintains a separate replication topology for each type of partition. Although a single bridgehead server can be responsible for replicating multiple directory partitions, the replication topology for each partition is maintained separately.

Domain controllers that operate as bridgehead servers have an additional workload that increases with the number and frequency of replication changes. As you should do with the ISTG, you should periodically monitor designated bridgehead servers to ensure that they do not become overloaded. You can list the bridgehead servers in a site by entering the following command at a command prompt:

```
repadmin /bridgeheads site:SiteName
```

Here, *SiteName* is the name of the site, such as:

```
repadmin /bridgeheads site:SacramentoSite
```

If current bridgehead servers become overloaded, or if you have domain controllers you would prefer to be bridgehead servers, you can designate preferred bridgehead servers to use. Once you designate a preferred bridgehead server for a site, the ISTG uses the preferred bridgehead server for intersite replication. If the preferred bridgehead server goes offline or is unable to replicate for any reason, intersite replication stops until the server is again available or you change the preferred bridgehead server configuration.

When you designate preferred bridgeheads, you should always configure multiple preferred bridgehead servers in each site. The ISTG will then choose one of the servers you've designated as the preferred bridgehead server. If this server fails, the ISTG would then choose another server from the list of preferred bridgehead servers.

You must configure a bridgehead server for each partition that needs to be replicated. This means you must configure at least one domain controller with a replica of each directory partition as a bridgehead server. If you don't do this, replication of the partition will fail and the ISTG will log an event in the Directory Services event log detailing the failure.

You can configure a domain controller as a preferred bridgehead server by following these steps:

1. In Active Directory Sites And Services, domain controllers associated with a site are listed in the site's Servers node. Press and hold or right-click the server you want to designate as a preferred bridgehead, and then tap or click Properties.

2. In the Properties dialog box, select the intersite transport protocol for which the server should be a preferred bridgehead in the Transports Available For Inter-Site Data Transfer list and then tap or click Add. Repeat as necessary to specify both IP and SMTP. Tap or click OK.

When you've designated preferred bridgehead servers, you can recover from replication failure in several ways. You can remove the failed servers as preferred bridgehead servers and then specify different preferred bridgehead servers, or you can remove all servers as preferred bridgehead servers and then allow the ISTG to select the bridgehead servers that should be used. To stop a server from being a preferred bridgehead for a particular transport protocol, follow these steps:

1. In Active Directory Sites And Services, domain controllers associated with a site are listed in the site's Servers node. Press and hold or right-click the server you want to stop using as a preferred bridgehead, and then tap or click Properties.

2. Select the transport protocol in the This Server Is A Preferred Bridgehead Server For The Following Transports list, and then tap or click Remove. Tap or click OK.

Troubleshooting Active Directory

As part of routine maintenance, you need to monitor domain controllers, global catalog servers, bridgehead servers, and site links. If you suspect problems with Active Directory, you should look at replication in most cases as the starting point for your diagnostics and troubleshooting. By configuring monitoring of Active Directory intrasite and intersite replication, you can diagnose and resolve most replication problems. Keep in mind, though, that Active Directory replication has several service dependencies, including LDAP, DNS, Kerberos version 5 authentication, and RPC.

These important services must be functioning properly to allow directory updates to be replicated. During replication, Active Directory relies on various TCP and UDP ports being open between domain controllers. By default, the ports used are as follows:

- LDAP uses TCP and UDP on port 389 for standard traffic, and TCP on port 686 for secure traffic.
- Global catalogs use TCP on port 3268. Kerberos version 5 uses TCP and UDP on port 88.
- DNS uses TCP and UDP on port 53.
- SMB over IP uses TCP and UDP on port 445.

Additionally, for replication of files in the System Volume (SYSVOL) shared folders on domain controllers, Active Directory uses either the file replication service (FRS) or the DFS Replication Service. The appropriate replication service must be running and properly configured to replicate the SYSVOL.

As mentioned earlier in the chapter, Active Directory tracks changes by using update sequence numbers (USNs). Any time a change is made to the directory, the domain controller processing the change assigns the change a USN. Each domain controller maintains its own local USNs and increments the value each time a change occurs. The domain controller also assigns the local USN to the object attribute that changed. Each object has a related attribute, usnChanged, which is stored with the object and identifies the highest USN that has been assigned to any of the object's attributes.

Each domain controller tracks its local USN and also the local USNs of other domain controllers. During replication, domain controllers compare the USN values received to what is stored. If the current USN value for a particular domain controller is higher than the stored value, changes associated with that domain controller need to be replicated. If the current value for a particular domain controller is the same as the stored value, changes for that domain controller do not need to be replicated.

You can monitor replication from the command line by using Repadmin. With Repadmin, most command-line parameters accept a list of the domain controllers you want to work with, called DSA_List. You can specify the values for DSA_List as follows:

- ***** A wildcard character that includes all domain controllers in the organization
- ***PartialName*** A partial server name followed by the * wildcard character to match the remainder of the server name
- **Site:*SiteName*** The name of the site for which you want to include domain controllers
- **Gc** All global catalog servers in the organization

Although Repadmin has many parameters and you can use it in many ways, you'll perform certain tasks more than others. To view detailed help for each task, enter the following example at the command prompt: **repadmin /?:kcc**. Table 8-2 shows some of these tasks.

TABLE 8-2 Common Replication Tasks and Commands

TASK	COMMAND
Forcing the Knowledge Consistency Checker (KCC) to recalculate the intrasite replication topology for a specified domain controller.	repadmin /kcc DSA_List [/async]
Listing bridgehead servers that match the DSA_List.	repadmin /bridgeheads [DSA_List] [/verbose]
Listing calls made but not yet answered by the specified server to other servers.	repadmin /showoutcalls [DSA_List]
Listing domains trusted by a specified domain.	repadmin /showtrust [DSA_List]
Listing failed replication events that were detected by the KCC.	repadmin /failcache [DSA_List]
Listing connection objects for the specified domain controllers. Defaults to the local site.	repadmin /showconn [DSA_List]

TASK	COMMAND
Listing computers that have opened sessions with a specified domain controller.	repadmin /showctx [DSA_List]
Listing the name of the ISTG for a specified site.	repadmin istg [DSA_List] [/verbose]
Listing replication partners for each directory partition on the specified domain controller.	repadmin /showrepl [DSA_List]
Listing a summary of the replication state.	repadmin /replsummary [DSA_List]
Listing server certificates loaded on the specified domain controllers.	repadmin /showcert [DSA_List]
Listing tasks waiting in the replication queue.	repadmin /queue [DSA_List]
Listing the time between intersite replications that are using the ISTG Keep Alive time stamp.	repadmin /latency [DSA_List] [/verbose]

Creating user and group accounts

Managing accounts is one of your primary tasks as a Windows administrator. Chapter 8, "Core Active Directory administration," discusses computer accounts. This chapter examines user and group accounts. With user accounts, you can enable individual users to log on to the network and access network resources. With group accounts, you manage resources for multiple users. The permissions and privileges you assign to user and group accounts determines which actions users can perform and which computer systems and resources they can access.

Although you might be tempted to give users wide access, you need to balance a user's need for job-related resources with your need to protect sensitive resources or privileged information. For example, you don't want everyone in the company to have access to payroll data. Consequently, you should be sure that only those who need that information have access to it.

In this chapter, you'll learn how to manage domain accounts. Although local system accounts are discussed, they are not the primary focus. For further discussion of configuring local system accounts, see Chapter 5, "Managing user access and security," in *Windows 8.1 Administration Pocket Consultant: Essentials & Configuration* (Microsoft Press, 2013). Keep in mind that Windows 8.1 adds a special type of local account called a *Microsoft account*. Microsoft accounts can be thought of as synchronized accounts. When you connect a local or domain account to a Microsoft account, the account becomes a connected local account or connected domain account.

Windows Server security model

You control access to network resources with the components of the Windows Server security model. The key components you need to know about are those used for authentication and access controls.

Authentication protocols

Windows Server authentication is implemented as a two-part process consisting of an interactive logon and network authentication. When a user logs on to a computer by using a domain account, the interactive logon process authenticates the user's logon credentials, which confirms the user's identity to the local computer and grants access to Active Directory Domain Services (AD DS). Afterward, whenever the user attempts to access network resources, network authentication is used to determine whether the user has permission to do so.

Windows Server 2012 R2 supports many network authentication protocols. Active Directory uses Kerberos V5 as the default authentication protocol. NTLM authentication is maintained only for backward compatibility. In Group Policy, you can control how NTLM is used with the security option Network Security: LAN Manager Authentication Level. The default authentication level in most cases is Send NTLMv2 Response Only. With this authentication level, clients use NTLM 2 for authentication and session security if the server supports it. Active Directory can also use client certificates for authentication.

A key feature of the Windows Server authentication model is that it supports single sign-on, which works as follows:

1. A user logs on to the domain by using a logon name and password, or by inserting a smart card into a card reader.

2. The interactive logon process authenticates the user's access. With a local account, the credentials are authenticated locally, and the user is granted access to the local computer. With a domain account, the credentials are authenticated in Active Directory, and the user has access to local and network resources.

3. The user can authenticate to any computer in the domain through the network authentication process.

With domain accounts, the network authentication process typically is automatic (through single sign-on). With local accounts, users must provide a user name and password every time they access a network resource.

Windows Server includes Active Directory Federation Services (AD FS), which extends single sign-on to trusted resources on the Internet. Using AD FS, organizations can extend their existing Active Directory infrastructure to provide access to trusted Internet resources, which can include third parties and geographically separated units of the same organization. After you configure federated servers, users at the organization can sign on once to the organization's network and are then automatically logged on to trusted web applications hosted by partners on the Internet. Federated Web Single Sign-On uses federated authorization for seamless access. In addition to user identity and account information, security tokens used in federated authorization include authorization claims that detail user authorization and specific application entitlement.

Access controls

Active Directory is object-based. Users, computers, groups, shared resources, and many other entities are all defined as objects. Access controls are applied to these objects with security descriptors. Security descriptors do the following:

- List the users and groups that are granted access to objects.
- Specify permissions the users and groups have been assigned.
- Track events that should be audited for objects.
- Define ownership of objects.

Individual entries in the security descriptor are referred to as *access control entries (ACEs)*. Active Directory objects can inherit ACEs from their parent objects. This means that permissions for a parent object can be applied to a child object. For example, all members of the Domain Admins group inherit permissions granted to this group.

When working with ACEs, keep the following points in mind:

- ACEs are created with inheritance enabled by default.
- Inheritance takes place immediately after the ACE is created and saved.
- All ACEs contain information specifying whether the permission is inherited or explicitly assigned to the related object.

Claims-based access controls

To the standard access controls, Windows Server 2012 R2 adds Kerberos armoring, compound identities, and claims-based access controls. *Kerberos armoring* improves domain security by allowing domain-joined clients and domain controllers to communicate over secure, encrypted channels. Compound identities incorporate not only the groups that a user is a member of, but also user claims, device claims, and resource properties.

Claims-based access controls can be configured in several ways. The most basic approach is to define conditions that limit access as part of a resource's advanced security permissions. Typically, these conditions add device claims or user claims to the access controls. User claims identify users; device claims identify devices. For example, to access the Human Resources share, you might add a device claim to ensure that the computer being used to access a resource is a member of HR Computers, and add a user claim that ensures that the user is a member of the HR Managers group.

Kerberos armoring, compound identities, and claims-based access controls can also work together as part of a new authorization platform that allows dynamic access to resources by configuring central access policies. With central access policies, you define central access rules in Active Directory, and those rules are applied dynamically throughout the enterprise. Central access rules use conditional expressions that require you to determine the resource properties required for the policy, the claim types and security groups required for the policy, and the servers where the policy should be applied.

Before you can define and apply an access rule, you'll likely need to define resource properties and claim types:

- Resource properties create property definitions for resources. For example, you might add Department and Country properties to files so that you can dynamically control access by department and country.

- Claim types create claim definitions for resources. For example, you might create a user claim to add Department and Country properties to User objects so that you can dynamically control access by department and country.

After you create resource properties and claim types and determine where the policy should be applied, you can create an access rule and then add it to a central access policy. Adding the rule to a policy makes the rule available for dynamic control. You then need to apply the policy across file servers by using Group Policy.

Claims-based policy must be enabled for Default Domain Controllers policy. You do this by enabling and configuring the KDC Support For Claims, Compound Authentication And Kerberos Armoring policy in the Administrative Templates policies for Computer Configuration under System\KDC. The policy must be configured to use a specific mode. Here are the available modes:

- **Supported**   Domain controllers support claims, compound identities, and Kerberos armoring. Client computers that don't support Kerberos armoring can be authenticated.

- **Always Provide Claims**   This mode is the same as Supported, but domain controllers always return claims for accounts.

- **Fail Unarmored Authentication Requests**   Kerberos armoring is mandatory. Client computers that don't support Kerberos armoring cannot be authenticated.

The Kerberos Client Support For Claims, Compound Authentication And Kerberos Armoring policy in the Administrative Templates policies for Computer Configuration under System\Kerberos controls whether the Kerberos client running on Windows 8.1 and Windows Server 2012 R2 requests claims and compound authentication. The policy must be enabled for compatible Kerberos clients to request claims and compound authentication for Dynamic Access Control and Kerberos armoring.

REAL WORLD Claims-based policy should be enabled for all domain controllers in a domain to ensure consistent application. A domain must have at least one domain controller running Windows Server 2012 R2, and file servers must run Windows Server 2012 R2. By default, domain controllers are placed in the Domain Controllers organizational unit (OU), and Default Domain Controllers policy has the highest precedence among Group Policy Objects (GPOs) linked to the Domain Controllers OU. If your organization uses a different approach, you need to ensure that the GPO with the highest precedence for the appropriate OU has claims-based policy enabled and configured properly.

Central access policies

Central access policies don't replace traditional access controls. Instead, they are designed to enhance existing access controls by defining very precisely the specific attributes users and devices must have to access resources. The easiest way to manage central access policy is to use Active Directory Administrative Center.

An overview of the policy creation and deployment process follows:

1. Open Active Directory Administrative Center. In the left pane, List View is selected by default. Tap or click Tree View to display the tree view. Next, expand Dynamic Access Control in the left pane, and then select Claim Types.

2. Use the Claim Types node to create and manage claim types. For example, right-click the Claim Types node, click New, and then select Claim Type to start creating a new claim type.

3. Use the Resource Properties node to create and manage resource properties. For example, right-click the Resource Properties node, click New, and then select Resource Property to start creating a new resource property.

   NOTE Resource properties are also added as classification definition properties on file servers.

4. Use the Central Access Rules node to create and manage central access rules. For example, right-click the Central Access Rules node, click New, and then select Central Access Rule to start creating a new access rule.

5. Use the Central Access Policies node to create and manage central access policies. For example, right-click the Central Access Policies node, click New, and then select Central Access Policy to start creating a new access policy.

To complete the deployment, you need to edit the highest precedence GPO linked to the OU where you put file servers and then enable central access policies. To do this, follow these steps:

1. In Group Policy Management, open the GPO for editing.

2. Browse Computer Configuration policies to Windows Settings\Security Settings\File System.

3. Press and hold or right-click Central Access Policy, and then tap or click Manage Central Access Policies. This opens the Central Access Policies Configuration dialog box.

4. In the Central Access Policies Configuration dialog box, available policies are listed in the left pane, and currently applied policies are listed in the right pane. To apply a policy, tap or click it in the left pane and then tap or click Add. To remove a policy, tap or click it in the right pane and then tap or click Remove. Tap or click OK.

After the Group Policy changes take effect on your servers, the dynamic controls are available. You can speed the refresh along by entering **gpupdate /force** at an elevated, administrator command prompt.

Servers that you want to apply dynamic controls to must have, at a minimum, the File And Storage Services role with the File Server, Storage Services, and File Server Resource Manager role services. You need the File Server Resource Manager role service and the related tools to apply classification property definitions to folders.

After you enable central access policy, and any time you update your classification property definitions, you need to wait for Global Resource Properties from Active Directory to refresh on your file servers. You can speed this along by opening Windows PowerShell and entering **update-fsrmclassificationpropertydefinition**. Do this on each file server where you want to configure central access policies.

To complete the deployment of central access policies, you need to edit the properties of each folder where you want a central access policy to apply and do the following:

1. Add the appropriate classification definitions on the folder's Classification tab. On the Classification tab, each resource property you created will be listed. Select each property in turn, and then set its value as appropriate.

2. Enable the appropriate policy by using advanced security settings for the folder. On the Security tab, tap or click Advanced, and then tap or click the Central Policy tab. Any currently selected or applied policy is listed along with a description that allows you to review the rules of that policy. When you tap or click Change, you can use the selection list provided to select a policy to apply, or you can choose No Central Access Policy to stop using the policy. Tap or click OK.

Repeat this process for each top-level or other folder where you want to limit access. Files and folders within the selected folder will inherit the access rule automatically unless you specify otherwise. As an example, if you create an access rule called "HR Managers in the US" and define Department and Country resource definitions, you could edit the HR folder's properties, select the Classification tab, and then use the options available to set Department to HR and Country to US. Then you could apply the "HR Managers in the US" policy by using the advanced security settings for the folder.

Differences between user and group accounts

Windows Server 2012 R2 provides user accounts and group accounts (of which users can be a member). User accounts are designed for individuals. Group accounts are designed to make the administration of multiple users easier. Although you can log on with user accounts, you can't log on with a group account. Group accounts are usually referred to simply as *groups*.

> **REAL WORLD** Windows Server supports the InetOrgPerson object. Essentially, this object is the same as a user object, and you can use it as such. However, the real purpose for the InetOrgPerson object is to allow for compatibility and transition from third-party X.500 and Lightweight Directory Access Protocol (LDAP) directory services that use this object to represent users. If you are migrating from a third-party directory service and end up with many InetOrgPerson objects, don't worry. These objects are security principals just like user accounts. You can set passwords for InetOrgPerson objects and change the object class if you want to. When you change the object class, the InetOrgPerson object is converted to a user object, and from then on it is listed as the User type in Active Directory Users And Computers.

User accounts

Two types of user accounts are defined in Windows Server:

- User accounts defined in Active Directory are called *domain user accounts*. Through single sign-on, domain user accounts can access resources throughout the domain. You create domain user accounts in Active Directory Users And Computers.

- User accounts defined on a local computer are called *local user accounts*. Local user accounts have access to the local computer only, and they must authenticate themselves before they can access network resources. You create local user accounts with the Local Users And Groups utility.

> **NOTE** In a domain, only member servers and workstations have local user and group accounts. On the initial domain controller for a domain, these accounts are moved from the local Security Accounts Manager (SAM) database to Active Directory and then become domain accounts.

Logon names, passwords, and public certificates

All user accounts are identified with a logon name. In Windows Server, this logon name has two parts:

- **User name**   The text label for the account
- **User domain or workgroup**   The workgroup or domain where the user account exists

For the user wrstanek, whose account is created in the cpandl.com domain, the full logon name is wrstanek@cpandl.com. The pre–Windows 2000 logon name is CPANDL\wrstanek.

When working with Active Directory, you might also need to specify the fully qualified domain name (FQDN) for a user. The FQDN for a user is the combination of the Domain Name System (DNS) domain name, the container or organizational unit that contains the user, and the user name. For example, for the user cpandl.com \users\wrstanek, *cpandl.com* is the DNS domain name, *users* is the container or organizational unit location, and *wrstanek* is the user name.

User accounts can also have passwords and public certificates associated with them. *Passwords* are authentication strings for an account. *Public certificates* combine a public and private key to identify a user. You log on with a password interactively. You log on with a public certificate by using a smart card and a smart card reader.

Security identifiers and user accounts

Although Windows Server displays user names to describe privileges and permissions, the key identifiers for accounts are *security identifiers (SIDs)*. SIDs are unique identifiers that are generated when you create accounts. Each account's SID consists of the domain's security ID prefix and a unique relative ID (RID), which is allocated by the relative ID master.

Windows Server uses these identifiers to track accounts independently from user names. SIDs serve many purposes. The two most important purposes are to allow you to change user names easily and to allow you to delete accounts without worrying that someone might gain access to resources simply by re-creating an account with the same name.

When you change a user name, you tell Windows Server to map a particular SID to a new name. When you delete an account, you tell Windows Server that a particular SID is no longer valid. Afterward, even if you create an account with the same user name, the new account won't have the same privileges and permissions as the previous one. That's because the new account will have a new SID.

Group accounts

In addition to user accounts, Windows Server provides groups. Generally speaking, you use groups to grant permissions to similar types of users and to simplify account administration. If a user is a member of a group that can access a resource, that particular user can access the same resource. Thus, you can give a user access to various work-related resources just by making the user a member of the correct group. Note that although you can log on to a computer with a user account, you can't log on to a computer with a group account.

Because different Active Directory domains might have groups with the same name, groups are often referred to by *domain\groupname*, such as cpandl \gmarketing for the *gmarketing* group in the *cpandl* domain. When you work with Active Directory, you might also need to specify the FQDN for a group. The

FQDN for a group is the concatenation of the DNS domain name, the container or organizational unit location, and the group name. For the group cpandl.com\users\gmarketing, *cpandl.com* is the DNS domain name, *users* is the container or organizational unit location, and *gmarketing* is the group name.

> **REAL WORLD** Employees in a marketing department probably need access to all marketing-related resources. Instead of granting access to these resources to each individual employee, you could make the users members of a marketing group. That way, they automatically obtain the group's privileges. Later, if a user moves to a different department, you simply remove the user from the group, thus revoking all access permissions. Compared to having to revoke access for each individual resource, this technique is pretty easy, so you'll want to use groups whenever possible.

Group types

Windows Server supports three types of groups:

- **Local** Groups that are defined on a local computer. Local groups are used on the local computer only. You create local groups with the Local Users And Groups utility.
- **Security** Groups that can have security descriptors associated with them. You define security groups in domains by using Active Directory Users And Computers.
- **Distribution** Groups that are used as email distribution lists. They can't have security descriptors associated with them. You define distribution groups in domains by using Active Directory Users And Computers.

> **NOTE** Most general discussions about groups focus on local groups and security groups rather than on distribution groups. Distribution groups are only for email distribution and are not for assigning or managing access.

Group scope

In Active Directory, groups can have different scopes—domain local, built-in local, global, and universal. That is, the groups are valid in different areas, as described here:

- **Domain local** Groups primarily used to assign access permissions to resources within a single domain. Domain local groups can include members from any domain in the forest and from trusted domains in other forests. Typically, global and universal groups are members of domain local groups.
- **Built-in local** Groups with a special group scope that have domain local permissions and, for simplicity, are often included in the term *domain local groups*. The difference between built-in local groups and other groups is that you can't create or delete built-in local groups. You can only modify built-in local groups. References to domain local groups apply to built-in local groups unless otherwise noted.

- **Global** Groups that are used primarily to define sets of users or computers in the same domain that share a similar role, function, or job. Members of global groups can include only accounts and groups from the domain in which they're defined.
- **Universal** Groups that are used primarily to define sets of users or computers that should have wide permissions throughout a domain or forest. Members of universal groups include accounts, global groups, and other universal groups from any domain in the domain tree or forest.

BEST PRACTICES Universal groups are very useful in large enterprises where you have multiple domains. If you plan properly, you can use universal groups to simplify system administration. You shouldn't change the members of universal groups frequently. Each time you change the members of a universal group, you need to replicate those changes to all the global catalogs in the domain tree or forest. To reduce changes, assign other groups rather than user accounts to the universal group. For more information, see the "When to use domain local, global, and universal groups" section later in this chapter.

When you work with groups, the group's scope restricts what you can and cannot do. Table 9-1 offers a quick summary of these items. For complete details about creating groups, see the "Adding a group account" section later in this chapter.

TABLE 9-1 How Group Scope Affects Group Capabilities

GROUP CAPABILITY	DOMAIN LOCAL SCOPE	GLOBAL SCOPE	UNIVERSAL SCOPE
Members	Accounts, global groups, and universal groups from any domain; domain local groups from the same domain only	Accounts and global groups from the same domain only	Accounts from any domain, in addition to global and universal groups from any domain
Member of	Can be put into other domain local groups and assigned permissions only in the same domain	Can be put into other groups and assigned permissions in any domain	Can be put into other groups and assigned permissions in any domain
Scope conversion	Can be converted to universal scope provided that it doesn't have as its member another group having domain local scope	Can be converted to universal scope provided that it's not a member of any other group having global scope	Can't be converted to any other group scope

Security identifiers and group accounts

As with user accounts, Windows Server tracks group accounts with unique SIDs. This means that you can't delete a group account, re-create it, and then expect all the permissions and privileges to remain the same. The new group will have a new SID, and all the permissions and privileges of the old group are lost.

Windows Server creates a security token for each user logon. The security token specifies the user account ID and the SIDs of all the security groups to which the user belongs. The token's size grows as the user is added to additional security groups, which has the following consequences:

- The security token must be passed to the user logon process before logon can be completed. As the number of security group memberships grows, the logon process takes longer.

- To determine access permissions, the security token is sent to every computer that the user accesses. Therefore, the size of the security token has a direct impact on the network traffic load.

NOTE Distribution group memberships aren't distributed with security tokens, so distribution group memberships don't affect the token size.

When to use domain local, global, and universal groups

Domain local, global, and universal groups provide many options for configuring groups in the enterprise. Although these group scopes are designed to simplify administration, poor planning can make them your worst administration nightmare. Ideally, you use group scopes to help you create group hierarchies that are similar to your organization's structure and the responsibilities of particular groups of users. The best uses for domain local, global, and universal groups are as follows:

- **Domain local** Groups with domain local scope have the smallest extent of all groups. Use groups with domain local scope to help you manage access to resources such as printers and shared folders.

- **Global** Use groups with global scope to help you manage user and computer accounts in a particular domain. Then you can grant access permissions to a resource by making the group with global scope a member of the group with domain local scope.

- **Universal** Groups with universal scope have the largest extent. Use groups with universal scope to consolidate groups that span domains. Typically, you do this by adding global groups as members. Then, when you change membership of the global groups, the changes aren't replicated to all global catalogs because the membership of the universal group didn't change.

TIP If your organization doesn't have two or more domains, you don't really need to use universal groups. Instead, build your group structure with domain local and global groups. Then, if you ever bring another domain into your domain tree or forest, you can easily extend the group hierarchy to accommodate the integration.

To put this in perspective, consider the following scenario. Suppose that you have branch offices in Seattle, Chicago, and New York. Each office has its own domain, which is part of the same domain tree or forest. These domains are called Seattle, Chicago, and NY, respectively. You want to make it easy for any administrator (from any office) to manage network resources, so you create a group structure that is very similar at each location. Although the company has marketing, IT, and engineering departments, let's focus on the structure of the marketing department. At each office, members of the marketing department need access to a shared printer called *MarketingPrinter* and a shared data folder called *MarketingData*. You also want users to be able to share and print documents. For example, Bob in Seattle should be able to print documents so that Ralph in New York can pick them up on his local printer, and Bob should also be able to access the quarterly report in the shared folder at the New York office.

To configure the groups for the marketing departments at the three offices, you'd follow these steps:

1. Create global groups for each marketing group. In the Seattle domain, create a group named **GMarketing** and add the members of the Seattle marketing department to it. In the Chicago domain, create a group named **GMarketing** and add the members of the Chicago marketing department to it. In the NY domain, create a group named **GMarketing** and add the members of the New York marketing department to it.

2. In each location, create domain local groups that grant access to the shared printers and shared folders. Name the printer group **LocalMarketingPrinter**, and name the shared folder group **LocalMarketingData**. The Seattle, Chicago, and NY domains should each have their own local groups.

3. Create a group with universal scope in the domain at any branch office. Name the group **UMarketing**. Add Seattle\GMarketing, Chicago\GMarketing, and NY\GMarketing to this group.

4. Add UMarketing to the LocalMarketingPrinter and LocalMarketingData groups at each office. Marketing users should now be able to share data and printers.

Default user accounts and groups

When you install Windows Server 2012 R2, the operating system installs default users and groups. These accounts are designed to provide the basic setup necessary to grow your network. Three types of default accounts are provided:

- **Built-in** User and group accounts installed with the operating system, applications, and services
- **Predefined** User and group accounts installed with the operating system
- **Implicit** Special groups, also known as *special identities*, created implicitly when accessing network resources

NOTE Although you can modify default users and groups, you can't delete default users and groups created by the operating system because you wouldn't be able to re-create them. The SIDs of the old and new accounts wouldn't match, and the permissions and privileges of these accounts would be lost.

Built-in user accounts

Built-in user accounts have special purposes in Windows Server. All Windows Server systems have several built-in user accounts, including the following ones:

- **LocalSystem**   A pseudoaccount for running system processes and handling system-level tasks. This account is part of the Administrators group on the server and has all user rights on the server. If you configure applications or services to use this account, the related processes have full access to the server system. Many services run under the LocalSystem account. In some cases, these services also have the privilege to interact with the desktop. Services that need alternative privileges or logon rights run under the LocalService or NetworkService account.

- **LocalService**   A pseudoaccount with limited privileges. This account grants access to the local system only. The account is part of the Users group on the server and has the same rights as the NetworkService account, except that it is limited to the local computer. Configure applications or services to use this account when related processes don't need to access other servers.

- **NetworkService**   A pseudoaccount for running services that need additional privileges and logon rights on a local system and the network. This account is part of the Users group on the server and provides fewer permissions and privileges than the LocalSystem account (but more than the LocalService account). Specifically, processes running under this account can interact throughout a network by using the credentials of the computer account.

When you install add-ons or other applications on a server, other default accounts might be installed.

Predefined user accounts

Several predefined user accounts are installed with Windows Server, including Administrator and Guest. With member servers, predefined accounts are local to the individual system they're installed on.

Predefined accounts have counterparts in Active Directory. These accounts have domainwide access and are completely separate from the local accounts on individual systems.

Administrator account

Administrator is a predefined account that provides complete access to files, directories, services, and other facilities. In Active Directory, the Administrator account has domainwide access and privileges. Otherwise, the Administrator account generally has access only to the local system. Although files and directories can be protected from the Administrator account temporarily, the Administrator account can take control of these resources at any time by changing the access permissions. By default, the Administrator account is enabled for use, but you can disable or rename it to enhance security.

SECURITY ALERT To prevent unauthorized access to the system or domain, be sure to give the Administrator account an especially secure password. Also, because this is a known Windows account, you might want to rename the account as an extra security precaution. If you rename the original Administrator account, you might also want to create a dummy Administrator account. This dummy account should have no permissions, rights, or privileges, and you should disable it.

You usually won't need to change the basic settings for the Administrator account. However, you might need to change its advanced settings, such as membership in particular groups. By default, the Administrator account for a domain is a member of these groups: Administrators, Domain Admins, Domain Users, Enterprise Admins, Group Policy Creator Owners, and Schema Admins. You'll find more information about these groups in the next section.

REAL WORLD In a domain environment, you use the local Administrator account primarily to manage the system when you first install it. This allows you to set up the system without getting locked out. You probably won't use the account after the system has been installed. Instead, you should make your administrators members of the Administrators group. This ensures that you can revoke administrator privileges without having to change the passwords for all the Administrator accounts.

For a system that's part of a workgroup where each individual computer is managed separately, you typically rely on this account any time you need to perform your system administration duties. Here, you probably don't want to set up individual accounts for each person who has administrative access to a system. Instead, use a separate administrator account on each computer.

Guest account

The Guest account is designed for users who need one-time or occasional access. Although guests have limited system privileges, you should be very careful about using this account. Whenever you use this account, you open the system to potential security problems. The risk is so great that the account is initially disabled when you install Windows Server.

The Guest account is a member of the Domain Guests and Guests groups by default. Note that the Guest account—like all other named accounts—is also a member of the implicit group Everyone. The Everyone group typically has access to files and folders by default. The Everyone group also has a default set of user rights.

SECURITY ALERT If you decide to enable the Guest account, be sure to restrict its use and change the password regularly. As with the Administrator account, you might want to rename the account as an added security precaution.

Built-in and predefined groups

Built-in groups are installed with all Windows Server systems. Use built-in and predefined groups to grant a user the group's privileges and permissions. You do this by making the user a member of the group. For example, you give a user administrative access to the system by making a user a member of the local Administrators group. You give a user administrative access to the domain by making a user a member of the Domain Admins group in Active Directory.

Implicit groups and special identities

Implicit groups are assigned implicitly during logon and are based on how a user accesses a network resource. For example, if a user accessed a resource through an interactive logon, the user is automatically a member of the implicit group named Interactive. Although you can't view the membership of special identities, you can grant membership in implicit groups to users, groups, and computers.

To reflect the modified role, implicit groups are also referred to as *special identities*. A special identity is a group whose membership can be set implicitly, such as during logon, or explicitly through security access permissions. As is the case with other default groups, the availability of a specific implicit group depends on the current configuration. Implicit groups are discussed later in this chapter.

Account capabilities

When you set up a user account, you can grant the user specific capabilities. You generally assign these capabilities by making the user a member of one or more groups, thus giving the user the capabilities of these groups. You withdraw capabilities by removing group membership.

In Windows Server, you can assign the following types of user rights as capabilities to an account:

- **Privileges** Grants permissions to perform specific administrative tasks. You can assign privileges to both user and group accounts. An example of a privilege is the ability to shut down the system.

- **Logon rights** Grants logon permissions. You can assign logon rights to both user and group accounts. An example of a logon right is the ability to log on locally.

- **Built-in capabilities** Assigned to groups and includes the group's automatic capabilities. Built-in capabilities are predefined and unchangeable, but they can be delegated to users with permission to manage objects, organizational units, or other containers. An example of a built-in capability is the ability to create, delete, and manage user accounts. This capability is assigned to administrators and account operators. Thus, if a user is a member of the Administrators group, the user can create, delete, and manage user accounts.

- **Access permissions** Defines the operations that can be performed on network resources. You can assign access permissions to users, computers, and groups. An example of an access permission is the ability to create a file in a directory.

As an administrator, you deal with account capabilities every day. To help track built-in capabilities, refer to the following sections. Keep in mind that although you can't change a group's built-in capabilities, you can change a group's default rights. For example, an administrator could revoke network access to a computer by removing a group's right to access the computer from the network.

Privileges

A *privilege* is a user right assignment that grants permissions to perform a specific administrative task. You assign privileges through group policies, which can be applied to individual computers, organizational units, and domains. Although you can assign privileges to both users and groups, you'll usually want to assign privileges to groups. In this way, users are automatically assigned the appropriate privileges when they become members of a group. Assigning privileges to groups also makes it easier to manage user accounts.

Table 9-2 provides a brief summary of each privilege you can assign to users and groups. To learn how to assign privileges, see the "Configuring user rights policies" section later in this chapter.

TABLE 9-2 Windows Server 2012 R2 Privileges for Users and Groups

PRIVILEGE	DESCRIPTION
Act As Part Of The Operating System	Allows a process to authenticate as any user and gain access to resources as any user. Processes that require this privilege should use the LocalSystem account, which already has this privilege.
Add Workstations To Domain	Allows users to add computers to the domain.
Adjust Memory Quotas For A Process	Allows users to adjust process-based memory usage quotas.
Back Up Files And Directories	Allows users to back up the system regardless of the permissions set on files and directories.
Bypass Traverse Checking	Allows users to pass through directories while navigating an object path regardless of permissions set on the directories. The privilege doesn't allow the user to list directory contents.
Change The System Time	Allows users to set the time for the system clock.
Change The Time Zone	Allows users to set the time zone for the system clock. All users have this privilege by default.

PRIVILEGE	DESCRIPTION
Create A Pagefile	Allows users to create and change the paging file size for virtual memory.
Create A Token Object	Allows processes to create token objects that can be used to gain access to local resources. Processes that require this privilege should use the LocalSystem account, which already has this privilege.
Create Global Objects	Allows processes to create global objects. LocalService and NetworkService have the privilege by default.
Create Permanent Shared Objects	Allows processes to create directory objects in the object manager. Most components already have this privilege; it's not necessary to specifically assign it.
Create Symbolic Links	Allows an application that a user is running to create symbolic links. Symbolic links make it appear as though a document or folder is in a specific location when it actually resides in another location. Use of symbolic links is restricted by default to enhance security.
Debug Programs	Allows users to perform debugging.
Enable Computer And User Accounts To Be Trusted For Delegation	Allows computers and users to change or apply the trusted-for-delegation setting, provided they have write access to the object.
Force Shutdown From A Remote System	Allows users to shut down a computer from a remote location on the network.
Generate Security Audits	Allows processes to make security log entries for auditing object access.
Impersonate A Client After Authentication	Allows Web applications to act as clients during the processing of requests. Services and users can also act as clients.
Increase A Process Working Set	Allows an application that a user is running to increase the memory that the related process working set uses. A process working set is the set of memory pages currently visible to a process in physical memory. Allowing for increases in memory pages reduces page faults and enhances performance.
Increase Scheduling Priority	Allows processes to increase the scheduling priority assigned to another process, provided that they have write access to the process.

PRIVILEGE	DESCRIPTION
Load And Unload Device Drivers	Allows users to install and uninstall Plug and Play device drivers. This doesn't affect device drivers that aren't Plug and Play, which can be installed only by administrators.
Lock Pages In Memory	Allows processes to keep data in physical memory, preventing the system from paging data to virtual memory on disk.
Manage Auditing And Security Log	Allows users to specify auditing options and access the security log. You must turn on auditing in the group policy first.
Modify An Object Label	Allows a user process to modify the integrity label of objects, such as files, registry keys, or processes owned by other users. This privilege can be used to lower the priority of other processes. Processes running under a user account can modify the label of any object the user owns without requiring this privilege.
Modify Firmware Environment Values	Allows users and processes to modify system environment variables.
Perform Volume Maintenance Tasks	Allows for the administration of removable storage, the disk defragmenter, and disk management.
Profile A Single Process	Allows users to monitor the performance of nonsystem processes.
Profile System Performance	Allows users to monitor the performance of system processes.
Remove Computer From Docking Station	Allows a laptop to be undocked and removed from the network.
Replace A Process Level Token	Allows processes to replace the default token for subprocesses.
Restore Files And Directories	Allows users to restore backed-up files and directories, regardless of the permissions set on files and directories.
Shut Down The System	Allows users to shut down the local computer.
Synchronize Directory Service Data	Allows users to synchronize directory service data on domain controllers.
Take Ownership Of Files Or Other Objects	Allows users to take ownership of files and any other Active Directory objects.

Logon rights

A *logon right* is a user rights assignment that grants logon permissions. You can assign logon rights to both user and group accounts. As with privileges, you assign logon rights through group policies, and you'll usually want to assign logon rights to groups rather than to individual users.

Table 9-3 provides a brief summary of each logon right you can assign to users and groups. Assigning logon rights is covered in the "Configuring user rights policies" section later in this chapter.

TABLE 9-3 Windows Server 2012 R2 Logon Rights for Users and Groups

LOGON RIGHT	DESCRIPTION
Access Credential Manager As A Trusted Caller	Grants permission to establish a trusted connection to Credential Manager. Credentials, such as a user name and password or smart card, provide identification and proof of identification.
Access This Computer From The Network	Grants remote access to the computer.
Allow Log On Locally	Grants permission to log on at the computer's keyboard. On domain controllers, this right is restricted by default and only members of the following groups can log on locally: Administrators, Account Operators, Backup Operators, Print Operators, and Server Operators.
Allow Log On Through Remote Desktop Services	Grants access through Remote Desktop Services. This right is necessary for remote assistance and remote desktop use.
Deny Access To This Computer From The Network	Denies remote access to the computer through network services.
Deny Logon As Batch Job	Denies the right to log on through a batch job or script.
Deny Logon As Service	Denies the right to log on as a service.
Deny Logon Locally	Denies the right to log on by using the computer's keyboard.
Deny Logon Through Remote Desktop Services	Denies the right to log on through Remote Desktop Services.
Log On As A Batch Job	Grants permission to log on as a batch job or script.
Log On As A Service	Grants permission to log on as a service. The Local-System account has this right. A service that runs under a separate account should be assigned this right.

Built-in capabilities for groups in Active Directory

The built-in capabilities that are assigned to groups in Active Directory depend on a computer's configuration. Using the Local Group Policy Editor, shown in Figure 9-1, you can view the capabilities that have been assigned to each group by expanding Computer Configuration\Windows Settings\Security Settings\Local Policies and then selecting the User Rights Assignment node.

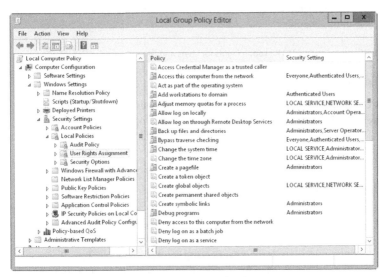

FIGURE 9-1 View the built-in capabilities that are used with groups.

Note that any action that's available to the Everyone group is available to all groups, including the Guests group. This means that although the Guests group doesn't have explicit permission to access the computer from the network, a member of the Guests group can still access the system because the Everyone group has this right.

Table 9-4 summarizes capabilities you can delegate to other users and groups. As you study the table, note that restricted accounts include the Administrator user account, the user accounts of administrators, and the group accounts for Administrators, Server Operators, Account Operators, Backup Operators, and Print Operators. Because these accounts are restricted, Account Operators can't create or modify them.

TABLE 9-4 Other Capabilities for Built-in and Local Groups

TASK	DESCRIPTION	GROUP NORMALLY ASSIGNED
Assign User Rights	Allows users to assign user rights to other users	Administrators
Create And Delete Groups	Allows users to create new groups and delete existing groups	Administrators, Account Operators
Create And Delete Printers	Allows users to create and delete printers	Administrators, Server Operators, Printer Operators
Create, Delete, And Manage User Accounts	Allows users to administer domain user accounts	Administrators, Account Operators
Manage Group Policy Links	Allows users to apply existing group policies to sites, domains, and organizational units for which they have write access to the related objects	Administrators
Manage Network Configuration	Allows users to configure networking	Administrators, Network Configuration Operators
Manage Performance Logs	Allows users to configure performance logging	Administrators, Performance Log Users
Manage Printers	Allows users to modify printer settings and manage print queues	Administrators, Server Operators, Printer Operators
Modify The Membership Of A Group	Allows users to add and remove users from domain groups	Administrators, Account Operators
Monitor Performance Logs	Allows users to monitor performance logging	Administrators, Performance Monitor Users
Perform Cryptographic Operations	Allows users to manage cryptographic options	Administrators, Cryptographic Operators
Read All User Information	Allows users to view user account information	Administrators, Server Operators, Account Operators
Read Event Logs	Allows users to read event logs	Administrators, Event Log Readers
Reset Passwords On User Accounts	Allows users to reset passwords on user accounts	Administrators, Account Operators

Using default group accounts

The default group accounts are designed to be versatile. By assigning users to the correct groups, you can make managing your Windows Server 2012 R2 workgroup or domain a lot easier. Unfortunately, with so many groups, understanding the purpose of each isn't easy. To help, let's take a closer look at groups used by administrators and groups that are implicitly created.

Groups used by administrators

An *administrator* is someone who has wide access to network resources. Administrators can create accounts, modify user rights, install printers, manage shared resources, and more. The main administrator groups are Administrators, Domain Admins, and Enterprise Admins. Table 9-5 compares the administrator groups.

TABLE 9-5 Administrator Groups Overview

ADMINISTRATOR GROUP TYPE	NETWORK ENVIRONMENT	GROUP SCOPE	MEMBERSHIP
Administrators	Active Directory domains	Domain local	Administrator, Domain Admins, Enterprise Admins
Administrators	Workgroups, computers not part of a domain	Local	Administrator
Domain Admins	Active Directory domains	Global	Administrator
Enterprise Admins	Active Directory domains	Global or Universal	Administrator
Schema Admins	Active Directory domains	Universal	Administrator

> **TIP** The Administrator account and the global groups Domain Admins and Enterprise Admins are members of the Administrators group. The Administrator account is used to access the local computer. Domain Admins membership allows other administrators to access the system from elsewhere in the domain. Enterprise Admins membership allows other administrators to access the system from other domains in the current domain tree or forest. To prevent enterprisewide access to a domain, you can remove Enterprise Admins from this group.

Administrators is a local group that provides full administrative access to an individual computer or a single domain, depending on its location. Because this account has complete access, you should be very careful about adding users to this group. To make someone an administrator for a local computer or domain, all you need to do is make that person a member of this group. Only members of the Administrators group can modify this account.

Domain Admins is a global group designed to help you manage resources in a domain. Members of this group have full control of a domain. This group has administrative control over all computers in a domain because it's a member of the Administrators group by default on all domain controllers, all domain workstations, and all domain member servers at the time they join the domain. To make someone an administrator for a domain, make that person a member of this group.

TIP The Administrator account is a member of Domain Admins by default. This means that if a user logs on to a computer as the administrator and the computer is a member of the domain, the user will have complete access to all resources in the domain.

Enterprise Admins is a global group designed to help you manage resources in a forest. Members of this group have full control of all domains in a forest. This group has administrative control over all domain controllers in the enterprise because the group is a member of the Administrators group by default on all domain controllers in a forest. To make someone an administrator for the enterprise, make that person a member of this group.

TIP The Administrator account is a member of Enterprise Admins by default. This means that if someone logs on to a computer as the administrator and the computer is a member of the domain, the user will have complete access to the domain tree or forest.

Schema Admins is a universal group designed to help you manage schema in Active Directory. Members of this group can work with and manage schema in the domain. Before someone can edit schema, they need to be a member of this group.

Implicit groups and identities

Windows Server defines a set of special identities you can use to assign permissions in certain situations. You usually assign permissions implicitly to special identities. However, you can assign permissions to special identities directly when you modify Active Directory objects. The special identities include the following:

- **Anonymous Logon**   Any user accessing the system through anonymous logon has the Anonymous Logon identity. This identity allows anonymous access to resources such as a webpage published on a corporate intranet server.

- **Authenticated Users**   Any user accessing the system through a logon process has the Authenticated Users identity. This identity allows access to shared resources within the domain, such as files in a shared folder that should be accessible to all the workers in the organization.

- **Batch** Any user or process accessing the system as a batch job (or through the batch queue) has the Batch identity. This identity allows batch jobs to run scheduled tasks, such as a nightly cleanup job that deletes temporary files.

- **Creator Group** Windows Server uses this special identity group to automatically grant access permissions to users who are members of the same group or groups as the creator of a file or a directory.

- **Creator Owner** The person who created the file or the directory is a member of this special identity group. Windows Server uses this identity to automatically grant access permissions to the creator of a file or directory.

- **Dial-Up** Any user accessing the system through a dial-up connection has the Dial-Up identity. This identity distinguishes dial-up users from other types of authenticated users.

- **Enterprise Domain Controllers** Domain controllers with enterprisewide roles and responsibilities have the Enterprise Domain Controllers identity. This identity allows them to perform certain tasks in the enterprise by using transitive trusts.

- **Everyone** All interactive, network, dial-up, and authenticated users are members of the Everyone group. This special identity group gives wide access to a system resource.

- **Interactive** Any user logged on to the local system has the Interactive identity. This identity allows only local users to access a resource.

- **Network** Any user accessing the system through a network has the Network identity. This identity allows only remote users to access a resource.

- **Proxy** Users and computers accessing resources through a proxy have the Proxy identity. This identity is used when proxies are implemented on the network.

- **Remote Desktop Services User** Any user accessing the system through Remote Desktop Services has the Remote Desktop Services User identity. This identity allows Remote Desktop Services users to access Remote Desktop Services applications and to perform other necessary tasks with Remote Desktop Services.

- **Restricted** Users and computers with restricted capabilities have the Restricted identity.

- **Self** The Self identity refers to the object itself and allows the object to modify itself.

- **Service** Any service accessing the system has the Service identity. This identity grants access to processes being run by Windows Server services.

- **System** The Windows Server operating system itself has the System identity. This identity is used when the operating system needs to perform a system-level function.

User account setup and organization

A key part of an administrator's job is to create accounts, and this chapter shows you how. User and group accounts allow Windows Server 2012 R2 to track and manage information about users, including permissions and privileges. To create user accounts, you primarily use the following two account administration tools:

- Active Directory Users And Computers, which is designed to administer accounts throughout an Active Directory domain
- Local Users And Groups, which is designed to administer accounts on a local computer

The most important aspects of account creation are account setup and account organization. Without the appropriate guidelines and policies, you might quickly find that you need to rework all your user accounts. Before you create accounts, determine the policies you'll use for setup and organization.

Account naming policies

A key policy you need to set is the naming scheme for accounts. User accounts have display names and logon names. The *display name* (or full name) is the name displayed to users and the name referenced in user sessions. The *logon name* is the name used to log on to the domain. Logon names are discussed briefly in the "Logon names, passwords, and public certificates" section earlier in this chapter.

Rules for display names

For domain accounts, the display name is normally the concatenation of the user's first name, middle initial, and last name, but you can set it to any string value. The display names must follow these rules:

- Local display names must be unique on an individual computer.
- Display names must be unique throughout a domain.
- Display names must be no more than 64 characters.
- Display names can contain alphanumeric characters and special characters.

Rules for logon names

Logon names must follow these rules:

- Local logon names must be unique on an individual computer, and global logon names must be unique throughout a domain.
- Logon names can contain as many as 256 characters. However, it isn't practical to use logon names that have more than 64 characters.
- A pre–Windows 2000 logon name is given to all accounts. By default, this logon name is set to the first 20 characters of the Windows logon name. The pre–Windows 2000 logon name must be unique throughout a domain.

- Users logging on to the domain by using a computer that runs Windows 2000 or a later release can use their standard logon names or their pre–Windows 2000 logon names, regardless of the domain operations mode.
- Logon names can't contain certain characters. The following characters are invalid:

  " / \ [ ] ; | = , + * ? < >
- Logon names can contain all other special characters, including spaces, periods, dashes, and underscores. Generally, however, it is not a good idea to use spaces in account names.

NOTE Although Windows Server stores user names in the case that you enter, user names aren't case sensitive. For example, you can access the Administrator account with the user name Administrator, administrator, or ADMINISTRATOR. Thus, user names are case aware but not case sensitive.

Naming schemes

Most small organizations tend to assign logon names that use the user's first or last name. But you can have more than one person with the same name in an organization of any size. Rather than having to rework your logon naming scheme when you run into problems, select a good naming scheme now and make sure that other administrators use it. You should use a consistent procedure for naming accounts—one that allows your user base to grow, limits the possibility of name conflicts, and ensures that your accounts have secure names that aren't easily exploited. If you follow these guidelines, the types of naming schemes you might want to use include the following:

- User's first name and last initial
- User's first initial and last name
- User's first initial, middle initial, and last name
- User's first initial, middle initial, and first five characters of the last name
- User's first name and last name

SECURITY ALERT In environments with strict security, you can assign a numeric code for the logon name. This numeric code should be at least 20 characters. Combine this strict naming method with smart cards and smart card readers to allow users to quickly log on to the domain without having to type in all those characters. Don't worry—users can still have a display name that humans can read.

Password and account policies

Domain accounts use passwords or private keys from certificates to authenticate access to network resources. This section focuses on passwords.

Using secure passwords

A *password* is a case-sensitive string that can contain more than 127 characters with Active Directory and up to 14 characters with the legacy Security Manager. Valid characters for passwords are letters, numbers, and symbols. When you set a password for an account, Windows Server stores the password in an encrypted format in the account database.

But simply having a password isn't enough. The key to preventing unauthorized access to network resources is to use secure passwords. The difference between an average password and a secure password is that secure passwords are difficult to guess and crack. You make passwords difficult to guess and crack by using combinations of all the available character types—including lowercase letters, uppercase letters, numbers, and symbols. For example, instead of using happydays for a password, you would use haPPy2Days&, Ha**y!day5, or even h*99Y%d*ys.

You might also want to use password phrases. With a password phrase, the password contains multiple words and punctuation, like a sentence. For example, you might use the password phrase *This problem is 99 times ten!* A password phrase that includes punctuation and numbers meets all complexity requirements and is incredibly difficult to crack.

Unfortunately, no matter how secure you make a user's password initially, the user will eventually choose his own password. Therefore, you should set account policies that define a secure password for your systems. Account policies are a subset of the policies configurable in Group Policy.

Setting account policies

As I mentioned in earlier chapters, you can apply group policies at various levels within the network structure. You manage local group policies in the manner discussed in the "Managing local group policies" section in Chapter 6, "Automating administrative tasks, policies, and procedures." You manage global group policies as explained in "Managing site, domain, and organizational unit policies," also in Chapter 6.

Account policies should be configured in the highest precedence GPO that is linked to a domain. By default, the highest precedence GPO linked to a domain is the Default Domain Policy GPO. After you access the Default Domain Policy GPO or other appropriate GPO, you can set account policies by following these steps:

1. In the Group Policy Management Editor, shown in Figure 9-2, open the Account Policies node by expanding Computer Configuration\Windows Settings\Security Settings. The console tree shows the name of the computer or domain you are configuring. Be sure that this is the appropriate network resource to configure.

   NOTE Domain policies have precedence over local policies. The GPO with a link order of 1 in the domain always has the highest precedence.

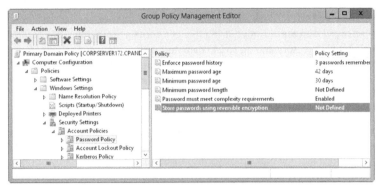

FIGURE 9-2 Use the Account Policies node to set policies for passwords and general account use.

2. You can now manage account policies through the Password Policy, Account Lockout Policy, and Kerberos Policy nodes. To configure a policy, double-tap or double-click its entry, or press and hold or right-click it and then tap or click Properties. This opens a Properties dialog box for the policy, shown in Figure 9-3.

FIGURE 9-3 Define and configure global group policies in the Properties dialog box.

All policies are either defined or not defined. That is, they are either configured for use or not configured for use. A policy that isn't defined in the current container could be inherited from another container.

NOTE Kerberos policies aren't used with local computers. Kerberos policies are available only with group policies that affect domains. For stand-alone servers, you can change the local policy settings. However, you cannot change the local policy settings for domain controllers or member servers.

3. Select or clear the Define This Policy Setting check box to specify whether a policy is defined.

TIP Policies can have additional options for configuration. Often these options are buttons labeled Enabled and Disabled. Tapping or clicking Enabled turns on the policy restriction. Tapping or clicking Disabled turns off the policy restriction. Some policies are negations, which means that by enabling them you are actually negating the item. For example, Disable Log On As A Service is the negation of the item Log On As A Service.

Specific procedures for working with account policies are discussed in the "Configuring password policies," "Configuring account lockout policies," and "Configuring Kerberos policies" sections later in this chapter.

Configuring account policies

As you learned in the previous section, there are three types of account policies: password policies, account lockout policies, and Kerberos policies. The sections that follow explain how to configure each of these policies.

Configuring password policies

Password policies, listed here, control security for passwords:

- Enforce Password History
- Maximum Password Age
- Minimum Password Age
- Minimum Password Length
- Password Must Meet Complexity Requirements
- Store Passwords Using Reversible Encryption

The uses of these policies are discussed in the following sections.

Enforce Password History

Enforce Password History sets how frequently old passwords can be reused. With this policy, you can discourage users from alternating between several common passwords. Windows Server can store up to 24 passwords for each user in the password history.

To disable this feature, set the value of the password history to 0. To enable this feature, set the value of the password history by using the Passwords Remembered box. Windows Server then tracks old passwords by using a password history that's unique for each user, and users aren't allowed to reuse any of the stored passwords.

NOTE To prevent users from bypassing settings for Enforce Password History, don't allow them to change passwords immediately. This stops users from changing their passwords several times to get back to an old password. You can set the time required to keep a password with the Minimum Password Age policy as discussed later in the chapter.

Maximum Password Age

Maximum Password Age determines how long users can keep a password before they have to change it. The aim is to force users to change their passwords periodically. When you use this feature, set a value that makes sense for your network. Generally, you use a shorter period when security is very important and a longer period when security is less important.

You can set the maximum password age to any value from 0 through 999. A value of 0 specifies that passwords don't expire. Although you might be tempted to set no expiration date, users should change passwords regularly to ensure the network's security. Where security is a concern, good values are 30, 60, or 90 days. Where security is less important, good values are 120, 150, or 180 days.

NOTE Windows Server notifies users when the password expiration date is approaching. Any time the expiration date is fewer than 30 days away, a warning is displayed when the user logs on stating that he or she has to change the password within a specific number of days.

Minimum Password Age

Minimum Password Age determines how long users must keep a password before they can change it. You can use this box to prevent users from bypassing the password system by entering a new password and then changing it right back to the old one.

If the minimum password age is set to 0, users can change their passwords immediately. To prevent this, set a specific minimum age. Reasonable settings are from three to seven days. In this way, you make sure that users are less inclined to switch back to an old password but are able to change their passwords in a reasonable amount of time if they want to. Keep in mind that a minimum password age could prevent a user from changing a compromised password. If a user can't change the password, an administrator has to make the change.

Minimum Password Length

Minimum Password Length sets the minimum number of characters for a password. If you haven't changed the default setting, you should do so immediately. The default in some cases is to allow empty passwords (passwords with zero characters), which is definitely not a good idea.

For security reasons, you'll generally want passwords of at least eight characters, because long passwords are usually more difficult to crack than short ones. If you want greater security, set the minimum password length to 14 characters.

Password Must Meet Complexity Requirements

Beyond the basic password and account policies, Windows Server includes facilities for creating additional password controls. These facilities enforce the use of secure passwords that follow these guidelines:

- Passwords must have at least six characters.
- Passwords can't contain the user name, such as stevew, or parts of the user's full name, such as steve.
- Passwords must use at least three of the four available character types: lowercase letters, uppercase letters, numbers, and symbols.

To enforce these rules, enable Passwords Must Meet Complexity Requirements.

Store Passwords Using Reversible Encryption

Passwords in the password database are encrypted. This encryption can't normally be reversed. The only time you would want to change this setting is when your organization uses applications that need to read the password. If this is the case, enable Store Password Using Reversible Encryption For All Users.

With this policy enabled, passwords might as well be stored as plain text—it presents the same security risks. With this in mind, a much better technique is to enable the option on a per-user basis and then only as required to meet the user's actual needs.

Configuring account lockout policies

Account lockout policies, listed here, control how and when accounts are locked out of the domain or the local system:

- Account Lockout Threshold
- Account Lockout Duration
- Reset Account Lockout Counter After

These policies are discussed in the sections that follow.

Account Lockout Threshold

Account Lockout Threshold sets the number of logon attempts that are allowed before an account is locked out. If you decide to use lockout controls, you should use a value that balances the need to prevent account cracking with the needs of users who are having difficulty accessing their accounts.

The main reason users might not be able to access their accounts properly the first time is that they forgot their passwords. If this is the case, they might need several attempts to log on properly. Workgroup users could also have problems accessing a remote system if their current passwords don't match the passwords that the remote system expects. For example, the remote system might record several bad logon attempts before a user receives a prompt to enter the correct password because Windows Server has attempted to automatically log on to the remote system. In a domain environment, this normally doesn't happen because of the single sign-on feature.

You can set the lockout threshold to any value from 0 to 999. The lockout threshold is set to 0 by default, which means that accounts won't be locked out because of invalid logon attempts. Any other value sets a specific lockout threshold. Keep in mind that the higher the lockout value, the higher the risk that a hacker might be able to break into your system. A reasonable range of values for this threshold is from 7 to 15. This is high enough to rule out user error and low enough to deter hackers.

Account Lockout Duration

If someone violates the lockout controls, Account Lockout Duration sets the length of time that the account is locked. You can set the lockout duration to a specific length of time by using a value between 1 and 99,999 minutes, or to an indefinite length of time by setting the lockout duration to 0.

The best security policy is to lock the account indefinitely. When you do, only an administrator can unlock the account. This prevents hackers from trying to access the system again and forces users who are locked out to seek help from an administrator, which is usually a good idea. By talking to the user, you can determine what the user is doing wrong and help the user avoid further problems.

> **TIP** When an account is locked out, open the Properties dialog box for the account in Active Directory Users And Computers. Tap or click the Account tab, and then select the Unlock Account check box.

Reset Account Lockout Counter After

Every time a logon attempt fails, Windows Server raises the value of a threshold that tracks the number of bad logon attempts. To maintain a balance between potential lockouts from valid security concerns and lockouts that could occur from simple human error, another policy determines how long to maintain information regarding bad logon attempts. This policy is called Reset Account Lockout Counter After, and you use it to reset the bad logon attempts counter to 0 after a certain waiting period. The way the policy works is simple: If the waiting period for Reset Account

Lockout Counter After has elapsed since the last bad logon attempt, the bad logon attempts counter is reset to 0. The bad logon attempts counter is also reset when a user logs on successfully.

If the Reset Account Lockout Counter After policy is enabled, you can set it to any value from 1 to 99,999 minutes. As with Account Lockout Threshold, you need to select a value that balances security needs against user access needs. A good value is from one to two hours. This waiting period should be long enough to force hackers to wait longer than they want to before trying to access the account again.

If the Reset Account Lockout Counter After policy isn't set or is disabled, the bad logon attempts counter is reset only when a user successfully logs on.

NOTE Bad logon attempts against a password-protected screen saver at a workstation don't increase the lockout threshold. Similarly, if you press Ctrl+Alt+Delete to lock a server or workstation, bad logon attempts against the Unlock dialog box don't count.

Configuring Kerberos policies

Kerberos V5 is the primary authentication mechanism used in an Active Directory domain. The Kerberos protocol uses tickets to verify the identification of users and network services. Tickets contain encrypted data that confirms identity for the purposes of authentication and authorization.

You can control ticket duration, renewal, and enforcement with the following policies:

- Enforce User Logon Restrictions
- Maximum Lifetime For Service Ticket
- Maximum Lifetime For User Ticket
- Maximum Lifetime For User Ticket Renewal
- Maximum Tolerance For Computer Clock Synchronization

These policies are discussed in the sections that follow.

SECURITY ALERT Only administrators with an intimate understanding of Kerberos security should change these policies. If you change these policies to inefficient settings, you might cause serious problems on the network. The default Kerberos policy settings usually work just fine.

Enforce User Logon Restrictions

Enforce User Logon Restrictions ensures that any restrictions placed on a user account are enforced. For example, if the user's logon hours are restricted, this policy enforces the restriction. By default, the policy is enabled and you should disable it only in rare circumstances.

Maximum Lifetime

Maximum Lifetime For Service Ticket and Maximum Lifetime For User Ticket set the maximum duration for which a service or user ticket is valid. By default, service tickets have a maximum duration of 600 minutes, and user tickets have a maximum duration of 10 hours.

You can change the duration of tickets. For service tickets, the valid range is from 0 to 99,999 minutes. For user tickets, the valid range is from 0 to 99,999 hours. A value of 0 effectively turns off expiration. Any other value sets a specific ticket lifetime.

A user ticket that expires can be renewed, provided that the renewal takes place within the time set for Maximum Lifetime For User Ticket Renewal. By default, the maximum renewal period is seven days. You can change the renewal period to any value from 0 to 99,999 days. A value of 0 effectively turns off the maximum renewal period, and any other value sets a specific renewal period.

Maximum Tolerance

Maximum Tolerance For Computer Clock Synchronization is one of the few Kerberos policies you might need to change. By default, computers in the domain must be synchronized within five minutes of one another. If they aren't, authentication fails.

If you have remote users who log on to the domain without synchronizing their clocks to the network time server, you might need to adjust this value. You can set any value from 0 to 99,999. A value of 0 indicates that there's no tolerance for a time difference, which means the remote user's system must be precisely time-synchronized or authentication will fail.

Configuring authentication policies

Authentication policies are an advanced configuration option for large enterprises. You use authentication policies to do the following:

- Restrict the authentication methods available to user, service, and computer accounts.
- Specify access control conditions that restrict the devices that can request Kerberos tickets for user, service and computer accounts.

Authentication policies and related options are available only when an Active Directory domain is operating at the Windows Server 2012 R2 or higher functional level. Authentication policies are enforced during initial Kerberos authentication and whenever a user, computer or service requests access to a server services. You use authentication policy silos to identify the users, computers, managed services accounts, and group managed service accounts to which you want to apply authentication settings; to fine-tune which accounts are to be protected; and to define explicitly permitted accounts.

Several object classes in the Active Directory schema were implemented to support authentication policies and silos, including:

- **Authentication Policies container**   Used to store Authentication Policy objects in Active Directory
- **Authentication Policy object**   Used to configure Kerberos Ticket Granting Ticket properties and specify authentication conditions based on account type
- **Authentication Policy Silos container**   Used to store Authentication Policy Silo objects in Active Directory Domain Services
- **Authentication Policy Silo object**   Defines the authentication policy or policies to be applied to accounts that inherit this object

NOTE A default Authentication Policies container is created under the System container in a domain and it stores the Authentication Policy objects (APOs). You add APOs to the Authentication Policies Container to define the various sets of authentication settings you want to use.

You use authentication policies in conjunction with the Protected Users security group. Any accounts that should have additional protections should be added to the Protected Users group, restricted by using an Authentication Policy object, and then optionally identified in an authentication policy silo to fine-tune the way controls are applied. Membership in the Protected Users group ensures that only Kerberos can be used for authentication. Otherwise, if NTLM is used for authentication, access control conditions that you define in policies will not be properly applied.

Both types of policies can be configured in auditing only or enforce mode. With auditing only mode, policy restrictions are audited rather than enforced. With enforced mode, policy restrictions are strictly enforced.

In Active Directory Administrative Center, you create and manage authentication policies by using the options in the Authentication\Authentication Policies node. To create an authentication policy, select the Authentication\Authentication Policies node in the left pane. Next, under Tasks, select New and then select Authentication Policy. In the Create Authentication Policy dialog box, use the options provided to define the new policy and specify access control conditions for each type of account to which the policy will apply.

Authentication Policy Silos allow you to apply authentication policies in several different ways. When you create the object, you can specify a single authentication policy to apply to all member accounts or use a separate authentication policy for each type of security principal. As part of creating the authentication policy silo, you also can specify explicitly permitted accounts.

In Active Directory Administrative Center, you create and manage authentication silos by using the options on the Authentication\Authentication Policy Silos node. To create an authentication policy silo, select the Authentication\Authentication Policies node in the left pane. Next, under Tasks, select New and then select Authentication Policy Silo. Use the options in the Create Authentication Policy Silo dialog box to create the authentication policy silo.

Configuring user rights policies

User accounts have built-in capabilities and user rights. Although you can't change built-in capabilities for accounts, you can manage user rights for accounts. Typically, you apply user rights to users by making them members of the appropriate group or groups. You can also apply rights directly, and you do this by managing the user rights for the user's account.

> **SECURITY ALERT** Any user who's a member of a group that's assigned a certain right also has that right. For example, if the Backup Operators group has the right, and jsmith is a member of this group, jsmith also has this right. Keep in mind that changes you make to user rights can have a far-reaching effect. Because of this, only experienced administrators should make changes to the user rights policy.

You assign user rights through the Local Policies node of Group Policy. As the name implies, local policies pertain to a local computer. However, you can configure local policies and then import them into Active Directory. You can also configure these local policies as part of an existing GPO for a site, a domain, or an organizational unit. When you do this, the local policies apply to computer accounts in the site, domain, or organizational unit.

To administer user rights policies, follow these steps:

1. Open the GPO you want to work with, and then open the Local Policies node by working your way down the console tree. To do so, expand Computer Configuration\Windows Settings\Security Settings\Local Policies.

2. Select User Rights Assignment to manage user rights. To configure a user rights assignment, double-tap or double-click a user right, or press and hold or right-click it and then tap or click Properties. This opens a Properties dialog box.

3. Configure the user rights. To configure local user rights, follow steps 1–3 in the "Configuring local user rights" section later in this chapter. To configure global user rights, follow steps 1–6 in the following section.

Configuring global user rights

For a site, a domain, or an organizational unit, you configure individual user rights by following these steps:

1. Open the Properties dialog box for the user right, which is similar to the one shown in Figure 9-4. If the policy isn't defined, select Define These Policy Settings.

FIGURE 9-4 In the Properties dialog box, define the user right, and then apply the right to users and groups.

2. To apply the right to a user or group, tap or click Add User Or Group. Then, in the Add User Or Group dialog box, tap or click Browse. This opens the Select Users, Computers, Service Accounts, Or Groups dialog box, shown in Figure 9-5.

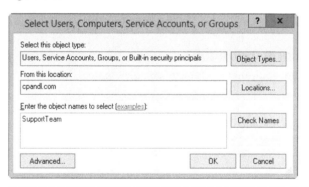

FIGURE 9-5 In the Select Users, Computers, Service Accounts, Or Groups dialog box, apply the user right to users and groups.

SECURITY ALERT Windows Firewall running on a domain controller might prevent you from using the Select Users, Computers, Service Accounts, Or Groups dialog box. This can occur when you aren't logged on locally to the domain controller and are working remotely. You might need to configure an exception on the domain controller for incoming TCP port 445. You can do this by expanding Computer Configuration\Administrative Templates\Network \Network Connections\Windows Firewall\Domain Profile. In the details pane, double-tap or double-click the Windows Firewall: Allow Inbound Remote Administration Exception policy, and then select Enabled. Alternatively, you can configure an exception by entering the following at a command prompt on the domain controller: **netsh firewall set portopening tcp 445 smb enable**. See Microsoft Knowledge Base Article 840634 (support.microsoft.com /default.aspx?scid=kb;en-us;840634) for more details.

3. Enter the name of the user or group you want to use in the box provided, and then tap or click Check Names. By default, the search is configured to find built-in security principals and user accounts. To add groups to the search, tap or click Object Types, select Groups in the list box, and then tap or click OK.

4. After you select the account names or groups to add, tap or click OK. The Add User Or Group dialog box should now show the selected accounts. Tap or click OK again.

5. The Properties dialog box is updated to reflect your selections. If you made a mistake, select a name and remove it by tapping or clicking Remove.

6. When you have finished granting the right to users and groups, tap or click OK.

Configuring local user rights

For local computers, apply user rights by following these steps:

1. Open the Properties dialog box for the user right, which is similar to the one shown in Figure 9-6. Remember that site, domain, and organizational unit policies have precedence over local policies.

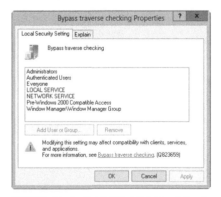

FIGURE 9-6 In the Properties dialog box, define the user right and then apply the right to users and groups. If you can't edit local user rights, you might be working with a domain controller.

2. The Properties dialog box shows current users and groups that have been given a user right. To remove the user right, select a user or group and then tap or click Remove.

3. You can apply the user right to additional users and groups by tapping or clicking Add User Or Group. This opens the Select Users, Computers, Service Accounts, Or Groups dialog box shown previously in Figure 9-5. You can now add users and groups.

Adding a user account

You need to create a user account for each user who wants to use your network resources. You create domain user accounts with Active Directory Users And Computers. You create local user accounts with Local Users And Groups.

Creating domain user accounts

Generally, you can create new domain accounts in two ways:

- **Create a completely new user account** Press and hold or right-click the container in which you want to place the user account, tap or click New, and then tap or click User. This opens the New Object - User Wizard, shown in Figure 9-7. When you create a new account, the default system settings are used.

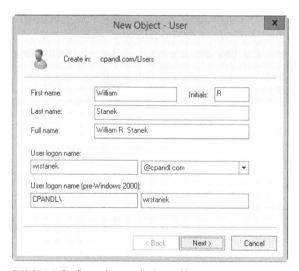

FIGURE 9-7 Configure the user display and logon names.

- **Base the new account on an existing account** Press and hold or right-click the user account you want to copy in Active Directory Users And Computers, and then tap or click Copy. This starts the Copy Object - User Wizard, which is essentially the same as the New Object - User Wizard. However, when you create a copy of an account, the new account gets most of its environment settings from the existing account. For more information about copying accounts, see the "Copying domain user accounts" section in Chapter 10, "Managing existing user and group accounts."

With either the New Object - User Wizard or the Copy Object - User Wizard, you can create an account by following these steps:

1. As shown in Figure 9-7, the first wizard page lets you configure the user display name and logon name. Enter the user's first name, middle initial, and last name in the boxes provided. These boxes are used to create the full name, which is the user's display name.

2. Make changes to the Full Name field as necessary. For example, you might want to enter the name in LastName FirstName MiddleInitial format or in FirstName MiddleInitial LastName format. The full name must be unique in the domain and must have 64 or fewer characters.

3. In the User Logon Name box, enter the user's logon name. Use the drop-down list to select the domain to associate the account with. This sets the fully qualified logon name.

4. The first 20 characters of the logon name are used to set the pre–Windows 2000 logon name. This logon name must be unique in the domain. If necessary, change the pre–Windows 2000 logon name.

5. Tap or click Next, and then configure the user's password on the page shown in Figure 9-8.

FIGURE 9-8 Use the New Object - User Wizard to configure the user's password.

The options for this page are as follows:

- **Password** The password for the account. This password should follow the conventions of your password policy.

- **Confirm Password** A box to ensure that you assign the account password correctly. Simply reenter the password to confirm it.

- **User Must Change Password At Next Logon** If selected, the user must change the password upon logon.

- **User Cannot Change Password** If selected, the user can't change the password.

- **Password Never Expires** If selected, the password for this account never expires. This setting overrides the domain account policy. Generally, it's not a good idea to set a password so that it doesn't expire—this defeats the purpose of having passwords in the first place.

- **Account Is Disabled** If selected, the account is disabled and can't be used. Use this check box to temporarily prevent anyone from using an account.

6. Tap or click Next, and then tap or click Finish to create the account. If you have problems creating the account, you receive a warning, and you need to use the Back button to reenter information in the user name and password pages as necessary.

After you create the account, you can set advanced properties for the account as discussed later in this chapter.

You also can create user accounts by using Active Directory Administrative Center. To do this, follow these steps:

1. In the Active Directory Administrative Center console tree, press and hold or right-click the container in which you want to place the user account, tap or click New in the container pane, and then tap or click User. This opens the Create User dialog box shown in Figure 9-9.

2. Enter the user's first name, middle initial, and last name in the boxes provided. These boxes are used to create the full name, which is the user's display name.

3. Make changes to the Full Name box as necessary. The full name must be unique in the domain and must have 64 or fewer characters.

4. In the User UPN Logon box, enter the user's logon name. Use the drop-down list to select the domain to associate the account with. This sets the fully qualified logon name.

5. The first 20 characters of the logon name are used to set the User Sam-AccountName Logon box. This is the user's pre–Windows 2000 logon name, which must be unique in the domain.

6. All other boxes in the dialog box are optional. Set and confirm the user's password, if desired. Optionally, select Protect From Accidental Deletion to mark the account as protected in Active Directory. Protected accounts can be deleted only if you remove the Protect flag prior to attempting to delete the account.

7. Tap or click OK to create the user account.

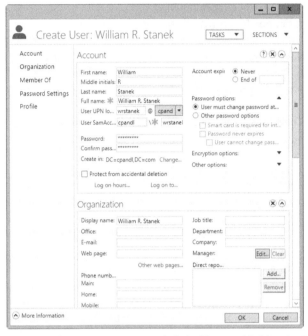

FIGURE 9-9 Create a new user account in Active Directory Administrative Center.

Creating local user accounts

You create local user accounts with Local Users And Groups. You can open this utility and create an account by following these steps:

1. In Server Manager, tap or click Tools and then tap or click Computer Management. Alternatively, you can press Windows+X and then click Computer Management.

2. Press and hold or right-click the Computer Management entry in the console tree, and then tap or click Connect To Another Computer. You can now choose the system whose local accounts you want to manage. Domain controllers don't have local users and groups.

3. Under System Tools, choose Local Users And Groups.

4. Press and hold or right-click Users, and then tap or click New User. This opens the New User dialog box, shown in Figure 9-10. You use each of the boxes in the dialog box as follows:

- **User Name**   The logon name for the user account. This name should follow the conventions for the local user name policy.
- **Full Name**   The full name of the user, such as William R. Stanek.
- **Description**   A description of the user. Typically, you enter the user's job title, such as Webmaster. You could also enter the user's job title and department.
- **Password**   The password for the account. This password should follow the conventions of your password policy.
- **Confirm Password**   A second entry to ensure that you assign the account password correctly. Simply reenter the password to confirm it.
- **User Must Change Password At Next Logon**   If selected, the user must change the password upon logon.
- **User Cannot Change Password**   If selected, the user can't change the password.
- **Password Never Expires**   If selected, the password for this account never expires. This setting overrides the local account policy.
- **Account Is Disabled**   If selected, the account is disabled and can't be used. Use this check box to temporarily prevent anyone from using an account.

FIGURE 9-10 Configuring a local user account is different from configuring a domain user account.

5. Tap or click Create when you have finished configuring the new account.

Adding a group account

You use group accounts to manage privileges for multiple users. You create global group accounts in Active Directory Users And Computers. You create local group accounts in Local Users And Groups.

As you set out to create group accounts, remember that you create group accounts for similar types of users. The types of groups you might want to create include the following:

- **Groups for departments within the organization** Generally, users who work in the same department need access to similar resources. You'll often create groups that are organized by department, such as Business Development, Sales, Marketing, and Engineering.

- **Groups for users of specific applications** Users often need access to an application and resources related to the application. If you create application-specific groups, you can be sure that users have proper access to the necessary resources and application files.

- **Groups for roles within the organization** You can also organize groups by user roles within the organization. For example, executives probably need access to different resources than supervisors and general users do. By creating groups based on roles within the organization, you can ensure that proper access is given to the users who need it.

Creating a global group

To create a global group, follow these steps:

1. Start Active Directory Users And Computers. Press and hold or right-click the container in which you want to place the user account, tap or click New, and then tap or click Group. This opens the - New Object - Group dialog box, shown in Figure 9-11.

2. The first 20 characters of the group name are used to set the pre–Windows 2000 group name. This group name must be unique in the domain. If necessary, change the pre–Windows 2000 group name.

3. Select a group scope (Domain Local, Global, or Universal).

4. Select a group type (either Security or Distribution).

5. Tap or click OK to create the group. After you create the account, you can add members and set additional properties, as discussed later in this chapter.

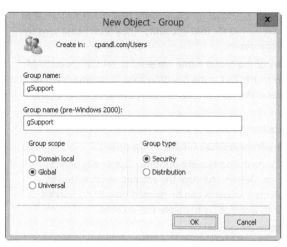

FIGURE 9-11 The New Object - Group dialog box allows you to add a new global group to the domain.

You also can create groups by using Active Directory Administrative Center. To do this, follow these steps:

1. In the Active Directory Administrative Center console tree, press and hold or right-click the container in which you want to place the group, tap or click New in the container pane, and then tap or click Group. This opens the Create Group dialog box shown in Figure 9-12.

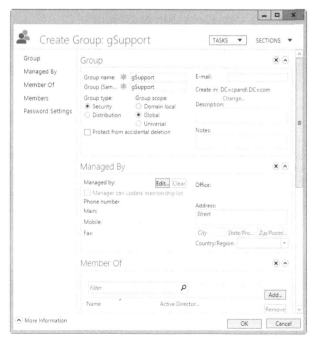

FIGURE 9-12 Create a new group in Active Directory Administrative Center.

2. Enter a name for the group. Global group account names follow the same naming rules as display names for user accounts. They aren't case sensitive and can be up to 64 characters.

3. The first 20 characters of the group name are used to set the group SAM-AccountName group name. This is the pre–Windows 2000 group name, which must be unique in the domain. Accept the default or enter a new value.

4. Select a group type (either Security or Distribution).

5. Select a group scope (Domain Local, Global, or Universal).

6. All other selections in the dialog box are optional. Optionally, select Protect From Accidental Deletion to mark the account as protected in Active Directory. Protected accounts can be deleted only if you remove the Protect flag prior to attempting to delete the account.

7. Tap or click OK to create the group.

Creating a local group and assigning members

You create local groups with Local Users And Groups. You can access this utility and create a group by following these steps:

1. In Server Manager, tap or click Tools and then tap or click Computer Management. Press and hold or right-click the Computer Management entry in the console tree, and then tap or click Connect To Another Computer. You can now choose the system whose local accounts you want to manage. Domain controllers don't have local users and groups.

2. Under System Tools, choose Local Users And Groups.

3. Press and hold or right-click Groups, and then tap or click New Group. This opens the New Group dialog box, shown in Figure 9-13.

FIGURE 9-13 In the New Group dialog box, you can add a new local group to a computer.

4. After you enter a name and description of the group, tap or click the Add button to add names to the group. This opens the Select Users dialog box.

5. In the Select Users dialog box, enter the name of a user you want to use in the Name box, and then tap or click Check Names. If matches are found, select the account you want to use, and then tap or click OK. If no matches are found, update the name you entered and try searching again. Repeat this step as necessary, and then tap or click OK.

6. The New Group dialog box is updated to reflect your selections. If you made a mistake, select a name and tap or click Remove.

7. Tap or click Create when you've finished adding or removing group members.

Handling global group membership

To configure group membership, you use Active Directory Users And Computers or Active Directory Administrative Center. When working with groups, keep the following points in mind:

- All new domain users are members of the group Domain Users, and their primary group is specified as Domain Users.
- All new domain workstations and member servers are members of Domain Computers, and their primary group is Domain Computers.
- All new domain controllers are members of Domain Controllers, and their primary group is Domain Controllers.

You manage group membership several ways:

- Manage individual memberships.
- Manage multiple memberships.
- Set primary group membership for individual users and computers.

Managing individual membership

You can quickly add a user or a group to one or more groups by pressing and holding or right-clicking the account and then selecting Add To Group. This opens the Select Groups dialog box. You can now choose groups that the currently selected account should be a member of.

You can manage group membership for any type of account by following these steps:

1. Double-tap or double-click the user, computer, or group entry in Active Directory Users And Computers or Active Directory Administrative Center. This opens the account's Properties dialog box.

2. On the Member Of tab or panel, groups that the user is currently a member of are listed. Tap or click Add to make the account a member of an additional group. This opens the Select Groups dialog box. You can now choose groups that the currently selected account should be a member of.

3. To remove the account from a group, select a group, and then tap or click Remove.

4. Tap or click OK.

If you're working exclusively with user accounts, you can add users to groups by following these steps:

1. Select the user accounts you want to work with in Active Directory Users And Computers or Active Directory Administrative Center.

   TIP To select multiple users individually, hold down the Ctrl key and then tap or click each user account you want to select. To select a sequence of accounts, hold down the Shift key, select the first user account, and then select the last user account.

2. Press and hold or right-click one of the selections, and then tap or click Add To A Group or Add To Group as appropriate. This opens the Select Groups dialog box. You can now choose groups that the currently selected accounts should be members of.

3. Tap or click OK.

Managing multiple memberships in a group

Another way to manage group membership is to use a group's Properties dialog box to add or remove multiple accounts. To do this, follow these steps:

1. Double-tap or double-click the group entry in Active Directory Users And Computers or Active Directory Administrative Center. This opens the group's Properties dialog box.

2. On the Members tab or panel, current members of the group are listed alphabetically. To add accounts to the group, tap or click Add. This opens the Select Users, Contacts, Computers, Service Accounts, Or Groups dialog box. You can now choose users, computers, service accounts, and groups that should be members of the currently selected group.

3. To remove members from a group, select an account, and then tap or click Remove.

4. Tap or click OK.

Setting the primary group for users and computers

Users who access Windows Server from Macintosh or POSIX-compliant applications use primary groups. When a Macintosh user creates files or directories on a system running Windows Server, the primary group is assigned to these files or directories.

NOTE All user and computer accounts must have a primary group regardless of whether the accounts access Windows Server systems through Macintosh. This group must be a group with global or universal scope, such as the global group Domain Users or the global group Domain Computers.

To set the primary group, follow these steps:

1. Double-tap or double-click the user or computer entry in Active Directory Users And Computers or Active Directory Administrative Center. This opens the account's Properties dialog box.

2. On the Member Of tab or panel, select a group with global or universal scope in the Member Of list.

3. Tap or click Set Primary Group.

All users must be a member of at least one primary group. You can't revoke membership in a primary group without first assigning the user to another primary group. To do this, follow these steps:

1. Select a different group with global or universal scope in the Member Of list, and then tap or click Set Primary Group.

2. In the Member Of list, tap or click the former primary group, and then tap or click Remove. The group membership is now revoked.

Implementing managed accounts

Microsoft Exchange Server, Microsoft Internet Information Services, Microsoft SQL Server, and other types of applications often use service accounts. On a local computer, you can configure the application to run as a built-in user account, such as Local Service, Network Service, or Local System. Although these service accounts are easy to configure and use, they usually are shared among multiple applications and services and cannot be managed on a domain level. If you configure the application to use a domain account, you can isolate the privileges for the application, but then you must manually manage the account password and any service principal names (SPNs) required for Kerberos authentication.

Windows 7 and all later releases of Windows support two additional types of accounts:

- Managed service accounts
- Managed virtual accounts

Managed service accounts are a special type of domain user account for managed services. These accounts reduce service outages and other issues by having Windows manage the account password and related SPNs automatically.

Managed virtual accounts are a special type of local computer account for managed services. These accounts provide the ability to access the network with a computer identity in a domain environment. Because the computer identity is used, no password management is required.

You can manage these accounts by using the Active Directory module for Windows PowerShell. Because the Active Directory module is not imported into Windows PowerShell by default, you need to import the module before you can use the cmdlets it provides. Although not originally available with Windows 7 and Windows

Server 2008 R2, Windows 8, Windows 8.1, Windows Server 2012, and Windows Server 2012 R2 support group managed service accounts. Group managed service accounts provide the same functionality as standard managed service accounts but extend that functionality over multiple servers. As an example, when a client computer connects to a service hosted by a server farm, mutual authentication cannot succeed unless all the instances of the services use the same principal. By using a group managed service account, you allow each server in the farm to use the same service principal, which is managed by Windows itself rather than individually by the administrator.

Group managed service accounts are, in fact, the default type of service account for Windows 8, Windows 8.1, Windows Server 2012, and Windows Server 2012 R2. Because of this, managed service accounts can span multiple computers by default. This means you can add the account to more than one computer at a time as necessary to support clustered nodes, network load-balancing server farms, and so on. If you want to restrict a managed service account to a single computer, you must now set the −RestrictToSingleComputer option when creating the account. Don't forget that a single computer can also have multiple managed service accounts.

In Active Directory schema, managed service accounts are represented by msDS-ManagedServiceAccounts. This object class inherits its attributes from the Computer object class, but the objects also are users. Managed service accounts use the same password-update mechanism as regular computer accounts. This means the password for the account is updated whenever the computer updates its password, which by default occurs every 30 days. Managed service accounts can automatically maintain their Kerberos SPN and support delegation.

> **TIP** Some applications, such as SQL Server and IIS, make use of Kerberos extensively and know how to register themselves with SPNs. If an application supports writing its own SPNs, managed service accounts will work for automatic SPN management.

> **NOTE** By default, all managed service accounts are created in the Managed Service Accounts container in Active Directory. This container is visible in Active Directory Users And Computers when you display advanced features.

Like computer accounts, managed service accounts do not use either domain or fine-grained password policies. Instead, they use a randomly generated 240-byte (120-character) password. Managed service accounts cannot perform inter-active logons or be locked out like user accounts can be. You can add managed service accounts to groups by using Active Directory Users And Computers or Add-ADGroupMember.

Creating and using managed service accounts

With managed service accounts, you create an actual account, which is stored by default in the Managed Service Accounts container in Active Directory. Next, you associate the account with a computer in Active Directory and then install the managed service account on a local server to add it to the account as a local user.

Finally, you configure the local service to use the account. Put another way, you must do the following:

1. Create the managed service account.
2. Associate the account with a computer in Active Directory.
3. Install the managed service account on the computer that was associated.
4. Configure the local service to use the account.

You can use Windows PowerShell cmdlets to install, uninstall, and reset passwords for managed service accounts. After a managed service account has been installed, you can configure a service or application to use the account and no longer have to specify or change passwords because the account password is maintained by the computer. You can also configure the SPN on the service account without requiring domain administrator privileges.

You create a managed service account by using New-ADServiceAccount. The basic syntax is as follows:

```
New-ADServiceAccount –DisplayName DisplayName -SamAccountName SAMName
–Name Name [-RestrictToSingleComputer]
```

DisplayName is the display name for the account, *SAMName* is the pre–Windows 2000 name of the account, and *Name* is the pre–Windows 2000 name of the account, such as:

```
New-ADServiceAccount –DisplayName "SQL Agent Account"
–SamAccountName sqlagent –Name "SQL Agent"
```

The account will be created as a group account by default. It will have a randomly generated 240-byte (120-character) password and be created in the Managed Service Accounts container. The account is also enabled by default, but you can create the account in a disabled state by adding –Enabled $false. If you need to pass in credentials to create the account, use the –Credential parameter, as shown in this example:

```
$cred = Get-Credential
New-ADServiceAccount –DisplayName "IIS App Pool 1"
–SamAccountName pool1 –Name "IIS Pool 1" –Credential $cred
```

Although the account is listed in Active Directory Users And Computers, you shouldn't use this management tool to work with the account. Instead, you should use the following Windows PowerShell cmdlets:

- Get-ADServiceAccount, to get information about one or more managed service accounts
- Set-ADServiceAccount, to set properties on an existing managed service account
- Remove-ADServiceAccount, to remove a managed service account from Active Directory

After you create a managed service account in Active Directory, you associate it with a target computer in Active Directory by using Add-ADComputerServiceAccount. You use Remove-ADComputerServiceAccount to remove a computer association from Active Directory.

The basic syntax for Add-ADComputerServiceAccount is as follows:

```
Add-ADComputerServiceAccount [-Identity] ComputerName
    [-ServiceAccount] MSAName
```

ComputerName is the name of the target computer, and *MSAName* is the name of the managed service account, such as:

```
Add-ADComputerServiceAccount IISServer84 WebServicesAccount
```

If you need to pass in credentials to create the account, use the –Credential parameter, as shown in this example:

```
$cred = Get-Credential
Add-ADComputerServiceAccount IISServer32 FarmFourServicesAccount
```

You can install the account on a local computer by using Install-ADServiceAccount. The basic syntax is this:

```
Install-ADServiceAccount [-Identity] ServiceAccountId
```

ServiceAccountId is the display name or SAM account name of the service account, such as:

```
Install-ADServiceAccount sqlagent
```

If you need to pass in credentials to create the account, use the –Credential parameter. Use Uninstall-ADServiceAccount to uninstall an account.

Configuring services to use managed service accounts

You can configure a service to run with the managed service account by following these steps:

1. In Server Manager, tap or click Tools, and then tap or click Computer Management.

2. As necessary, connect to the computer you want to manage. In the left pane, press and hold or right-click the Computer Management node, and then tap or click Connect To Another Computer. Enter the host name, fully qualified domain name, or IP address of the remote server, and then tap or click OK.

3. In the left pane, expand the Services And Applications node, and then select the Services node.

4. Press and hold or right-click the name of the service you want to work with, and then tap or click Properties.

5. On the Log On tab, select This Account, and then enter the name of the managed service account in the format *DomainName\AccountName*; or tap or click Browse to search for the account.

6. Confirm that the password box is blank, and then tap or click OK.

7. Select the name of the service, and then tap or click Start to start the service, or tap or click Restart to restart the service as appropriate. Confirm that the newly configured account name appears in the Log On As column for the service.

NOTE A dollar sign ($) appears at the end of the account name in the Services snap-in console. When you use the Services snap-in console to configure the logon as an account, the Service Logon Right logon right is automatically assigned to the account. If you use a different tool, the account has to be explicitly granted this right.

Removing managed service accounts

If a managed service account is no longer being used on a computer, you might want to uninstall the account. Before you do this, however, you should check the Services snap-in to ensure that the account isn't being used. To uninstall a managed service account from a local computer, use Uninstall-ADServiceAccount. The basic syntax is shown here:

```
Uninstall-ADServiceAccount -Identity ServiceAccountId
```

ServiceAccountId is the display name or SAM account name of the service account, such as:

```
Uninstall-ADServiceAccount -Identity sqlagent
```

If you need to pass in credentials to uninstall the account, use the –Credential parameter.

Managed service account passwords are reset on a regular basis based on the password reset requirements of the domain, but you can reset the password manually if needed. To reset the password for a managed service account, use Reset-ADServiceAccountPassword. The basic syntax is as follows:

```
Reset-ADServiceAccountPassword -Identity ServiceAccountId
```

ServiceAccountId is the display name or SAM account name of the service account, such as:

```
Reset-ADServiceAccountPassword -Identity sqlagent
```

If you need to pass in credentials to reset the password, use the –Credential parameter. You can modify the default password change interval for managed service accounts by using the domain policy Domain Member: Maximum Machine

Account Password Age under Local Policies\Security Options. Group Policy settings under Account Policies\Password Policy are not used to modify managed service account password-reset intervals, nor can the NLTEST /SC_CHANGE_PWD command be used to reset managed service account passwords.

Moving managed service accounts

To move a managed service account from a source computer to a new destination computer, you need to do the following:

1. On the source computer, configure any services that are using the managed account to use a different account, and then run Uninstall-ADServiceAccount.

2. On the new destination computer, run Install-ADServiceAccount, and then use the Services snap-in console to configure the service to run with the managed service account.

To migrate a service from a user account to a managed service account, you need to do the following:

1. Create a new managed service account in Active Directory by using New-ADServiceAccount.

2. Install the managed service account on the appropriate computer by using Install-ADServiceAccount, and then use the Services snap-in console to configure the service to run with the managed service account.

3. You also might need to configure the access control lists on the service resources for the service management account.

Using virtual accounts

Virtual accounts require very little management. They cannot be created or deleted, and they do not require any password management. Instead, they exist automatically and are represented by the machine identity of the local computer.

With virtual accounts, you configure a local service to access the network with a computer identity in a domain environment. Because the computer identity is used, no account needs to be created and no password management is required.

You can configure a service to run with a virtual account by following these steps:

1. In Server Manager, tap or click Tools, and then tap or click Computer Management.

2. As necessary, connect to the computer you want to manage. In the left pane, press and hold or right-click the Computer Management node, and then tap or click Connect To Another Computer. Enter the host name, fully qualified domain name, or IP address of the remote server, and then tap or click OK.

3. In the left pane, expand the Services And Applications node, and then select the Services node.

4. Press and hold or right-click the name of the service you want to work with, and then tap or click Properties.

5. On the Log On tab, select This Account, and then enter the name of the service account in the format *SERVICE\ComputerName*.

6. Confirm that the password box is blank, and then tap or click OK.

7. Select the name of the service, and then tap or click Start to start the service, or tap or click Restart to restart the service. Confirm that the newly configured account name appears in the Log On As column for the service.

NOTE A dollar sign ($) appears at the end of the account name in the Services snap-in console. When you use the Services snap-in console to configure the logon as an account, the Service Logon Right logon right is automatically assigned to the account. If you use a different tool, the account has to be explicitly granted this right.

Managing existing user and group accounts

I n a perfect world, you could create user and group accounts and never have
to touch them again. Unfortunately, we live in the real world. After you create
accounts, you'll spend a lot of time managing them. This chapter provides guidelines
and tips to make that task easier.

Managing user contact information

Active Directory Domain Services (AD DS) is a directory service. When you create
user accounts, those accounts can have detailed contact information associated
with them. The contact information is then available for anyone in the domain tree
or forest to use as criteria to search for users and to create address book entries.

Setting contact information

You can set a user's contact information in Active Directory Users And Computers by following these steps:

1. Double-tap or double-click the user name in Active Directory Users And Computers. This opens the account's Properties dialog box.

2. Tap or click the General tab, shown in Figure 10-1. Set general contact information in the following boxes:

   - **First Name, Initials, Last Name**   The user's full name.
   - **Display Name**   The user's display name as shown in logon sessions and in Active Directory.
   - **Description**   A description of the user.
   - **Office**   The user's office location.
   - **Telephone Number**   The user's primary business telephone number. If the user has other business telephone numbers you want to track, tap or click Other, and then enter additional phone numbers in the Phone Number (Others) dialog box.
   - **E-Mail**   The user's business email address.
   - **Web Page**   The URL of the user's home page, which can be on the Internet or on the company intranet. If the user has other webpages you want to track, tap or click Other, and then enter additional webpage addresses in the Web Page Address (Others) dialog box.

FIGURE 10-1 Configure general contact information for the user on the General tab.

TIP   You must fill in the E-Mail and Web Page boxes if you want to use the Send Mail and Open Home Page features of Active Directory Users And Computers. For more information, see the "Updating user and group accounts" section later in this chapter.

3. Tap or click the Address tab. Set the user's business or home address in the boxes provided. You'll usually want to enter the user's business address. You can then track the business locations and mailing addresses of users at various offices.

NOTE **You need to consider privacy issues before you enter users' home addresses. Discuss the matter with your human resources and legal departments. You might also want to get user consent before releasing home addresses.**

4. Tap or click the Telephones tab. Enter the primary telephone numbers that should be used to contact the user, such as home, pager, mobile, fax, and IP phone.

5. You can configure other numbers for each type of telephone number. Tap or click the associated Other buttons, and then enter additional phone numbers in the dialog box provided.

6. Tap or click the Organization tab. As appropriate, enter the user's job title, department, and company.

7. To specify the user's manager, tap or click Change, and then select the user's manager in the Select User Or Contact dialog box. When you specify a manager, the user shows up as a direct report in the manager's account.

8. Tap or click Apply or OK to apply the changes.

You also can set contact information by using Active Directory Administrative Center. Double-tap or double-click the user name. In the account's Properties dialog box, tap or click Organization to display the Organization panel. As Figure 10-2 shows, this panel provides a one-stop location for setting general, address, telephone, and organization details.

FIGURE 10-2 The Organization panel provides a one-stop location for setting general, address, telephone, and organization details.

The Web Page box sets the URL of the user's home page, which can be on the Internet or on the company intranet. If the user has other webpages you want to track, tap or click Other Web Pages and then enter additional webpage addresses in the Web Page Address (Others) dialog box.

Under Phone Numbers, enter the primary telephone numbers that should be used to contact the user, such as main, home, mobile, fax, pager, and IP phone. You can configure other numbers for each type of telephone number. Tap or click Other Phone Numbers, and then enter additional phone numbers in the dialog box provided.

If the user has a manager set, this is listed in the Manager box. If no manager is set or you want to change the manager, tap or click the Edit button next to Manager to specify the user's manager in the Select User Or Contact dialog box. When you specify a manager, the user shows up as a direct report in the manager's account.

If the user has direct reports, they are listed under Direct Reports. You can add and remove direct reports by using the related Add and Remove buttons. To add a direct report, tap or click Add, specify the direct report in the Select User Or Contact dialog box, and then tap or click OK. To remove a direct report, tap or click the name in the list, and then tap or click Remove.

Searching for users and groups in Active Directory

Active Directory makes it easy for you to find users and groups in the directory, which you can do by following these steps:

1. In Active Directory Users And Computers, press and hold or right-click the domain or container, and then tap or click Find.

2. In the Find Users, Contacts, And Groups dialog box, the In list shows the previously selected domain or container. If you want to search the entire directory instead, select Entire Directory, or tap or click Browse to select a domain or container to search.

3. On the Users, Contacts, And Groups tab, enter the name of the user, contact, or group you want to search for.

4. Tap or click Find Now to begin the search. If matches are found, the search results are displayed, as shown in Figure 10-3. Otherwise, enter new search parameters and search again.

5. To manage an account, press and hold or right-click its entry. If you press and hold or right-click an account entry and then select Properties, you can open the account's Properties dialog box.

FIGURE 10-3 Search for users in Active Directory, and then use the results to create address book entries.

You can also search for users and groups by using the filter and global search features of Active Directory Administrative Center. For more information, see the "Active Directory Administrative Center and Windows PowerShell" section in Chapter 8, "Core Active Directory administration."

Configuring the user's environment settings

User accounts can also have profiles, logon scripts, and home directories associated with them. To configure these optional settings, double-tap or double-click a display name in Active Directory Users And Computers, and then tap or click the Profile tab, shown in Figure 10-4. On the Profile tab, you can provide the following settings:

- **Profile Path** The path to the user's profile. Profiles provide the environment settings for users. Each time a user logs on to a computer, that user's profile is used to determine desktop and Control Panel settings, the availability of menu options and applications, and more. Setting the profile path is covered in the "Managing user profiles" section later in this chapter.

- **Logon Script** The path to the user's logon script. Logon scripts are batch files that run whenever a user logs on. You use logon scripts to set commands that should be executed each time a user logs on.

- **Home Folder** The directory the user should use for storing files. Here, you assign a specific directory for the user's files as a local path on the user's system or on a connected network drive. If the directory is available to the network, the user can access the directory from any computer on the network, which is a definite advantage.

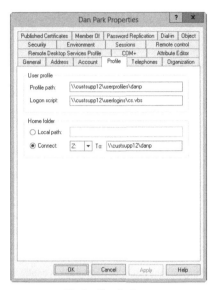

FIGURE 10-4 The Profile tab allows you to create a user profile and thereby configure the network environment for a user.

In Active Directory Administrative Center, you configure a user's environment settings by using the options in the Profile panel. To configure these settings, double-tap or double-click a display name in Active Directory Administrative Center, and then tap or click Profile to display the Profile panel, shown in Figure 10-5.

FIGURE 10-5 Configure the user's environment settings by using the options in the Profile panel.

System environment variables

System environment variables are often helpful when you're setting up the user's environment, especially when you work with logon scripts. You use environment variables to specify path information that can be dynamically assigned. You use the following environment variables the most:

- **%SystemRoot%** The base directory for the operating system, such as C:\Windows. Use it with the Profile tab of the user's Properties dialog box and logon scripts.

- **%UserName%** The user account name, such as wrstanek. Use it with the Profile tab of the user's Properties dialog box and logon scripts.

- **%HomeDrive%**   The drive letter of the user's home directory followed by a colon, such as C:. Use it with logon scripts.
- **%HomePath%**   The full path to the user's home directory on the respective home drive, such as \Users\Mkg\Georgej. Use it with logon scripts.
- **%Processor_Architecture%**   The processor architecture of the user's computer, such as x86. Use it with logon scripts.

Figure 10-6 shows how you might use environment variables when creating user accounts. Note that by using the %UserName% variable, you allow the system to determine the full path information on a user-by-user basis. If you use this technique, you can use the same path information for multiple users, and all the users will have unique settings.

FIGURE 10-6 When you use the Profile tab, environment variables can lessen the information you need to enter, especially when you create an account based on another account.

Logon scripts

Logon scripts set commands that should be executed each time a user logs on. You can use logon scripts to set the system time, network drive paths, network printers, and more. Although you can use logon scripts to execute one-time commands, you shouldn't use them to set environment variables. Any environment settings used by scripts aren't maintained for subsequent user processes. Also, you shouldn't use logon scripts to specify applications that should run at startup. You should set startup applications by placing the appropriate shortcuts in the user's Startup folder.

Normally, logon scripts contain Windows commands. However, logon scripts can be any of the following:

- Windows PowerShell scripts with a .ps1 or other valid extension
- Windows Script Host files with .vbs, .js, or another valid script extension
- Batch files with the .bat extension
- Command files with the .cmd extension
- Executable programs with the .exe extension

One user or many users can use a single logon script. As the administrator, you control which users use which scripts. As the name implies, logon scripts are accessed when users log on to their accounts. You can specify a logon script by following these steps:

1. Open the user's Properties dialog box in Active Directory Users And Computers, and then tap or click the Profile tab.
2. Enter the path to the logon script in the Logon Script box. Be sure to set the full path to the logon script, such as \\Zeta\User_Logon\Eng.vbs.

Creating logon scripts is easier than you might think, especially when you use the Windows command language. Just about any command you can enter into a command prompt can be set to run in a logon script. The most common tasks you'll want logon scripts to handle are to set the default printers and network paths for users. You can set this information with the NET USE command. The following NET USE commands define a network printer and a network drive:

```
net use lpt1: \\zeta\techmain
net use G: \\gamma\corpfiles
```

If these commands were in the user's logon script, the user would have a network printer on LPT1 and a network drive on drive G. You can create similar connections in a script. With Microsoft Visual Basic Scripting Edition (VBScript), you need to initialize the variables and objects you plan to use and then call the appropriate methods of the Network object to add the connections. Consider the following example:

```
Option Explicit
Dim wNetwork, printerPath
Set wNetwork = WScript.CreateObject("WScript.Network")

printerPath = "\\zeta\techmain"
wNetwork.AddWindowsPrinterConnection printerPath
wNetwork.SetDefaultPrinter printerPath

wNetwork.MapNetworkDrive "G:", "\\gamma\corpfiles"

Set wNetwork = vbEmpty
Set printerPath = vbEmpty
```

Here, you use the AddWindowsPrinterConnection method to add a connection to the TechMain printer on Zeta, and you use the SetDefaultPrinter method to set the printer as the default for the user. You then use the MapNetworkDrive method to define a network drive on drive G.

Assigning home directories

Windows Server 2012 R2 lets you assign a home directory for each user account. Users can store and retrieve their personal files in this directory. Many applications use the home directory as the default for File Open and File Save As operations, which helps users find their resources easily. The command prompt also uses the home directory as the initial current directory.

Home directories can be located on a user's local hard drive or on a shared network drive. On a local drive, the directory is accessible only from a single workstation; however, shared network drives can be accessed from any computer on the network, which makes for a more versatile user environment.

> **TIP** Although users can share home directories, doing so is not a good idea. You'll usually want to provide each user with a unique home directory.

You don't need to create the user's home directory ahead of time. Active Directory Users And Computers automatically creates the directory for you. If there's a problem creating the directory, Active Directory Users And Computers will instruct you to create it manually.

To specify a local home directory, follow these steps:

1. Open the user's Properties dialog box in Active Directory Users And Computers, and then tap or click the Profile tab.

2. Select Local Path in the Home Folder section, and then enter the path to the home directory in the associated box, such as C:\Home\%UserName%.

To specify a network home directory, follow these steps:

1. Open the user's Properties dialog box in Active Directory Users And Computers, and then tap or click the Profile tab.

2. In the Home Folder section, select the Connect option, and then select a drive letter for the home directory. For consistency, you should use the same drive letter for all users. Also, be sure to select a drive letter that won't conflict with any currently configured physical or mapped drives. To avoid problems, you might want to use Z as the drive letter.

3. Enter the complete path to the home directory by using Universal Naming Convention (UNC) notation, such as \\Gamma\User_Dirs\%UserName%. You include the server name in the drive path to ensure that the user can access the directory from any computer on the network.

NOTE If you don't assign a home directory, Windows Server 2012 R2 uses the default local home directory.

Setting account options and restrictions

Windows Server 2012 R2 gives you many ways to control user accounts and their access to the network. You can define logon hours, permitted workstations for logon, dial-in privileges, and more.

Managing logon hours

Windows Server 2012 R2 lets you control when users can log on to the network. You do this by setting their valid logon hours. You can use logon hour restrictions to tighten security and prevent system cracking or malicious conduct after normal business hours.

During valid logon hours, users can work as they typically do. They can log on to the network and access network resources. During restricted logon hours, users can't work. They can't log on to the network or make connections to network resources.

If users are logged on when their logon time expires, what happens depends on the account policy you've set for them? Generally, one of two things happens to the user:

- **Forcibly disconnected** You can set a policy that tells Windows Server to forcibly disconnect users when their logon hours expire. If this policy is set, remote users are disconnected from all network resources and logged off the system when their hours expire.

- **Not disconnected** Users aren't disconnected from the network when their logon hours expire. Instead, Windows Server doesn't allow them to make any new network connections.

Configuring logon hours

To configure the logon hours, follow these steps:

1. Open the user's Properties dialog box. In Active Directory Users And Computers, tap or click the Account tab, and then tap or click Logon Hours. In Active Directory Administrative Center, tap or click Log On Hours in the Account panel.

2. You can now set the valid and invalid logon hours by using the Log On Hours dialog box, shown in Figure 10-7. In this dialog box, you can turn on or off each hour of the day or night:

   - Hours that are allowed are filled in with a dark bar—you can think of these hours as being turned on.

   - Hours that are disallowed are blank—you can think of these hours as being turned off.

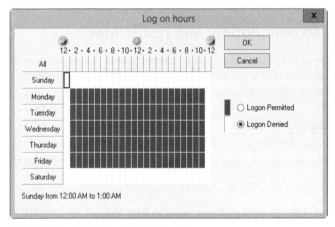

FIGURE 10-7 Configure logon hours for users.

3. To change the setting for an hour, tap or click it and then select either Logon Permitted or Logon Denied.

Table 10-1 lists Log On Hours dialog box options.

TABLE 10-1 Log On Hours Dialog Box Options

FEATURE	FUNCTION
All	Allows you to select all the time periods
Days of the week buttons	Allow you to select all the hours in a particular day
Hourly buttons	Allow you to select a particular hour for all the days of the week
Logon Permitted	Sets the allowed logon hours
Logon Denied	Sets the disallowed logon hours

TIP When you set logon hours, you'll save yourself a lot of work in the long run if you give users a moderately restricted time window. For example, rather than explicit 9:00 A.M. to 5:00 P.M. hours, you might want to allow a few hours on either side of the normal work hours. This lets early birds onto the system and allows night owls to keep working until they finish for the day.

Enforcing logon hours

To forcibly disconnect users when their logon hours expire, follow these steps:

1. Access the Group Policy Object (GPO) you want to work with, as detailed in the "Managing site, domain, and organizational unit policies" section in Chapter 6, "Automating administrative tasks, policies, and procedures."

2. Open the Security Options node by working your way down through the console tree. Expand Computer Configuration\Windows Settings\Security Settings. In Security Settings, expand Local Policies, and then select Security Options.

3. Double-tap or double-click Network Security: Force Logoff When Logon Hours Expire. This opens a Properties dialog box for the policy.

4. Select the Define This Policy Setting check box, and then tap or click Enabled. This turns on the policy restriction and enforces the logon hours. Tap or click OK.

Setting permitted logon workstations

Windows Server 2012 R2 has a formal policy that allows users to log on to systems locally. This policy controls whether a user can log on to the computer while sitting at the computer's keyboard. By default, you can use any valid user account, including the Guest account, to log on locally to a workstation.

As you might imagine, allowing users to log on to any workstation is a security risk. Unless you restrict workstation use, anyone who obtains a user name and password can use them to log on to any workstation in the domain. By defining a permitted workstation list, you close the opening in your domain and reduce the security risk. Now, not only must hackers find a user name and password, but they must also find the permitted workstations for the account.

For domain users, you define permitted logon workstations by following these steps:

1. Open the user's Properties dialog box. In Active Directory Users And Computers, tap or click the Account tab, and then tap or click Log On To. In Active Directory Administrative Center, in the Account panel, tap or click Log On To.

2. For the This User Can Log On To option, select The Following Computers, as shown in Figure 10-8.

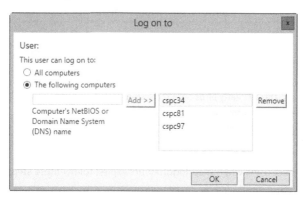

FIGURE 10-8 To restrict access to workstations, specify the permitted logon workstations.

3. Enter the name of a permitted workstation, and then tap or click Add. Repeat this procedure to specify additional workstations.

4. If you make a mistake, select the erroneous entry and then tap or click Remove.

Setting dial-in and VPN privileges

Windows Server 2012 R2 lets you set remote access privileges for accounts on the Dial-In tab of the user's Properties dialog box. These settings control access for dial-in and virtual private networks (VPNs). Remote access privileges are controlled through Network Policy Server (NPS) Network Policy by default. This is the preferred method of controlling remote access. You can explicitly grant or deny dial-in privileges by selecting Allow Access or Deny Access. In any event, before users can remotely access the network, you need to follow these steps:

1. In Server Manager, add the role of Network Policy And Access Services.

2. To enable remote access connections, access the GPO for the site, domain, or organizational unit you want to work with, as specified in the "Managing site, domain, and organizational unit policies" section in Chapter 6. In the policy editor, expand User Configuration\Administrative Templates\Network. Select Network Connections, and then configure the Network Connections policies as appropriate for the site, domain, or organizational unit.

3. Configure remote access by using Routing And Remote Access. In Computer Management, expand Services And Applications, and then select Routing And Remote Access. Configure Routing And Remote Access as appropriate.

REAL WORLD Binaries needed to install roles and features are referred to as payloads. With Windows Server 2012 R2, you remove the payloads for roles and features that you are uninstalling by using the –Remove parameter of the Uninstall-WindowsFeature cmdlet. Restore a removed payload by using the Install-WindowsFeature cmdlet. By default, payloads are restored via Windows Update. Use the –Source parameter to restore a payload from a Windows Imaging (WIM) format mount point. In the following example, you restore the NPS and Routing And Remote Access Service (RRAS) binaries via Windows Update:

```
install-windowsfeature -name npas-policy-server
-includemanagementtools

install-windowsfeature -name remoteaccess
-includeallsubfeature -includemanagementtools
```

After you grant a user permission to access the network remotely, follow these steps to configure additional dial-in parameters on the Dial-in tab of the user's Properties dialog box (as shown in Figure 10-9):

1. If the user must dial in from a specific phone number, select Verify Caller-ID, and then enter the telephone number from which this user is required to log on. Your telephone system must support Caller ID for this feature to work.

NOTE In Active Directory Administrative Center, the Dial-in tab is accessed from the Extensions panel. Tap or click Extensions and then tap or click Dial-in.

2. Define callback parameters by using the following options:

   ■ **No Callback** Allows the user to dial in directly and remain connected. The user pays the long-distance telephone charges, if applicable.

   ■ **Set By Caller** Allows the user to dial in directly, and then the server prompts the user for a callback number. Once the number is entered, the user is disconnected, and the server dials the user back at the specified number to reestablish the connection. The company pays the long-distance telephone charges, if applicable.

   ■ **Always Callback To** Allows you to set a predefined callback number for security purposes. When a user dials in, the server calls back the preset number. The company pays the long-distance telephone charges, if applicable, and reduces the risk of an unauthorized person accessing the network.

NOTE You shouldn't assign callback numbers for users who dial in through a switchboard. The switchboard might not allow the user to properly connect to the network. You also shouldn't use preset callback numbers with multilinked lines. The multilinked lines won't function properly.

If necessary, you can also assign static IP addresses and static routes for dial-in connections by selecting Assign Static IP Addresses and Apply Static Routes, respectively.

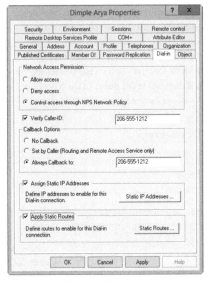

FIGURE 10-9 Dial-in privileges control remote access to the network.

Setting account security options

The Account tab/panel of the user's Properties dialog box has the following options, which are designed to help you maintain a secure network environment and control how user accounts are used:

- **User Must Change Password At Next Logon**   Forces the user to change his password when the user logs on next.
- **User Cannot Change Password**   Doesn't allow the user to change the account password.
- **Password Never Expires**   Ensures that the account password never expires, which overrides the normal password expiration period.

    CAUTION   Selecting this option creates a security risk on the network. Although you might want to use Password Never Expires with administrator accounts, you usually shouldn't use this option with normal user accounts.

- **Store Password Using Reversible Encryption**   Saves the password as encrypted clear text.
- **Account Is Disabled**   Disables the account, which prevents the user from accessing the network and logging on (Active Directory Users And Computers only).

- **Smart Card Is Required For Interactive Logon**   Requires the user to log on to a workstation by using a smart card. The user can't log on to the workstation by entering a logon name and password at the keyboard.

- **Account Is Sensitive And Cannot Be Delegated**   Specifies that the user's account credentials cannot be delegated by using Kerberos. Use this for sensitive accounts that should be carefully controlled.

- **Use Kerberos DES Encryption Types For This Account**   Specifies that the user account will use Data Encryption Standard (DES) encryption.

- **This Account Supports Kerberos AES 128 Bit Encryption**   Specifies that the account supports Advanced Encryption Standard (AES) 128-bit encryption.

- **This Account Supports Kerberos AES 256 Bit Encryption**   Specifies that the account supports AES 256-bit encryption.

- **Do Not Require Kerberos Preauthentication**   Specifies that the user account doesn't need Kerberos preauthentication to access network resources. Preauthentication is part of the Kerberos V5 security procedure. The option to log on without it allows authentication from clients who are using a previous, or nonstandard, implementation of Kerberos.

REAL WORLD   AES is one of several encryption standards. Another encryption standard is Data Encryption Standard (DES). Most computers running earlier versions of Windows support DES.

Computers running current releases of Windows support AES, which provides more secure encryption than DES. Although US versions support both 128-bit and 256-bit AES, versions exported for use outside the United States typically support only 128-bit encryption.

Managing user profiles

User profiles contain settings for the network environment, such as desktop configuration and menu options. Problems with a profile can sometimes prevent a user from logging on. For example, if the display size in the profile isn't available on the system being used, the user might not be able to log on properly. In fact, the user might get nothing but a blank screen. You could restart the computer, go into VGA mode, and then reset the display manually. However, solutions for profile problems aren't always this easy, and you might need to update the profile itself.

Windows Server 2012 R2 provides several ways to manage user profiles:

- You can assign profile paths in Active Directory Users And Computers or Active Directory Administrative Center.

- You can copy, delete, and change the type of an existing local profile with the System utility in Control Panel.

- You can set system policies that prevent users from manipulating certain aspects of their environment.

Local, roaming, and mandatory profiles

In Windows Server 2012 R2, every user has a profile. Profiles control startup features for the user's session, the types of programs and applications that are available, the desktop settings, and a lot more. Each computer that a user logs on to has a copy of the user's profile. Because this profile is stored on the computer's hard disk, users who access several computers have a profile on each computer. Another computer on the network can't access a locally stored profile—called a *local* profile—and, as you might expect, this has some drawbacks. For example, if a user logs on to three different workstations, the user could have three very different profiles—one on each system. As a result, the user might get confused about what network resources are available on a given system.

Working with roaming and mandatory profiles

To reduce the confusion caused by multiple profiles, you can create a profile that other computers can access. This type of profile is called a roaming profile. By default, with a roaming profile, users can access the same profile no matter which computer they're using within the domain. Roaming profiles are server-based and can be stored on any server running Windows. When a user with a roaming profile logs on, the profile is downloaded, which creates a local copy on the user's computer. When the user logs off, changes to the profile are updated both on the local copy and on the server.

> **REAL WORLD** When your organization uses the Encrypting File System (EFS) to make file access more secure, the use of roaming profiles becomes extremely important for users who log on to multiple computers. This is because encryption certificates are stored in user profiles, and the encryption certificate is needed to access and work with the user's encrypted files. If a user has encrypted files and doesn't have a roaming profile, that user won't be able to work with these encrypted files on another computer—unless she uses credential roaming with Digital ID Management Service (DIMS).

As an administrator, you can control user profiles or let users control their own profiles. One reason to control profiles yourself is to make sure that all users have a common network configuration, which can reduce the number of environment-related problems.

Profiles controlled by administrators are called *mandatory profiles*. Users who have a mandatory profile can make only transitory changes to their environment. Any changes that users make to the local environment aren't saved, and the next time they log on, they're back to the original profile. The idea is that if users can't permanently modify the network environment, they can't make changes that cause problems. A key drawback to mandatory profiles is that the user can log on only if the profile is accessible. If, for some reason, the server that stores the profile is inaccessible and a cached profile isn't accessible, the user normally won't be able to log on. If the server is inaccessible but a cached profile is accessible, the user receives a warning message and is logged on to the local system using the system's cached profile.

Restricting roaming profiles

Typically, users can access their roaming profiles no matter which computer they're using within the domain. Windows 8.1 and Windows Server 2012 R2 allow you to modify this behavior by specifying from which computers a user can access roaming profiles and redirected folders. You do this by designating certain computers as primary computers and then configuring domain policy to restrict the downloading of profiles, redirected folders, or both to primary computers.

A *primary computer* is a computer that has been specifically designated as permitted for use with redirected data. You designate a primary computer by editing the advanced properties of a user or group in Active Directory and then setting the msDS-PrimaryComputer property to the name of the permitted computers. You then turn on the primary computer restriction for roaming profiles by enabling the Download Roaming Profiles On Primary Computers Only policy found in the Administrative Templates policies for Computer Configuration under System \User Profiles. You also can turn on the primary computer restriction for redirected folders by enabling the Redirect Folders On Primary Computers Only policy found in the Administrative Templates policies for Computer Configuration under System \Folder Redirection.

The goal of these policies is to protect personal and corporate data when users log on to computers other than the ones they use regularly for business. Data security is improved by not downloading and caching this data on computers a user doesn't usually use. To set the msDS-PrimaryComputer of a user or group, follow these steps:

1. In Active Directory Administrative Center, open the Properties dialog box for the user or group and then tap or click Extensions. Or in Active Directory Users And Computers, ensure Advanced Features is selected on the View menu, and then open the Properties dialog box for the user or group.

2. On the Attribute Editor tab, scroll through the list of attributes. Tap or click msDS-PrimaryComputer and then tap or click Edit.

3. In the Multi-Valued String Editor dialog box, enter the name of the first primary computer and then click Add. Repeat this process until you've added all primary computers. Tap or click OK twice.

Creating local profiles

User profiles are maintained either in a default directory or in the location set by the Profile Path box in the user's Properties dialog box. For Windows 7 and later, the default location for profiles is %SystemDrive%\Users\%UserName%\. A key part of the profile is the Ntuser.dat file in this location, such as C:\Users\wrstanek\Ntuser.dat. If you don't change the default location, the user will have a local profile.

Creating roaming profiles

Roaming profiles are stored on servers running Windows. When users log on to multiple computers and use EFS, they need a roaming profile to ensure that the certificates necessary to read and work with encrypted files are available on computers other than their primary work computers.

If you want a user to have a roaming profile, you must set a server-based location for the profile directory by following these steps:

1. Create a shared directory on a server running Windows Server, and make sure that the group Everyone has at least Change and Read access.

2. In Active Directory Users And Computers or Active Directory Administrative Center, open the user's Properties dialog box, and then access the Profile tab/panel. Enter the path to the shared directory in the Profile Path box. The path should have the form \\server name\profile folder name\user name. An example is \\Zeta\User_Profiles\Georgej, where Zeta is the server name, User_Profiles is the shared directory, and Georgej is the user name.

   The roaming profile is then stored in the Ntuser.dat file in the designated directory, such as \\Zeta\User_Profiles\Georgej\Ntuser.dat.

   NOTE You don't usually need to create the profile directory. The directory is created automatically when the user logs on, and NTFS permissions are set so that only the user has access. You can select multiple user accounts for simultaneous editing. One way to do this is by holding down the Shift key or the Ctrl key when tapping or clicking the user names. Then when you right-click one of the selected users and then tap or click Properties, you can edit properties for all the selected users. Be sure to use %UserName% in the profile path, such as \\Zeta\User_Profiles\%UserName%.

3. As an optional step, you can create a profile for the user or copy an existing profile to the user's profile folder. If you don't create an actual profile for the user, the next time the user logs on, he will use the default local profile. Any changes the user makes to this profile are saved when the user logs off. The next time the user logs on, he has a personal profile.

Creating mandatory profiles

Mandatory profiles are stored on servers running Windows Server. If you want a user to have a mandatory profile, you define the profile as follows:

1. Follow steps 1 and 2 in the procedure in the previous section, "Creating roaming profiles."

2. Create a mandatory profile by renaming the Ntuser.dat file as %UserName%\Ntuser.man. The next time the user logs on, she will have a mandatory profile.

NOTE Ntuser.dat contains the registry settings for the user. When you change the extension for the file to Ntuser.man, you tell Windows Server to create a mandatory profile.

Using the System utility to manage local profiles

To manage local profiles, you need to log on to the user's computer. Then you can use the System utility in Control Panel to manage local profiles. To view current profile information, tap or click System And Security in Control Panel and then tap or click System. On the System page in Control Panel, tap or click Advanced System Settings. In the System Properties dialog box, under User Profiles, tap or click Settings.

As shown in Figure 10-10, the User Profiles dialog box displays information about the profiles stored on the local system. You can use this information to help you manage profiles. The dialog box lists the following information:

- **Name** The local profile's name, which generally includes the name of the originating domain or computer and the user account name. For example, the name ADATUM\Wrstanek tells you that the original profile is from the domain adatum and the user account is wrstanek.

   NOTE If you delete an account but don't delete the associated profile, an entry that says Account Deleted or Account Unknown might be displayed. Don't worry—the profile is still available for copying if you need it, or you can delete the profile here.

- **Size** The profile's size. Generally, the larger the profile, the more the user has customized the environment.
- **Type** The profile type, which is either local or roaming.
- **Status** The profile's current status, such as whether it's from a local cache.
- **Modified** The date that the profile was last modified.

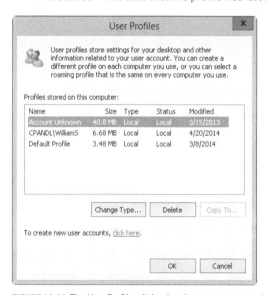

FIGURE 10-10 The User Profiles dialog box lets you manage existing local profiles.

Creating a profile manually

Sometimes you might want to create the profile manually. You do this by logging on to the user account, setting up the environment, and then logging off. As you might guess, creating accounts in this manner is time consuming. A better way to handle account creation is to create a base user account, set up the account environment, and then use this account as the basis of other accounts.

Copying an existing profile to a new user account

If you have a base user account or a user account you want to use in a similar manner, you can copy an existing profile to the new user account. To do this, follow these steps to use the System Control Panel utility:

1. Start the System Control Panel utility. On the System page in Control Panel, tap or click Advanced System Settings. In the System Properties dialog box, under User Profiles, tap or click Settings.

2. Select the profile you want to copy from the Profiles Stored On This Computer list. (See Figure 10-10.)

3. Copy the profile to the new user's account by tapping or clicking Copy To. In the Copy Profile To box, shown in Figure 10-11, enter the path to the new user's profile directory. For example, if you were creating the profile for georgej, you'd enter \\Zeta\User_Profiles\Georgej.

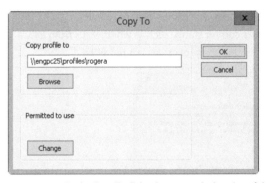

FIGURE 10-11 In the Copy To dialog box, enter the location of the profile directory and assign access permissions to the user.

4. Now you need to give the user permission to access the profile. In the Permitted To Use area, tap or click Change, and then use the Select User Or Group dialog box to grant access to the new user account.

   TIP If you know the name of the user or group you want to use, you can save time by entering it directly into the Name box.

5. Tap or click OK to close the Copy To dialog box. Windows then copies the profile to the new location.

Copying or restoring a profile

When you work with workgroups where each computer is managed separately, you often have to copy a user's local profile from one computer to another. Copying a profile allows users to maintain environment settings when they use different computers. Of course, in a Windows Server domain, you can use a roaming profile to create a single profile that can be accessed from anywhere within the domain. The problem is that sometimes you might need to copy an existing local profile to replace a user's roaming profile (when the roaming profile becomes corrupt), or you might need to copy an existing local profile to create a roaming profile in another domain.

You can copy a profile to a new location by following these steps:

1. Log on to the user's computer, and start the System Control Panel utility. On the System page in Control Panel, tap or click Advanced System Settings. In the System Properties dialog box, under User Profiles, tap or click Settings.

2. In the Profiles Stored On This Computer list, select the profile you want to copy.

3. Copy the profile to the new location by tapping or clicking Copy To, and then enter the path to the new profile directory in the Copy Profile To box. For example, if you're creating the profile for janew, you could enter **\\Gamma \User_Profiles\Janew**.

4. To give the user permission to access the profile, tap or click the Change button in the Permitted To Use area, and then grant access to the appropriate user account in the Select User Or Group dialog box.

5. When you have finished, tap or click OK to close the Copy To dialog box. Windows then copies the profile to the new location.

Deleting a local profile and assigning a new one

Profiles are accessed when a user logs on to a computer. Windows Server uses local profiles for all users who don't have roaming profiles. Generally, local profiles are also used if the local profile has a more recent modification date than the user's roaming profile. Therefore, sometimes you might need to delete a user's local profile. For example, if a user's local profile becomes corrupt, you can delete the profile and assign a new one. Keep in mind that when you delete a local profile that isn't stored anywhere else on the domain, you can't recover the user's original environment settings.

To delete a user's local profile, follow these steps:

1. Log on to the user's computer by using an account with administrator privileges, and then start the System utility.

2. Tap or click Advanced System Settings. In the System Properties dialog box, under User Profiles, tap or click Settings.

3. Select the profile you want to delete, and then tap or click Delete. When asked to confirm that you want to delete the profile, tap or click Yes.

You can't delete a profile that's in use. If the user is logged on to the local system (the computer you're deleting the profile from), the user needs to log off before you can delete the profile. In some instances, Windows Server marks profiles as in use when they aren't. This typically results from an environment change for the user that wasn't properly applied. To correct this, you might need to restart the computer.

The next time the user logs on, Windows Server does one of two things. Either the operating system gives the user the default local profile for that system, or it retrieves the user's roaming profile stored on another computer. To prevent the use of either of these profiles, you need to assign the user a new profile. To do this, you can do one of the following:

- Copy an existing profile to the user's profile directory. Copying profiles is covered in the "Copying or restoring a profile" section earlier in this chapter.
- Update the profile settings for the user in Active Directory Users And Computers. Setting the profile path is covered in the "Creating roaming profiles" section earlier in this chapter.

Changing the profile type

With roaming profiles, the System utility lets you change the profile type on the user's computer. To do this, select the profile and then tap or click Change Type. The options in this dialog box allow you to do the following:

- **Change a roaming profile to a local profile**   If you want the user to always work with the local profile on this computer, specify that the profile is for local use. All changes to the profile are then made locally, and the original roaming profile is left untouched.
- **Change a local profile (defined originally as a roaming profile) to a roaming profile**   The user will use the original roaming profile for the next logon. Windows Server then treats the profile like any other roaming profile, which means that any changes to the local profile are copied to the roaming profile.

NOTE   If these options aren't available, the user's original profile is defined locally.

Updating user and group accounts

Active Directory Administrative Center and Active Directory Users And Computers are the tools to use when you want to update a domain user or group account. If you want to update a local user or group account, use Local Users And Groups.

When you work with Active Directory, you'll often want to get a list of accounts and then do something with those accounts. For example, you might want to list all the user accounts in the organization and then disable the accounts of users who have left the company. One way to perform this task is to follow these steps:

1. In Active Directory Users And Computers, press and hold or right-click the domain name and then tap or click Find.

2. In the Find list, select Custom Search. This updates the Find dialog box to display a Custom Search tab.

3. In the In list, select the area you want to search. To search the enterprise, select Entire Directory.

4. On the Custom Search tab, tap or click Field to display a menu. Select User, and then select Logon Name (Pre–Windows 2000).

   TIP Be sure to select Logon Name (Pre–Windows 2000). Don't use Logon Name. User accounts aren't required to have a logon name, but they are required to have a pre–Windows 2000 logon name.

5. In the Condition list, select Present, and then tap or click Add. If prompted to confirm, tap or click Yes.

6. Tap or click Find Now. Active Directory Users And Computers gathers a list of all users in the designated area.

7. You can now work with the accounts one by one or several at a time. One way to select multiple resources not in sequence is to hold down the Ctrl key and then click each object you want to select. One way to select a series of resources at one time is to hold down the Shift key, click the first object, and then click the last object.

8. Press and hold or right-click a user account, and then select an action on the shortcut menu that's displayed, such as Disable Account.

   TIP The actions you can perform on multiple accounts include Add To Group (used to add the selected accounts to a designated group), Enable Account, Disable Account, Delete, Move, and Send Mail. By choosing Properties, you can edit the properties of multiple accounts.

Use this same procedure to get a list of computers, groups, or other Active Directory resources. With computers, do a custom search, tap or click Field, choose Computer, and then select Computer Name (Pre–Windows 2000). With groups, do a custom search, tap or click Field, choose Group, and then select Group Name (Pre–Windows 2000).

The sections that follow examine other techniques you can use to update (rename, copy, delete, and enable) accounts and change and reset passwords. You'll also learn how to troubleshoot account logon problems.

Renaming user and group accounts

When you rename a user account, you give the account a new label. As discussed in Chapter 9, "Creating user and group accounts," user names are meant to make managing and using accounts easier. Behind the scenes, Windows Server uses security identifiers (SIDs) to identify, track, and handle accounts independently from user names. SIDs are unique identifiers that are generated when accounts are created.

Because SIDs are mapped to account names internally, you don't need to change the privileges or permissions on renamed accounts. Windows Server simply maps the SIDs to the new account names as necessary.

One common reason for changing the name of a user account is that the user gets married and decides to change her last name. For example, if Heidi Steen (heidis) gets married, she might want her user name to be changed to Heidi Jensen (heidij). When you change the user name from heidis to heidij, all associated privileges and permissions will reflect the name change. If you view the permissions on a file that heidis had access to, heidij now has access (and heidis is no longer listed).

To simplify the process of renaming user accounts, Active Directory Users And Computers provides a Rename User dialog box you can use to rename a user's account and all the related name components. This dialog box currently isn't in Active Directory Administrative Center, so you need to open the Properties dialog box and enter the new name properties for each box as appropriate.

To rename an account, follow these steps:

1. Find the user account you want to rename in Active Directory Users And Computers.

2. Press and hold or right-click the user account, and then tap or click Rename. Active Directory Users And Computers highlights the account name for editing. Press Backspace or Delete to erase the existing name, and then press Enter to open the Rename User dialog box, shown in Figure 10-12.

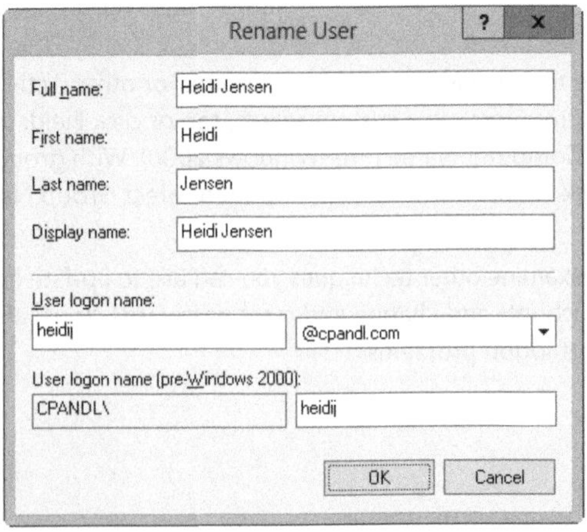

FIGURE 10-12 Fully rename an account.

3. Make the necessary changes to the user's name information, and then tap or click OK. If the user is logged on, a warning prompt is displayed telling you that the user should log off and then log back on by using the new account logon name.

4. The account is renamed, and the SID for access permissions remains the same. You might still need to modify other data for the user in the account Properties dialog box, including the following:

- **User Profile Path**   Change the Profile Path in Active Directory Users And Computers, and then rename the corresponding directory on disk.

- **Logon Script Name**   If you use individual logon scripts for each user, change the Logon Script Name in Active Directory Users And Computers, and then rename the logon script on disk.

- **Home Directory**   Change the home directory path in Active Directory Users And Computers, and then rename the corresponding directory on disk.

NOTE   Changing directory and file information for an account when a user is logged on might cause problems. You might want to update this information after hours or ask the user to log off for a few minutes and then log back on. You can usually write a simple Windows script that can perform the tasks for you automatically.

Copying domain user accounts

Creating domain user accounts from scratch can be tedious. Instead of starting anew each time, you might want to use an existing account as a starting point. This option currently isn't in Active Directory Administrative Center. To do this in Active Directory Users And Computers, follow these steps:

1. Press and hold or right-click the account you want to copy, and then tap or click Copy. This opens the Copy Object—User dialog box.

2. Create the account as you would any other domain user account, and then update the properties of the account as appropriate.

As you might expect, when you create a copy of an account, Active Directory Users And Computers doesn't retain all the information from the existing account. Instead, Active Directory Users And Computers tries to copy only the information you need and to discard the information that you need to update. The following properties are retained:

- City, state, postal code, and country values set on the Address tab
- Department and company set on the Organization tab
- Account options set by using the Account Options boxes on the Account tab
- Logon hours and permitted logon workstations
- Account expiration date
- Group account memberships
- Profile settings
- Dial-in privileges

NOTE If you used environment variables to specify the profile settings in the original account, the environment variables are also used for the copy of the account. For example, if the original account used the %UserName% variable, the copy of the account will also use this variable.

Importing and exporting accounts

Windows Server 2012 R2 includes the Comma-Separated Value Directory Exchange (CSVDE) command-line utility for importing and exporting Active Directory objects. For import operations, CSVDE uses a comma-delimited file as the import source. You can run CSVDE by using these general parameters:

- **–i** Turns on import mode (rather than export, which is the default mode)
- **–f *filename*** Sets the source for an import or the output file for an export
- **–s *servername*** Sets the server to use for the import or export (rather than the default domain controller for the domain)
- **–v** Turns on verbose mode

For import operations, the source file's first row defines the list of Lightweight Directory Access Protocol (LDAP) attributes for each object defined. Each successive line of data provides the details for a specific object to import and must contain exactly the attributes listed. Here is an example:

```
DN,objectClass,sAMAccoutName,sn,givenName,userPrincipalName
"CN=William Stanek,OU=Eng,DC=cpandl,DC=com",user,williams,William,Stanek,
williams@cpandl.com
```

Given this listing, if the import source file is named newusers.csv, you could import the file into Active Directory by entering the following command at an elevated command prompt:

```
csvde -i -f newusers.csv
```

For export operations, CSVDE writes the exported objects to a comma-delimited text file. You can also run CSVDE by using the general parameters listed previously as export-specific parameters, which include the following:

- **–d *RootDN*** Sets the starting point for the export, such as -d "OU=Sales,DC=domain,DC=local". The default is the current naming context.
- **–l *list*** Provides a comma-separated list of attributes to output.
- **–r *Filter*** Sets the LDAP search filter, such as −r "(objectClass=user)".
- **–m** Configures output for the Security Accounts Manager (SAM) rather than Active Directory.

To create an export file for the current naming context (the default domain), you could enter the following at an elevated command prompt:

```
csvde -f newusers.csv
```

However, this could result in a very large export dump. Thus, in most cases, you should specify at a minimum the RootDN and an object filter, as shown here:

```
csvde -f newusers.csv -d "OU=Service,DC=cpandl,DC=com" −r
"(objectClass=user)"
```

Deleting user and group accounts

Deleting an account permanently removes the account. After you delete an account, you can't create an account with the same name to restore the same permissions. That's because the SID for the new account won't match the SID for the old account.

Because deleting built-in accounts can have far-reaching effects on the domain, Windows Server 2012 R2 doesn't let you delete built-in user accounts or group accounts. You can remove other types of accounts by selecting them and pressing the Delete key, or by pressing and holding or right-clicking and selecting Delete. When prompted, tap or click Yes.

With Active Directory Users And Computers, one way to work with multiple accounts is by doing one of the following:

- Select multiple user names for editing by holding down the Ctrl key and tapping or clicking each account you want to select.
- Select a range of user names by holding down the Shift key, selecting the first account name, and then tapping or clicking the last account in the range.

NOTE When you delete a user account, Windows Server 2012 R2 doesn't delete the user's profile, personal files, or home directory. If you want to delete these files and directories, you have to do it manually. If this is a task you perform routinely, you might want to create a script that performs the necessary procedures for you. However, don't forget to back up files or data that might be needed before you do this.

Changing and resetting passwords

As an administrator, you often have to change or reset user passwords. This usually happens when users forget their passwords or when their passwords expire.

To change or reset a password, follow these steps:

1. Open Active Directory Users And Computers, Active Directory Administrative Center, or Local Users And Groups (whichever is appropriate).

2. Press and hold or right-click the account name, and then tap or click Reset Password or Set Password.

3. Enter a new password for the user and confirm it. The password should conform to the password-complexity policy set for the computer or domain.

4. User Must Change Password At Next Logon forces the user to change his password when the user logs on next. If you don't want the user to have to change his password, clear this check box.

5. The Account Lockout Status On This Domain Controller property shows whether the account is locked or unlocked. If the account is locked, select Unlock The User's Account to unlock it. Tap or click OK.

Enabling user accounts

User accounts can become disabled for several reasons. If a user forgets her password and tries to guess it, the user might exceed the account policy for bad logon attempts. Another administrator could have disabled the account while the user was on vacation, or the account could have expired. The following sections describe what to do when an account is disabled, locked out, or expired.

Account disabled

Active Directory Users And Computers and Active Directory Administrative Center depict disabled accounts with an arrow next to the user icon in the main view. When an account is disabled, follow these steps to enable it:

1. Open Active Directory Users And Computers, Active Directory Administrative Center, or Local Users And Groups (whichever is appropriate).

2. Press and hold or right-click the user's account name. Select the appropriate option for the tool you are using, either Enable or Enable Account.

TIP To quickly search the current domain for disabled accounts, enter **dsquery user –disabled** at a command prompt.

You can select multiple accounts at the same time and then use the options on the shortcut menu to enable or disable them. In Active Directory Users And Computers, enable all selected accounts by using the Enable Account option, or disable them by selecting Disable Account. In Active Directory Administrative Center, enable the accounts by using the Enable All option, or disable them by using Disable All.

Account locked out

When an account is locked out, follow these steps to unlock it:

1. Open Active Directory Users And Computers, Active Directory Administrative Center, or Local Users And Groups (whichever is appropriate).

2. Double-tap or double-click the user's account name, and then select the Unlock Account check box. In Active Directory Users And Computers, this check box is on the Account tab.

In Active Directory Administrative Center, you can unlock multiple accounts at the same time. Simply select the accounts and then use the Unlock All option on the shortcut menu to unlock the accounts.

NOTE If users frequently get locked out of their accounts, consider adjusting the account policy for the domain. You might want to increase the value for acceptable bad logon attempts and reduce the duration for the associated counter. For more information about setting account policy, see the "Configuring account policies" section in Chapter 9.

Account expired

Only domain accounts have an expiration date. (Local user accounts don't have an expiration date.) When a domain account expires, follow these steps to change the expiration date:

1. Open Active Directory Users And Computers or Active Directory Administrative Center.

2. Double-tap or double-click the user's account name. Open the Account tab or panel.

3. Under Account Expires, select End Of, and then tap or click the arrow on the related list box. With Active Directory Users And Computers, this displays a calendar you can use to set a new expiration date. With Active Directory Administrative Center, enter the date in the format shown.

Managing multiple user accounts

You can use Active Directory Users And Computers to modify the properties of multiple accounts simultaneously. Any changes you make to the property settings are applied to all the selected accounts. When you press and hold or right-click the selected accounts, the following options are available:

- **Add To A Group**   Displays the Select Group dialog box, which you can use to designate the groups the selected users should be members of
- **Disable Account**   Disables all the selected accounts
- **Enable Account**   Enables all the selected accounts
- **Move**   Moves the selected accounts to a new container or organizational unit
- **Cut**   Moves the selected accounts to a new container or organizational unit when you later select Paste
- **Delete**   Deletes the selected accounts from the directory
- **Properties**   Allows you to configure a limited set of properties for multiple accounts

In Active Directory Administrative Center, the options are similar. Add To Group, Disable All, Enable All, Unlock All, Move, Delete, and Properties are displayed.

The Properties option is the one you'll examine in the sections that follow. As shown in Figure 10-13, the Properties For Multiple Items dialog box has a different interface from the Properties dialog box for standard users.

FIGURE 10-13 The Properties dialog box has a different interface when you work with multiple accounts.

NOTE The examples shown here and in the sections that follow are for Active Directory Users And Computers. The management techniques are similar for Active Directory Administrative Center.

You should note the following differences:

- Account name and password boxes are no longer available. You can, however, set the Domain Name System (DNS) domain name (user principal name [UPN] suffix), logon hours, computer restrictions, account options, account expiration, and profiles.

- You must specifically select properties you want to work with by selecting the properties' check boxes. After you do this, the value you enter in the box is applied to all the selected accounts.

Setting profiles for multiple accounts

You set the profile information for multiple accounts with the options on the Profile tab. One of the best reasons to work with multiple accounts in Active Directory Users And Computers is that you can set all their environment profiles by using a single interface. To do this, you usually rely on the %UserName% environment variable, which lets you assign paths and file names that are based on individual user names. For example, if you assign the logon script name as %UserName%.cmd, Windows replaces this value with the user name, and it does so for each user you're managing. Thus, the users named bobs, janew, and ericl would all be assigned the following unique logon scripts: Bobs.cmd, Janew.cmd, and Ericl.cmd.

Figure 10-14 shows an example of setting environment profile information for multiple accounts. Note that the %UserName% variable is used to assign the user profile path, the user logon script name, and the home folder.

FIGURE 10-14 Use the %UserName% environment variable to assign paths and file names based on individual user names.

Although you might want all users to have unique file names and paths, sometimes you want users to share this information. For example, if you're using mandatory profiles for users, you might want to assign a specific user profile path rather than one that's dynamically created.

Setting logon hours for multiple accounts

When you select multiple user accounts in Active Directory Users And Computers, you can manage their logon hours collectively. To do this, follow these steps:

1. Select the accounts you want to work with in Active Directory Users And Computers.

2. Press and hold or right-click the highlighted accounts, and then tap or click Properties. In the Properties dialog box, tap or click the Account tab.

3. Select the Logon Hours check box, and then tap or click Logon Hours. You can then set the logon hours as discussed in "Configuring logon hours" earlier in the chapter.

NOTE Active Directory Users And Computers doesn't tell you the previous logon hour designations for the selected accounts, and it doesn't warn you if the logon hours for the accounts are different.

Setting permitted logon workstations for multiple accounts

You set the permitted logon workstations for multiple accounts with the Logon Workstations dialog box. To open this dialog box, follow these steps:

1. Select the accounts you want to work with in Active Directory Users And Computers.

2. Press and hold or right-click the highlighted accounts, and then tap or click Properties. In the Properties dialog box, tap or click the Account tab.

3. Select the Computer Restrictions check box, and then tap or click Log On To.

4. If you want to allow the users to log on to any workstation, select All Computers. If you want to specify which workstations users are permitted to use, tap or click The Following Computers button, and then enter the names of the workstations. When you tap or click OK, these settings are applied to all the selected user accounts.

Setting logon, password, and expiration properties for multiple accounts

User accounts have many options that control logon, passwords, and account expiration. You set these values on the Account tab of the Properties dialog box. When you work with multiple accounts, you must enable the option you want to work with by selecting the corresponding check box in the leftmost column. You now have two choices:

- Enable the option by selecting its check box. For example, if you are working with the Password Never Expires option, a flag is set so that the password for the selected users won't expire when you tap or click OK.

- Don't set the option, which effectively clears the option. For example, if you are working with the Account Is Disabled option, the accounts for the selected users are reenabled when you tap or click OK.

If you want to set the expiration date of the selected accounts, start by selecting Account Expires, and then select the appropriate expiration value. The Never option removes any current account expiration values. Select the End Of option to set a specific expiration date.

Troubleshooting logon problems

The previous section listed ways in which accounts can become disabled. Active Directory Users And Computers shows disabled accounts with a red warning icon next to the account name. To enable a disabled account, press and hold or right-click the account in Active Directory Users And Computers, and then tap or click Enable Account.

You can also search the entire domain for users with disabled accounts by entering **dsquery user –disabled** at a command prompt. To enable a disabled account from the command line, enter **dsmod user *UserDN* –disabled no**.

When a user account has been locked out by the Account Lockout policy, the account cannot be used for logging in until the lockout duration has elapsed or an administrator resets the account. If the account lockout duration is indefinite, the only way to unlock the account is to have an administrator reset it as discussed previously.

Windows Server 2012 R2 can record logon success and failure through auditing. When you enable account logon failure auditing, logon failure is recorded in the security log on the login domain controller. Auditing policies for a site, domain, or organizational unit GPO are found under Computer Configuration\Windows Settings\Security Settings\Local Policies\Audit Policy.

When a user logs on to the network by using his domain user account, the account credentials are validated by a domain controller. By default, users can log on by using their domain user accounts even if the network connection is down or no domain controller is available to authenticate the user's logon.

The user must have previously logged on to the computer and have valid, cached credentials. If the user has no cached credentials on the computer, and the network connection is down or no domain controller is available, the user will not be able to log on. Each member computer in a domain can cache up to 10 credentials by default.

Authentication can also fail if the system time on the member computer deviates from the logon domain controller's system time by more than is allowed in the Kerberos Policy: Maximum Tolerance For Computer Clock Synchronization. The default tolerance is five minutes for member computers.

Beyond these typical reasons for an account being disabled, some system settings can also cause access problems. Specifically, you should look for the following:

- **A user gets a message that says that the user can't log on interactively** The user right to log on locally isn't set for this user, and the user isn't a member of a group that has this right.

  The user might be trying to log on to a server or domain controller. If so, keep in mind that the right to log on locally applies to all domain controllers in the domain. Otherwise, this right applies only to the single workstation.

  If the user is supposed to have access to the local system, configure the Logon Locally user right as described in the "Configuring user rights policies" section in Chapter 9.

- **A user gets a message that the system could not log on the user** If you've already checked the password and account name, you might want to check the account type. The user might be trying to access the domain with a local account. If this isn't the problem, the global catalog server might be unavailable, which means that only users with administrator privileges can log on to the domain.

- **A user has a mandatory profile and the computer storing the profile is unavailable** When a user has a mandatory profile, the computer storing the profile must be accessible during the logon process. If the computer is shut down or otherwise unavailable, users with mandatory profiles might not be able to log on. See the "Local, roaming, and mandatory profiles" section earlier in this chapter.

- **A user gets a message saying the account has been configured to prevent the user from logging on to the workstation** The user is trying to access a workstation that isn't defined as a permitted logon workstation. If the user is supposed to have access to this workstation, change the logon workstation information as described in the "Setting permitted logon workstations for multiple accounts" section earlier in the chapter.

Viewing and setting Active Directory permissions

As you know from previous discussions, user, group, and computer accounts are represented in Active Directory as objects. Active Directory objects have standard and advanced security permissions. These permissions grant or deny access to the objects.

Permissions for Active Directory objects aren't as straightforward as other permissions. Different types of objects can have sets of permissions that are specific to the type of object. They can also have general permissions that are specific to the container they're defined in.

You can view and set standard security permissions for objects by following these steps:

1. Start Active Directory Users And Computers, and then display advanced options by choosing Advanced Features from the View menu. Next, press and hold or right-click the user, group, or computer account you want to work with, and then tap or click Properties.

2. In the Properties dialog box, tap or click the Security tab. As shown in Figure 10-15, a list of groups and users that have been assigned permissions on the object you previously selected is displayed. If the permissions are unavailable, it means the permissions are inherited from a parent object.

3. Users or groups with access permissions are listed in the Group Or User Names list box. You can change permissions for these users and groups by doing the following:
   - Select the user or group you want to change.
   - Grant or deny access permissions in the Permissions list.
   - When inherited permissions are not available, override inherited permissions by selecting the opposite permissions.

4. To set access permissions for additional users, computers, or groups, tap or click Add. In the Select Users, Computers, Service Accounts, Or Groups dialog box, add users, computers, or groups.

5. In the Group Or User Names list, select the user, computer, or group you want to configure. In the check boxes in the Permissions area, allow or deny permissions. Repeat this step for other users, computers, or groups.

6. Tap or click OK when you have finished.

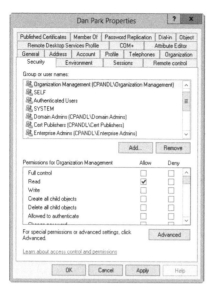

FIGURE 10-15 View and configure object permissions on the Security tab.

CAUTION Only administrators who have a solid understanding of Active Directory and Active Directory permissions should manipulate object permissions. Setting object permissions incorrectly can cause problems that are very difficult to track down.

One way to view and set advanced security permissions for objects is by following these steps:

1. Start Active Directory Users And Computers, and then display advanced options by choosing Advanced Features from the View menu. Next, press and hold or right-click the user, group, or computer account you want to work with, and then tap or click Properties.

2. In the Properties dialog box, tap or click the Security tab, and then tap or click Advanced. A list of individual permission entries for the previously selected object is displayed. Permission entries that are inherited are listed as being inherited from a specific parent object.

3. To view and set the individual permissions associated with a permission entry, select the entry, and then tap or click Edit. You can change advanced permissions for the selected user or group by granting or denying access permissions in the Permissions list. When inherited permissions are not available, override inherited permissions by selecting the opposite permissions.

4. Tap or click OK twice when you have finished.

Index

Symbols and Numbers

32-bit operating systems, upgrading to
Windows Server 2012 R2 from, 48
$ (dollar sign), in managed service account
names, 317

A

access control entries (ACEs), 267
access control lists (ACLs), 220
access controls, 267–269
access permissions, 279
account lockout
    duration, 296, 353
    policies, 156, 296
    resetting lockout counter, 296
    resetting passwords and, 347
    threshold, 295
accounts. *See* domain user accounts; group
accounts; user accounts
    Administrator, 277, 278, 286
    computer, 186, 220, 221, 223, 227–236
    configuring policies, 293–299
    deleting, 347
    enabling, 348
    Guest, 278
    managed service, 313–319
    naming policies, 289, 290
    options and restrictions, 329–335
    restricted, 284
    service, 108
    setting policies, 291, 292
    troubleshooting logon, 353
    unlocking, 348
    virtual, 186, 318
ACEs (access control entries), 267
ACLs (access control lists), 220
ACPI (Advanced Configuration and Power
Interface)
    cooling modes, 8
    described, 7
    processor states, 9
activating Windows Server, 46, 47, 76, 77
active cooling, 8
Active Directory Administrative Center
    account expiration dates, changing, 349
    authentication policies, 299
    authentication silos, 299
    central access policies, 269

computer account properties, 231
creating computer accounts, 228, 229
creating groups, 309
creating user accounts, 305
described, 224–227
enabling user accounts, 348
global group membership, 311, 312
opening, 187
OUs, 250
primary computers, 337
raising functional levels, 204
recovering deleted objects, 215
remote access privileges, 333
resetting locked computer accounts,
233
roaming profiles, 338
setting contact information, 323
unlocking accounts, 348
Active Directory-based activation, 188
Active Directory-based Group Policy, 155
Active Directory Certificate Services (AD CS),
14, 33
Active Directory Domains And Trusts
    described, 193
    transferring domain naming master
role, 243
Active Directory Domain Services (AD DS)
    adding role to server, 184
    AD FS and, 33
    administration tools, 217, 218, 220
    described, 15, 33, 183
    DNS and, 18, 19, 183–185
    domain controllers and, 197, 238–240
    domains, 14, 197
    Group Policy and, 146
    LDAP and, 209
    permissions, 354
    replication and, 208, 209
    restartable, 17
    schema, 243
    searching, 222, 225, 226, 324, 325, 343
    structure, 205–211
    support tools, 219, 220
    troubleshooting, 261
Active Directory Federation Services (AD FS)
    AD DS and, 33
    described, 15, 33
    single sign-on, 267

G

X

Z

About the author

WILLIAM STANEK (*www.williamstanek.com*) is the award-winning author and series editor of the bestselling Pocket Consultant series. William is one of the world's leading technology experts and has more than 20 years of hands-on experience with advanced programming and development. Over the years, his practical advice has helped millions of programmers, developers, and network engineers all over the world. Dubbed "A Face Behind the Future" in 1998 by *The Olympian*, William has been helping to shape the future of the written word for more than two decades. William's 150th book was published in 2013, and more than 7.5 million people have read his many works. William's current books include *Windows Server 2012 Inside Out* and the *Pocket Consultants* for Exchange Server 2013, Windows Server 2012 R2, and Windows 8.1.

William has been involved in the commercial Internet community since 1991. His core business and technology experience comes from more than 11 years of military service. He has substantial experience in developing server technology, encryption, and Internet solutions. He has written many technical white papers and training courses on a wide variety of topics. He frequently serves as a subject matter expert and consultant.

William has an MS with distinction in information systems and a BS in computer science, magna cum laude. He is proud to have served in the Persian Gulf War as a combat crew member on an electronic warfare aircraft. He flew on numerous combat missions into Iraq and was awarded nine medals for his wartime service, including one of the United States of America's highest-flying honors, the Air Force Distinguished Flying Cross. Currently, he resides in the Pacific Northwest with his wife and children.

William recently rediscovered his love of the great outdoors. When he's not writing, he can be found hiking, biking, backpacking, traveling, or trekking in search of adventure with his family!

Find William on Twitter at WilliamStanek and on Facebook at *www.facebook.com /William.Stanek.Author*. Please visit *www.Pocket-Consultant.com* to find links to stay in touch with William.

Now that you've read the book...

Tell us what you think!

Was it useful?
Did it teach you what you wanted to learn?
Was there room for improvement?

Let us know at http://aka.ms/tellpress

Your feedback goes directly to the staff at Microsoft Press,
and we read every one of your responses. Thanks in advance!

 Microsoft

CPSIA information can be obtained at www.ICGtesting.com
Printed in the USA
LVOW01s1649060314

376317LV00003B/3/P